Unbecoming Persons

Unbecoming Persons

THE RISE AND DEMISE OF
THE MODERN MORAL SELF

Ladelle McWhorter

THE UNIVERSITY OF CHICAGO PRESS
CHICAGO AND LONDON

The University of Chicago Press, Chicago 60637
The University of Chicago Press, Ltd., London
© 2025 by The University of Chicago
All rights reserved. No part of this book may be used or reproduced in any manner whatsoever without written permission, except in the case of brief quotations in critical articles and reviews. For more information, contact the University of Chicago Press, 1427 E. 60th St., Chicago, IL 60637.
Published 2025

34 33 32 31 30 29 28 27 26 25   1 2 3 4 5

ISBN-13: 978-0-226-84358-2 (cloth)
ISBN-13: 978-0-226-84359-9 (paper)
ISBN-13: 978-0-226-84360-5 (e-book)
DOI: https://doi.org/10.7208/chicago/9780226843605.001.0001

Library of Congress Cataloging-in-Publication Data

Names: McWhorter, Ladelle, 1960– author.
Title: Unbecoming persons : the rise and demise of the modern moral self / Ladelle McWhorter.
Description: Chicago : The University of Chicago Press, 2025. | Includes bibliographical references and index.
Identifiers: LCCN 2025004379 | ISBN 9780226843582 (cloth) | ISBN 9780226843599 (paper) | ISBN 9780226843605 (e-book)
Subjects: LCSH: Philosophical anthropology. | Persons.
Classification: LCC BD450 .M372 2025 | DDC 128—dc23/eng/20250407
LC record available at https://lccn.loc.gov/2025004379

Authorized Representative for EU General Product Safety Regulation (GPSR) queries: **Easy Access System Europe**—Mustamäe tee 50, 10621 Tallinn, Estonia, gpsr.requests@easproject.com

Any other queries: https://press.uchicago.edu/press/contact.html

*Whoever cannot seek the unforeseen sees nothing,
for the known way is an impasse.*

HERACLITUS, FRAGMENT 7

Contents

INTRODUCTION
The Question of How to Live · 1

CHAPTER ONE
"God Is No Respecter of Persons": The Modern Person's Ancestors from the Ancients to the English Civil Wars · 15

CHAPTER TWO
Subject of/to Judgment: John Locke and God's Three Persons · 45

CHAPTER THREE
Imposing Personhood: African Enslavement and Indigenous Resistance · 77

CHAPTER FOUR
Sovereign Persons, Nonpersons, and Corporate Persons: The United States in the Nineteenth Century · 103

CHAPTER FIVE
Questioning Ownership · 135

CHAPTER SIX
Questioning Individuality · 167

CHAPTER SEVEN
Imagining Life After Personhood · 196

Acknowledgments 229
Notes 231
Works Cited 257
Index 271

[INTRODUCTION]

The Question of How to Live

I do not know how to live. For years, on and off, I came to this realization and felt more or less troubled by it. Now and then, it just befell me. Whenever it did, I worried over it. But then, usually, I shoved it away because I didn't really know how to deal with it—meaning not only that I didn't know how to answer the question, but that I didn't even know how to pursue it as a question.

I suspected that most people around me labored in the fog of a similar ignorance, although I couldn't be sure because I didn't have the words or the courage to ask most of them. There is just no nonchalant way to bring up the question of how to live in the course of a normal conversation.

It wasn't that I didn't know how to take care of myself. I'm as self-sufficient as most adults, reasonably healthy, gainfully employed. I own property. I vote. I am a tolerable cook and a licensed driver of automobiles. I have basic social skills, a spouse, and a few very good friends. I easily and often pleasantly get through the average day. Even on a day that is not average, a day when injury or illness strikes, I know how to apply a handful of home remedies to suffice until an expert can be sought. I am also materially prepared for a variety of natural as well as anthropogenic disasters. My house is equipped with a propane generator in case of power failure attendant upon an ice storm or a hurricane. In accordance with former Vice President Richard Cheney's instructions, in 2001 I purchased and stored enough 6 mil polyethylene and duct tape to seal my windows in case of terrorist attack. Clearly, self-maintenance and preservation are high on my list of daily priorities. Anyone to whom I might have put my question about how to live would most likely have known this about me and, consequently, would have known that my question wasn't about anything glaringly practical.

But what *was* it about? Was it about something like "lifestyle choice" or concern over my career path or finding the right balance between leisure and work? Yes, all those things and, no, none of them. Something deeper, then, maybe a desire to make a mark and a fear that I hadn't and wouldn't as I confronted my mortality? Or maybe a vague sense of guilt over my relatively privileged location in the world? Yes, maybe, but not really.

No, it was that, somehow, living had become a problem for me—a problem not in the sense of a dilemma, but in the sense of something that seemed to need genuine attention. I kept stumbling over it, like a vacuum cleaner left on the living room floor. There it is again. I surely ought to find time to do something about that. But—in the case of life as opposed to the vacuum cleaner—what?

Over time, not knowing how to live made me uneasy, impatient, short-tempered, sleepless, and sometimes just the slightest bit frantic. Or maybe not knowing how to live was not the cause of this conduct but, rather, the conduct just *was* the not knowing. Life just didn't get lived smoothly anymore. There were constant interruptions in its flow, like peeling flakes of paint as you run your hand along the enameled surface of an old doorframe. And the source of these cracks and flakes seemed, somehow, to be me.

I. How Living Became a Problem: A True Story

Here is a story about how this question crept up on me. In the early years of the present century, I began to read and listen to news reports again. I had stopped near the end of the last century out of disgust with the various Clinton-era sex scandals that dominated the media, and I subsequently extended this moratorium out of depression over the egregious manipulations of the 2000 US presidential election and a visceral revulsion to George W. Bush's voice and face. But on September 11, 2001, like everybody else, I kept the television on all day and night and stayed in front of it, staring, for hours. In the aftermath, I tuned my car radio to National Public Radio every day for the duration of my thirty-five-minute commute to work and back. October of that year brought the Enron scandal, and I found my interest piqued by, of all things, the business news. After Enron came WorldCom, which was a veritable soap opera of a corporate collapse. I was hooked. Listening to the financial news became a daily habit. And like so many habits (if people who make anti-drug-use training films are to be believed), it led beyond itself to something more hardcore. By early 2003 I was listening not only to the financial news, but to the national and international news as well (though I still switched off the channel at the first strains of Dubya's dubious drawl).

At some point, I became aware of plans to deregulate electric power in my region. In light of all I had learned about the machinations of companies like Enron, I searched frantically for a way to get off the grid before rates skyrocketed. I read up on solar and wind power. I hired a consultant to advise me on ways to make my home more energy efficient. I analyzed every facet of our household energy consumption and cut out everything inessential. I was determined not to lay my neck in the ruthless hands of any enormous corporation with no governmental restraints and a strong disposition to squeeze. But none of the technological alternatives proved feasible, and after just a few adjustments in our tightly built new house, we hit a conservationist wall. One day, when my spouse insisted that we use our clothes dryer, I burst into tears. "They've got us," I wailed. "There's no way around it. They control our lives. We can't get free of them."

Of course, they don't really control our lives. But they—meaning huge corporations without scruples or faces—*can* make us feel powerless and insignificant at the same time they make themselves indispensable and rich. Who hasn't spent an afternoon trying to get through to the customer service department of a mega-utility or a too-big-to-fail financial institution or a retailer with a multi-thousand-mile supply chain whose product didn't measure up to expectations, only to realize in the process that corporate voicemail menu options are not a set of genuine possibilities but instead barricades to meaningful exchange? Who hasn't just gone ahead and paid an erroneous credit card fee rather than fight through all the red tape to contest it, recognizing all the while that this is exactly what that red tape was meant to persuade people to do? Who doesn't at least at times feel managed, manipulated, cheated, channeled, and worn down into complicity by the massive corporations that pump their so-called "goods" and "services" into our lives at every hour of every day? We can avert our eyes and cultivate apathy or beat our heads against a wall, but what we cannot seem to do is establish an existence independent of them.

The "rational" response to such defeats is acquiescence. What difference did it make, after all, if we used the dryer that day? Or the next day, or the one after that? Not using the dryer today or tomorrow would not make us any freer. Dominion Energy had beaten me. I admitted it. And I suffered a double humiliation in my acknowledgment that they had beaten me without ever even registering the fact that I was putting up a fight. I felt puny and bereft. But there was nothing to do, it seemed, except get used to it. So, when WorldCom resurrected itself as Verizon and promised a good deal (by market standards) on a bundled package of long distance and DSL,[1] I signed a contract with nary a whimper. Now most months we pay more for telephone and internet service than we pay for electricity, and I resent every check I write.[2]

The realization that at least some aspects of my life were in the grip of huge transnational corporations, especially ones I thought were ruthless and for all practical purposes above the law, compelled me to take stock of my consumption habits. Do I really need all the things I purchase? Could I maybe satisfy some of those needs by purchasing from local vendors and manufacturers instead of transnational ones? Could I raise or make some of those goods myself? To what degree could I disentangle myself from a global economy? That question led to a less immediately practical question, a question about my existence as an element—perhaps even an actor, puny though I might be—in something called a "global economy." What, after all, *is* a global economy, and just what *is* my place in it? And what place in the world do I aspire to occupy instead? What place is my attempt at disentangling supposed to move me to?

If my anger at big corporations set me on the path toward existential confusion, the US invasion of Iraq in March 2003 moved me several steps further along it. However terrible Sadaam Hussein's Ba'ath regime was, it was clear to me that there were no weapons of mass destruction under his control and that he had had no involvement in the September 11, 2001, attacks on US territory. There was no justification for war. Yet we were at war, aggressors intent on taking control of what was not ours—primarily the oil fields, perhaps, but certainly the land itself as a strategic location from which to gain some control over the entire Middle East politically and dominate it economically.

I was ashamed of my country, ashamed of its greed, and felt sick about its disregard for human life. I was angry at Bush and Cheney and Rumsfeld. But the shame far outweighed the anger once the war began—because once the decision was made and the Senate voted and the tanks rolled over the desert sand, it wasn't just their war anymore; it was mine, too. And if it was wrong, the wrong was mine as well, even though I had not willed it and could not stop it from happening.

Taking on the guilt for the war makes no sense from a deontological point of view, I know. Immanuel Kant very famously asserted that "ought" implies "can"; no one is blameworthy for something they did not choose and cannot help. But my psyche isn't Kantian. It is American instead. As a US citizen, I feel implicated in and to some degree responsible for its foreign policy decisions.[3]

I grew up in a small town named after the nineteenth-century naval hero Stephen Decatur, whose words were emblazoned across the local newspaper's masthead: "My country—may she ever be right, but, right or wrong, my country." My WWII veteran father taught me the words when I was very small; other than my name, they were the first words I learned to read. I don't recall anything that my father may have said about their meaning, but they do have a meaning for me. It isn't the apparent one, namely that we ought to commit ourselves to stand behind our country's policies and actions regardless of what they are. I don't read the sentence as a declaration of total loyalty or, for that matter, as any kind of moral principle at all. I read it, rather, as a statement of fact about what it is to be a citizen of a democratic republic. It is that no matter how much I deplore and oppose what the United States government does, I'm still an American.[4] This is still my country, and whatever this country does is still somehow my doing. The US government isn't the nation, but insofar as it is a government by the people, the United States of America is—we Americans are—responsible for that government's actions. A citizen can't escape that responsibility by saying, "Well, I voted against those guys."[5] *We*—remember us, the People?—in effect vote *for* the whole apparatus over and over again all our lives, even if we never set foot in a polling booth. A bunch of *We* established it; this current generation of *We* sustains it; our tax dollars pay for it; and none among us except a few crazies seems inclined to try to blow it up.[6] I'm certainly not so inclined, despite at times feeling raging anger and terrible despair. So there I was in March 2003, furious with my government, ashamed of my country, and confronting myself as a responsible party in a military venture that would have profound effects on people in every corner of the globe.

Two years after the US invasion of Iraq, the departmental administrative assistant where I taught emailed me an article she had read in *Rolling Stone*.[7] Dutifully, I read it, thinking of nothing more than to be able to engage her in casual conversation at work the next day. But its contents shook me thoroughly. The author claimed that 2005 was most likely the year of peak global oil extraction, which meant that ever after, even as demand for oil grew, the world's supply would diminish and the price would inevitably go up. Oh, and somewhere along the way, civilization would tumble into chaos.

There was no question in my mind that if the oil wells stopped producing that day, we would be in trouble. We didn't yet have hydrogen cars, and the refineries weren't geared up to make enough biofuel for our gasoline-burning ones. But down the road? Weren't there people working on that? Weren't we gradually going to replace all our oil-burning machines with other . . . things? I guess I just hadn't thought about it, really. Of course the world's supply of petroleum would run out someday, at least that portion of it that human beings could get their hands on. There was—there had to be—a finite amount. But I had thought that time was far away, too far to worry about. However, this author was saying—and not he alone, I soon discovered, but many others as well—that what matters is not when we run out but when we get to the halfway point and people start competing for and fighting over the diminishing quantity that's left. And that time was not far away at all.

I wasn't so shocked and upset about the oil per se. After all, I was alive and cognizant in the 1970s, when US domestic oil production peaked (given the technology of the day) and began to decline, and people began to talk seriously about energy conservation. No, what shocked and upset me was the result of the author's invitation to contemplate what in our lives now would be irreplaceable in a world without oil. I accepted that invitation and took a look around my study, my kitchen, my clothes closet, my medicine chest. And I reached the truly shocking realization that, indeed, almost everything I own or use is made of petroleum, or made in a process that involves petroleum, or made accessible to me by means of petroleum. In other words, most of what I have absolutely depends on the world's oil supply. Most of what I do on a given day absolutely depends on the world's oil supply. Most of who I am in this world is unsustainable in the absence of the world's oil supply. Petroleum is the platform upon which virtually all of modern civilization is built.

That was not always true. As late as the mid-nineteenth century, no aspect of civilization depended on petroleum. And yet there were printing presses, railroads, and telegraphs. There were stock markets and universities and free elections and judicial systems. People did many of the things people do now: They traveled; they studied; they conducted scientific experiments; they made music and art. Then, in 1854 at Titusville, Pennsylvania, an attorney named George Bissell, a bank president named James Townsend, and a retired railroad conductor called "Colonel" Edwin Drake began developing what in 1857 became the first commercially successful oil well. In a move toward conjuring up a market, they hired a Yale chemistry professor, Benjamin Silliman, to study possibilities for transmuting crude oil into something actually usable.[8] Silliman's studies showed that crude oil distilled into a substance called kerosene (which local entrepreneur Samuel Kier had been producing since 1853) might eventually compete with the illuminant camphene (a derivative of turpentine, a product of tree sap). The partners launched a vigorous promotional campaign, and for many years thereafter, petroleum was most commonly used at night to read by.[9]

Less than a century later, however, life without oil—civilization without oil—had become unthinkable and indeed practically impossible. Nowadays every industry, every household, every school, every governmental institution requires a constant stream of petroleum just to function, petroleum transmuted into everything from the plastics in our computers to the lubricants in our door hinges. Even the machinery we think of as providing alternatives to fossil fuels—wind turbines, solar panels, electric cars—are currently manufactured and maintained through the use of petroleum. In just over three decades between the beginning of World War I and the end of

World War II, almost without comment, civilization picked up and moved itself off its foundations on water, wind, wood, animal, and human labor power and settled itself firmly down on petroleum power supplemented by coal, and then it proceeded to expand and expand and expand. Could it maybe downsize a bit and move back? I wasn't sure. Would it? No. Nuclear power was the only known option that might close the gap between what nineteenth-century energy sources could supply and what twenty-first-century civilization required. And there were all sorts of practical problems with that option, including that the construction and maintenance of nuclear power plants are currently impossible without petroleum.

What is likely to happen, then, as supplies fall short of demand is that prices will fluctuate with a strong tendency to rise, creating terrible economic dislocations—that is, many people will fall into poverty—and there will be wars. Meanwhile, as easily accessible, higher-quality supplies grow scarce and rising prices provide incentive for further exploitation of more remote "reserves," oil companies will extract and sell dirtier petroleum whose refinement and use will create much more pollution per barrel than the petroleum burned thus far.[10] And the process of extracting this petroleum will be more dangerous. For example, companies will need to drill deeper, in more extreme temperatures, and farther out to sea, where stress on laborers and equipment will be far greater and thus where accidents resulting in loss of human and other forms of life will become far more commonplace.[11]

We will also use up the second half of the world's supply of petroleum much faster than we used up the first half—which apparently took about 150 years. How much faster? How much time do we have to move our civilization onto some other "energy platform"? A hundred years? Fifty? Twenty-five? I read whatever I could find on the subject, but firm answers were not forthcoming.[12]

It was 2005. The president of the United States was an oilman. I had thought before that he was greedy, shady, and a little bit benighted. He had squandered some brain cells in his fraternity days; in middle age, he preferred brush cutting to reading; he only ever thought about the short run. And his anti-intellectualism allowed him to reject the claims of scientists who said that our heavy use of fossil fuels is destabilizing the earth's climate. He just didn't understand. But after I read that article, I realized I had underestimated him. He did understand. That's why he had built a well-fortified family compound in Texas that was a model of conservation and environmental friendliness—green as green could be. The oilmen, of all people, surely did know that the end was coming. The president knew. So did the president's father, the former president and CIA director; he surely knew. Their close friend Vice President Cheney knew.[13] And they knew there would be terrible consequences—environmental devastation, violence, poverty—as well as plenty of profit to be made. They knew all this long before I did, and for a while already they had been planning ahead so that they and theirs would not suffer the worst of those consequences.

Would I and mine? I expected to live another thirty years, possibly forty, and my spouse as well. My students would live another sixty-five. Our godson, not quite nine years old at the time, might well live another seventy-five. What sort of world would we live to see?

That spring semester I was teaching a course on environmental ethics. I had agreed to do it because a colleague in the Department of Religious Studies who usually taught it was on sabbatical. Having no time to research the topic in advance, I had simply adopted his syllabus and all semester had been reading the material just a few days ahead of the students. I thought I knew what I was getting into. The last time I had looked at environmental ethics textbooks, many years before, their chapters were concerned with issues familiar from my own college years: conservation, pollution, animal rights. Those topics still prevailed in the first half of this course, but the second half was filled with dire warnings and impending disasters. Climate change was the culmination, and by the time we got there, it was clear why. After reading all this material, I made it my business to find out *exactly* how many feet above (the current) sea level my property lay. Once I determined that it would most likely remain above sea level through the rest of the twenty-first century, I planted a dozen fruit and nut trees on the hunch that they were a better investment for old age than any financial expert's retirement savings plan.

Global climate change, global economies built on global oil supplies—my life is in fact utterly inextricable from all of that. I don't so much live in a place, on a plot of ground, and in a neighborhood, as I live in a human-constructed, worldwide web of circulating currencies, commodities, technologies, and information (true, false, and fuzzy), as well as the very stuff of life itself: air, water, food, and energy, and, along with all that, the jet-setting microbes that make every epidemic a potential pandemic. I can't escape from that web. I can't "get back to nature" or "get off the grid." I myself am a product of that human construct—my education, my sensibilities, my desires, my life expectancy, the state of my health, the very fillings in my teeth. Despite my love of trees and birds and bright blue sunny days, despite my dabbling in organic gardening and my concern over the loss of species and habitats, I'm not really part of any place. I may have fantasies of connection to this or that piece of earth, but I'm not really rooted anywhere. My feet barely reach the ground. I am global to the bone.

II. Choice Without Freedom, Responsibility Without Control

That is the story of how I came to find my life itself problematic. Even now, years later, I still don't know how to be a good global person. Given the way I've adumbrated the concept "global" in my narrative, I'm not sure that a "global *person*" is even a logical possibility. The concept of personhood that has come down to us from the Enlightenment involves something like autonomy. A person, as opposed to a thing (says Kant), is an individual entity with the freedom and intelligence necessary to set the principles by which it will act and live. I was taught to believe that adults were in fact persons in this sense, responsible for what they thought and did, and blameworthy when they abdicated that responsibility. While of course they might be dependent upon others or indebted to them for certain things at certain times, their values and judgments were their own to make and hold. In the moral realm, each person was in effect the equivalent of a sovereign state. My education was designed to facilitate my emerging personhood, my eventual assumption of this sovereign autonomy; I learned to think for myself and to face the consequences of my own actions precisely because they were mine—conceived, undertaken, and carried out by none other than me.

The figurative vacuum cleaner I stumble over on the metaphorical living room floor seems to consist, in part, in the realization that I am not a person in that sense. My non-Kantian psyche feels that as an American I act in Iraq and elsewhere in ways I don't choose or control or sometimes even know about. My relatively recent attention to macroeconomics has demonstrated to me that much of my conduct and even my desires are conditioned by political and economic forces quite alien to any principles or values that I could ever hold. I want to save the environment. I want world peace. I want everyone to have clean, safe drinking water. I want children to stop starving to death. But my life is built on an energy platform that makes all those professions of charity and concern moot. What I actually do, despite myself, is use up resources faster than any human being ever before in the 300,000-year history of humanity, emit more pollution than any human being ever before in the 300,000-year history of humanity, and in the process of doing so directly threaten the lives and health of several billion members of the current population of human beings on this planet, not to mention untold trillions of other organisms.

If I *were* a person in that Enlightenment sense, I could choose to stop— without thereby killing myself, I mean. If I *were* a person in the Enlightenment sense, I could decide to live in accord with my convictions. No doubt it would not be easy; it would take a lot of effort to identify all the things I do that are inconsistent with my principles and a lot of discipline to change my ways. But I could do it.

And this is what most people—decent, reasonable people—keep trying to do. We want to act in accord with our moral principles. We want to exert our autonomous wills and conduct ourselves as upright human beings. Therefore, when we find out that Corporation X runs sweatshops, we stop buying its merchandise; when we find out that polar bears are threatened with extinction because of polar ice melt, we take the train or drive hybrid cars so we can stop putting so much greenhouse gas in the atmosphere; when our government exploits attacks on US territory to invade foreign countries as a means to further the financial interests of a few billionaire contractors, we campaign for the bastards' opponents in the next election. We want to be persons. We try hard to act as if we are persons. But the hard truth is: We're not. We are not in control. We don't even understand our own situation, the real conditions of our own existence, in this globalized world. We do not know who or what we are, much less how we should, or even could, conduct ourselves. We don't know how to live.

As a result, it's hit-or-miss. After the Deepwater Horizon disaster in April 2010, I boycotted BP, so I bought my gasoline from Valero. I voted for the Democrats, because they were not the warmongering, contractor-funded, xenophobic, racist Republicans. And I kept tending my fruit and nut trees. But I still felt uneasy, irritable, wary, out of sorts, and sometimes just the slightest bit frantic because, try as I might to deny it, at some level I was ever aware that a gulf the size of the planet yawns between who I am and who I am supposed to be.

It is hard to admit all this, because, at least from a Kantian perspective, the alternative to asserting personhood is pretty terrible. If you're not a person—if you're not autonomous, if your conduct is predicated upon and governed by forces outside your control—then what you are is a thing, a thing like any other thing, a thing like a stick or a rock or a turd. What direction you head, where you land, and how much impact you have—none of that is up to you; it's all a matter of physics... or some broadened account of the laws of nature. You are not free; you could not do otherwise; you are just a thing.

Some of us embrace this idea, at least when other people disapprove of what we do. "I can't help it; it's just how I am." But most of us don't really believe it. We *feel* like we make our own decisions. We exercise our right to choose. We individuate and express ourselves through the choices we make, and we take a fair measure of pride in that. We are persons, we think (and as evidence we have the fact that after some careful research, we selected the Prius over the Subaru, or vice versa). If somebody tries to coerce or bribe us, we are insulted. If we discover that we have been managed or manipulated, we are outraged.

But it happens all the time. The conditions under which we choose are in fact stringently managed and manipulated. Our cooperation and oftentimes our beliefs, whether we like it or even know it or not, are generally up for sale. Despite our professed values, we buy the cheaper imports without investigating the labor conditions at the factories where they were produced or the environmental impact those factories and supply chains might have. We allow our 401(k)s to be invested in ways we don't even bother to keep up with. We cave in and pay the erroneous credit card fee. We toss the defective piece of retail merchandise into the landfill and buy a replacement for it rather than stand in the long line at the big box store and wrangle at length with the minimum-wage-earning clerk who is not authorized to give us our money back. We keep paying our taxes knowing that the money supports wars of greed and aggression. We keep voting for the lesser of the evils. And, sometimes at least, we dry our clothes in the electric clothes dryer. We are constantly bribed and coerced—or incentivized and reminded of the better part of valor—and thus our acts of free choice, the expressions and manifestations of our supposed autonomy, become the instruments through which are perpetrated a great many of the wrongest wrongs in the world, wrongs to which we would sincerely like to put a stop. When we pay a little bit of attention here or there, we try to do the right thing. But we dare not look too long and hard, because when we do, we see plainly that we have failed—because we can't boycott every evil corporation, because we can't stop burning fossil fuels, because we can't withdraw without an exit strategy, and because the bottom line is that the power we feel we exercise is really just streaming through us and will cease to be ours as soon as we try to divert the flow.

I don't know how to live. I was born into a world where I was expected to become a person. I was educated to be a person. And I've been trying and failing to be one for a very long time now. I'm tired. I think most of the people I know are tired, even if they wouldn't describe the situation in quite the same way. Surely some of the recent dramatic rise in depression and anxiety diagnoses, addiction to painkillers, and attempts at or death by suicide are a result of this moral exhaustion. Yes, of course, it is also true that wherever there is a product to sell—such as antidepressants and painkillers—demand will be created. But capitalism and advertising cannot account for the fact that in 2009 the number of deaths by suicide in the United States rose higher than the number of traffic fatalities. The trend continued in 2010, with 33,687 deaths from traffic accidents and 38,364 from suicides.[14] Chad

Lavin has suggested that the 1999 Columbine High School shooting—a mass murder/double suicide—might have been partially motivated by this sort of frustration. Citing passages from teenage killer Eric Harris's journal, Lavin writes: "The frustrations of Harris's life are accentuated by a failure to attain the sort of autonomy he had been promised. His violent reaction reflects a desperate attempt to take control of his situation" (Lavin 2008, 131). I am unwilling to speculate about Harris's and Klebold's motives, and what Lavin describes sounds more like frustrated white male entitlement than moral despair, but insofar as we are all expected to assume the responsibilities attendant upon autonomous personhood and to the extent that we find that assumption impossible, we feel an uncomfortable glimmer of recognition in Harris's words.

Whatever may have precipitated any given individual's addiction, suicide, road rage, shooting spree, or hate crime, one way or another, it seems to me, a whole lot of people these days are renouncing or abdicating their claims to personhood. They don't know how to live, so they opt out. Would it be any surprise if some of them took some of the rest of us with them?

Thank goodness, my life is too good for me to resort to pills or put a gun to my head. When I'm not worrying over the impact of my consumer choices or how to endure a sweltering old age, I can sit on my back patio on an early summer evening, smell the mimosa blossoms, listen to the tree frogs, and share a wonderful bottle of wine with the woman I love. Life just does not get any better than that, ever, for anybody. That is perfect bliss. And it fills me with gratitude.

So, gratitude and anguish—gratitude for what I have, anguish for what my having takes from others and for what we all might lose in an ever-nearer future—these experiences motivate me to pursue the question of how to live. I want to keep on living; I want other people to keep on living; I want the mimosas and the tree frogs to keep on living. And I think the *ethos* we have—the morality of modern personhood—isn't going to allow us that, not for very long.

III. Refusal, Curiosity, Innovation: A Different Ethos

In 1980 the French philosopher Michel Foucault had a conversation with a Berkeley undergraduate student named Michael Bess, an excerpt of which was published in the university newspaper, *The Daily Californian*.[15] In the course of it, young Mr. Bess expressed some anxiety about the fact that Foucault's approach to history suggested that nothing is absolute, that everything we think we know is wrapped up in limited perspectives and relations of power, that there is no definitive right or wrong. Although he didn't put the question in these words, Bess was basically asking Foucault how he could possibly live and work in such uncertainty. Foucault described what he termed "three elements in my morals" that together marked out "the field of values within which I situate my work." Those elements were (1) refusal, (2) curiosity, and (3) innovation. He refused to take for granted principles and truths that were commonly accepted, particularly ones that he felt trapped him in ways of thinking and acting that were frustrating or painful. Instead of just assuming these principles and truths were a given, he took an interest in their histories; he asked when they emerged and how they gained ascendance and acceptance, and he tried to see how people thought and lived without them before they existed—because it turns out, when you look into it, there usually is a *before*. And as those principles and truths began to seem less inevitable and less essential, he found it possible to begin to imagine alternatives, and he offered his "genealogies" to others to help them free themselves from painful or frustrating assumptions so that they might begin to imagine alternatives. This was Foucault's "morality," not telling people (including himself) what is right or good, but shaking the ground underneath our assumptions enough to expose the possibility of something different—different ways to think, different ways to act, different ways to live.

As the foregoing likely made very clear, by the time I read this interview with Foucault in 2014, I had already cultivated the virtue of refusal. Indeed, I had reached the point where I couldn't *not* refuse. I needed something more to do. What I did, then, was start writing this book. The first four chapters are fueled by curiosity; they explore the genealogy of modern moral personhood, pursuing the questions of how people became persons like me (failed though we may be at the project), of how we came to think of ourselves as persons and as accountable as such, and of how we came to hold each other responsible as persons. As these chapters make clear, for most of human history, people were not persons in the contemporary sense and many were not persons at all, yet they sometimes got along with each other and in the world reasonably well. Personhood emerges in these pages as a historically formed subject position that took shape beginning in the late seventeenth century, as a way of understanding and conducting ourselves that is neither an absolute fact of human nature or civilization nor an essential foundation for living a good life. Pursuing this genealogy disturbed my sense of who and what I am, and we are, just enough to make it possible to reorient toward other possibilities.

Genealogy alone never provides other possibilities, however. By disturbing settled and unquestioned assumptions, it enables a process of transformation, but as Foucault's comments in the above-cited interview suggest, real change requires more. He called that something more "innovation," a word I dislike because of its overuse by corporate executives and the university administrators who mimic them, so I will call it, instead, creative experimentation. Ownership and individualism are key components of modern moral personhood, so chapters 5 and 6 analyze our assumptions about them, explore existing alternatives, and experimentally reimagine selves and relationships in light of serious challenges to them. Chapter 7 concludes the study by offering a set of ethical improvisations that may help us imagine, discover, and eventually inhabit other possibilities for thinking and conducting ourselves.

Failure to become or be good persons surely need not mean that we are doomed to be, simply, bad or failed persons. There are other ways to live. My aim in writing this book is to get free enough from the bonds and assumptions of modern moral personhood—its extreme possessiveness, its preoccupation with self-identity, its often-exclusive concern with individual enrichment or salvation—to discover and create ways to live well together in this world. My hope is that we, or at least people not too many generations after us, will become something for whom personhood is an ancestor rather than an aspiration.

[CHAPTER ONE]

"God Is No Respecter of Persons"

The Modern Person's Ancestors from the
Ancients to the English Civil Wars

Could we be something other than persons? Is there any possibility that we could throw off the form of subjectivity that we have inherited, that we try to inhabit, and that we have been taught to revere and, instead, learn to live otherwise? And might some such other way help position us to grapple with the ills of our world less painfully and more effectively than personhood does?

Before I can even begin to pursue those questions, I must acknowledge that even to suggest to people raised in the prevailing Western worldview that they might occupy a position other than that of person is likely to inspire fear, and reasonably so. We all know of human beings who have been declared nonpersons, and we know the consequences for them were not of the sort any of us would wish for ourselves. Loss or denial of the status of personhood has meant loss or denial of membership in the moral community wherein lives have value, wherein we have a right to insist that we be treated with consideration and respect. While I stand on the verge of challenging and possibly repudiating personhood, most crusaders for social justice are embracing it and trying hard to expand the category to encompass more and more beings, to force the law and society to treat all human beings and many nonhuman beings with the consideration and respect that is officially accorded to persons.[1] Personhood is powerful. To forfeit it is to relinquish any access to the protective power that it affords.

It is not safe to question—let alone undermine—personhood *if* there is no other way for people to live together on Earth in peace and reciprocity. Caution is definitely in order. At the same time, however, it is good to consider that beings who fall outside the category of personhood are treated in ways we want to avoid—as commodities, resources, garbage, for example—not so much at the hands of one another but at the hands of persons. Beings are commodities because there are other beings who can buy, own, and sell or consume them—that is, persons. Beings can be exploited because there are other beings who own and command systems that confer the right of and the means for exploitation upon them—again, persons. In this society, one rightly fears losing the status of personhood because one knows what those who are persons do to beings without that status. This fear reveals the awesome power of personhood, for both protection and destruction. If people found ways to live otherwise than as persons, maybe there wouldn't be so much destruction.

Before considering alternative ways of being, however, it would be wise to confront and investigate that awesome power. What generates it? What maintains it? What, if anything, has ever opposed it? How did personhood come to have this power to order the world? How did it acquire this near monopoly on the conferral of value in its various forms? Has it always been so?

We each use the tools we know how to use. The tool I know how to use to investigate formations or networks of power—which is what I have suggested personhood is, or at any rate is an important aspect of—is what Michel Foucault called genealogy. One begins genealogical work with the postulation that values, concepts, institutions, and ways of thinking and living form and transform over time. I call this a postulation, because it is not universalizable as an ontological truth; a genealogist does not claim that *all* values, concepts, institutions, et cetera are contingent or historical in nature. Universal being is not within the scope of genealogical inquiry. Genealogy is always localized, focused on a particular ensemble of values, institutions, practices, and so on. It begins with the postulation that the network of forces composing a particular ensemble came together at some point in time, before which there were other configurations, perhaps involving some of the same elements, that enabled a different range of knowledge and practices. For example, in the nineteenth century, Friedrich Nietzsche set out to investigate the concept of evil. He assumed at the outset that evil, as a concept that underwrites a set of practices and institutions (e.g., moral condemnation and legal punishment), must have formed at some point in time. As a classicist and a linguist, he was able to describe a configuration of meaning in the distant past where evil had no place, a time when value judgments were made in terms of good and bad or noble and vulgar, but not in terms of evil. He then searched for turning points when one configuration of value transformed in ways that eventually gave rise to another. Nietzsche called this work genealogical as opposed to historical because what one traces through time are sequences of predecessors of a present thing, not that self-identical thing in various guises through history. One traces how multiple and disparate events and forces gave rise to what is present now as something different from what preceded it.

There was a time before evil existed, Nietzsche found. Then, at a certain point, there was evil. Evil did not come out of nowhere; it had forebears. But those forebears did not aim to engender evil any more than my great-grandparents aimed to engender me. My great-grandparents met by chance, fell in love, and had children, who were not them. Evil's ancestors likewise came together without a master plan, responded to changing forces impinging upon them, and passed away leaving something different from themselves. Evil and I are similar in that regard and so, I postulate, might modern moral personhood be.

If personhood is historically emergent, as I postulate, then in principle one could find a time *before*, a time when people lived differently, valued differently, interacted with and understood themselves in relation to each other and to nonhuman beings differently. One might also be able to begin to imagine a time *after*.² Tracing the disparate forces that gave rise to a division of the world into persons with intrinsic or moral value and nonpersons without such value can alter our view of personhood in ways that reduce its power. In this way, if in no other, it might be transformative. Beyond that, however, it can reveal possibilities for living good lives in ways other than those that a person/nonperson dichotomy and hierarchy of value dictates.

I. The Diggers and King James

The first step in genealogical work usually consists in simply attending to a moment of seeming disconnection. One discovers something in history that just does not fit with one's own ways of making sense of things. I had such an experience a few years before I began to think about doing a genealogy of personhood. At that time, I was working on a book now published as *Racism and Sexual Oppression in Anglo-America*, in which I analyzed portions of Michel Foucault's 1976 lecture course published in English as *"Society Must Be Defended"* (1997). In some of those lectures, Foucault discusses political tracts written by so-called Diggers, seventeenth-century English commoners who protested against land enclosure by occupying and cultivating land they did not own. When I dove into those tracts, I encountered locutions that puzzled me. The Diggers did not seem to use the word *person* quite as I did.

I knew that the Diggers' countryman, philosopher John Locke, did use the word *person* very much as I did in his writings at the end of the seventeenth century. In fact, Locke's work is still very much alive in ethical and especially epistemological debates in the present century. Less than forty years elapsed between Gerrard Winstanley's *The Law of Freedom in a Platform* (1652) and Locke's *Essay Concerning Human Understanding* (1689).

Locke was already a young adult when Winstanley's book was published. How could his conception of personhood seem so familiar and contemporary, while the Diggers' conception seemed so archaic and strange?

A few years later, having decided to do a genealogy of modern moral personhood and remembering my earlier puzzlement, I returned to seventeenth-century England as a starting point, on the hunch that modern moral person's parentage might be discovered in that tumultuous period of English history. Somehow, I supposed, the political and religious upheavals before, during, and after the Civil War must have brought some important linguistic and conceptual upheavals with them. Realignments of power, it stood to reason, would involve reconfigurations of language as well.

The first job, I thought, was to get as clear a sense as possible of what the Diggers were saying in those pamphlets, a sense of the personhood they invoked and how that personhood functioned in the context of their self-positioning, their political demands, and their ethical and religious concerns. I will start, though, with a brief description of their protests.

A. THE DIGGERS' PROTEST

The 1640s was probably the most turbulent decade in English history. That decade brought war with both Scotland and Ireland, civil war within England, violent religious schism, and economic catastrophe. With supplies of food cut off by the wars, people literally died of starvation in the streets of London. The hardship in the countryside compounded the terrible effects of decades of land enclosure and consequent loss of the common fens, forests, and pastureland that previously made small farms sustainable. Disease, including plague, also claimed many lives. Political conflict and war brought the business of government to a halt; courts of law ceased to operate. Clergy fled their parishes to avoid mobs of dissenters sick of supporting them by paying mandatory tithes drawn from their meager resources and of taking orders from dubious spiritual superiors. Parliament declared itself sovereign and fought, captured, and ultimately executed the king. The world, as so many scholars of seventeenth-century English history put it, had turned itself upside down.[3] It was a time of both great misery and great license, and of the innovation that comes of desperation.

Near the end of that tumultuous decade, in the spring of 1649, a small group of impoverished men and women, grasping for any means to feed themselves and their children, staged an occupation of St. George's Hill. Despite having no legal right to work the land, these people built huts and broke ground for cultivation of crops, earning them the somewhat derogatory label "Diggers." They called themselves "True Levellers," in contrast to the self-styled Levellers, who agitated for political rights (including universal manhood suffrage) but not for land reform or redistribution of property. Nevertheless, history remembers the True Levellers, when it remembers them at all, as the Diggers.

Three weeks later, the occupiers of St. George's Hill issued a declaration entitled *The True Levellers Standard Advanced*. That pamphlet, dated April 20, 1649, and signed by fifteen men, declares in part:

> The work we are going about is this, To dig up *Georges-Hill* and the waste Ground thereabouts, and to Sow Corn, and to eat our bread together by the sweat of our brows.
>
> And the First Reason is this, That we may work in righteousness, and lay the Foundation of making the Earth a Common Treasury for All, both Rich and Poor, That every one that is born in the Land, may be fed by the Earth his Mother that brought him forth, according to the Reason that rules in the Creation. Not Inclosing any part into any particular hand, but all as one man, working together, and feeding together as Sons of one Father, members of one Family; not one Lording over another, but all looking upon each other, as equals in the Creation; so that our Maker may be glorified in the work of his own hands, and that every one may see, he is no respecter of Persons, but equally loves his whole Creation. . . .
> (Winstanley et al. 1649, 12 13)

By May, the occupation had become a village with families, dwellings, gardens, and livestock. Through the next year, at least ten similar groups took over so-called wasteland and commons in the south Midlands.[4] The claim that God is "no respecter of Persons" recurs in Digger pamphlets, as well as in Digger leader Winstanley's 1652 monograph *The Law of Freedom in a Platform* (Winstanley [1652] 1973, 283). It may have been a common locution at the time, but the Diggers' primary reference is the King James Bible. I will turn to that source momentarily to elucidate the concept, but, first, the rest of the Diggers' story.

Landowners in the vicinity of the Diggers' occupation at St. George's Hill were incensed. At first, they called upon military leaders to disperse the community, but after a brief investigation, General Thomas Fairfax dismissed their concerns and told them to work through the courts (some of which had been restored by that time). They did not follow this suggestion but instead launched a series of attacks against the settlement, repeatedly pulling down huts, destroying crops, and killing animals. On June 1, 1649, the Diggers responded by issuing their second pamphlet, *A Declaration from the Poor oppressed People of England*. It opens with these lines:

> We whose names are subscribed do in the name of all the poor oppressed people in England declare unto you that call yourselves lords of manors and lords of the land that in regard the King of righteousness, our maker, hath enlightened our hearts so far as to see that the earth was not made purposefully for you to be lords of it, and we to be your slaves, servants and beggars; but it was made to be a common livelihood to all, without respect of persons. (Winstanley 1973, 99)

Forty-five men at St. George's Hill signed this Declaration, which ends by calling for a free commonwealth without division of land. In response, landowners had the Diggers charged with trespassing.

Legal action posed a new problem for the Diggers. In the 1640s, ordinary English people could not simply appear in court and speak for themselves. As commoners, they did not have legal standing. It was not possible to enter a plea, therefore, unless one hired an attorney, usually for an exorbitant fee. The Diggers despised attorneys in principle, because they were the younger sons of landowners. (Prevented from inheriting their fathers' estates by the law of primogeniture, younger sons received Oxford or Cambridge educations and lucrative positions at court or in the national Church hierarchy, positions that brought them income and often land as well.) The Diggers did not hire an attorney, so they were sentenced without a hearing. They were fined ten pounds per man plus court costs, but of course they had no money, so their animals were seized. Despite all this hardship, the Diggers held their contested ground.

Landowners were not satisfied with the court settlement and continued to press for decisive action to oust the occupation. In July 1649, General Fairfax received instructions to arrest the alleged ringleader, Gerrard Winstanley, and to disperse the people by force. The group abandoned St. George's Hill and moved to Cobham Heath, but they were harassed there too, arrested, and fined. In November troops were called in, houses pulled down, crops destroyed, and participants beaten by landowners (or their representatives) as soldiers stood by. Many Diggers were imprisoned. Similar events occurred at the other settlements through the spring of 1650; by the beginning of 1651, the Digger movement was destroyed.

B. THE PERSONS OF KING JAMES

The Diggers' assertion that people should not respect persons sounds very strange, because it reverses the currently commonplace moral imperative to respect each and every person qua person, the assumption that personhood in and of itself commands basic respect. Shouldn't the Diggers have asserted the opposite, namely that God respects all persons and that the law and the landowners should have respected *them* and heeded their concerns because they were persons? If people were not supposed to respect persons, then persons must have been something different from what they are now.

The Diggers often cited scripture in support of this claim, using, of course, the King James Bible, wherein variations on the phrase occur repeatedly. Consider, for example, the Acts of the Apostles 10:34–35: "Then Peter opened his mouth and said, Of a truth I perceive that God is no respecter of persons: / But in every nation he that feareth him, and worketh righteousness, is accepted with him." Here, after Jesus's crucifixion, resurrection, and ascension, the disciple Peter is preaching in the house of the gentile Cornelius to a non-Jewish gathering. A vision has led him to extend the gospel beyond the Jewish people to other peoples, to gentiles, and so he finds it necessary to emphasize that God does not favor any one nation over any other. The phrase in question is a translation from the Greek προσωποληπτής (*prosopoleptes*), which comes from προσωπολεμσια (*prosopolemsia*), and is commonly rendered in subsequent translations as *partiality*.[5] God shows no partiality; regardless of nationality, all are equal before God. Likewise, human beings should not hold some above others. All must be seen and treated as equal in worth, as the Apostle Paul makes clear in James 2:9: "But if ye have respect to persons, ye commit sin, and are convinced of the law as transgressors"[6] (εἰ δέ προσωποληπτέω ἁμαρτία ἐργάζομαι ἐλέγχω ὑπό ὁ νόμος ὡς παραβάτης). It is sinful to believe and behave as if some people are worth more than others in God's eyes.[7]

Why did King James's translators not say, simply, that God is not partial to the members of one nation over another, nor should people favor one group above another? Why say, instead, that God is no respecter of persons and that neither should we be? The translators and the Digger pamphleteers could have used those words—in fact, the early sixteenth-century William Tyndale translation actually sounds more modern than the more recent King James: "Then Peter opened his mouth and sayde: Of a trueth I perseave that God is not parciall."[8] Nevertheless, in the seventeenth century, an apparently preferable way to say "do not show partiality to some people over others" was "do not respect persons." We know what the phrase in its entirety meant, but how did those words actually function together in order to generate that meaning?

Clearly "to respect" does not mean what it most commonly means in modern English—something like "to behave toward someone with civility and consideration for their dignity and concerns." For the Diggers, it apparently means something more like "to distinguish between" or "to discriminate among." Modern English has remnants of that sense of *respect*, when we speak of distinguishing among different parts or dimensions of something, as for example when one says, "In this respect, X is a problem, but in other respects it is not." The difference is that when we use the term that way, we refer to differing dimensions of the object of concern, whereas King James's translators refer to an action of the subject, the differentiating act itself.

The puzzle intensifies if we examine a larger range of these odd passages. Consider the following: "Let me not, I pray you, accept any man's person, neither let me give flattering titles unto man" (Job 32:21); "And when they were come, they say unto him, Master, we know that thou art true, and carest for no man: for thou regardest not the person of men . . ." (Mark 12:14); and ". . . their mouth speaketh great swelling words, having men's persons in admiration because of advantage" (Jude 1:16). In all of these passages, the persons that are not to be respected, regarded, accepted, or admired are distinct from the men whose persons they are; these passages speak of "any man's person" and "the person of men," as if personhood were a possession, quality, or aspect of individuals rather than the individuals themselves. Person is not simply one member of the class of people; it seems to be something more specific.

In contemporary English, we occasionally separate someone's person from the rest of that someone's being, as in: "Kindly remove your hands from my person!" In such cases, one's person seems to be one's living physical body. Likewise, we speak of appearing in person or meeting in person, meaning being present in body. Bodies and bodily presentation may have been part of what was at issue in these seventeenth-century phrases, but for the most part, something else seems to be at stake, even when physical appearance is clearly discussed. James 2:1–4 comes nearest to using the term *person* to mean *body*. "My brethren, have not the faith of our Lord Jesus Christ, the Lord of glory, with respect of persons. / For if there come unto your assembly a man with a gold ring, in goodly apparel, and there come in also a poor man in vile raiment; / And ye have respect to him that weareth the gay clothing, and say unto him, Sit thou here in a good place; and say to the poor, Stand thou there, or sit here under my footstool: / Are ye not then partial in yourselves, and are become judges of evil thoughts?" We could imagine that what is denounced here is judging the worth of an individual on the basis of physical appearance. Instead of judging by appearance, First Peter 1:17 asserts that God "without respect of persons judgeth according to every man's work. . . ." It might be, then, that we are being warned not to discriminate among people because of how they look or because of the way they present themselves physically; rather, we should treat them in accordance with how they conduct themselves and what they accomplish. This passage from James is exceptional, however, in describing a situation where appearance is primary. Most of the passages where this locution occurs refer not simply to how someone *appears*—specifically whether they *seem* to be wealthy or poor—but to how someone *is*, to their actual social or economic status, whether expressed in physical appearance or not. Deuteronomy 1:17 cautions Israel's leaders: "Ye shall not respect persons in judgment; but ye shall hear the small as well as the great. . . ." Similar passages in Deuteronomy (see especially 16:19) warn against taking bribes from the wealthy to settle disputes in their favor. It seems more plausible, then, that *person* refers not so much to how the individual appears in public but to the status that their appearance likely indicates.

In seventeenth-century England, as noted above, in at least one important respect, social status and public appearance were closely connected: If people lacked an elevated status conferred by birth and reinforced by land and wealth, they could not appear in courts of law; commoners had no right of juridical self-presentation. Likewise, they had no right of political representation—no right to vote for representation in, let alone stand for election to, Parliament. Officially speaking, they had no public face, no persona. In both a legal and a political sense, it seems, they were not persons. If we read the biblical passages with these facts in mind, to have respect for persons would be to favor people who have titles and wealth and to disregard those who do not. On this reading, *person* not only refers to the fact of differential social or class status; it *is* a status. To respect persons was to favor people with land, wealth, and title and to disfavor people without. The word *person* was a name for a *particular* status, one that most people in the Diggers' day did not have. The Diggers were not simply low-status persons; they were not persons at all.

If the Diggers did not understand themselves and each other primarily as persons, then not one of them was striving to be a good person, even if they all were striving to live good lives. Although it may be impossible to know precisely how their system of values was configured or how it operated, we can at least draw the conclusion that contemporary systems based on a modern concept of personhood as the seat of moral value and responsibility are contingent on historical forces that can change and perhaps already are changing in ways that create the moral anguish that I and others experience.

The rest of this chapter further examines one strand of the prehistory—one line of various ancestors—of modern moral personhood. In other words, the chapter moves backward in time, rather than forward toward Locke's more familiar concept of personhood. There are two reasons for what might be seen as a detour. One reason for going into such genealogical depth is simply to reinforce my claim that personhood as we know it was not in evidence before the seventeenth century. The ways the term was used become less and less familiar, even if not altogether unfamiliar, the further back in time we go. A second reason—of equal if not of more importance—is to identify several historically separate elements or traits that now exist in compound in our concept of personhood. Chapter 2 will then offer an account of how those elements and others came together in the decades after the Diggers' protests to form the more modern moral personhood that plays a key role in the ethical and political philosophy of Locke and his followers, the concept of personhood that gradually shaped the moral world as so many of us now experience it.

II. Four Types of Evidence That Personhood Was an Exclusive Status

In what follows I discuss four discursive domains that lend plausibility to the idea that the word *person* often (though not always) functioned as a social status that not every human being in seventeenth-century England enjoyed—in other words, to the idea that some people at that time were not persons in some important ways. These four are (1) the homology between the words *person* and *parson* in the context of massive and sometimes violent uprisings against the Anglican clergy; (2) the gradual displacement of the Middle English word *wight* with the Norman-French word *person* that was not yet complete in the seventeenth century; (3) the integration of Roman law into English law after the twelfth century, including the legal category of the person; and (4) the legal existence of nonhuman persons, taken over from Roman law, that enabled the formation, amid much controversy, of corporate persons in English law (and then in US law, which has been especially controversial since the 2010 US Supreme Court decision in *Citizens United* and the 2011 Occupy Movement). While (1) probably has only minor significance, and my research into (2) is somewhat limited by my lack of training in the relevant linguistic fields, (3) and (4) are quite compelling, and the four taken together paint a picture of seventeenth-century English personhood as a highly contested political, economic, and social formation and suggest that the Diggers were not simply decrying inequality but were denouncing personhood per se. Their vision of a just and godly society was one in which no one claimed the status of personhood, an egalitarian society in which personhood did not exist. Unlike some social justice crusaders today, the Diggers did not want to make personhood all-inclusive; on the contrary, they wanted to abolish it.

A. OF PERSONS AND PARSONS

In the seventeenth century, English speakers pronounced the word *person* as we pronounce the word *parson*, just as they pronounced the word *clerk* as *clark* (eventuating in the surname Clark); the words *person* and *parson* were homonyms.[9] For people like the Diggers, that was no doubt a happy coincidence, for they opposed the distinguished status of Anglican clergymen as much as they opposed the distinguished status of attorneys and lords. Not only did clerics enforce the strictly hierarchical state religion at the local level, but they lived off the mandatory tithes of those who resided within their parishes. Many did no physical labor themselves, and quite a few neglected their official duties as well. They were the sons of the lords and gentry, sons of landowners and frequently landowners themselves, which was reason enough for the Diggers to detest them, but anger and dissent were not confined to the lower classes.[10] Verbal abuse of and physical assaults upon clergy were commonplace. Many clerics were run out of their parishes. Historian David Cressy goes so far as to assert, "The disintegration of the Church of England was the most startling and disturbing feature of the English Revolution" (Cressy 2006, 129).

At first the angry attacks were launched only against individual holders of positions within the episcopacy, not the episcopacy itself; the dominant demand was for national church reform, not overthrow. But with challenges to the holders of the highest positions in the hierarchy, the hierarchy itself was also under attack. The object of some of the most intense rage was Archbishop William Laud, who had led a years-long effort to make the hierarchy more secure and the liturgy more formal—some said more Roman Catholic. The extremely ill-fated war with Scotland in the summer of 1640 (during which the Scots seized all of Northumberland and Durham, including the crucial coal fields) was frequently referred to as the Bishops' War and was believed to be the result of Laud's handiwork—Laud having allegedly convinced King Charles to impose the English Book of Common Prayer on the Scottish church. Just a few weeks before the war broke out, when the Church Convocation had met in April 1640, the archbishop and his associates—many in the highest ranks of the Anglican episcopate and in professorships at Oxford and Cambridge—had issued the *Constitutions and Canons Ecclesiastical*. Discontent had been growing for years, but these two events brought it to a head. When Charles summoned Parliament in November 1640—an action made necessary by the Scots' encroachment on the north and the consequent need to raise taxes to finance an army—a large number of members of Parliament began officially to dismantle "Laudianism" in the Anglican Church. Some demanded that the *Canons* be burned. Twelve of the bishops who participated in drawing it up were impeached (Cressy 2006, 152), and in December Parliament had Laud himself charged with treason. On January 10, 1645, the archbishop was executed by decapitation.

By the time the Diggers broke ground on St. George's Hill at the beginning of April 1649, both Laud and Charles were dead, Charles by a scant two months. Both had been executed by their own people—Laud, the archbishop of Canterbury, the supreme parson of the land;[11] Charles, the sovereign king of Great Britain and Ireland, the supreme person of the land. What a mere decade before was utterly unthinkable had come to pass: the top of the hierarchy had been lopped off, and the intermediate echelons were in terrible disarray. Dissenter religious sects and communities abounded; in some instances, commoners took over churches and preached their radical doctrines from the pulpits. Both the countryside and the towns were full of Ranters, Quakers, Muggletonians, Fifth Monarchists, and myriad other groups, some of which proclaimed total sex equality as well as common ownership of land. And with the collapse of censorship, religious and political views once entirely banned were published and discussed openly from one end of the former kingdom to the other. In the midst of all this, the Diggers' dream of true leveling, of a fundamental equality among all people—the dream that no one would go cold or hungry or homeless while others claimed exclusive rights to fertile land—was more realistic in England in 1649 than it had ever been.

That dream died in the 1650s. Within eleven years, both the Stuart monarchy and the Church of England were restored. The parsons/persons regained their hold on the country's political machinery. The Diggers lost. Nevertheless, and despite the term "restoration," things had changed and were changing. Religious and political ideas, practices, and communities that came to expression while censorship was suspended may have been substantially eliminated from public life—thanks to ongoing exercising of force—but they still circulated among the populous, ready to surge forward at the slightest opportunity.[12] Things could not return to any prewar status quo (whatever that might have been), and those who wished for such a thing knew that fact very well. When the world turned upside down, too many things came loose and fell out of place; inverting it again only brought more dislocation. To contain and manage the mess over the next several decades, new political institutions and technologies had to be invented, one of which, I will argue in the next chapter, was the modern moral person.

Although perhaps it is a minor point in the vast sweep of seventeenth-century English history, surely the constant denunciation of "parsons" put commoners in mind of persons as well and of the generally elevated status of those who had the rights to parliamentary representation and to present themselves before the law and use it to secure their property and harass and deprive their poorer neighbors. That close aural connection must have intensified commoners' sense that they—as neither parsons nor propertied persons—were a thing apart. Whether they thought of themselves in opposition simply as people, as souls, or as children of God—or perhaps as *wights*, as the next section will suggest—they must have been adamant that they were not persons/parsons.

B. BEFORE PERSONS—CHAUCERIAN WIGHTS

If there were English-speaking human beings to whom the word *person* did not apply in the seventeenth century and before, how did they refer to themselves and each other in the singular? By the seventeenth century, the word *person* could be and was used simply to mean individual human being. However, before that time, English had a perfectly good word for individual people, the word *wight*. *Wight* was a common word in Chaucer's fourteenth-century English, and it still existed into the seventeenth century. A wight was straightforwardly an individual human being, just as a modern person is. Why, then, has *person* completely displaced *wight* in modern English?

I believe that an answer lies in the different associations surrounding *wight* and *person* in how each word situates individual human beings. To demonstrate this point, I will start with a little etymology. *Wight* was derived from the Old English and Old High German word *wiht*. According to *Webster's New World Dictionary* (1988), *wiht* is akin to the German *wicht*, meaning "creature," and the Goth *waihts* and Indo-European *wekti*, both meaning "thing." There are cognates in Dutch, Swedish, Danish, and Icelandic. But in addition to indicating an individual human being, the Middle English *wight* could also mean something like *vigorous, active, brave*, or *strong*. In this sense, it comes from Old Norse, meaning "skilled in fighting" or "of age" and from the Old English *wigan*, "to fight." We can see both these uses in Chaucer's "Monk's Tale" (lines 2263–70):

> She dorste wilde beestes dennes seke,
> And rennen in the montaignes al the nyght,
> And slepen under a bussh, and she koude eke
> Wrastlen, by verray force and verray might,
> With any yong man, were he never so wight.
> Ther myghte no thyng in hir armes stonde.
> She kepte hir maydenhod from every wight;
> To no man deigned hire for to be bonde.

The young woman in the story is quite feral, visiting wild beasts' dens and sleeping under bushes, running in the mountains all night. She can overpower any young man, no matter how strong (*wight*); she has such strength in her arms that nothing can stand against her. She preserves her virginity from everyone (every *wight*) and will not be bound to any man. Here and elsewhere, the word *wight* does not function exactly as the word *person* does in modern English. For example, it does not clearly distinguish between human and nonhuman creatures; its emphasis seems to fall on animation and vitality rather than on species identification. It conveys a continuity across living beings rather than a distinction among humans in social status, although in some contexts it was used to refer to a social inferior and not to a social superior. For instance, in the context of intimate relationships, *wight* might be used to refer to a female beloved but not to a male lover (Farrell 2015, 184–86), and, like the German word *wicht*, it could refer to children. The dominant meaning of *wight* in the fourteenth century, however, made it a synonym for *creature*, a living being made by a Creator God. As we will see in the next subsection of this chapter, *person* has a very different derivation and situates individual human beings very differently in relation to other beings.

Wight was far less common a word in the seventeenth century than it had been in Chaucer's day.[13] It was still used, but instead of referring to the vitality of animate creatures, it seems to have focused attention instead on their vulnerability, mortality, or misery. In his 1626 poem "On the Death of a Fair Infant Dying of a Cough," for example, John Milton refers to the sick child as a "mortal wight." *Webster's New World Dictionary* points out that by then the word was often used "in a patronizing or commiserating sense." If a person was a rights-bearer and proprietor worthy of respect (as we will see more definitively in what follows), a wight seems to have been something more like a poor wretch properly pitied if not simply despised. *Wight* seems to have come to refer not to all individual human (and other living) beings as it once did, but specifically to individual humans of a low social status.

Unlike *wight*, *person* is not an Anglo-Germanic word; it descends from the Latin word *persona*. *Persona* has cognates in modern romance languages, such as *persona* in Spanish and Italian and *personne* in French. The first documented uses of the word *person* in English's lineage occur in the thirteenth century in Anglo-Norman, which was the hybridized language of the Norman-French conquerors and their Anglo-Saxon subjects. When the Normans arrived in England in the eleventh century, they were persons I suppose, but the Anglo-Saxons were wights or wihts—and for some time thereafter each group must have retained its own word. Eventually, though, the two groups of people merged, and so did their two languages, creating the Anglo-Norman of the thirteenth century, much as English and Spanish are merging in many communities in the United States today. By the eighteenth century, there are no wights anymore, only persons. A foreign word had become so deeply incorporated into English that the English word ceased to function at all.

We might suspect that when a language incorporates a foreign word, it is because people find the foreign word better for conveying a concept than the range of words available to them in their own language (or because use of the foreign word signifies one's refined taste or projects high status). English has incorporated the French word *entrepreneur*, for example, and people now understand and use it freely as if it were an English word. It serves an important purpose, precisely because English previously had no word for the range of meanings covered by the French word *entrepreneur*. Before the seventeenth century, there were no English entrepreneurs. When it became important to talk about people who were not merely merchants, adventurers, or investors but something similar to yet slightly different from all three, the English just borrowed the French word and kept it.

Something similar must have happened with the word *person*. The fact that the word also appears in modern Germanic languages, including both German and English, suggests that at some point in their history, those languages had no word that would serve the purposes that the Latin word served. Yet all had words for an individual human being, the singular of *people*. The question, then, is what purpose the Latin word served for English speakers that *wight* could not. I believe an answer lies in the fact that *wight* took its meaning from a discursive network in which human beings were not radically distinguished from nonhuman animals and in which status likely depended more on animacy and strength than on wealth and land ownership. Each of these discursive networks is entangled with a different configuration of power relations. As England's social, political, and economic arrangements changed, the discursive arrangements that included personhood gained ascendancy over those that included wight-ness. The word *wight* was losing any place in the configurations of power and discourse that were forming from the fifteenth through the seventeenth centuries, just as peasants were losing their literal places through land enclosure.

C. PERSON AS LEGAL STATUS

As noted above, *person* derives from the Latin *persona*, English having taken it over almost intact within a few decades after the Norman Conquest. The Latin could at times be used to mean "individual human being"; however, as this section will demonstrate, its fundamental and core meanings gave it a much more limited extension. In Roman philosophy, at least in Cicero's *De Officiis*, a work that was widely read and cited in England in the Middle Ages, one human being could have multiple personae. In Roman law, brought to England soon after its rediscovery in Italy in the twelfth century, some people were personae as a matter of status for some part of their lives and most people were never personae. There is no reason to think, then, that the English word *person*, newly derived from *persona*, bore the modern meaning of, simply, human individual. It makes much more sense to assume that in its first English uses, *person* remained much closer to the meaning in Latin legal discourse, particularly since, as we have already noted, there was already a perfectly good English word for the singular of *people*, namely, *wight*. The adoption of *person* into English suggests that either existing English words did not suffice to carry the meaning that the Latin word carried or use of the Latinate term was a mark of high status in itself. In either case, *person* did not mean what it means now and likely did not apply to a wide range of human beings. In the English language as well as in Roman law, *person* most often named an elevated status that most people did not enjoy.

To take the measure of the Latin word, it is helpful to examine a few strands of its prehistory and early uses. Although its precise etymology is unsettled, many scholars hold that *persona* can be traced back to the Etruscan *phersu*, meaning mask. The Etruscan word is a plausible source for the Latin both because of the similarity in sound and also because the Etruscans were longtime neighbors of the Latin peoples of southern Italy and ruled the Romans for at least a century, until 509 BCE. Undoubtedly, they imparted many words to the Latin language. Marcel Mauss offers some evidence that the Etruscan word is in turn a garbled version of the Greek word πρόσωπον (*prosōpon*) (Mauss 1938, 274),[14] which meant face or countenance in Homeric Greek but certainly by the fourth century BCE did mean mask or in some cases portrait.[15] At any rate, whether or not the Etruscans took their word from the Greek and whether the Latin word came from the Etruscan or (directly) from the Greek, one thing we know for certain is that the Romans regularly used their word *persona*, mask, to translate the Greek πρόσωπον, and the histories of both words affected the development and significance of our English word *person* (as well as the German *Person* and the French *personne*). In the sixth century, Boethius explained that *persona* was derived from *personando*, "sounding through," because stage actors' masks amplified and sometimes altered the pitch of their voices to help them differentiate characters by age and sex (Marshall 1950, 472). Thomas Aquinas repeats this derivation in *The Summa Theologica* I, q. 29, a. 1, 2, 3. More recently, along the same lines, Paul J. Fenwick has held that the Latin word breaks down into *per* + *sona*, "sounding through" (Fenwick 2005, x), which, again, alludes to theatrical masks. In all three ancient cultures—Etruscan, Greek, and Roman—actors always wore masks onstage, through which, obviously, they spoke their lines. Siegmund Schlossmann presents a great deal of evidence that theatrical practices are the locus of both the Greek and Latin words' emergence in his in-depth study *Persona und Πρόσωπον im Recht und im Christlichen Dogma*.[16]

There may well also have been some slippage even in the theatrical use of the terms quite early on between the mask and the role the mask represented. Several centuries later, Christian authors such as John the Scot, Abelard, Simon of Tournai, and Thomas Aquinas took *persona* to have meant, in addition to mask: role, representation, and even the personage represented by the mask/actor. John the Scot and Simon of Tournai also took the words to mean the actor who played the role (Marshall 1950, 477). Aquinas at one point suggests that when famous men were represented onstage, a considerable honor apparently, these men themselves were then called persons (Marshall 1950, 478; see *Summa Theologica* I, q. 29, a. 1, 2, 3).

By the second century BCE, Greek grammarians were using πρόσωπον in their analyses of verb inflections. Aristarchus of Samothrace (ca. 156 BCE), the fifth head of the library at Alexandria and a scholar of Homeric literature, is the first known to have done so, although he may well have adopted the practice from earlier Stoic grammarians. His pupil Dionysius Thrax, who employed the word as well, wrote a book that became the basis for all succeeding ancient grammars (Trendelenburg 1910, 350); thus did πρόσωπον and then its Latin translation, *persona*, become a technical term in grammatical analysis.[17] Our English terms *first person, second person,* and *third person* for categories of pronoun, as well as verb inflection, descend from these Alexandrian Greeks. The inspiration for this adaptation of πρόσωπον for analytic purposes seems to have come from the Greek theater's "three-actor rule"—the rule that, no matter how many different speaking parts there might be in a given play, the play had to be written for no more than three actors.[18] (This meant not only that no more than three speaking actors appeared onstage simultaneously, but also that if one actor played more than one role, his characters would never appear onstage at the same time.) At all times, therefore, there were no more than three speaking masks onstage (not counting the chorus). Accordingly, whichever role had the opening speech was called the first πρόσωπον, the first mask. The role to which this speech was addressed was called the second πρόσωπον, the second mask. The third character, or mask, to come onto the stage was called the third πρόσωπον, and quite often that character would be the object of the initial discussion. The parallel with grammar is obvious: The one speaking—and the verbs inflected—is the first person; the one spoken to is the second person; and the one spoken about, the object, is the third person (see Trendelenburg 1910, 349–50).

Roman grammarians took up this usage, simply translating the Greek πρόσωπον with the Latin *persona*, as we see in the work of the prolific Roman scholar Marcus Terentius Varro (116–128 BCE), who was described as "the most learned of the Romans" (Trendelenburg 1910, 351n1). Varro writes, "Since the persons of the verb were likewise of three natures, the one who was speaking, the one to whom the speaking was done, and the one about whom the speaking took place, there are three derivative forms of each and every verb" (Varro 1938, 387).

By Varro's time, the meaning of the word *persona* had expanded considerably; it had come to designate not only grammatical inflections and theatrical roles, but social roles as well. One could be a son, a father, a military officer, a priest, and so on. Such "roles" brought with them sets of duties, expectations, and privileges. Each individual might have several personae, and the number could increase or decrease as one's circumstances changed. Cicero's *De Officiis* (*On Duties*), composed in the last months before his assassination in 44 BCE, provides insight into the word's broadened philosophical meaning. There Cicero explains that everyone has a rational persona, which distinguishes human beings from "brute creatures." So here we see *persona* indicating something a bit more substantial than a changeable social role. In addition, each of us has an individual persona that distinguishes us from one another (Cicero 1991, 42). This latter seems to involve basic bodily and mental dispositions that might be referred to colloquially as one's "temper" or "nature." A well-lived life involves expression of the common persona, the rational, but also the expression of the particular persona. Cicero also attributes two other types of personae to human individuals. One type includes that which one takes on in consequence of chance occurrences or contingent circumstances, and these may be multiple and shifting. The other includes those we acquire as the result of our decisions. "Kingdoms, military powers, nobility, political honours, wealth and influence, as well as the opposites of these, are in the gift of chance and governed by circumstances. In addition, assuming a role [*persona*] that we want ourselves is something that proceeds from our own will; as a consequence, some people apply themselves to philosophy, others to civil law, and others again to oratory, while even in the case of the virtues, different men prefer to excel in different of them" (Cicero 1991, 45). In the Latin of Cicero's time, in sum, the individual was not a person; the individual was many persons (and presumably also exceeded his or her many persons).[19]

Perhaps not surprisingly, given attempts like Cicero's quasi-legalistic efforts to determine which duties adhered to which personae, a close connection between *personae* and legal roles and duties or offices shows up in Roman jurisprudence over the next two centuries. At first the word may have been used simply for the roles of different individuals at court. The individual who brought suit (whom we might call the plaintiff) and the individual against whom the suit was brought (the defendant) would enter plea and counterplea before the court in a ritualized manner that was reminiscent of actors onstage. Accordingly, their roles were called *personae*. This usage appears in Gaius's highly influential *Institutiones*, which was written around the year 161 CE, in book IV, section 86.[20]

It is, however, the work of legal scholars commissioned by the Emperor Justinian I that directly influenced English law from the twelfth century onward. Soon after assuming office in 527 CE, Justinian began preparations to reunite and restore the Roman Empire to its second-century glory.[21] Within three years, he waged a successful military campaign against the Vandals to take the entirety of the North Africa coast (Louth 1995b, 123). Not long thereafter, he sent troops to retake Italy from the Ostrogoths. They attacked from the south through Sicily, where the ruling Ostrogoths were weakest, another very successful strategy. Soon Justinian's troops held Rome, and Milan was razed (Louth 1995b, 125). Then they pushed on to reclaim the Visigoth's region of southern Spain.[22] Taking the territory was crucial to his plan; however, Justinian knew that holding on to the empire required much more than military might and efficient tax collection. He needed a systematized, updated legal system.

Even before his military successes, within months after assuming office, Justinian officially announced to the Senate his intention to have a new law code drawn up. He commissioned ten men to update and clarify existing law, reconciling contradictions and eliminating irrelevancies, a massive project considering what had accumulated over the course of the last thousand years of Roman rule.[23] Thousands of laws existed by that time, from innumerable scattered sources. The first known written laws were called the Twelve Tables, which were lost in their entirety during Celtic invasions in the fourth century BCE, but the content remained available for several centuries. (Cicero reports that he memorized and could recite the Twelve Tables as a student in the first century BCE. Not surprisingly then, references and fragments in later work are plentiful.) In addition, however, unwritten laws came into being as times changed and new needs arose, and these were known as the *ius civile*. Further, once Rome became an empire encompassing many non-Romans, provincial governors made laws to protect and manage those people, a highly varied mass of laws known as the *ius honorarium*, and emperors issued ordinances called "constitutions." The presence of travelers through Roman territories also called for regulations and protections that would apply to all people regardless of their status in the empire, the *ius gentium* or law of nations. Justinian expected his commission to reconcile and systematize all these laws.

Despite the enormity of the challenge, the commission completed the ten-book *Codex Constitutionum* by 529 and a twelve-book revision, the *Codex Repetitae Praelectionis*, by 534. (The ten-book edition is no longer extant, but copies of the latter edition still exist.) Between 530 and 533, a group of sixteen lawyers compiled and edited all the known writings of all authorized Roman jurists in a fifty-book *Digesta* as a commentary upon the laws. Additionally, they produced a legal textbook, the *Institutes*, which was a revision of the second-century jurist Gaius's commentaries, for use in training jurists at the two official schools of law at Constantinople and at Berytus (now Beirut). (A fourth compilation, produced by Constantinople law professor Julianus for his students in 556 and called the *Novellae*, would contain the constitutions Justinian issued after publication of the second edition of the *Codex* in 534.) All these works were published in Latin, although in fact Justinian, as emperor of the Eastern Empire (the Western having fallen into Germanic hands earlier on), spoke and issued later laws in Greek.

In undertaking these juridical tasks, Justinian pointedly assumed law giving and judging as paramount duties of an emperor. Such duties were, therefore, a personal means of imperial self-assertion. Much more importantly, however, they gave Justinian the opportunity, as Andrew Louth puts it, "to delineate a worldview, enshrining the inheritance of Roman civilization, the embrace of Christian orthodoxy, and the paramount position of the emperor. This was an enduring legacy, and at its heart was a vision of the complementarity of empire and priesthood, *basileia* and *hierosynē*, *imperium* and *sacerdotium*" (Louth 1995a, 100). Justinian's vision would help to shape both the ecclesiastical and juridical institutions of Latin-speaking western Europe for centuries to come. After a revival of Justinian's unified body of law, first in Bologna and Florence in the eleventh century and within another century at Oxford and Cambridge, the idea of the persona, the person as a legal status, was perpetuated in Western thought.

The story of the development and spread of Roman law is rich and fascinating in and of itself, but what is important here is the conception of personhood embedded in and disseminated along with it, for it is this that figures into a genealogy of modern moral personhood as it emerged in seventeenth- and eighteenth-century England. Classicist J. B. Moyle discusses Roman jurists' use of the term in his translator's introduction to book I of the *Institutes*:

What did the Romans mean by 'persona'? It is clear there is some relation between persona and homo: for the leading division of the 'ius quod ad personas pertinet' (i.3.pr.) is that all men are either free or slaves. It is equally clear that they did not regard all men as persons; it is not said all persons, but all *men* are either free or slaves. . . . An essential element in the conception of 'persona' is the capacity of acquiring or possessing legal rights, and . . . a slave could have no legal rights of any kind whatsoever. In other words, a persona is a man regarded as invested with legal rights, or as capable of acquiring them, so that our attention is drawn away from the man to the rights, or to the capacity of having them in virtue of which he is a persona. (Moyle 1912, 85–86)[24]

Italian political theorist Roberto Esposito notes, "No one in Rome was a full-fledged person from the beginning of life nor did one remain a person forever. Some became persons, as *filii* became *patres*; others were excluded because they were prisoners of war or were debtors" (Esposito 2012a, 24).[25] Theoretically, at least, an individual could be and then not be a person of one sort or another several times throughout one's lifetime. And as one's status changed, so did one's legal rights.[26] Roman law, therefore, both personalized and depersonalized. A person who lost his property and plunged into debt, for instance, was legally depersonalized.

Far from signaling moral equality, then, as the term *person* purports to do in contemporary ethical theory and practice, the concept of persona in Roman law was a tool for differentiating and even for oppressing a majority of human beings. Its function and purpose were to mark, intensify, and even to produce inequality. To acquire the status of person was to have bestowed upon one a set of rights and responsibilities not granted to other human beings. And, as both Moyle and Esposito note, prominent among the rights it bestowed was the right to own and/or dispose of the living bodies of nonpersons, including other human beings.[27]

Esposito contends that the category of personhood in Rome (and in later legal discourses informed by Roman law) was not simply applied but wielded to ensure the dominance of some individuals over others and the continuation of certain networks of power despite onslaughts of resistance. While I embrace Esposito's claim, I must also note that the situation in Rome was a bit more complex than his rather abbreviated account suggests. Nonpersons, including women and slaves, did have some legal protections.[28] And even among free adult males, personhood was a matter of degree; full personhood involved the rights of *libertas*, *civitas*, and *familia* and was only had by heads of households. A son was not a full person until his father's death and his assumption of his father's persona, which gave him the rights of a paterfamilias. Until that point, the son had citizens' privileges but no property rights of his own; everything he had or acquired belonged to his father. A prepubescent son whose father died could not assume full personhood and so had to have a "tutor," who "was a person who supplied something that was wanting, who filled up the measure of his pupil's *persona*" (Sandars 1941, xl). Only upon his entry into manhood could the son assume the status of a full legal person with property rights. And no daughter ever could. Still, Esposito's point holds: Roman legal personhood was not a general term for individual human beings; personhood was a mechanism of power. This was as true in seventeenth-century England as it had been in sixth-century Rome.

By the third generation after the Norman Conquest, Englishmen were avid students of Roman law.[29] Many journeyed to Bologna, where rediscovery of copies of Justinian's work had ignited a revival of civil jurisprudence alongside study of canon law. In the 1130s, John de Bohun, bishop of Salisbury, went to Bologna to study. Thomas Beckett, later archbishop of Canterbury, studied there in the 1140s. In 1145 then-archbishop of Canterbury Theobald of Bec brought over the Lombard legal scholar Vacarius to serve as his adviser. Vacarius incited much enthusiasm for Roman law in Theobald's circle and began offering lectures at Oxford. Soon courses were being offered at other English schools, and copies of the *Institutes*, *Digest*, and other Roman works as well as commentaries were available in both cathedral and monastic libraries (for lists, see Turner 1975, 8). By the end of the twelfth century, most educated Englishmen had some basic knowledge of Roman law even if jurisprudence was not their primary course of study. And along with the law came the legal concepts, such as *persona*, through which it was organized.

Henry II introduced reforms that gave English common law its shape beginning in 1166. Although at this time, the English court was well versed in Roman law, the procedures Henry adopted—such as trial by jury—were not based on it. Canon law as practiced in England, however, was far more deeply indebted to Roman law. As Ralph V. Turner puts it, "Canon law was the child of Roman law and, naturally, a close connection of the two continued" (1975, 10). Alongside common law, canon law remained in force until the time of Henry VIII, and in modified form even after the break with the Roman Catholic Church, until it was suspended during the Civil Wars. Regardless of the extent of Roman law's direct impact on English legal forms, however, it is clear that Roman legal concepts like *persona* circulated among educated Englishmen as long as Latin remained the language of scholarship. In England, as in Rome, personhood was an elevated status that excluded a vast majority of the people, especially common people like the Diggers.

D. FROM *UNIVERSITAS* TO *LEVIATHAN*: NONHUMAN PERSONS

So far it may appear that personhood as a category or class of entity in Rome and in seventeenth-century England was a subset of the category of human being; a person was a certain kind of human being, much as an aristocrat was a certain kind of human being. Moreover, it might seem, since the seventeenth century there has been a laudable trend toward broadening the category to include more and more human beings, with the egalitarian-minded working for the day when the categories of human and person become absolutely coextensive. But such an eventuality only seems possible if we ignore the existence of nonhuman persons.

In the lineage here examined, the concept of *person* bore no necessary relation to *human being* at all. It did not pick out a subset of humanity. Even when human beings were included in its extension, it referred to something other than their being as human. And because it referred to something other, its extension always could, and did, include beings that were not human, beings that were not conscious actors, beings that were not even alive. (In this last sense, if not in others, *person* is obviously not a good translation of *wight*; wights were always living beings, even if they were nonhuman animals or demons.) The *persona* that originated in ancient Roman law and reappeared in medieval canon law was an entity that could appear and act in civil society. Like personae onstage, Roman legal personae could appear and state their business, but now in courts of law, where they could assert their rights. However, appearing and speaking were not the essence of these legal personae; most fundamentally, Roman legal personae were proprietors, rightful owners who had the rightful powers of *usus* and *dominium* over economies of non-personae. When necessary, legal personae could be represented in court and spoken for; they did not have to appear "in person" themselves. In fact, they did not even have to have a "person" in the corporeal sense; living flesh was entirely optional.

Many nonhuman entities in Rome owned things. Municipalities, for example, owned land and buildings, archives, movable goods, tax money, and, of course, human slaves. They could take cases to court. They could enter into contracts. The Roman state itself was such an owner. These institutions were personae. By the second century BCE, incorporation of business enterprises was expanding. Some corporations, called *universitates* in Latin, received contracts for public works. There were also mining operations in Macedonia and Spain. Public land could be contracted out for such purposes, and contractors could form joint-stock companies with limited liability (see Patterson 1983, 93). Craft guilds were also incorporated.[30] By the second century CE, *universitates* held contracts to provision the military and to build public buildings and infrastructure. Roman government became quite dependent on them, and many were absorbed into the state machinery—even to the point that membership was made hereditary so that contracts vital to the government's interests could be perpetuated. As the empire declined in the West over the next couple of centuries, the corporate form declined there also, but it remained in the East and so found its way into Justinian's Code.[31] The key feature was that these institutions held property that did not belong to the human beings who might populate, organize, invest in, or staff them. The entities themselves bore property rights protected by the state. Sandars sums this up:

> Many *personae* had no physical existence. The law clothed certain abstract conceptions with an existence, and attached to them the capability of having, and being subject to, rights. The law, for instance, treated the State as a *persona*, capable, for example, of owning land or slaves (*ager publicus, servi publici*). So, a corporation, or an ecclesiastical institution, was a *persona*, quite apart from the individual *personae* who formed the one and administered the other. Even the *fiscus*, or imperial treasury, as being the symbol of the abstract conception of the emperor's claims, was spoken of as a *persona*. (Sandars 1941, xxxvi)

Corporate personhood is not a recent invention, then, as many opponents of the US Supreme Court's ruling in *Citizens United v. Federal Election Commission* (2010), seem to think; on the contrary, it is one of the oldest institutions in the Western world. In Roman law, corporations had more claim to personhood than most human beings did.

In the Middle Ages, the concept of *universitas*, corporate personhood, was absorbed into the canon law, especially as a mechanism to handle property and contracts associated with monasteries. As Max Radin writes, "It was quite within the medieval tradition that . . . the corporation aggregate might well own lands and enter into contracts, although every single person who composed it could do neither. That question had been fought out in regard to the mendicant orders, since any monastic community might be a great landed proprietor, while the individuals could have no property whatever, but were civilly dead, that is to say, no persons at all" (Radin 1932, 648). (We will revisit this fight, as Radin terms it, in chapter 5, when we examine Francis of Assisi's ultimately futile effort to defy the property regime that was developing in the Mediterranean world in the thirteenth century.) Soon thereafter, in the twelfth and thirteenth centuries via the *Institutes* of Justinian and the canon law derived from it, Roman legal thinking entered English courts, English law, and, increasingly, English thought. English municipalities were legal persons, much as Roman municipalities had been. By 1540 there were forty-four incorporated cities and boroughs in England, four in Wales, and thirty-five royal boroughs in Scotland (Withington 2007, 1027).

And, just as in Rome, eventually there were commercial corporations in England, too. The first chartered companies operated as umbrellas for bands of merchants; they functioned much like craft guilds, setting standards and collecting fees for shared services like docks and warehouses. By the sixteenth century, charters were issued for companies of merchant-adventurers in the hope that England might compete internationally in the spice trade, namely, the Muscovy Company (1555) and the Levant Company (1581). This trend continued in the seventeenth century as Britain entered the fur and slave trades with the Virginia Company (1606), the Company of Royal Adventurers Trading to Africa (1663), the Hudson's Bay Company (1670), and the Royal African Company (1672) (see Robins 2012, 23). Most famous and influential of all, of course, was the East India Company, chartered by Queen Elizabeth I on December 31, 1600.

The queen hoped that the company would bring spices from the East Indies to England by sea, which theoretically would be much less expensive than the overland route then in use from the Levant. Of course, the initial investment in such a venture was large, and the venture itself was risky, not only because all long sea voyages were risky but also because other European powers were already trading in the area and would respond with force to protect their interests. Still, over the preceding twenty years, Elizabeth had learned from experience that there were great riches to be had in transcontinental trade (or piracy, as the case may be). She had been the largest investor in Francis Drake's three-year around-the-world expedition on the *Golden Hind* (1577–80), which brought back jewels, gold, spices, and other goods worth so much that the average investor saw a return of 5,000 percent. Elizabeth herself saw an enormous return. The East India Company might prove to be equally lucrative.

The joint-stock model overcame some of the challenges of raising capital for the first voyage and then for voyages thereafter. (For the first fifty-seven years, the company sold stock for each separate voyage; only under the charter issued by Oliver Cromwell in 1657 did it begin to sell stock in the company per se.) The pool of potential investors was enlarged by the fact that company management was separated from investment; investors did not have to play any role in actually running the operation. The joint-stock model also limited the risk each investor took; if the venture failed to produce a profit, each would only lose his initial capital and would not be liable for any debt beyond that amount. Finally, as Nick Robins explains, "trading was conducted by the joint-stock company on its own behalf, rather than by the members themselves. This gave the company a separate identity and its own legal personality—one that could conduct business strategies that went beyond the interests of individual merchants" (Robins 2012, 24). In other words, the company became a legal person, a legal actor and bearer of property rights. The East India Company was a person, then, at a time when most of Elizabeth's subjects had no such status.

In addition to its long-standing use as a way of giving municipalities and other public institutions legal proprietary status and its value as a form for commercial ventures, Roman personhood—specifically, nonhuman corporate personhood—played another very important role in Britain in the seventeenth century: it provided the means for rethinking sovereignty in the aftermath of the Civil Wars. English political theorists looked to the legal concept of corporate personhood to free them from the sovereign personhood of the monarch, on the one hand, and the chaos of popular rule, on the other. A perfect example comes from Thomas Hobbes, whose *Leviathan* demonstrates his knowledge of the Roman concept of personhood and his assumption that his readers were familiar with the concept as well. *Leviathan* was published in 1651, the same year that the Diggers were finally ousted from their settlements. Like the Diggers, and probably like most other people in England in the 1650s, Hobbes was very tired of civil strife and economic disruption. He wanted peace. He wanted stability. And he wanted both to last. Where he differed from the Diggers and other like-minded radicals was in what he believed lasting peace and stability required. In his view, equality was the problem, not the solution to social strife and upheaval. To keep the peace, someone (or some group of people) had to occupy a station sufficiently above all others so that fear of this authority would compel obedience to law.

A sovereign was essential, then, but the recent unpleasantness made clear that this sovereign could not declare its authority and legitimacy on the basis of Divine Right or even Right of Conquest. Hobbes had to distinguish sovereign authority from what his contemporaries saw as tyranny; otherwise, the state and its laws would be, as radicals had long claimed (and as Foucault discusses at some length in *"Society Must Be Defended"* 1997), nothing other than war by other means. Hobbes needed a theory that would make the sovereign's authority originate in the authority of the people to be governed by it; the sovereign somehow had to represent their will, even when they disliked the laws or deliberately violated them. In *Leviathan*, chapter 16, entitled "Of Persons, Authors, and Things Personated," Hobbes undertakes to distinguish and clarify the concepts of person, actor, and author in order to explain how one individual can legitimately represent another to the point of creating obligations that will be binding upon that other. This is a necessary step in his argument that a multitude of individuals can be bound together into one person, the sovereign, and bound to obey that sovereign's decrees.

Hobbes uses something like the Roman legal notion of persona to explain transfer of authority from one individual to another, such as the authority to enter into contracts that will be binding upon the first individual. In other words, if Jones designates Smith as his agent, Jones gives Smith the authority to sign contracts on Jones's behalf, as Jones's representative, so that Jones is the one who is obligated to fulfill the contract. In designating Smith as his representative, Jones transfers his authority to Smith. Hobbes explicitly relates ownership (which he refers to in Latin as *dominus*) of words and actions to ownership of property. One owns one's authority to give one's word, a type of ownership that Hobbes calls authorship (Hobbes 1958, 133). In a case of authorized representation, the actor Smith "personates" the author Jones, the owner of the words spoken or written in contract.

Hobbes notes that the Latin word *persona* "signifies the *disguise* or *outward appearance* of a man, counterfeited on the stage, and sometimes more particularly that part of it which disguises the face, as a mask or vizard; and from the stage has been translated to any representer of speech and action, as well in tribunals as theaters. So that a *person* is the same that an *actor* is, both on the stage and in common conversation . . ." (Hobbes 1958, 132). What is transferred when one becomes the authorized agent of another, he claims, is the personhood of one individual to another.

There are two types of person, then: (1) those who act on their own authority and who are thus both the owner of the words/action and the actor—these Hobbes calls natural persons—and (2) those who act by prior covenant in the place of another. In the latter case, the actor bears the personal authority of the owner's words or actions but is a distinct individual— these Hobbes calls feigned or artificial persons. Personhood is a matter of authority, and in particular of the authority to make binding promises, covenants, or contracts. It is alienable and is not coextensive with selfhood.

By means of this legal concept of persona, Hobbes explains how a multitude of individuals can be unified under a single, undivided sovereign without having recourse to the controversial Stuart doctrine of Divine Right. "A multitude of men are made *one* person when they are by one man or one person represented. . . . For it is the *unity* of the representer, not the *unity* of the represented, that makes the person *one*. And it is the representer that bears the person, and but one person . . ." (135). This sort of authority is the only hope for security against foreign invasion and against injury by one's neighbors; everyone must "confer all their power and strength upon one man, or upon one assembly of men that may reduce all their wills, by plurality of voice, unto one will; which is to as much as to say, to appoint one man or assembly of men to bear their person . . ." (142). This one person is Leviathan, who "has the use of so much power and strength conferred on him that, by terror thereof, he is enabled to form the wills of them all to peace at home and mutual aid against their enemies abroad." Further, "he that carries this person is called SOVEREIGN and said to have *sovereign power*; and everyone besides, his SUBJECT" (143). This one sovereign person may be one individual or a collection of individuals as in a parliament. Hobbes discusses the advantages and disadvantages of each type of government, although he clearly favors the model of the single individual.

Regardless of the form it takes, Hobbes insists, sovereignty once constituted must not be challenged. Subjects are not to pass judgment on the decisions or actions of government, for subjection to a sovereign authority is incompatible with the exercise of personal judgment. Hobbes thus banishes private conscience from political life, calling the very idea "that every private man is judge of good and evil actions" a "disease of the commonwealth" proceeding "from the poison of seditious doctrines" (253). Whatever authority an individual might hold over his life and property would henceforth be granted to him by the sovereign power and could always be revoked by it. Once sovereignty was established, Hobbes insisted, all other legal and political authority—all other personhood—existed only by leave of that sovereign power.

There are human beings without any authority, human beings who are not even "natural persons," Hobbes says. He mentions "children, fools, and madmen" (134). Although they are not and cannot be persons in themselves, the sovereign can authorize means by which they can be personated; the sovereign can create a person to act on their behalf. Hobbes notes, for example, that a legally authorized guardian can personate a child. This authorization does not confer personhood upon the child; it simply establishes a new "feigned" or "artificial" person borne by the guardian. (Recall the Roman designation of "tutor" discussed above.) Sovereign authority can create persons at will, wherever it sees a need for authorization to act. It can even cause inanimate objects to be personated. For example, Hobbes says, a rector can personate a church.[32] Here we can see how the currently controversial corporate person might arise. The sovereign power can grant the status of personhood—that is, the authority and right to act—to a group of people united in a common enterprise so that the person is borne not by the several individuals as an aggregate but by the enterprise as a legal entity.

This power of civil law to grant authority for personation can even extend to the personating of nonexistent things, Hobbes notes, such as the heathen personation of false gods. He is quick to assert, though, that Moses's personation of the One True God was duly authorized and nonfictional, as is the personation of God that occurs in the Holy Spirit and Jesus Christ.

Hobbes's political views were controversial, but not because of his understanding of personhood as legal agent and rights-bearer. Those ideas were commonplace among educated Englishmen of his time. Personhood—even "natural personhood"—was not a status all human beings had by virtue of species membership, and in its artificial form it could extend to anything on which a corporately generated sovereign had need of conferring rights.

∴

In sum, based on these various evidentiary domains, I believe it is fair to say that persons in seventeenth-century England were proprietors, and the laws protected them as such whether they were humans or nonhumans. The laws did not protect humans as such, however; on the contrary, by protecting proprietors, the laws left humans to starve to death or die of the disease and violence that run rampant among the materially deprived. The law was a respecter of persons, even though God was not.

III. Conclusion: Return to Moral Anguish

By this point, I think, my claim that mid-seventeenth-century English personhood was not the same as a human being or human individual is abundantly plausible. At some point in the not terribly distant past, people in my own cultural and linguistic lineage could and presumably many did lead good lives without being good persons. My desire to be a good person and my anguish over not being so arise out of a particular history marked by particular social, political, and economic arrangements. Those arrangements are historical formations and as such are historically contingent. I exist within formations of power that subjectify me as a person; I am a person, even though I am not very good at it, and I don't know how to be otherwise, even though this emerging awareness suggests that some aspects of my life are already otherwise. Anything that arises in history can erode or collapse in history. The configurations of forces that produce me and other Westerners as persons are not absolute and unchangeable, nor are they all-encompassing. In fact, my moral anguish at my inability to be a good person, as well as my ability to question that anguish and the complex of meanings and arrangements of forces that condition and generate it, could both be indications that alternatives are possible and change is already afoot.

Before exploring such possibilities, however, we will look further at how what was once clearly an elite status having to do with property, law, rights, and representation became the personhood that today involves moral agency and responsibility, consciousness and conscience, and individual identity and freedom. Those are the aspects of personhood that moral anguish problematizes, not the status of rights-bearer or owner of property (at least, not thus far). How did an exclusive legal status become an all-embracing moral status? In the next chapter, I will locate the emergence of the modern moral person at the turn of the eighteenth century and argue that we can interpret its appearance then as a solution to a particular set of political, legal, economic, and theological problems within specific networks of power and knowledge.

[CHAPTER TWO]

Subject of/to Judgment
John Locke and God's Three Persons

The sense of personhood I came to experience (and so often feel myself failing at) involves some kind of self-reflexivity or something like consciousness, selfness, ownness, or mineness, and, of course, responsibility, which in turn involves both self-control and accountability. *Person* designates a decision-maker and an actor that recognizes itself as such through time. Immanuel Kant's 1797 definition of *person* in *The Metaphysics of Morals* is classic: "A *person* is a subject whose actions can be *imputed* to him" (1996, 16). When we blame or praise someone, when we indict or convict someone, when we hand out medals of valor or science fair ribbons, when we claim authorship of books, we engage in practices of imputation. Many of these practices are closely related to practices of ownership and involve epistemic apparatuses for discerning true or proper ownership. A person is a being capable of owning its past actions, emotions, preferences, and plans for the future. As such, it is also capable of owning material goods and intellectual property and of keeping promises and fulfilling terms of contracts. Connected with this is the idea that persons bear certain legal rights and obligations. A person is an individual rights-bearer, a proprietor, then, as Hobbes assumed in the mid-seventeenth century, but unlike the legal person known to Hobbes and his contemporaries, it is also a self-conscious and deliberate actor. All of this culminates in the ever-present possibility of judgment, both a person's own judgment and, often more importantly, the person's susceptibility to the judgment of others.

In the preceding chapter, we saw ancestors of moral personhood in Roman law and its applications and manifestations in seventeenth-century England. From that Roman lineage, modern personhood inherited its proprietorship and legal standing as rights-bearer, but not its subjection to social, religious, and moral accountability or the dictates of conscience. Rights-bearing and property-owning persons in that Roman lineage need not even be living beings, let alone self-aware human beings capable of deliberation. Kant's eighteenth-century definition of *person*, despite its undertones of ownership, would make little sense in the ancient Roman context. Something happened, then, between the mid-seventeenth century when the Diggers wrote their tracts and the end of the eighteenth century when Kant wrote his tomes. Somehow the status of proprietorship and the capacities for deliberation and responsibility came together in a new configuration of meaning—which was, as we will see in this chapter and the next two, inextricable from new configurations of power.

This chapter has two aims: To explore another lineage of the modern moral person, the lineage from which it inherits at least some aspects of what we might call its consciousness, and to describe the two lineages' confluence. First, then, I will suggest that modern personhood's particular form of self-awareness comes from the evolving Christian Doctrine of the Holy Trinity, God in Three Persons, particularly as it took shape in the Church settlement struggles of seventeenth-century England. Second, I will provide a plausible account of the unlikely marriage of Roman legal personhood and Christian Trinitarian theology and of the delivery of their offspring as performed primarily and notably (although certainly not single-handedly) by the English philosopher, political theorist, and physician John Locke.

The first section of this chapter recounts Locke's discussion in *An Essay Concerning Understanding* (bk. II, sec. xxvii), wherein he introduces his concept of personal identity, and it provides some of the historical context in which his theory was conceived and presented. The second section recounts the long history of Trinitarian doctrine, highlighting the shifting networks of institutional forces that shaped that doctrine as both a site of contestation and, at times, a tool for social control through the Middle Ages. The third section focuses on struggles over the doctrine as the Anglican Church tried to reestablish itself in the aftermath of the English Civil Wars. Then the final section of the chapter examines one move in that long, high-stakes game that was made by Locke's friend William Sherlock at the end of the seventeenth century, a move that rested on a novel account of divine personhood and suggests that Locke used his friend's proposed solution to the Trinitarian controversy, in combination with the concept of person generated within the Roman legal tradition, to solve an interrelated set of problems in theology, ethics, and government that were extremely important to him and to his generation of educated Englishmen. It is in this effort of Locke's, as I will show, that we see the birth of the modern moral person.

I. John Locke's Account of Personhood

Étienne Balibar has called Locke's concept of personhood "the first great modern doctrine of the individual subject" (Balibar 2013, 44). And, indeed, it was a first. Introduced with the publication of the second edition of Locke's *Essay Concerning Human Understanding* in 1694, this new concept of personhood was met with considerable confusion. In the late seventeenth century, human beings were usually individuated most fundamentally as souls, not as persons in the way that Locke promoted. As a result, some readers seriously misunderstood his analysis; some feared it would lead to denial of the soul's existence and, therefore, immorality or even atheism. Only after a few years of discussion and published debate did the dimensions and functions of the concept become clear to a wide readership, but once it did, Locke's concept of person took strong hold. The concept met a set of intellectual needs that made it indispensable once its contours were fully appreciated. The fact that it also enabled a range of new ways of exercising power, which the next chapter will explore, certainly did not hinder its acceptance, either.

The first edition of Locke's *Essay* appeared in December 1689 (although the publisher stamped it with the date of 1690), and almost immediately it made a major impact. It went through four editions in the decade and a half between its appearance and Locke's death in 1704 (Huyler 1995, 325n119), which indicates its astonishing popularity if not its intellectual influence. Its influence was no less astonishing, however. One measure of that influence is the trouble subsequent writers took to position themselves in relation to its arguments and conclusions, whether in support or in opposition (see Carey 2006, 183). Gary McDowell characterizes *An Essay Concerning Human Understanding* as "the most influential book of the eighteenth century, with the sole exception of the Bible" (McDowell 2010, 169). Even Garry Wills, who argues that Locke's *Two Treatises* influenced American revolutionaries far less than his predecessors had assumed, acknowledges the great impact of the *Essay*, noting that "Locke was, for men of Jefferson's period, the Newton of the mind—the man who revealed the workings of knowledge, the proper mode of education, and the reasonableness of belief" (Wills 1978, 171). The intellectual, social, and ultimately political importance of the *Essay* cannot be overstated.

For the second edition, Locke added a new section (bk. II, sec. xxvii) addressing the question of personal identity, which he included in all editions thereafter. On this topic specifically, one twentieth-century commentator has asserted that all subsequent philosophy is just a footnote to Locke (Noonan 1989, 30), and another terms Locke's account of personal identity "revolutionary" (Uzgalis 2018). The book as a whole was pivotal, and this additional section has proven to be so in its own right, so much so that Balibar terms it a treatise in itself (2013, 1).

Despite, or perhaps because of, the concept's groundbreaking nature, Locke was reluctant to publish this material. He included it in the second edition apparently only at the strenuous urging of his friend William Molyneux, Furthermore, it appears there not as an explicit theory of personhood but rather as a theory of persistent identity—that is, of what it takes for someone to be considered the same person in the present as in the past and future in practices of imputation, judgment, and punishment—and is presented as simply a solution to a problem raised before the Royal Society by another of Locke's friends, Sir Robert Boyle. Its immediate function is to reconcile scientific fact with a particular point of Christian theology. Of course, its implications and uses are far, far broader, but it is important to attend to the argument in context to grasp it fully.

The question that Boyle posed to the Royal Society concerned God's Final Judgment. At the End of Days, according to the prevailing Christian doctrine of the time, God will raise the dead in order to evaluate their deeds and determine their eternal fate. (Most people in seventeenth-century Britain believed that this resurrection would involve restoration of each individual soul to its material body; intact bodies would literally rise from their graves to stand before the Almighty Judge.) Yet, Boyle pointed out, upon death, bodies begin to disintegrate and disperse, and over time their particles become parts of other beings. This makes the job of corporeal reconstruction extremely difficult, although perhaps not impossible for an omnipotent being. Boyle, however, added a serious complication: What if an individual is eaten by a cannibal? Then the same particles belong to two different human bodies, both of which must be reconstructed and exist simultaneously on Judgment Day.[1] What would the deity do about that?

What would there be of either individual to be judged? In what would either individual's self-sameness or personal identity consist? René Descartes's work could have furnished a basis for an answer. According to Descartes, the entity to be judged is a thinking thing, an immaterial substance, not a body at all. If we adopt this view, we can hold that God could bring both individuals' immaterial substance forth and judge them even without their material bodies. This view, with a variety of nuances, was not uncommon among English and Scottish philosophers of the seventeenth and eighteenth centuries.[2] Locke was not eager to adopt such a position, however; he had spent the first book of his *Treatise* refuting the Cartesian doctrine of innate ideas and distinguishing his own position from Continental rationalism. Furthermore, as Locke well knew, this Cartesian answer posed significant practical problems of its own: If the entities to be held accountable are immaterial, God could certainly hold them accountable for their actions, but human beings and courts of law could not, quite simply because mere mortals would be unable to tell whether the individual at court was *the same* as the individual who perpetrated a past action. A distinctively embodied man with a clearly recognizable countenance might rob someone this week and then that same body could be hauled into court for prosecution a few weeks from now, but even with eyewitnesses who could recognize the body, there would be no way for a human judge to know that this same body was currently attached to the same immaterial being who committed the robbery. If individual people are not recognizable by some criterion accessible to human beings' physical senses, law enforcement—indeed civil law and the civil government whose primary purpose is to make and administer it[3]—is worthless.[4]

The dilemma was this: On the one hand, a judgeable individual could not be just a body (that would run afoul of both theology and science), but, on the other hand, a judgeable individual could not be a pure thinking being with no essential attachment to a body and its material history (that would make a mockery of earthly jurisprudence). Locke's *Essay* sought to provide a different sort of answer.[5]

He began by distinguishing three different types of identity through time. First is that of a nonliving object. Second is that of a living, and therefore constantly changing, body. Third is the identity through time of what he calls a person. We can say, as Boyle's question implied, that a nonliving object is the same through time because its parts, or particles, remain together. Living bodies are another matter. Carrying Boyle's scientific observation even further, Locke points out that the particles of our bodies do not disperse *only* upon death; we and all living beings are constantly shedding old particles and adding new ones throughout our lives. That being the case, whatever it is that makes a living being the same being now that it was last week cannot be the particles of its body. What, then, is it? Locke's answer is that sameness is a matter of a living being's organized form, coupled with the emergence of that form at a given point in time. That oak tree there is the particular oak tree that it is because it sprouted right there in that spot forty years ago, and it has retained basically the same form throughout those forty years—although of course material has been added and subtracted continually over the seasons and decades. The identity of any living being is a matter of formal continuity.[6] The organization of living beings operates in such a way over time to assimilate new matter to the same form;

basically, living beings actively organize and recreate themselves continually.[7] This is what Locke refers to as "the same life" (*Essay* II.xxvii.4, 298).

What is true of an oak tree is true of a man (a human body). A man is the same man because of the singularity of his emergence in time and space and because of the continuity of his form, regardless of the material that composes him at any given moment. This is the identity of a *man*; however, Locke maintains, a man is not the same thing as a person. *Personal* identity is, as Locke puts it, "the sameness of a rational being: and as far as this consciousness can be extended backwards to any past action or thought, so far reaches the identity of that *person*; it is the same *self* now it was then; and 'tis by the same *self* with this present one that now reflects on it, that that action was done" (*Essay* II.xxvii.9, 302). In other words, the persistence and unity of awareness (not soul or an immaterial thinking being, but also not particles and not bodily form) are the criteria of personal identity.[8] A particular consciousness may or may not inhere in a particular immaterial thinking substance as Descartes said; it simply does not matter one way or the other. Nor does it matter whether the consciousness inheres in the *very same* material object or body, even if experience tells us it does. What matters is the capacity for—or more precisely the act of—self-attribution over time. A person is a being who recognizes past actions, passions, and perceptions as its own. A person who exists now is the same person who existed yesterday if now it can recognize events that happened to it yesterday—including what it witnessed, what it underwent, and what it did—as part of its own past. Note that this means the person is essentially embodied in living material form, causing and undergoing material events; the person is embodied, but it is not reducible to "mere" body, to specific material configuration.

This persistence of consciousness over time, this personhood, is what enables us to hold people responsible for what they did, for their actions—what enables us, as both Locke and, later, Kant put it, to impute to them. And on Judgment Day, God can also impute to us, as long as resurrection of formally identical bodies also restores our conscious awareness of a past set of acts united with the present. As Locke says: "The sentence shall be justified by the consciousness all persons shall have, that they *themselves*, in what bodies soever they appear, or what substances soever that consciousness adheres to, are the *same* that committed those actions, and deserve that punishment for them" (*Essay* II.xxvii.26, 312). So, both the cannibal and his/her victim meal will come before God at the End of Days. Problem solved.

Questions obviously remain, however, and commentators over the centuries have raised a great many. People can take themselves to be conscious of having committed a past action when in fact they have not or can fail to retain a past action in consciousness. And under such circumstances people can blame themselves for or take pride in things they never did or fail to make right or take credit for things they really did do. But Locke's account incorporates those factual, historical mistakes into those people's persons as readily as it incorporates their real choices and acts. He leaves this problem unaddressed.[9]

To sum up, for Locke, *person* "is a forensic term appropriating actions and their merit; and so belongs only to intelligent agents capable of a law, and happiness and misery. This personality extends it*self* beyond present existence to what is past, only by consciousness, whereby it becomes concerned and accountable, owns and imputes to it*self* past actions, just upon the same ground, and for the same reason that it does the present" (*Essay* II.xxvii.26, 312). A person, in other words, is an intelligent agent, a being that can deliberate before making a decision and taking action, which, as a result, is based upon that prior deliberation; hence, among other characteristics, a person is essentially consciousness or awareness persisting through time. Bare consciousness alone is not enough for full personhood, however; without some experience in the world, consciousness would lack a realized ability to deliberate. (If I have no experience of a situation, I cannot perceive my options for action within it and so cannot deliberate among them.) Fortunately, consciousness's temporal duration makes it possible to accumulate experience, which also allows it to develop preferences and motivations. An enduring consciousness knows not merely pleasure and pain, which are momentary sensations, but also more long-lasting happiness and misery, which provide it with an impetus or motive to reflect on its behavior and learn from the consequences of it. Having learned through experience to anticipate consequences, consciousness acquires the ability to follow rules (or deliberately break them) and to plan future actions accordingly. Nobody is born a person, therefore; in the first few years of life, children become persons.[10] Persons are beings with enough experience and skill to be able to hold themselves accountable and to be held accountable by others, both morally and legally, for what they have done.[11]

These points must be stressed: A person, according to Locke in 1694, is a conscious being who has learned to deliberate and decide before doing. This means that personhood is not a fleeting, momentary phenomenon, nor is it something that can exist outside of time in an eternal present; a person persists through time. A person is, by definition, a thoughtful awareness unified across different moments, hours, and days. That sameness through time is personal *identity*, the topic of Locke's chapter. In the course of explaining personal identity, Locke also makes the point that a person is a producer of material effects, and he/she/it recognizes these effects as having originated with him/her/it, understands these effects as being in some sense his/her/

its own. Personhood is also, and by definition therefore, ownership of actions. All this taken together renders a person a being who is accountable.

Locke's concept of personhood was strange to his contemporaries, many of whom believed he was denying the existence of the soul. He was not, but his analysis did render souls irrelevant for all practical purposes; souls do not come before courts of law or even clerical confessors. Furthermore, it is the persons, not the souls, upon whom God will pass final judgment. Souls might well exist; they might even be somehow ontologically necessary for consciousness to come into being and persist. For Locke's moral and legal purposes, however, we can leave that set of issues aside.

Theological worries over Locke's claims died away, and his concept of personhood eventually prevailed in European and then in Euro-American thought. Protestant Christians, in particular, embraced individual personal responsibility for economic and political as well as spiritual life (although the concept of individual soul did retain a place alongside personhood and sometimes was conflated with it, despite Locke's distinction). Locke had introduced something new into the world, but it quickly found a central place and function within a set of discourses and practices that had been, unwittingly, in need of it for some time. There had been no such person in that world before Locke introduced one, but a world in which modern moral persons were comfortably absent had undergone serious disruptions for several decades so that a place had opened for just such a creature to be recognized and to take pride of place in Locke's time. Such was the birth of modern moral personhood.

II. Modern Moral Personhood's Other Parent: The Doctrine of the Trinity

New ideas and ways of being do not come out of nowhere; they have precursors or analogues, or they arise from motivated reversals of ideas and practices already in use. Furthermore, new ways of thinking and living have no impact if the world is not ready to take them up; a place for them and a need for them must already exist. So, while I put the invention of modern moral personhood down to Locke, we must keep in mind the historical and social context within which he arrived at it and the conditions of its uptake then and its practice—that is, its realization as a subject position—in subsequent decades. Chapter 1 examined Roman personhood, which in modified form existed in English law from the late twelfth century forward. The rights-bearing, property-owning person was a Latin concept familiar to educated Englishmen of the period, who of course studied Latin in school and read Latin classics even if they were not trained in the law. In this section, we will examine the other discourse in which personhood was prominent in England both before and during the seventeenth century, Christian theology's Doctrine of the Holy Trinity, the Three Persons of God.

Versions of such a doctrine can be traced back to the turn of the third century CE, and no version was ever free of controversy, or at least not for very long. Adherence to whichever version happened to be the official doctrine at a given time was often used as a test of "true" Christianity, and departure from it was often punished as heresy. This was as true in seventeenth-century England as it had been in fourth-century Constantinople, and Locke was very aware of both the debates and the dangers of taking a public stance. In fact, he never publicly declared his views on these doctrinal issues and never publicly professed belief in either Trinitarianism or Unitarianism. Nevertheless, as I will show below, he drew on Trinitarian ideas published by his friend William Sherlock in 1690 (and no doubt discussed in private circles that included Locke long before that year) to formulate his concept of personal identity. To make that case, I will first recount the origins of the doctrine and its history of controversy and then describe Locke's borrowings and amendments.

A. WHY THE ONE GOD NEEDED ALSO TO BE THREE: EARLY CHRISTIANITY'S BIG PROBLEM

The earliest followers of Jesus of Nazareth had no need to formulate a Trinitarian theology, because, as monotheistic Jews, they did not believe that their assassinated leader was either *the*, or even *a*, god. While they certainly believed that Jesus was the Messiah, they understood him as the *anointed* son of the One God, as his ancestor King David had been, not as God himself or as God's literal offspring. It was only around the beginning of the second century that some began to maintain that Jesus himself was divine.

This departure from Jewish monotheism may have been set in motion in part (and if so certainly inadvertently) by the missionary work of Paul of Tarsus in the mid-first century.[12] While most of Paul's converts were diaspora Jews and their non-Jewish sympathizers (known as the God-fearers) so that the congregations he founded and facilitated remained largely Jewish in tradition and tone, Paul did aspire to bring Hellenistic pagans into this new religious movement. Although he had little (if any) respect for the cults of Mithras, Osiris, Attis, and Hercules, when he preached to pagans he formulated his message in terms he knew would resonate, at times fusing pagan concepts and imagery with aspects of Jewish scripture and tradition (Hillar 2012, 111). His efforts were very successful; over the next two centuries many pagans did join the people who began to call themselves Christians.[13] With these gentile converts, however, came many more elements of Greco-Roman practice, terminology, and intellectual and affective commitments. Since Greek and Roman religions had always assumed the existence of multiple deities and tales of divine acts of reproduction were commonplace, many of these new converts to Christianity had no trouble understanding the son of God as himself a god.

The new ideas may have taken hold first at Antioch; Ignatius, bishop of Antioch, is known to have discussed Jesus's deification in letters he wrote between 98 and 117 CE. The subject can also be found in the writings of Pliny the Younger in 112 CE (Hillar 2012, 129–30). Belief in Jesus's divinity was apparently fairly widespread by the middle of the second century.[14] And so, it would appear, there were two. Furthermore, scriptures compiled and circulated during this time also speak of a Holy Spirit sent after Jesus's resurrection, apparently yet a third deity. Christianity in the broadened context of the Roman Empire was on its way to becoming a polytheistic religion.

Many Jewish Christians were not at all pleased with this development.[15] Early on, predominantly Jewish congregations were racked over the issue; there were expulsions and schisms. Some gentile Christians broke off and established their own congregations and sought new converts (Hillar 2012, 122). The only hope for the Christian movement to retain its unity was to find a way to reconcile the convictions that, on the one hand, Jesus, the Holy Spirit, and the omnipotent Creator were all divine beings distinct from one another and, on the other hand, there is but one God. Three had ultimately, somehow, to be One while, at the same time, remaining Three.

B. HOW THE THREE GODS COULD ALSO BE ONE: A LONG TALE OF HERETICS AND THE TRINITARIANS WHO REBUKED THEM

The theological solution that eventually emerged in the Greek-speaking East was that there is one God, but that one God has three πρόσωπα (*prosopa*) or ὑπόστασις (hypostasis) and, in the Latin-speaking West, that there is one God, but that one God has three personae. The trick was to explain exactly what those three πρόσωπα or ὑπόστασις or personae were and what it means to say the one God "has" them. And that trick was made even more complicated by the fact that, as we saw in the previous chapter, these words carried a wide range of different definitions and applications in theatrical, grammatical, and jurisprudential discourses that had been in circulation already for several centuries.

One prominent solution to the three divinities problem—the Modalist solution, whose most prominent advocates were the Greek-speakers Noetus, Praxeas, and Sabellius—was that the Son and the Father were merely different modes or faces (πρόσωπα) of one substance. Sabellius explicitly equated them with different masks worn by the same actor (Armstrong 1993, 99). In other words, for the Modalists, the Messiah was not simply the anointed one, as he was for the monotheistic Christian Jews, nor was he a separate, second deity, as some pagan converts would have it. Like the Father and the Holy Spirit, Jesus was in fact the one true God (see Phan 2011, 6). The apparently different entities were in fact just the same being (ὁμοουσία, homoousia), each presenting a different aspect or wearing a different mask (πρόσωπον, *prosōpon*). Many early Christians were satisfied with this answer.

It did not satisfy everybody, however, for the Modalist solution entailed that the one true God, masked as the Son, had actually died on the cross. How could a God die? That thought—and its obvious alternative, namely that Jesus's death was faked—was utterly unacceptable to many Christians, including the Stoic jurist Tertullian (160-220 CE).[16] He decided a better solution was called for.

Tertullian's home was Carthage, which was not a major center of Christianity at that time—the major centers being Antioch, Alexandria, and Rome—and unlike the important Christian writers of his and earlier days, he did not speak and write primarily in Greek; although he could and sometimes did use Greek, his preferred language was Latin.[17] When he challenged the Modalist view in *Adversus Praxean* and *Apologetics*, he translated their πρόσωπον as *persona*.[18] Just as his Roman predecessor Cicero had asserted that one human being may have multiple personae, some emanating from his nature and others acquired or produced at identifiable historical moments, Tertullian asserted that one divine being could (and did) have multiple personae.[19] Contrary to Sabellius, however, these personae were not mere masks, false faces that would obscure the true being of God; they were real roles, as distinct from one another as the different roles one actor might play onstage or as the different roles (son, father, statesman) that Cicero might play in the course of his life. Those roles were really God's roles, not masks used to project an illusion. Understanding personae as roles preserved distinctions among Father, Son, and Holy Spirit, while still allowing Christians to rest assured that underlying those distinct roles was one divine actor, who did not die.

Tertullian did not develop the concept of God's personae in great logical detail, instead relying extensively on metaphor: As the sun emanates rays of light or as the roots send forth the tree, the Godhead sends forth the Word; the Word is the prolation, or emanation, of the Father, and the Holy Spirit is the prolation, or emanation, of the Word. Many readers found this reasoning abstruse and unconvincing (for, it seems to me, obvious reasons). Nevertheless, Tertullian's work provided a basis for the Latin versions of the Doctrine of the Holy Trinity that would emerge in the next century, after Christianity became a legal religion in the Roman Empire. He even gave the doctrine its name. It was Tertullian who coined the term *trinitas*, basing this neologism on the Greek term τρίας, *trias*, the term that Theophilus of Antioch had used to name the divine trio around 180 CE (Hillar 2012, 243).

No one should be surprised to learn that Tertullian's largely metaphorical account of God's threeness in oneness did not settle the matter. The emperor Constantine's conversion (in 312) and subsequent legalization of Christianity (in 313) meant that the new religion could now be institutionalized. Who would have authority in this new set of institutions, and who would control their development? With so much more at stake in the question of who did and did not count as a true Christian believer, controversies over Jesus's status intensified.

In that atmosphere in 318, a presbyter at Alexandria, one Arius, drew a growing number of followers by asserting that the Son is a creature of God and God's instrument for creating the world; in other words, although the Son is perfect and above all other creatures, he is not eternal (having had a beginning in time) and not of one substance with the Father. In making these claims, Arius was not trying to undermine Christianity; on the contrary, he held that the Son's status as creature offered hope for us creaturely mortals; if we imitated Jesus, we, too, might approach perfection (Armstrong 1993, 110). But Church officials at Alexandria found Arius's assertion (and, no doubt, his growing number of followers) deeply disturbing and moved to excommunicate him and his associates later that year. Excommunication did not stop the spread of Arius's ideas, however. (He apparently set them to music, producing a tune catchy enough that it was picked up and sung by sailors and thereby spread around the Mediterranean—see Armstrong 1993, 107). Schism looked imminent, which annoyed Constantine, who called a council at Nicaea to settle the doctrinal matter.

The Council of Nicaea began meeting on May 20, 325, with at least 220 participants. Most of the participants started out as moderates perhaps open to compromise, but the new patriarch of Alexandria, Athanasius, whose views were deeply opposed to those of his Alexandrian colleague Arius, was able to sway the assembly. The creed they ultimately produced (with only three dissenting votes) declared that the Son was fully divine, and the Father and Son were ὁμοουσία, homoousia (which would be translated into Latin as "same *substantia*"). The Christ was generated, not created as the Arians said, and so existed from eternity (Fortman 1972, 65). Thus was doctrinal unity supposedly achieved, and Arianism was declared a heresy.

It was unity in name only, however, as bishops returning to their congregations upon the council's conclusion simply continued preaching whatever theologies they preferred. In truth, it appeared that various Arian-like factions and others who opposed the Nicene Creed together made up a majority of Christian thinkers in the mid-fourth century,[20] and they began to hold synods and produce their own creeds. Far from uniting the Church and thereby putting an end to schism, the Council of Nicaea, as led by Athanasius, seems to have attempted simply to cover over differences of opinion more or less by force, an approach that just did not work.

Many anti-Nicenes disliked the term ὁμοουσία (homoousia), which did not appear in the Scriptures and which had been used by Sabellius in his version of Modalism (Phan 2011, 8). Some preferred to speak of the status of Father and Son (and Holy Spirit) using the term ὑπόστασις (hypostasis), which does occur in Scripture.[21] Back in the second century, Origen had used this word in its ancient meaning of "single concrete being" and had rejected consubstantiality. Some of the anti-Nicenes may have been attempting to rehabilitate this older meaning of the term, while still holding to the thesis of ultimate consubstantiality. The problem was that by the time of the Council of Nicaea, ὑπόστασις had simply become a synonym of οὐσία, both words translating into Latin as *substantia*, which made use of the term to differentiate Father from Son quite confusing. An alternative was tried by the Council of Antioch in 345 in developing the "Long-Lined Creed," which omitted the terms οὐσία, ὁμοουσία, and ὑπόστασις altogether and referred to Father, Son, and Holy Spirit as three πρόσωπα (*prosopa*) (see Athanasius, *De Synodis* 26). The council sent this creed to the Western Church at Milan, knowing the word πρόσωπα would be translated easily as *personae*, the word favored since Tertullian by members of the Latin-speaking Church (Fortman 1972, 71.) And so we arrive again at the term we translate as *person*, no more the wiser.

Acrimonious doctrinal debates raged on for more than fifty years. In 381 the emperor Theodosius I convened what became known as the Second Council of Constantinople. The ostensible idea was to establish a single doctrine and unify all factions of the Church, but this council was hardly representative. It excluded the Roman pope—he was not invited—and no Western bishops attended, either; it was strictly an action of the Eastern Church, and therefore a conference of speakers of Greek. Furthermore, while at least 186 bishops arrived for the council, 36 of them left shortly thereafter when they were given to understand that a pledge of faith to the

Nicene Creed was a prerequisite for participation in the discussion (Fortman 1972, 84). The remaining 150 bishops worked out a doctrinal understanding that largely reflected the work of the Cappadocian Fathers—Basil of Caesarea, his younger brother Gregory of Nyssa, and their friend and colleague Gregory of Nanzianzus. Remarkably (after a certain amount of politicking), the doctrine they produced did satisfy most Greek-speaking theologians and thus, surprisingly enough, brought unity to the Eastern Church.²² But Western, Latin-speaking theologians were never happy with the Cappadocian doctrine. Saint Jerome, for one, disliked it because for him the crucial Greek word ὑπόστασις retained its Nicene-era synonymy with ὀυσία (see Armstrong 1993, 116). Western theologians continued to speak of God as one *substantia* with three personae, but they had no coherent, widely accepted Latin account. Some serious Latin theology was definitely called for.

C. SOME SERIOUS LATIN THEOLOGY: AUGUSTINE, BOETHIUS, AND AQUINAS ON THE NATURE OF THE PERSONAE

So things stood in the Latin West for the next several decades. The Big Problem was still a Big Problem, still causing strife and acrimony, still pitting Christian against Christian in struggles for control over souls, congregations, and the levers of institutional power. Then, in the early fifth century, into this mess stepped Augustine of Hippo, who offered a new perspective in his *De Trinitate*.

Edmund Fortman offers a helpful overview of Augustine's approach, as opposed to that of both his Greek and Latin predecessors, to the issue of the One God's Threeness. He writes:

> The dogma of the Trinity involves two elements: numerical unity of nature and real distinction of the three Persons. Hence it can be presented in two ways, both perfectly orthodox but resulting in quite different attitudes toward the mystery. One way, that of the Greek Fathers and of the Latin Fathers before Augustine, starts from the plurality of Persons and proceeds to the assertion that the three really distinct Persons subsist in a nature that is numerically one. Their problem was how to arrive at 'one' from 'three,' how to move from the plurality of persons to the unity of nature, and the answer they gradually developed was in terms of the 'consubstantiality' of the Son and Holy Spirit with the Father. In this approach the danger to be avoided was subordinationism, for by concentrating too

much on the real distinction of the Persons one could endanger the unity of nature and the perfect equality of the three (as Apologists and Origen and Arians did in varying degrees). The advantage of this way is that in it God is not simply the God of the philosophers or of the Old Testament, but the specifically Christian God: Father, Son and Holy Spirit. The other way starts out from the unity of nature and moves to the trinity of Persons. It first affirms that there is numerically one divine nature and then that this one nature subsists in three really distinct Persons. Here the unity of nature is in the foreground, the trinity of Persons in the background. Now the problem is how to arrive at 'three' from 'one' and how to show that 'three' are compatible with this 'one.' This approach immediately negates subordinationism and Tritheism, but the danger it must avoid is Modalism. (Fortman 1972, 140)

Augustine chose this second way, beginning with the perfect unity of the Godhead and working toward an account of the three personae. He asked: How can we understand this differentiation that occurs in the perfectly unitary God?

Augustine's answer (greatly oversimplified here) is relation.[23] The Father is distinct from the Son and the Spirit, and they are distinct from each other, not in nature but in relation. The Father is characterized and distinguished by the paternal relation; the Son is characterized and distinguished by the filial relation; the Holy Spirit is characterized and distinguished by the gift relation. It is not that the personae are relations (as Fortman takes pains to make clear—see 1972, 144), but that the Godhead occurs in dynamic self-relation. We may refer to the Godhead by referring to substance—God—or to one or another of that substance's unchanging relations—Father, Son, and Holy Spirit. These three latter names refer to eternally subsisting relations (or perhaps we should say "relatings" or "eternal events of relating"), not to ontologically independent beings.[24]

Obviously, these personae of God bear no resemblance to what we call persons today. If the Doctrine of the Holy Trinity had solidified with Augustine's account of personae, it would not have contributed to the lineage of modern moral personhood.

Despite the wide and persistent appeal of Augustine's work, questions about the nature or being of the divine personae remained. About a century later, therefore, the Roman scholar Boethius (c. 480–525) took up the subject. While serving as consul under Theodoric, the second Ostrogoth ruler of Italy, Boethius translated some of the works of Aristotle and wrote his *Theological Tractates*.[25] It was in the latter (drawing on ideas in the former) that he supplied a definition of *persona* that gained more credence than many of its predecessors. It is also, clearly, one of our modern person's distant ancestors.

A persona, Boethius wrote, is a *naturae rationalibis individua substantia*, an individual substance of a rational nature (Boethius 1962, 84). He arrived at this definition by first distinguishing between essence, or *natura* (the Greeks' ὀυσία), and substance, *substantia*. For example, Boethius writes, Cicero's *natura* is that of human—a kind of rational—being; whatever else he might be and whatever might change about him, he remains human as long as he remains in existence. Cicero's *substantia*, by contrast, is Cicero insofar as he is a concrete individual thing that can serve as a substrate for other things. Cicero, the *substantia*, is an individual thing that is a substrate for a number of accidents such as the color of his hair. His essence is his unchanging *natura* (which he shares with other humans), whereas his substance is simply the unity that underlies his changing qualities (and that is his alone). Cicero, then, is an individual substance of a rational nature, a persona. And he is but one persona, despite what Cicero himself might have thought.

Now, what of God? Is not God, too, an individual *substantia* of a rational *natura*? Why is it that God is able to have multiple personae whereas Cicero can only have, or be, one? Although at times Boethius refers to God as *substantia*, when discussing this issue he specifies that God is actually *superstantia* (Boethius 1962, 16–19, 90–91). God does not serve as the substrate for accidents. It is true that we can predicate of God such qualities as omnipotence, omniscience, eternality, and so forth. But in fact those qualities are not accidents of God. God is pure form without matter, pure substance or "superstance" (Boethius 1962, 10–11). God has no accidents. The qualities of God are integral to God's nature. So, what of the three persons? Neither persons nor Trinity is properly predicated of God either as accidental or as integral to God's essence. Whereas God is pure form (subsistence and superstance), the persons are concrete substances (Boethius 1962, 90–91). They participate in the nature of God, but they differ in that they serve as substrates for attributes.

Boethius points out, as did so many others in this long debate, that the word *persona* originally referred to theatrical masks that enabled one actor to play more than one role in the same play (84–87). Each role had individuating characteristics—sex, age, station, and so on; in other words, each role presented the accidents of a given substance. Given that the acting of these roles was the presentation of individual rational beings, it makes sense, Boethius says, to use the term *persona* for what the Greeks call ὑποστασις (hypostasis), the Cappadocian Fathers' term for the concrete individual that is able to bear a proper name. When we encounter a human individual, we perceive his or her characteristics, the accidents of a substance that we in fact posit rather than directly experience. In watching a theatrical production, we do the same thing; we encounter characteristics for which we could posit a substance, although in the case of the theatrical presentation, we know that there really is no substance apart from the actor of the role. The actor is simply creating the illusion of a substance's presence distinct to his own for the duration of the play. Although Boethius embraces the word *persona* in its derivation from *mask*, he does so with emphasis not on the illusion of substance but on the indirect presentation of substance, persona, through a collection of accidents.

Whatever its merit as theology (which fortunately is not the issue here), Boethius's account clearly links *persona* to its ancient roots while facilitating a notable transformation in meaning. His person is not a mask or a role but a real being (*substantia*), and each one of us has, or is, a (single) person, who is truly who we are (beneath our accidents). So it might seem that Boethius, centuries before Locke, discovered or invented our concept of personhood and, therefore, that the "modern" person is not very modern after all. But such a conclusion would be premature. First of all, Boethius's person only makes sense in the context of scholastic metaphysics; it is a substance, meaning that it is something like an essential substrate or a soul by definition not directly available to human perception. This is exactly what Locke rejected. Locke's person—the judgeable, accountable, embodied actor—is emphatically not a substance. It is part of the empirical, material world. It is what it does in this world and, more importantly, what it is conscious of having done and undergone.

Boethius's account of human personae was not even unanimously accepted in the substance-loving Middle Ages. Even though he agreed with Boethius's account of the Trinity, Thomas Aquinas, perhaps the most influential scholastic of the period, insisted that human individuals are not personae. Persona as *individua substantia* involves three notions, Aquinas said: substance, completeness, and separate existence. If we add to this *rationalis naturae*, we get five features that together constitute personhood: (1) substance (not mere accident or quality); (2) completeness of *natura* (here meaning an intrinsic principle of activity); (3) *per se subsistens*—existence in and for itself (meaning the entity the subject of all its attributes); (4) separateness (whereby Aquinas excludes universals from existence as persons); and (5) *rationalis naturae*, which excludes non-intelligent beings from personhood. Human individuals do not meet these criteria. They have subsistence, but they have no *natura* apart from their human bodily forms. (This is why the body must be resurrected for the soul to have eternal life.[26]) Contra

Boethius, human beings are not persons, Aquinas concludes; the only persons are the Three Persons of God.

III. More Heresies, More Bloodshed: The Holy Trinity in Locke's Time

Trinitarian controversies raged on for centuries, with an accumulation of grisly effects. Protestant sects were as embroiled in them as the old Latin and Greek churches had been. The particular wave of acrimony and violence that led directly to the upheavals in seventeenth-century England began in Strasburg in 1531, when a young Spaniard named Michael Servetus (1509–1553) published *De Trinitatis erroribus* (*Concerning the Errors of the Trinity*). In this work and a second published in 1532, Servetus articulated a position very like Sabellian Modalism (Hillerbrand 2007, 134), the view that the persons of the Trinity are different masks all worn by one single deity. The reaction was negative, to understate the matter, resulting in Servetus adopting the alias of Michel de Villeneuve, moving to Paris, and taking up the study of medicine. There he lived for nearly two decades as a devout Catholic and came to have some prominence as a physician, but in secret he worked on his magnum opus, *Christianismi Restitutio* (*The Restitution of Christianity*), which was to be a counter to John Calvin's book *Christianismi Institutio*. He also began to correspond with Calvin in the hope of persuading him to change his views. When Servetus's book was published anonymously in 1553, Calvin informed the Inquisition at Vienne of the author's identity. Servetus was arrested but escaped to (most unwisely) Calvin's Geneva. He was apprehended there, brought to trial, and burned at the stake (Hillerbrand 2007, 135). Although Servetus's views might not have been popular while he was alive, his spectacular death, orchestrated by John Calvin himself, ignited an enormous controversy that brought much attention to his thought.[27] Writers such as Sebastian Castellio and Guillaume Postel stepped up to defend his views, and other supporters followed suit. Eventually a group of Italian anti-Trinitarians banded together and established a home base in Raków, Poland. Under the leadership of Faustus Socinus (1539–1604), their community flourished and their theological writings proliferated in the relatively tolerant Polish atmosphere, where they became known as the Socinians.

The Socinians held, in distinct contrast to orthodox Calvinism's doctrine of salvation by grace alone, that conduct lies at the heart of the Christian religion. Jesus did not come to atone for our sins but to instruct through speech and example. With the life and words of Jesus available to us through the New Testament, we have a choice to make: Will we choose to follow Jesus or to reject his moral teachings? Scripture makes the terms of the choice very clear, if only we will take the time to study it and reason through what it says, and if we weigh our options reasonably, we will in fact model our lives on that of Christ. But nothing in our nature compels us to do this; human beings have nothing like an "instinct" for religious belief or an innate idea of deity, as demonstrated by the fact that there are whole societies in the world where no one believes in a god of any sort. A choice to follow Jesus, or not, must be made deliberately and rationally, and we are fully responsible for that choice. Furthermore, said the Socinians, not only are the Calvinist doctrines of atonement and salvation by grace rather than works not scriptural, but there is nothing in Scripture supporting the claim that Jesus was divine. It is more reasonable to assume that he was a historical figure through whom God promised eternal life to those who obeyed his laws. Obviously, then, the Socinians had no use for any version of Trinitarian doctrine.

In keeping with their emphasis on human freedom of conscience and choice, the Socinians also held that God is absolutely free. This meant that God is not bound to punish all sins but can choose to forgive as he wishes. God has a right to punish, but no one, God included, is obligated to act on all their rights. Rights are not duties. This is why no atonement through sacrifice was necessary: God chose to offer human beings a teacher; he did not send a lamb for slaughter in humanity's stead. God chooses to be merciful to those who follow his anointed son. The Socinians went on to draw a very controversial conclusion from this notion of radical freedom: Although we have a right to preserve ourselves, we have no duty to do so. This was controversial on two fronts. In the immediate situation, it was controversial because Poland was at war, and the Socinians preached pacifism. Their thinking was that defending material goods—even home and body—was immoral if it required taking another's life; after all, Jesus did not resist his captors by force of arms. Less immediately, but no less significantly, it was controversial because it drove a wedge between Christianity and natural law, wherein the right to self-preservation figures prominently, to say the least. That right is derived from the duty to preserve God's creation in oneself, a duty that cannot be forsaken. But, according to the Socinians, Christ's teachings need not and in fact did not conform to the natural law tradition that had undergirded Christian theology for generations and would continue to do so in many quarters for some time to come.[28]

In 1609 the Socinians produced their Racovian Catechism, setting forth these very radical ideas. Believing that they had more support in England than they actually did, they dedicated the catechism to James I, who was outraged and had it burned in 1614 (Mortimer 2010, 39). Those events produced interest in Socinian writing in England for a short time, as did Martin Ruar's visit to the island in 1618, but the issue died down there for a couple of decades. Not so on the Continent. Protestants and Catholics alike were incensed as the catechism and its teachings spread through Europe. Meanwhile, a younger generation of Socinians—including Ruar (1589–1657), Jonas Schlichting (1592–1661), and Johan Crell (1590–1633)—moderated some of the group's earlier positions, including the position on the immorality of lethal self-defense (Mortimer 2010, 31). As their views evolved, the Socinians began to see affinities between themselves and the Dutch Remonstrants—such as Hugo Grotius and Simon Episcopius—with whom they were in contact. When the political climate in Poland became more hostile in 1638, many made plans to settle in Holland and continue their work there, a prospect that inspired the horror of Dutch Calvinists (Mortimer 2010, 104).

Although the Socinians rejected the Doctrine of the Trinity, their theology did incorporate an important understanding of God's personhood. There was one God, they believed, and that God had to be one person. Socinus's view was based on his knowledge of Roman law and in particular on the work of the Roman jurist Gaius (fl. 130–180 CE), whose *Institutes* furnished the basis for the sixth-century *Institutes* of Justinian. Gaius had made it clear that all Roman law had to do with persons, things, or actions and had implied, at least according to some, that personhood characterized active entities. For Socinus that meant, as Mortimer puts it, that "only if God were a person could he be an active agent..." (2010, 35). His critique of the Trinity was based in great part on this understanding of personhood. God had to be a person in that God was active, but the word *God* was not actually a proper name designating a unique individual being. Divinity was a power or authority, and it could be transferred. This view is consistent with Roman law, in which the personhood of the paterfamilias is transferred to the son and in which individuals can carry the personhood of another individual before the law. Thus, the relationship between God and Jesus could be understood in legal rather than scholastic philosophical terms: Christ was the delegate of God, and their essences were simply irrelevant.

Socinus's views were to have great influence in Holland and England through his young German follower, Johan Crell. Crell's *Ethica Christiana*, originally published in 1635, was reissued in Amsterdam in 1650, and many copies found their way to England (Mortimer 2010, 213), where they influenced parties to the heated post–Civil War discussions over the question of Church settlement (the question of whether there would be a national church and, if so, what its doctrines would be).

Socinianism from abroad was not the only source and inspiration for the growing skepticism of the Trinity in England. Radical sects grew powerful as mechanisms of censorship collapsed during the mid-century political upheavals. Ranters, for example, saw God as a pervasive presence that might well manifest in any individual as he had in Jesus. "God is all in one, and so is in everyone," asserts Ranter Richard Coppin in his 1649 tract *Divine Teachings* (Hill 1972, 177). As an incarnation of God, Jesus was in no way unique. Abiezer Coppe (1619–1672), a Baptist army chaplain, awoke from a four-day trance in 1647 to find himself infused with God. This experience, coupled perhaps with the news of the execution of three Leveller soldiers at Burford in May 1649, compelled him to go to London to preach. In his publication *A Fiery Flying Roll*,[29] he speaks in the voice of the Almighty (see, e.g., Coppe 1649, 14), denouncing both "fat parsons" (3) and the murderers of Leveller soldiers (11) and calling for "universall love" and "equality, or free community" (14). (Coppe was arrested in 1650, and Parliament ordered all copies of his book to be burned, although clearly not all were.) Like the Ranters, Seekers, Quakers, and other radical religious groups, including some Diggers, rejected Trinitarian distinctions in favor of a divinity manifest anywhere and everywhere in innumerable multiplicity and communality.

Lest we imagine these views existed only among disaffected foreigners or the less-than-rational British underclasses, it is important to note that radical anti-Trinitarianism (or "non-trinitarianism," as Paul Lim [2012] calls it) was also embraced by many educated Englishmen. In 1647 Paul Best (1590–1657) published *Mysteries Discovered*, and John Biddle (1615/16–1662) published *Twelve Arguments*. Best and Biddle were homegrown, Oxbridge-educated Englishmen, and both not only denied the prevailing Doctrine of the Trinity but went so far as to decry it as heresy. As sophisticated interpreters of Scripture who took a reasoned approach to theology and religious doctrine, these two English anti-Trinitarians exercised significant persuasive power over an elite audience, contributing to an atmosphere in which many respectable Englishmen expressed skepticism of the doctrine. John Fry (c. 1609–1656/7), a member of Parliament and one of the commissioners at King Charles's trial, publicly expressed doubts about the Trinity in 1649. His dispute with another commissioner, Colonel John Downes (1609–1666), as well as the parliamentary debates that resulted in his ouster in February 1651, were widely known and discussed. The proceedings against Fry were covered in detail by the most influential newsbook of the period, the *Mercurius Politicus*, which had a very wide circulation in and outside of London (Mortimer 2010, 164–65).

By the time the twenty-year-old John Locke arrived at Oxford in 1652, anti-Trinitarian ideas were part of the very atmosphere. In the aftermath of civil war, the Church hierarchy was barely functional, and canon law was not enforced. Socinian writings were widely available in Latin and some in English and were in circulation at the university. In that year alone, the Bodleian Library purchased some fifty Socinian books, and it already owned several, including the 1635 edition of Crell's *Ethica Christiana*. Oxford students—and we must assume young Locke included—were also avidly reading and discussing Grotius's Remonstrant (Socinian-influenced) biblical commentaries by 1656. University Vice-Chancellor John Owen did his best to turn his students against all these heretical ideas in favor of an orthodox Calvinism, publishing two refutations of Socinianism (*Diatriba de Institia Divina* in 1653 and *Vindiciae Evangelium* in 1655) and giving a series of lectures on the subject between November 1652 and March 1653. But his efforts actually helped to keep the controversial ideas alive not only for Oxford students but for the men who were then negotiating a postwar settlement for the Church of England. Whether the reinstituted state Church would be Trinitarian or Unitarian was an open question in the 1650s.[30]

The issue of Church settlement came to the political fore in 1652, as soon as other, even more pressing aspects of postbellum recovery had been more or less successfully addressed. Oliver Cromwell's son-in-law Henry Ireton's funeral on February 6 occasioned the first round of open controversy. It drew many army officers and chaplains to London, including Ireton's friend John Owen. In town from Oxford to give the funeral sermon, Owen used the opportunity to push for a Trinitarian settlement. He petitioned Parliament for an official condemnation of the Racovian Catechism—which had recently been reissued—and presented a document called *The Humble Proposals*. His actions inflamed his opposition. Many people, whether Trinitarian in their beliefs or not, did not want civil magistrates to rule on cases of alleged heresy, as *The Humble Proposals* would have it. There were some who did want religious authorities to have this power, but there were also advocates for liberty of conscience—including Roger Williams (1606–1683), Henry Vane Jr. (1613–1662), Marchamont Nedham (1620–1678), and John Milton (1608–1674)—who insisted that religious belief must be free of all state control. (Vane went on to challenge the Doctrine of the Trinity in particular that summer in *Zeal Examined*.) Clearly Owen and his allies had misjudged their opposition and might have lost the cause had Cromwell not dissolved the Rump Parliament before it finished considering *The Humble Proposals* in the spring of 1653. And they did lose considerable ground when Cromwell, Lord Protector by early 1654, adopted the Instrument of Government, under which all who professed faith in God through the revelations of Jesus Christ were granted religious liberty—whether or not they believed in the Doctrine of the Trinity.

With the question of a final Church settlement still open, two rival plans emerged. One came from the camp to which Owen belonged. It allowed civil magistrates to enforce core Church doctrines and required all state-supported ministers to subscribe to a single confession of faith. A second came from Richard Baxter and his allies in the Association movement. It suggested the Apostles' Creed and Ten Commandments as the only requirements for Church membership, with all else being matters of liberty of conscience. Although the Apostles' Creed does contain the words *Father*, *Son*, and *Holy Spirit*, it does not contain the word *Trinity* and says nothing about the nature or substance of God's person or persons. When Owen perceived the tide to be turning in favor of the Baxter plan, he and his allies hamstrung proceedings to prevent any decision being made that year (Mortimer 2010, 220).

Luckily for the strict Trinitarians, Biddle published his even more radical *Two-Fold Catechism* in 1652, and officials in Cromwell's administration asked Owen to write a refutation. Publication of his *Vindiciae Evangelium* (1655) gave Owen an opportunity to strike fear into the hearts of all the decision-makers by driving home the point that allowing religious toleration would license extremists like Biddle and his ilk (Mortimer 2010, 225). Owen's point was reinforced when Quaker leader James Nayler (1618–1660) rode into Bristol naked on a colt to symbolize the equality of all men with Christ, an act of blasphemy. Parliament served up severe corporal punishment for him and, for the rest of the country, Lord Broghill's *Humble Petition and Advice* to replace the Instrument of Government. This proposal outlawed both anti-Trinitarian and non-Trinitarian beliefs and gave magistrates the power to enforce the law. Cromwell accepted it in 1657, and the matter was settled—for a time.

Then came the Restoration. In 1660 Charles Stuart ascended to the throne as Charles II. At first, the new government's focus was on purging the Church of dissenters and squelching radical sects. In 1661 Charles and the Convention Parliament restored bishops to the House of Lords and reinstated all Church courts except for the Court of High Commission. Then, between 1661 and 1665, Parliament passed the four acts of the Clarendon Code. (The king tried to mitigate the repressive effects of these acts, but his efforts came to naught.) The Corporation Act of 1661 effectively excluded Nonconformists from public office. The Act of Uniformity of 1662 made the newly revised Anglican Prayer Book mandatory for all Church of England worship services. (This resulted in expulsion of nine hundred clergymen.[31]) In 1664 the Conventicle Act made it illegal to attend a meeting of more than five people for the purpose of worship without use of the Prayer Book. And in 1665 the Five Mile Act prohibited any ejected or unlicensed preachers from coming within five miles of their former parishes or any town or city.

The main threat was no longer Ranters or Quakers or even Presbyterians, however; now it was Catholicism. In 1662 Charles married the daughter of King João IV of Portugal, Catarina Henriqueta de Braganza, in a secret Catholic ceremony and in a public Anglican one. As part of the marriage agreement, Catherine, as she was known in England, retained the right to worship freely as a Catholic. By the 1670s, Protestant officials were putting pressure on Charles to divorce her. Not only was Catherine openly Catholic and kept Catholics in her retinue, but she had also had three miscarriages and produced no heir. Divorce would enable Charles to legitimize a son by his mistress Barbara Castlemaine—James, Duke of Monmouth. But Charles refused, which left his younger brother James Stuart, a Catholic himself, in line for the throne.[32]

A tremendous amount of intrigue ensued as anti-Catholics conspired to prevent James from ascending. Locke's patron Anthony Ashley Cooper, the newly minted first Earl of Shaftesbury, led a movement within Parliament to exclude professed Catholics from the throne. Three successive Parliaments entertained bills designed to prevent James's succession, but each time Charles dissolved Parliament before they could be passed. In 1681 Shaftesbury was arrested for high treason for his part in the intrigue. Although prosecution was dropped several months later, Shaftesbury, fearing for his life, fled to Amsterdam. His death in January 1683 left Locke without political protection in England, so soon thereafter he, too, fled to the Netherlands. Despite great effort, anti-Catholics could not prevent James Stuart from ascending to the throne upon Charles's death in February 1685. Subsequent efforts to depose him—the most violent of which was the Monmouth Rebellion in June of that year—also failed.

Through his brief reign, James tried to reduce the repression of Catholicism. In 1686 he issued a Direction to Preachers that he hoped would prevent anti-Catholic sermonizing. He also appointed many Catholics to offices and took steps to gain control over Church courts. To many, it appeared that he intended to make England a Catholic country. In June 1688 seven opposition leaders sent the Protestant William of Orange an invitation to invade England and take over the government of his father-in-law. That November, William and his forces landed at Torbay, and James left London for Salisbury. A few weeks later he fled to France, and the Convention Parliament declared the throne empty. In February 1689 William and his wife, James's daughter Mary, accepted the Parliament's offer of joint sovereignty under the Declaration of Rights. The political situation was resolved (and Locke returned from exile, having insinuated himself into Queen Mary's retinue as her personal physician), but the doctrinal situation was not.

The Trinitarian debate of the 1680s was minor by comparison with the theological free-for-all during the Interregnum, but it led directly to Locke's formulation of personhood. Court-sponsored Catholic writers did their best under Charles and then James to undermine the Anglican rule of faith, which held that reason was instrumental in the effort to understand the Scripture. Catholics asserted that because human reason is inadequate and its conclusions may vary from reader to reader, religious authority and tradition must take precedence. Anglicans might disparage the Socinians and other anti-Trinitarians, their Catholic opponents maintained, but their refusal to renounce individual reason in favor of the infallible authority of the Catholic Church was itself a significant step toward Socinianism. Anglicans rejected the Doctrine of Transubstantiation of the elements at Holy Communion because they said it was repugnant to reason, but was not the Doctrine of the Trinity equally so? What could not be comprehended by reason simply had to be accepted on faith, the Catholics insisted, both the Doctrine of the Trinity and the Doctrine of Transubstantiation. The Anglican orthodoxy had to answer these accusations. A group began to gather to discuss strategy, often at the London home of William Sherlock, who was then master of the Temple. Locke was an associate of many of the men who gathered and was likely present for some of discussions before his exile and after his return, although he refused to take a public stand on the Trinity. Whether present or not, he was undoubtedly quite familiar with the details of debate. In the three years of James II's reign, the group produced at least two hundred tracts against "popery" (Sirota 2013, 31–32).

Public debate was not limited to comparisons and contrasts between the epistemic and fideistic status of the two doctrines (the Trinity and Transubstantiation), however. There were some genuine Unitarians involved, including Stephen Nye, whose anonymous *A Brief History of the Unitarians* appeared in 1687. Nye argued that the Catholics were right; the Trinity stands or falls with Transubstantiation. He believed it should fall, but he called for Protestant unity across doctrinal differences in the face of the Catholic threat (Sirota 2013, 34–35).

With the overthrow of James II in 1688, the Catholic threat diminished, but the Trinitarian controversy continued as once again the question of Church settlement—which would now occur under the leadership of a Dutch Presbyterian king—came to the fore. In the spring of 1689, Parliament passed the Toleration Act, suspending prosecution of Protestant Nonconformists, and King William issued writs calling for a Church

Convocation. Among other business, the convocation deliberated over whether to include the Athanasian Creed in the liturgy. The London liberal, Low Church majority decided to rewrite part of it and not to require it for membership, which greatly angered High Church conservatives. On top of that, the Unitarian Nye asserted that no one could believe in nonsense (i.e., a God who is one and also is three), and the rector of Exeter College, Arthur Bury, condemned metaphysical speculation and reduced the gospel to repentance and faith as opposed to belief in doctrine in *The Naked Gospel* (1690). With such enormous differences coming to the fore, all hope of Protestant reconciliation (or "comprehension") drained away. By 1691 Church settlement was complete; there would be no comprehension and only a lackluster toleration.

IV. SHERLOCK'S SOLUTION AND LOCKE'S ADAPTATION OF IT

The Trinitarian debate might have died down at that point, despite the unanswered logical questions, but Locke's friend Sherlock, whose 1690 book *A Vindication of the Doctrine of the Holy and Ever Blessed Trinity* kept the conversation alive. Sherlock's point-by-point refutation of Nye's *Brief History* and an anonymous pamphlet entitled *Brief Notes on the Creed of St. Athanasius* promised a clear account of the Trinity (that is, one amenable to reason), and indeed the book was initially hailed as "a masterpiece of theological reasoning" (Sirota 2013, 45). Whether or not it was indeed that, it certainly did provide an account of mortal personhood that Locke adopted.

Three persons in one substantial being is not self-contradictory, Sherlock insisted, because a person is not the same thing as a substantial being. (Note the rejection of Boethius's view.) This truth is evident, if we ask what it is that makes any substance unified in itself. In a material being, oneness consists in the hanging together of parts that do not hang together with something else (Sherlock 1690, 48). But that way of conceiving of oneness cannot serve for immaterial beings. In what, then, does the unity of a spirit being consist? Here is Sherlock's answer: "Now this Self-unity of the Spirit, which has no Parts to be united, can be nothing else but Self-consciousness: that it is conscious to its own Thoughts, Reasonings, Passions, which no other finite Spirit is conscious to but itself: This makes a finite Spirit numerically One, and separates it from all other Spirits, that every Spirit feels only its own Thoughts and Passions, but is not conscious to the Thoughts and Passions of any other Spirits" (49). What makes a spirit being be itself is its consciousness of itself, its self-relation, and its lack of consciousness of what is not itself. This is a finite spirit's personhood. Apart from Sherlock's spirit-material dualism (which is no small thing in itself), this is the basis of Locke's forensic person in a nutshell.[33] Before I elaborate further, however, I will describe how Sherlock used his conception of finite personhood to defend the Doctrine of the Holy Trinity against the Unitarians.

Consciousness to itself also demarcates infinite spirit's personhood, says Sherlock. The person that is the Son is its self-consciousness as the Son, its comprehension of all that belongs to the Son. This is the Son's personhood, and the same for the Father and the Holy Ghost. They are separated as distinct persons by the fact that they experience within their self-consciousnesses different sets of things. The Son's self-consciousness includes his life on Earth and his torture and death, whereas the Holy Spirit's self-consciousness does not. Nevertheless, the infinite spirit, being infinite, also comprehends all else, so all three of the infinite divine persons comprehend and are intimately conscious to one another as they are to themselves. This mutual consciousness means that they are one substantial being. How, then, do they remain distinct as persons? First of all, each one owns its own intellect, will, and actions as its own; it distinguishes itself from the other divine persons just as it distinguishes itself from the finite spirits whose thoughts and affects it also comprehends. Its distinctness is an aspect of that to which it is conscious, and therefore its distinctness is an aspect of itself (Sherlock 1690, 67).

More importantly, however, personhood, whether infinite or finite, is a matter of agency, of acting. The mortal person acts temporally and often (Locke will say *always*) in the medium of matter. The Godhead is pure eternal activity with no admixture of passive material. God is pure agency. Sherlock writes:

3. That Original Mind and Wisdom, and the Knowledge of it self, and love of it self, and its own Image, are distinct Acts, and never can be One simple individual Act. They are distinct Powers and Faculties in Men, Knowledge, Self-reflection, and Love, and are so distinct, that they can never be the same: Knowledge is not Self-reflection, nor Love either Knowledge or Self-reflection, though they are inseparably united, they are distinct.
4. Therefore these three Acts, which are so distinct, that they can never be the same, must be three substantial Acts in God; that is, three Divine subsisting Persons; for there is nothing but Essence and Substance in God; no Accidents, or Faculties, as there are in Creatures.
5. That these are the true and proper Characters of the distinct Persons in the ever blessed Trinity. The Father is Original Mind and Wisdom; the Son the Word and Wisdom of the Father; that is, the reflex

Knowledge of himself, which is the perfect Image of his own Wisdom; the Holy Ghost, that Divine Love which Father and Son have for each other....

6. From hence it is clear, That these Three Divine Persons, Father, Son, and Holy Ghost, are One God, as these Three Powers, of Understanding, Self-reflection, and Self-love are One Mind: For what are meer Faculties and Powers in created Spirits, are Persons in the Godhead, really distinct from each other, but as inseparably united into One, as Three different Powers are essentially united in One Mind. (130, 135–36)

Sherlock thus gave his contemporaries a supposedly reasonable account of the Trinity (as opposed to the supposedly unreasonable Doctrine of Transubstantiation). But in the process, he also gave an account of both the unity and the individuation of the mortal person: an essentially temporal and embodied but non-substantial unifying force with finite scope. This was a new entity, neither a body nor a soul but also not simply a legal status and construct. It was a finite, individuated power of comprehension. It was just what Locke needed.

Locke had at least two reasons to choose the Latinate term *persons* (rather than, for example, the Anglo-Germanic term *selves*) to account for the fact that we experience ourselves as distinct, temporally enduring beings.[34] First, although he didn't cite Sherlock, those in his intellectual circle would have seen the association immediately, perhaps helping to diminish the new concept's unfamiliarity. Second, the Latinate word had long and close relations with ownership; Locke's selfsame individual is an owner of sensations and ideas. The person is, then, the site where knowledge forms, the seat and subject of knowledge, as his *Essay* makes clear. As such, it plays a crucial role in Locke's epistemology. But Locke's epistemological concerns cannot be disentangled from his theological, moral, and political concerns, where his concept of personhood also takes center stage. To appreciate fully the centrality of Locke's person in the entirety of his philosophy and its impact in the eighteenth century and beyond, we need to understand the configuration of ideas of which it is a part. These include the deeply entwined concepts of action, law, and duty.

Action must first of all be distinguished from mere behavior. When a boulder rolls down a mountainside, there is no action on the part of the boulder. It merely responds to preceding events, such as a lightning strike or a seismic tremor. Inanimate things behave in accordance with the order that God has imposed on creation. We can see the rolling of the boulder as an effect of a physical cause. By contrast, an action is an event that occurs as a result not of a physical cause but of a process of thinking. An action is the execution of a deliberate choice. Only a creature that can deliberate, therefore, can act. A person, Locke declares, is a creature that can deliberate and choose among its ideas. It is capable, therefore, of actions. Just as a person owns its ideas, then, it owns its actions. A person's action belongs to that person; that person is responsible for conceiving of that action and for choosing it out of a range of possibilities. Whereas no one owns behaviors, not even the creatures that enact them, actions are always owned by some person. And it is as the owner of actions that Locke's self, as a person, can appear before a judge, divine or earthly, and be held responsible.

As tightly bound up with Locke's concept of personhood and his concept of action is his concept of and commitment to natural law, which provides the criteria for judgment and should provide the criteria for deliberation as well. There is good reason to believe that Locke shared his close friend Robert Boyle's position on the nature of law, as outlined in the latter's 1690 treatise *The Christian Virtuoso*, which Locke likely read and commented upon in manuscript form as early as 1681.[35] In that work, Boyle declared that law is "a Moral, not a Physical, Cause," a claim that might seem odd coming from a man renowned for his discovery of the law of gases, which of course purports to be a formulation of physical law. But Boyle believed that the word *law* can be applied to non-rational beings and inanimate bodies, including gases, only metaphorically.[36] Law is, he writes, "but a Notional thing, according to which, an intelligent and free Agent is bound to regulate his Actions" (1690, 36). Strictly speaking, then, there are no *laws* of nature. The hawk spots the field mouse, swoops, kills, and eats it. The order of nature established by God, "as the Sovereign Rector of the World" (40), *causes* the hawk to kill and eat the mouse; the hawk does not freely decide to swoop and kill. A finite rational being, by contrast, deliberates and then executes a planned action. There is natural law, however, in the sense that we can investigate nature and discern there through reason God's order and decrees to rational beings. In fact, we must do so if we are to know the moral law, because (as Locke argues in book I of the *Essay*) there are no principles innate in the human mind; principles can only be arrived at through experience and reflection on nature and Scripture.

Reflection, Locke asserts, tells us that we are not the source of our own existence. Three truths can be drawn from this. First, we are creatures of some being far greater than ourselves (*Essay* IV.x, 547–56). Second, because we are creatures rather than self-creators, no one of us has priority over anyone else; we are all of equal worth before the power that created us. Third, having been created by this power other than ourselves, we do not belong to ourselves and have no authority to destroy or harm ourselves or others. These truths in turn yield natural moral laws:

> Every one, as he is *bound to preserve himself*, and not to quit his station willfully, so by the like reason, when his own preservation comes not in competition, ought he, as much as he can, *to preserve the rest of mankind*, and may not, unless it be to do justice to an offender, take away, or impair the life, or what tends to the preservation of the life, the liberty, health, limb, or goods of another. (*Second Treatise* II.6, 9)

These laws are not writ upon our hearts, as natural law theorists in the Thomist tradition might have it, but must be arrived at through experience and reasoned reflection. Reason likewise shows us that we are obliged to follow them—not because the order of nature compels us to, but because it would be unreasonable to do otherwise; it would bring long-term pain and misery, if not in this life, then certainly in the next. Reason shows us that we have a duty to preserve our own lives and a duty to preserve the lives of other rational creatures.

To carry out the duty to preserve ourselves, we must eat, drink, and secure shelter. But God has given all the world to all in common, has he not? Does that not mean that, as the Diggers and others claimed, the common stock must remain commonly inhabited and used? What gives any one individual the right to take a particular fruit for food or spot of ground for a dwelling place and exclude others from it? Obviously, one must have a right to do what duty requires. Indeed, Locke holds the belief, common to his times, that natural rights are nothing but the means to comply with the demands of natural law; if we had no natural duties, we would have no natural rights.[37] But he offers another justification as well. In the *Second Treatise*, Locke tells us that God has not in fact given all the world to all in common. He has already given us individual property.

> Though the Earth, and all inferior Creatures be common to all Men, yet every Man has a *Property* in his own *Person*. This no Body has any Right to but himself. The *Labour* of his Body, and the *Work* of his Hands, we may say, are properly his. Whatsoever then he removes out of the State that Nature hath provided, and left it in, he hath mixed his *Labour* with, and joyned it to something that is his own, and thereby makes it his *Property*. It being by him removed from the common state Nature placed it in, hath by this *labour* something annexed to it, that excludes the common right of other Men. For this *Labour* being the unquestionable Property of the

Labourer, no Man but he can have a right to what that is once joyned to, at least where there is enough, and as good left in common for others. (*Second Treatise* V.27)

From the beginning, then, there has been private property. From the moment a person acts to appropriate for self-preservation in accordance with duty, the world in its totality is no longer common stock. The existence of persons—rational, acting, embodied beings—entails private property, material ownership, just as private property entails persons, individual beings who are proprietors in their very essence.[38]

It might be objected that the word *person* in this passage should not be construed in the same way as the word in the *Essay*. Many readers have seen it here in the *Second Treatise* as a synonym for *body*. It is true that people in Locke's time used the term *person* in that manner, just as we sometimes do. But in light of the interpretation of personhood in the *Essay* offered above, another reading of the passage is also possible. In fact, the word *body* never appears in this passage or elsewhere in chapter V as a synonym of *person*, and careful reading shows that what Locke actually says human beings own is their labor.[39] Labor is a species of activity—purposeful, deliberate activity according to a plan. Laboring, like reasoning, is a temporal phenomenon; it unfolds through time, but its elements or steps must be held together and in correct order in pursuit of its end. We could, then, read *person* in this key passage not as *body* but rather as that to which belong processes of deliberative or reasoned action. If so, the word functions in this text much as it functions in the *Essay* (II.xxvii). Embodiment is a necessary condition for personhood in both texts—because actions create material effects in the world—but personhood is not reducible to body in either one.[40] A fundamental characteristic of personhood in both texts is individual ownership of actions through time. One's person is the unified consciousness of one's actions, which include one's labor. Thus, Locke's theory of labor and his theory of moral responsibility are mutually reinforcing.

One's duty is not merely to preserve one's own life but, insofar as possible without seriously jeopardizing that life, to preserve the lives of others, for the law of nature "willeth the peace and *preservation of all mankind*" (*Second Treatise* II.7). Reason shows us that we can preserve ourselves and others best not through basic and repetitive appropriation out of nature, but through improvement upon nature. Rational beings can cultivate the land rather than just take from it. We can dam the stream and irrigate the field or build a mill to grind grain that can be stored as flour for bread in winter. We can domesticate animals, make tools, and build dwellings and fences and barns. And we can invent money to make exchange easier across distances and seasons. While natural law dictates labor in the service of preservation, and not in the service of accumulation for its own sake,[41] accumulation of material property is necessary for extensive and complex cultivation and industry in the pursuit not only of continued bare existence with its fleeting moments of pleasure but of the sustained pleasure and diminution of pain that is, for rational beings, happiness. Property is at one with the pursuit of happiness. Persons have a natural right to accumulate as much property as they can in their efforts to fulfill their duties.[42]

To sum up then, in this early version, the modern person is a being that is essentially self-aware, rational, free, and (at least minimally) propertied. For Locke, ownership of property was an essential ingredient in the sustenance, expression, cultivation, and maintenance of persons. The person has a duty to preserve its own life and, where possible, the lives of all humankind and to use its reason to improve those lives—that is, the person has a duty to pursue happiness, not merely fleeting pleasures or absence of pain, through cultivation and industrious transformation of the natural stock of resources. This duty gives it the right not only to defend itself and innocent others against assault but also to accumulate property, in particular productive property, to whatever extent it can. Persisting through time, the Lockean person is fundamentally conscious; it deliberates over its future actions, makes plans in light of its experience, takes ownership of its past deeds, and is able to account for these past deeds to itself, its peers, and its Creator. And, perhaps most importantly, it is perfectly suited for judgment, both to make judgments and to be judged. The modern person is fundamentally a subject of judgment.

[CHAPTER THREE]

Imposing Personhood

African Enslavement and Indigenous Resistance

In attributing property in person to every individual human being with self-awareness, John Locke managed to make far more people persons than any version of Roman personhood ever did. The only exceptions were infants, "Lunaticks," and "Ideots" (*Second Treatise* VI.60, 350)—people in whom self-awareness had not developed or who had lost continuity or unity of self-awareness. Every being who is able to recognize its ideas and acts as its own through time is a person. Within a few years, Locke's admiring readers had followed him in extending the status of personhood even to servants and homeless beggars. Locke's world had embraced his account of moral equality for all. This was not, however, the equality that the Diggers and other radicals at mid-century had sought. They wanted equality not in individuality but in community, not a formal equality of distributed duties and their attendant rights, but a material equality of mutual care—which entailed common stewardship rather than private ownership of forests and open land. In short, they wanted an equality without personhood. What they—or rather, their successors, we—got instead was a broadly inclusive, refurbished personhood, still tied firmly to privatized propriety.

Although heralded as a forerunner of political liberalism and honored for his theory that legitimate government is a contract among natural equals, Locke never thought peasants, servants, laborers, or women should enjoy the civil liberties or stand as the political equals of educated professional men and landed gentry. His conferral of personhood upon women and commoners made them fully and individually morally accountable just as great landowners were, subject to moral judgment and divine punishment, but it left them with no more power to determine the course of their lives than they had had before. And it was never supposed to. On the contrary. Personhood was meant to function as a mechanism of capture. By definition, there was nothing about a person that could not be inventoried; everything could be identified and recorded. According to Locke's definition, nothing of a person's identity exceeded his or her conscious awareness.

The more one identified one's self with one's person, the more one detached one's self from anything that could not be accounted for, called to account, and judged—and rewarded or punished. The person's constant companion was the judge.

Locke was able to assert equal accountability under moral law while denying political, legal, and material equality in great part because he held to a doctrine of intellectual inequality. Every person is self-aware and able to deliberate by definition (every person has a natural capacity for reason), but the quality of actual deliberation varies from person to person depending on the range of experience from which the person may draw, the amount of training received in the use of reason as well as education in various subject matters, and the amount of time the person has to think. Persons who have spent all their days engaged in manual labor and childcare are not able to deliberate as thoroughly and well as persons who have had the opportunity for education, have applied themselves to that endeavor, and have leisure to pursue long trains of ideas and argumentation. Thus, circumstances of life can render people able to reason only to the point that they recognize the authority of masters, pastors, and magistrates. Such is the case, Locke thinks, with most of humanity.

> The greatest part of mankind want leisure or capacity for demonstration, nor can carry a train of proofs (which in that way they must always depend upon for conviction), and cannot be required to assent to, until they see the demonstration.... And you may as soon hope to have all the day-laborers and tradesmen, the spinsters and dairymaids, perfect mathematicians, as to have them perfect in ethics in this way. Hearing plain commands is the sure and only course to bring them to obedience and practice. The greatest part cannot *know*, and therefore they must *believe*. (Locke 1695, 178–79)

Hardworking, uneducated people will never be able to derive the moral law through reason from Scripture or nature for themselves. Given their station, the most reasonable option for them is simply to assent to the rules that their betters reveal to them and choose to act in compliance. They are morally responsible persons, then, just not rightfully autonomous ones. As such, they are properly subject not only to God, but also to external human authority.

Well-educated men of relative leisure are likewise responsible for obeying or failing to obey the moral law, but they are not dependent upon other men to provide them with it. They are amply equipped to discern it for themselves, so they need not place themselves under the command of mortal superiors. Here, therefore, among this fraternity of well-equipped rational persons of great attainment, equality *and* genuine liberty prevail. Under the just authority of no man (unless they freely so contract), these persons are under the authority of Almighty God alone. In this way, Locke reinforced sex and class domination even while propounding natural equality.

Lockean personhood clearly had tremendous value for educated English gentlemen at the turn of the eighteenth century. It had epistemological value, in that it could help locate and account for knowledge and truth; it had theological value, in that it could support a Christian theory of divine judgment in an age of scientific discovery; it had political value, in that it could serve as a basis for membership in or exclusion from a polity; and it had ethical value, in that it could ground radically individualized responsibility, condemnation, and righteous punishment. Meanwhile, it could retain its legal and economic value as a basis for privatized land rights, yet, despite the great breadth of its modern application, it could do so without distributing those rights to all. By spanning those different domains, personhood also had the power to help unify them both conceptually and practically. It could smooth over conflicts between capitalist pursuits and religious practices, for example; where Christian opposition to usury and embrace of charity and poverty as signs of a holy life had impeded capitalist development, a new emphasis on radically individuated personal moral responsibility and individual ownership made lending money at interest palatable and generosity toward the poor morally suspect. Its breadth and inclusiveness brought everyone into a new world of scientific discovery and capitalist economy.

Throughout this genealogical study so far, we have seen that personhood in its many ancestral forms functioned as a mechanism of exclusion, division, or differentiation. In spite of that ancestry, however, most people today place their faith in personhood as a category of inclusion, solidarity, and justice. Across a wide swath of the political spectrum, activists and moral theorists believe that the antidote to oppression is recognition of the personhood of the oppressed. Persons are to be accorded basic respect; they are not to be exploited, dispossessed, trafficked, enslaved, or abandoned to suffer and die. If only we would recognize the personhood of migrants, the unhoused, people of color, queer people, people with disabilities, fetuses, nonhuman primates, and so on, we would cease to deny them respect, rights, liberty, moral consideration, sustenance, habitat, a chance to grow. Yet, for more than a century after modern moral personhood was introduced and accepted, slavery and slave trafficking were legal, widespread, and profitable, and colonial dispossession and exploitation of Indigenous populations meant the suffering and deaths of millions of people (not to mention environmental destruction and wanton disregard for nonhuman animals and plants[1]). Most people assume those horrors were incompatible with recognition of personhood and therefore were the result of irrationality, immorality, or self-deceptive hypocrisy. In this chapter, I will argue that they were no such thing. The personhood of enslaved people and Indigenous people was widely recognized by European explorers and colonists, but it did not command respect and did not ensure equality.[2] It was never supposed to.

Section I will show that Locke—and perhaps also the eight men with whom he worked to colonize the territory of North America between the Virginia Colony and the Spanish-held lands to the south—believed that "Indians" were persons who owned their actions, including their labor, and who could appropriate and own material resources. This belief presented no obstacle in their efforts to take Indigenous land, however. Indeed, Locke and his colleagues believed they were entitled and perhaps even obligated to do so, not only in spite of but in part because of Indians' moral status as persons. As I will show, given Locke's theories, it was God's will that Carolina be put under cultivation by English methods, and if the Indians refused to do it, the English and their Scottish employees should. Section II presents evidence that enslaved Africans were persons in the eyes of a majority of their enslavers (although they most likely did not understand themselves as such in the early stages of their captivity), and their descendants who grew up in European custody were self-aware as persons in the Lockean lineage. These first two sections are intended to support my claim that personhood as it was conceived in the late seventeenth and eighteenth centuries did not preclude dispossession and enslavement; on the contrary, it enabled justification of those practices.

In the third section, I turn to North American Indigenous peoples' refusal to instantiate personhood, particularly their resistance to colonial regimes of criminal justice and property in land, resistance that in some quarters continues to this day. Attending to this resistance helps to highlight the fact that modern moral personhood is a product of western Europe that arose and took hold under very particular historical, political, and economic conditions; it is not a universal state or fact about human beings, and there have always been good reasons to question and challenge it. There have also always been alternatives to it for self-aware human beings and communities, even if we modern moral persons today cannot quite imagine now what those alternatives were or might yet be.

I. Dispossessing and Enslaving Persons

Locke embraced the idea that people native to the Americas were persons; they deliberated, executed plans, and learned from consequences. Just like

Europeans, therefore, they could possess property derived from their labor. In fact, one of the *Second Treatise*'s examples of the acquisition of property in its most basic form is the action of an Indigenous hunter: "Thus this Law of reason makes the Deer, that *Indian's* who hath killed it; 'tis allowed to be his goods who hath bestowed his labour upon it, though before, it was the common right of every one" (II.VII.30). Locke says the hunter labors. Labor is action, not mere behavior; a woodpecker extracting insects from tree bark does not labor; it merely behaves, in Locke's view. By contrast, deliberating beings choose, plan, and execute actions that change the material world around them. The Indian hunter labors for his deerskin and meat. Labor, reasoned action, is owned by the self who planned it and carried it out. The laborer is always, by definition, a proprietor, a person. Therefore, the laborer also owns what he or she appropriates from out of the common stock.

It is almost impossible to define personhood as Locke and his English successors defined it and not recognize the personhood—and therefore the moral status—of European women and people indigenous to the Americas, Africa, the Pacific Islands, and elsewhere. Yet, in practice, as we know, members of all these groups were routinely brutalized and violated, sometimes by those very same men. We could accuse them of self-contradiction, of hypocrisy, and leave it at that. But I believe there is much to be gained by taking them seriously.

The Lord Proprietors of Carolina, eight Englishmen who included Locke's patron the first Earl of Shaftesbury, intended that their colony be put under cultivation by enslaved Africans, supervised by the English and Scottish settlers whom they commissioned.[3] The *Fundamental Constitutions*, written largely if not wholly by Locke and adopted by the Lords Proprietors in 1669, gave each free colonist "absolute power and authority over his negro slaves" (see Welchman 1995, 72). Clearly, enslaved labor in Carolina did not merely evolve, as it had in Virginia over the previous decades; it was deliberately established from the beginning. For his work in setting up the governance structure for the colony, the Lord Proprietors awarded Locke the status of landgrave (a title used in the Holy Roman Empire equivalent to that of count) and the 48,000-acre tract of land in the Carolina Colony that went with it. Though he was an absentee landlord with undeveloped holdings, Locke was part of the landed nobility of the Carolina Colony, an African-slave-owning colony from its inception. There is no record or reason to believe that Locke directly purchased any human beings himself, but he did invest in the Royal African Company in early 1671, a slave-trading enterprise as set forth in charter, which Locke would have read carefully prior to investing. In 1672 he joined ten others to establish the Bahamas Adventurers, a company dedicated to developing trade in that region, including slave trade; initially Locke was one of eleven investors but soon held a double share and may have increased his holdings beyond that (Glausser 1990, 201). Locke certainly saw some material benefit from these investments; he sold his shares in the Royal African Company in 1677 at a good profit (Hinshelwood 2013, 577). It would seem that Locke was either a moral hypocrite, or he saw nothing morally wrong with enslaving people (or both).[4]

It is possible that Locke did not fully understand just how brutal colonial slavery could be. Paying servants in nothing but room and board was not an uncommon labor practice in England. A servant who received no wages, who was at the beck and call of a master at all hours, who could not leave the master's premises without permission, and who was contracted for a year or more at a time was, in effect, a temporary slave. Similarly, apprentices served masters without pay or liberty to leave for years on end and were often subject to severe physical abuse. The difference was, of course, that an English master could not sell a servant or an apprentice; they were labor only, not capital, and theoretically they did not serve for life. They were also living in their home communities, speaking their native language, surrounded by family; they were not ripped from their homeland, divested of every facet of their culture, and always in danger of yet another exile through the mechanisms of the market. Locke may have imagined that enslaved Africans lived and worked as English servants did, and he obviously had no objections to that. (In fact, he strongly favored amending the Elizabethan poor laws to make forced labor the norm for all impoverished people in England above the age of three years.[5]) The master/servant relationship was analogous to the sovereign/subject relationship; the servant was subject to the master's command, and that was as it should be. Liberty was definitely not for all. Still, lifelong enslavement was morally permissible according to Locke only as a consequence of war (and hereditary slavery was never permissible); only a vanquished aggressor could justly be enslaved (the justification being that enslavement would be an act of mercy on the part of a righteous victor who had the natural right to kill his defeated adversary). Most of the Africans brought to the colony were not members of defeated armies of aggression, however, as Locke and the Lord Proprietors certainly knew. No matter how gentle an institution Locke believed colonial slavery to be, if these people were persons, this treatment would seem to be absolutely immoral, an affront to the divine Creator in whom these men professed to believe and who served as the foundation of Locke's entire political theory and the classical liberalism that grew from it. Locke was transgressing against his own principles when he profited off the African slave trade. How did he justify this to himself?

A detour through actual practices in Carolina will help illuminate this issue. Africans were not the only enslaved people in the Carolina Colony, as Locke and the Lord Proprietors also well knew. In 1671, after a colonist killed a member of their tribe, the Coosa retaliated by destroying the settlers' crops. Colonists and Coosa entered treaty negotiations, but they soon deadlocked. At that point, the Carolina Grand Council declared war and began taking Coosa prisoners and selling them in Charlestown to slave traders, who took them to the West Indies sugar colonies. Carolina had no professional army, so this "work" of capture fell to individual planters, who quickly learned that capturing and selling human beings was much easier and more lucrative than farming. The Lord Proprietors were not happy with this turn of events, since they had hoped that the Coosa would become reliable trading partners rather than commodities and that the Goose Creek plantations would produce agricultural products for both the local and world markets. Nevertheless, the "Goose Creek men" (as they came to be called) had other ideas and resisted their appeals. By 1675, having realized that the Lord Proprietors believed enslavement was justified as a consequence of unjust aggression—in other words, having realized that if the Coosa attacked settlements, settlers could justifiably enslave the aggressors for life—the Goose Creek men took to provoking conflicts and even to claiming they had been attacked when they had not. The Carolina Colony soon became the center of the Indigenous slave trade in British North America, operating under the protection of the thinnest veil of just war theory.[6]

Locke might have felt a bit uncomfortable with how things were playing out in Carolina—his patron Shaftesbury was quite unhappy that the Goose Creek men were putting less time into agriculture and trade than into capturing warriors for market—but his theories of government, labor, and moral obligation were nothing if not capacious. He had at his disposal a way to argue that placing Indigenous peoples—including Indigenous Africans, I will argue below—into lifelong servitude was morally better than leaving them to lead their hand-to-mouth unproductive lives. Recall from the last section of chapter 2 that natural law dictates not only that we preserve our own lives but also that, in every way possible without endangering ourselves, we act to preserve the lives of other rational beings (*Second Treatise* II.6, 9). To Locke, the latter obligation meant that we must not only labor to appropriate straight out of nature's bounty for our own immediate needs (as he suggested Indigenous people did), but that we move beyond subsistence hunting and gathering to cultivation and development. Security and prosperity for everyone required production of a surplus. Swamps must be drained and forests felled to put land to use. Fences must be built and cattle bred. On Locke's view, reasonable land management and agriculture could only look like the enclosure movement that was ongoing in his homeland; it could not look like the eminently more sustainable strategies and practices of forest and land management and agriculture that actually existed in North America and West Africa. Indigenous peoples were not in fact living hand-to-mouth; they had long-standing and proven strategies for resilience through weather fluctuations and other disruptions in routine. And they had little or no need to plan for market fluctuations (which in Europe were arguably more profound than local weather fluctuations). But Locke, enamored as he was with the latest technologies of seventeenth-century England, could not see the wisdom of what Indigenous farmers and foresters were doing. He condemned them as unproductive and judged them lax in their moral duty to improve the world for the benefit and security of all rational creatures of God. They were morally condemnable in their neglect of production for surplus, and they were even more morally condemnable for hoarding land and preventing the more industrious Europeans from enclosing and farming it. No one has a right to prevent the cultivation and improvement of land. Land rightly belongs to those who will develop it for the advancement of rational beings—persons—in general. Given these intellectual starting points, one could easily deduce that rational, industrious Europeans had a moral obligation to take American land and put it to use for self-enrichment and for domestic and international markets. People without the deliberative skill to understand this obligation to (over-) produce ought not be allowed to live at liberty; they ought to bow to masters who could command them. Yes, those lazy Indigenous peoples were persons; they were persons fittingly judged to be derelict of duty. It was in their very personhood that they stood condemned and in need of subjection, just like lazy Englishmen and -women and lazy Scots and Irish as well.

In addition to the right to take land from people who are not developing it, Locke holds that in a state of nature, the duty to preserve rational creation entails the right to kill or enslave anyone who presents a credible threat to the life of another rational being. This argument begins in the *Second Treatise* (II.7). "And that all men may be restrained from invading others['] rights, and from doing hurt to one another, and the law of nature be observed, which willeth the peace and *preservation of all mankind*, the *execution* of the law of nature is, in that state, put into every man's hands, whereby every one has a right to punish the transgressors of that law to such a degree, as may hinder its violation." It continues in paragraph 11:

> ... every man, in the state of nature, has a power to kill a murderer, both to *deter* others from doing the like injury, which no reparation can compensate, by the example of the punishment that attends it from every

body; and also to secure men from the attempts of a criminal, who having renounced reason, the common rule and measure God hath given to mankind, hath, by the unjust violence and slaughter he hath committed upon one, declared war against all mankind; and therefore may be destroyed as a *lion* or a *tyger*, one of those wild savage beasts, with whom men can have no society nor security. (*Second Treatise* II.11)

Aggression transforms the state of nature into a state of war, as Locke describes it in the next chapter. In such a state, Locke's just war theory applies even if the aggressor is just one individual rather than an army; once the aggressor is captured, he may justly be killed or enslaved. "Indeed, having by his fault forfeited his own life, by some act that deserves death; he, to whom he has forfeited it [and this can be anybody who is acting to enforce the natural law], may (when he has him in his power) delay to take it, and make use of him to his own service, and he does him no injury by it: for, whenever he finds the hardship of his slavery outweigh the value of his life, it is in his power, by resisting the will of his master, to draw on himself the death he desires" (*Second Treatise*, IV.23).

Jennifer Welchman argues that this is how Locke's theory accommodates African slavery. Locke saw Africa, like the Americas, as being in a state of nature. "Consequently, it would be sufficient cause to enslave a man in sub-Saharan Africa if he was known to have threatened at least one person or if he had tolerated or concurred in one such assault. It would not be necessary that the captor be the person attacked, nor would it be necessary that the captive remain in his captor's hands. Being property, the captive might be sold, bartered, or given to whom ever his captor pleased—even Europeans" (Welchman 1995, 79). It would have been easy for Locke to assume that most, if not all, the people brought out of Africa as captives had at some point, while living in a state of nature, threatened someone else's well-being by theft if not by assault or by simply not punishing someone else who presented such a threat when they could have. This could easily be true not only of men but also of women and children. Since Locke also thought that, in general, uneducated people without masters exercised poor judgment, he might imagine that the average African was a frequent violator of natural law—in other words, a criminal.

Given contemporary political assumptions, one might suppose that people who profited off colonialism in the modern period justified their actions by denying the personhood of those they exploited, dispossessed, enslaved, and killed. I submit, to the contrary, that (1) Locke and his compatriots had no logical need to do so, and (2) they saw plenty of benefit in recognizing Americans and Africans as persons responsible for various sorts of action or inaction that they deemed immoral. We must remember that Locke's explicit reason for defining personhood as he did was to explain how all people with even the slightest capacity for practical reason were fully subject as individuals to authoritative judgment and discipline. Extending personhood to non-Europeans gave Europeans the right to judge, condemn, and dominate them all. It was a wonderful tool for colonists and the investors who profited from their work.

II. African Americans in the Eighteenth and Nineteenth Centuries

Given the utility of modern moral personhood as a tool of subjection, we should not be surprised to discover that eighteenth-century British colonists imposed it upon their labor force and their American successors perpetuated the project into the nineteenth century. With the status of personhood came the duty to preserve God's rational creation through labor. As noted above, that included not only providing for one's own subsistence but also producing surplus for the sake of security into the future and developing the resources at hand to provide surplus for what was evolving as an international capitalist market system. Failure to perform these duties according to European models and standards of productivity invited intervention in the form of confiscation of potentially productive resources and subordination of moral laggards to masters who could enforce duty and discipline.

For the most part, this strategy worked with enslaved Africans. Stripped of their own heritages, languages, kinship systems, and religions and introduced into the modern Euro-American system of private property, many Africans eventually succumbed to individuation as modern moral persons under European subjection. They or at least their Christianized descendants came to experience themselves that way, just as their white owners perceived them. It worked far less well with Indigenous North Americans, most of whom (despite the efforts of the Goose Creek men and other colonists) were not severed from their kin and transported to foreign soil; collectively, many Indigenous groups fiercely resisted assimilation into the European system of private ownership and fought to protect and preserve their traditional non-property relation to land and non-privatized relations to other goods and beings. I will examine some aspects of that resistance in the next section of this chapter. Here I take up the issue of personhood under slavery.

My claim that personhood was imposed on enslaved people as an integral aspect of their subjection runs counter to the liberal idea that the institution of slavery denied its victims their true personhood and depersonalized them with its brutality. That idea holds great power in the present day. Slavery, specifically the institution of slavery in British North America and the United States, is usually taken to be the very paradigm of depersonalization, which is why I will expend a good bit of effort here in examining slavery in descriptions offered by some of those who suffered under it. Only by laying to rest the objection that enslavement meant depersonalization will the power functions of modern moral personhood be evident. Personhood was not only compatible with enslavement; it often proved to be an effective tool in helping to maintain the institution. The status of personhood is empowering in some contexts, but it is horrifically disempowering in others. If we refuse to see the latter, we will remain trapped in a moral worldview and in ethical practices that are increasingly out of touch with our real needs as individuals and as communities and polities.

Unless one has taken the trouble to read a good amount of scholarship on slavery in the English colonies and in US history or at least a variety of memoirs by enslaved people, one is likely to have a monochrome mental picture of the institution, as if it were the same set of practices across differences of place, time, market fluctuations and commodities produced, technological innovations, and political tensions. According to that picture, slaves lived in slave quarters and slave owners lived in big plantation houses nearby. Slaves worked hard either in the house as servants always on call or in the fields from dawn to dusk. At night and on Sundays, they sang spirituals. If they failed to obey an order or fell behind in their work, or just if their master was in a bad mood, they might be whipped half to death. Slaves had no personal possessions, little privacy, and no education. Masters could rape enslaved women (and men and children) with impunity. And all enslaved families lived in fear of being sold separately and parted forever. There is much truth in this picture, of course, but it is simplistic and incomplete.

There were variations in living conditions from plantation to plantation, city to city, and industry to industry. Enslaved people worked not only in fields but also in hotels and taverns, shops, mills, and brothels. The two biggest factors conditioning most enslaved people's lives were the type of work they had to do and the character of the individuals who owned and supervised them. Of course, by far the greatest number did agricultural work primarily and lived for most or all of each year on a plantation of one sort or another. But what sort of plantation, and especially what sort of labor management system employed there, did matter.[7] Edward Baptist (2014) has described three different labor management systems used on plantations by the nineteenth century: the task system, the gang system, and the pushing system.

According to Baptist, the task system was prevalent in the lowlands of South Carolina and Georgia, where the primary crop was rice. There each person was given a specific task to complete for the day, such as to cultivate an acre, and once that task was finished, s/he could stop working for the owner for the day. This provided an incentive to work steadily, even without direct supervision and constant surveillance. Productivity did not increase over time, but planters saved the expense of a crew of overseers (Baptist 2014, 115–16). It was possible, therefore, for people enslaved in the lowlands to grow their own crops or work at some other trade in free hours, sometimes earning money for doing so. In the mid-Atlantic—Maryland, Virginia, North Carolina, and Kentucky—the gang system was the preferred method of labor management. Owners divided the people they enslaved into groups or gangs and assigned them to different fields for work under an overseer, who was usually white, or sometimes a driver who was him-/herself enslaved. Fields might be quite distant from one another with woods or hills between them. On large plantations, different sets of slave quarters might be located near different fields. The main cash crop was tobacco, but many other crops were also raised, including corn and wheat. All forms of slave labor management could be horrifically brutal, but the level of white surveillance varied. With the task system, enslaved people might be alone or within sight of only other enslaved people for hours at a time. This, obviously, cut down greatly on the amount of violence they suffered and the number of hours per day they had to fear it. With the gang system, some were under the constant surveillance of a white overseer at the edge of the field or walking or riding horseback around them with his whip, but they might also be under the supervision of another slave and therefore far away from white people's eyes for days at a time (Baptist 2014, 116). James Madison's plantation in Orange County, Virginia, can serve as an example. According to historian Elizabeth Dowling Taylor, "slave life at Montpelier was typical for the time and place" (2012, 21). Trusted and skilled enslaved people, such as Moses and Sawney, were foremen, Moses in the plantation blacksmith shop and Sawney on one of the tobacco farm quarters. Sawney also raised cabbage, sweet potatoes, chickens, and other crops, which he sold to the Madisons for cash (Taylor 2012, 23). Several of the Madisons' enslaved men and women were literate and sent written reports about conditions at the farm when the Madisons were in Washington.

Working conditions were fundamentally different in cotton country, Baptist asserts, where labor was managed under the pushing system, because there white overseers (often employed by absentee owners) exercised constant surveillance over vast flat fields and "whipped up" workers who did not keep up with their row leaders. It was not a matter of getting a job done; owners wanted slaves working harder and ever harder, because the global cotton market could absorb all they could produce and much more. Without any mechanical or agricultural innovation, productivity per field worker jumped almost 400 percent from 1800 to 1860 (Baptist 2014, 128). The only recorded innovation was, Baptist writes, "innovation in violence," which "was the foundation of the widely shared pushing system" (117). This included a new kind of whip; instead of the short cat-o'-nine-tails in use in the East, cotton overseers' whips were ten feet of plaited cowhide, giving overseers a much longer reach and more power per strike. But torture of laborers was not limited to whipping; overseers and owners also used carpentry tools, chains, handsaws, branding irons, pokers, tongs, and so on. "Every modern method of torture was used at one time or another: sexual humiliation, mutilation, electric shocks, solitary confinement in 'stress positions,' burning, even waterboarding" (Baptist 2014, 141). Mary Ella Grandberry described one method to interviewer Levi Shelby in Sheffield, Alabama, in the 1930s: "Iffen you weren't whipped, you was put in de 'nigger box' and fed corn bread what was made withouten salt and with plain water. De box was just big 'nough for you to stand up in, but it had air holes in it to keep you from suffocatin'. . . . Iffen you had done a bigger 'nough thing you was kept in de 'nigger box' for months at a time, and when you got out you was nothin' but skin and bones and scarcely able walk" (Yetman 2002, 62–63).[8] And of course there was also outright killing of slow workers in the field, sometimes by shooting, sometimes by locking people in stocks and whipping them. As Mary Reynolds told a WPA interviewer in Dallas in the 1930s, "They cut the flesh most to the bones, and when they taken some of them out of stock and put them on the beds, they never got up again" (Yetman 2002, 105).

Unrecorded were all the little innovations the workers themselves contrived to make it possible to go from picking a couple dozen pounds per day to a couple hundred, all to meet ever-rising quotas and avoid the lash. People were forced to work from dawn till night, as long as they could see to distinguish between bolls and leaves. Overseers weighed each one's daily total and recorded the amounts in record books against the total from the day before. Those who failed to meet their quotas received a lash for each pound they were short. There was every incentive to train oneself to pick with great speed, preferably with both hands at once, and not to stop any more than absolutely necessary. Similar procedures were used to speed hoeing, putting the fastest workers at the head of the row and forcing all others to keep up with them for hours at a time, with the overseer on horseback, wielding a whip, and literally bringing up the rear. Solomon Northup describes the cultivation of cotton in Louisiana in the 1840s. It took all year to raise a crop from planting to picking, with four rounds of hoeing through the first half of year and several rounds of picking from September into January; pickers could hardly bring in one crop from the enormous fields before it was time to plant the next crop (see Northup 1859, 118–21). No matter how fast enslaved people worked, the owners and overseers made them work faster, and they did so by making their very lives depend on their speed and efficiency. All their other chores had to be done at night, so that they rarely ate their evening meal until midnight and had to get up an hour before dawn to avoid getting whipped for being late to the field (Northup 1859, 121–23). In addition, then, to the heavy labor, malnutrition, insufficient clothing, and torture, cotton hands were always sleep-deprived.

Life in bondage on a cotton plantation was far more brutal and dehumanizing than life on most tobacco or rice plantations, although sadistic overseers and owners could be found in every segment of the slave-owning class.[9] To fully understand American slavery, we must let go of that old monochrome picture and take account of these and other differences. My purpose here is not to argue that enslavement in any part of the United States was gentle or that people in bondage anywhere were treated humanely, let alone justly. I am concerned, rather, with countering the view that people of African descent in the United States in the nineteenth century were universally denied personhood. My contention is that in most cases, on the contrary, enslaved African Americans were recognized as persons by their owners and experienced themselves as such. In what follows, I will support that contention with examples, but first I will emphasize once again that if my claim is correct, the benefits of being included in the class of modern moral persons have been tremendously exaggerated.

Like so many of the more than two thousand former slaves interviewed during the 1930s by employees of the New Deal's Works Progress Administration, some of whom are quoted above, Solomon Northup provides clear examples of slavery's depersonalization in his memoir *Twelve Years a Slave*, written soon after he was rescued from a Louisiana cotton plantation in 1853. Northup was lured to Washington, DC, from Saratoga Springs, New York, where he was a free man, with the promise of a temporary job playing violin for a circus. Once in the nation's slave-holding capital city, his supposed employers drugged him and chained and locked him in a prison known as Williams' slave pen within site of the US Capitol Building. There, his new "owner," slave-dealer James Burch, beat him with a cat-o'-nine-tails and a paddle because he refused to agree that he was a runaway slave from Georgia. Long after Northup was unable to speak anymore, Burch stopped beating him but declared "with an admonitory shake of his fist in my face, and hissing the words through his firm-set teeth, that if ever I dared to utter again that I was entitled to my freedom, that I had been kidnapped, or any thing whatever of the kind, the castigation I had just received was nothing in comparison with what would follow. He swore that he would either conquer or kill me" (Northup 1859, 34).

At this point in Northup's ordeal, he was a person, and James Burch knew it. It was Burch's intention to change that. Although Burch succeeded in selling Northup to a planter in Louisiana, he did not succeed in stripping him of his personhood. After Burch, Northup's first owner was William Ford, of whom Northup writes, "There was never a more kind, noble, candid, Christian man.... He never doubted the moral right of one man holding another in subjection.... Nevertheless, he was a model master, walking uprightly, according to the light of his understanding, and fortunate was the slave who came to his possession" (68). Ford did not treat the people he enslaved as nonpersons; he treated them as subjects, just as Locke suggests that women and common laborers should be treated. Northup himself never doubts "the inherent wrong at the bottom of the system of Slavery" (68); slavery was oppressive in the extreme, but it is clear that modern moral personhood could exist within such a system of subjection, and Ford's slaves retained that status in his view. He counted on their ability to deliberate, plan, and execute actions and appreciated their innovations—such as when Northup suggested getting lumber to market by barge, which he knew how to make and pilot, instead of overland (73). Ford's slaves were laborers, not tools. They were moral persons, responsible for their decisions and actions; they were simply not equal in legitimate authority to him.

Northup's next two owners were not benevolent sovereigns. The carpenter John Tibeats acquired him when Ford "became embarrassed in his pecuniary affairs" (77). Tibeats, according to Northup, "was without standing in the community, not esteemed by white men, nor even respected by slaves. He was ignorant, withal, and of a revengeful disposition" (76). And he clearly felt threatened in his lowly status by the obviously stronger, smarter, and far more talented Solomon Northup, known since the New Orleans slave auction as "Platt." The first time Tibeats commanded "Platt" to strip for a whipping, Northup refused. A fight ensued, which Northup won, lashing Tibeats with the latter's own whip until his right arm ached (81). With the aid of former owner William Ford's white overseer and eventually Ford himself, Northup evaded Tibeats's several attempts to murder him thereafter and was then sold to Edwin Epps (116).

As odd as it sounds to say, William Ford recognized and respected Solomon Northup as a person. John Tibeats, too, recognized Northup as a person and hated him for it. Edwin Epps lived in a different universe. When he bought "Platt" in 1842, Epps did not own his own land but leased a small plantation on Bayou Huff Power. His principal crop was cotton. He enslaved Northup there for two years until he had amassed enough money to buy his own plantation at Bayou Boeuf. Then he moved Northup and eight other slaves to the new property. Epps had been a slave driver and then an overseer before he had enough money to go into business for himself, and for the ten years that he held Northup, he saved money by acting as his own overseer. Apparently he was quite good at the job, "the requisite qualifications" for which "are utter heartlessness, brutality and cruelty. It is [an overseer's] business to produce large crops, and that if is accomplished, no matter what amount of suffering it may have cost" (Northup 1859, 159–60). And of course in terms of physical suffering and mental anguish, it cost a tremendous amount. Overseers usually went to the fields on horseback, equipped with pistols, bowie knives, whips, and dogs. The whip was applied liberally. Dogs were sicced on people who ran away or were too weak to work and to bear the whip. Under each overseer were drivers, usually slaves themselves, who both worked and whipped anyone who slowed down. Drivers wore their whips around their necks; if they failed to apply them, the overseer whipped them. Drivers also were responsible for dragging heat-exhausted slaves to shade to pour water on them until they could work again. At Bayou Boeuf, Epps made Northup a driver, thus forcing him into the role of torturer. "It is the literal, and unvarnished truth," he later wrote, "that the crack of the lash, and the shrieking of slaves, can be heard from dark till bed time, on Epps' plantation, any day almost during the entire period of the cotton-picking season" (129). For something as trivial as breaking the branch of a cotton plant or leaving a piece of boll in the cotton basket, a slave received twenty-five lashes. For idleness, the number was one hundred. Northup bore many of those lashes, but he also meted them out to his eight companions.

Northup got skillful enough that, when Epps was far enough away not to see him clearly, he could crack the whip within a hair's breadth of another slave's skin without actually landing a lash. The one "whipped" would then pretend injury. But when Epps was close by, the lashes were real, and Northup was the perfect instrument of Epps's torture. He records refusing to comply only one time and only after administering forty or more blows to young Patsey, who was staked, naked, to the ground.[10] His refusal did Patsey no good, because Epps simply picked up the whip Northup had thrown away and beat her himself until she was unconscious and, as Northup described it, "literally flayed" (183). Amazingly enough, she survived, but, thereafter in constant terror and despair, she was never the same.

To Epps, a slave was a non-reasoning beast that could be trained to respond to his wishes, be they for labor or for sex. He looked upon Patsey, who could pick five hundred pounds of cotton a day and whom he raped repeatedly for years, "merely as a valuable and handsome animal" (184), and he obviously looked upon his animals of all species as mere tools. If slaves resisted his commands, they were simply obstinate, like any draft animal that might prefer rest to work. Their actions were mere reactions, not the product of deliberation. Before he reached his teenage years, Epps's oldest son frequently corrected and whipped slaves while mimicking his father's attitude and gestures. "Mounted on his pony, he often rides into the field with his whip, playing the overseer, greatly to his father's delight. Without discrimination, at such times, he applies the rawhide, urging the slave forward with shouts, and occasional expressions of profanity, while the old man laughs, and commends him as a thorough-going boy.... He looked upon the black man simply as an animal, differing in no respect from any other animal, save in the gift of speech and the possession of somewhat higher instincts, and, therefore, the more valuable" (186). From the perspective of the Epps family and undoubtedly thousands of others like them, slaves were tools merely, not thoughtful, reasoning beings. They had none of the characteristics of modern moral personhood.

Northup managed to retain his own sense of personal responsibility and agency, despite the ten years of degradation at Epps's hands. He describes other enslaved people who did as well. But the pushing system and the white sadism and reigns of terror that it indulged and indeed called forth effectively extinguished that sense of self in some. Baptist describes the zombie phenomenon, slaves so degraded that they seemed dead, except that they continued to move mechanically through their days and nights, working like the others (Baptist 2014, 145–48). Baptist's example is Lucy Thurston, who turned back on her path toward death because of the kindness of other enslaved people and was able to recall the state she was in eighty years later. Others did not survive. Northup describes the decline of Eliza, whom he met when they were both imprisoned in Williams' slave pen in Washington, DC. She had been the concubine of a wealthy Virginia planter, kept in her own house with her son by an enslaved man and her daughter by her owner; he promised her and her children emancipation. But the planter's fortunes declined, and she passed eventually to his daughter's husband, who took her and the children to Washington on the pretense of signing her emancipation papers but instead sold them all to James Burch. As her children were subsequently sold away from her, her grief was more than she could bear. Even at Ford's plantation, where conditions were better than most in Louisiana, she deteriorated, going from house slave to field hand to being sold away for a pittance because she could barely work at all. Broken in both body and spirit, she lost any sense of her own agency; she could no longer claim any of her behavior as her own action. Her grief, despair, and utter powerlessness finally killed her (Northup 1859, 78, 115).

It is certain that slavery blotted out any semblance of personhood of many, people like Eliza and thousands of others who lived and died in total impotence, unable to act ever as anything more than the tool of another human being. And it is equally certain that those who were not utterly instrumentalized were so constrained that many of their deeds were entirely out of their control, making them not actors in their own lives but merely tools in someone else's hands. But for people like Solomon Northup and most of the other enslaved people whom he describes, some decisions and actions were still possible. They were still able to deliberate and plan, to care for each other, and to hold themselves and each other as individuals responsible for what they willingly did. They were still individuated moral agents whose actions mattered to those around them.

Most masters of enslaved people also understood them to have moral responsibilities (although certainly not all, as will be obvious below). Obedience was a moral duty, not just a result of training or just the best option under threat of violence. And violence was thought to be justified as punishment. Enslaved people were not, for the most part, depersonalized; they were personalized (which is one condition for the possibility of depersonalization). Masters held them morally responsible as individuals for the choices they made and the actions they took. And this individuated moral equality was held to be utterly distinct from the massive inequality of the material situation, as it had been from the beginning. Unlike Roman persons, modern moral persons could be enslaved, bought and sold, brutalized, raped, and worse, all without contradiction and without diminishing their accountability for everything they might do in response. The moral of this story for activists today is this: Do not expect your personhood to save you.

III. Indigenous Resistance to the Imposition of Personhood

The first European colonists in the Americas arrived before the category of modern moral personhood came into existence. Some were persons in the legal, proprietary, and civic sense in their countries of origin. Others were not, although many aspired to become so by taking land and claiming landed property rights in the colonies they helped to establish. By the nineteenth century, however, white Americans of all classes were modern moral persons, as were their free African American neighbors and, as I have argued above, a great many of their African American slaves. The same cannot be said about the majority of Indigenous people on the North American continent.[11] As will be discussed below, some whites attributed no moral significance to Indigenous people at all and treated them like vermin, but in many situations whites assumed Indigenous personhood and, increasingly in the nineteenth century, sought to impose its requirements of individualized proprietorship. Most Native peoples vigorously resisted the individualism of European American morality and justice, however, as well as European American assumptions about property in land, and along with it, implicitly at least, they resisted personhood.

I must quickly reiterate that not being persons or resisting the process of "personation" does not mean that these people were irresponsible, antisocial, wantonly violent, or fundamentally evil. They had working social systems that, in many instances at least, seem much less intolerant and cruel than European social systems of the same period. Most took care of their sick, injured, disabled, and elderly. In many groups, women were not relegated to subordinate positions but rather held positions of dignity and authority. They also had systems of diplomacy for handling disputes with other groups. In short, many of these peoples knew how to get along with one another without severely curtailing anyone's ability to live meaningfully.[12] That fact bespeaks some fairly clear visions of what makes for good lives and how to ensure for everyone the possibility of leading a good life. None of this required that they consider themselves or each other persons. None of it required that they be persons. They did not need to own their individual thoughts and actions; they did not need to be proprietors of themselves.

There were plenty of settlers along the western frontier of the British colonies and then of the United States who viewed so-called Indians as irrational "savages" incapable of the most rudimentary civil conduct. They were pests, like the vermin that infested their ships and towns and the wild animals that destroyed their crops. Such people would kill "Indians" as guiltlessly as they would kill a snake or a groundhog.[13] And at times governmental policies encouraged them to do so, just as they would later encourage the killing of wolves in the West. To these people and these policymakers, the Indigenous peoples of North America were not persons and, therefore, in a Euro-American post-Lockean world, they had no moral significance.[14]

A number of colonial and then local and state governments and even the federal government put bounties on the heads of Indigenous people from the 1630s (before the advent of Lockean personhood) and onward.¹⁵ But these policies were not confined to the seventeenth century before Euro-Americans accepted Locke's views; they continued well into the eighteenth century. During George Washington's campaign against the Haudenosaunee (Iroquois) Confederacy, for example, Pennsylvania offered generous bounties for scalps of women and children, regardless of tribal affiliation.¹⁶ Probably the most egregious and ongoing bounty campaigns occurred during and after the California Gold Rush in the mid-nineteenth century. Historian Brendan Lindsay recounts it as follows:

> Legislators passed laws to please their constituents, often violating the Treaty of Guadalupe-Hidalgo and usually ignoring the primacy of the federal government in regulating Indian affairs in order to deliver Native American lands and resources into the hands of covetous settlers. The governors of California signed these bills into law, called for the funding of volunteer campaigns to devastate Native groups, and used their influence as commander in chief of the state militia to make sure weapons and ammunition flowed to the sites of conflict. The judiciary, far from exercising judicial review to correct inconsistencies of state laws or conflicts with federal law or the U.S. Constitution, supported actions against Native Americans by ignoring the predicament they faced under an assault that if taking place between a white and white one would otherwise call criminal. Moreover even though it was technically illegal to kill Native Americans unless in self-defense, California law did not allow nonwhite testimony against whites, typically allowing injustice to reign in cases where whites were brought to trial for crimes against Native people. Perhaps worst of all, local governments acted as something akin to governing boards of avaricious homeowners associations in response to their constituencies' demands, as local leaders and authorities petitioned the state for arms and money to kill Indians, set scalp and head bounties, and looked the other way as their citizens kidnapped, raped, and murdered local Native people. Taken together the acts of local, regional, and state governments in California show them to be complicit in the genocide of Native peoples. (Lindsay 2012, 28)

Government-sponsored head and scalp bounty programs at the very least disregarded the personhood of the people targeted and may actually have precluded recognition of them as persons or even as distinct individuals. Such policies reduce human beings to the status of non-moral objects like boulders on a highway, obstacles or obstructions that must be cleared away.

It was not so everywhere and always, however. As long as Indigenous groups wielded political, economic, and military power, most government policies toward them were similar to policies toward the peoples of other nations, including European nations. The Spanish, French, and British all entered into negotiations with tribal leaders at one point or another; they made treaties and alliances that reflected a recognition of the moral authority of those leaders. And it is not unusual in the historical record to see white diplomats, negotiators, and agents express admiration and respect for Indigenous individuals. The Crown's superintendent John Stuart had a longstanding relationship with the Upper Creek leader Emistisiguo that seems to have been as much mutual friendship and respect as expedient political alliance (see Kokomoor 2018, 42). Similar relationships grew up between US representatives to Indigenous nations in the years after the Revolution. For example, in 1793 James Seagrove described Creek leader White Lieutenant as "a virtuous, good man, and his friendship to our country is not equaled by any in this land" (Kokomoor 2018, 212). Most whites did not hold Creeks or other Indigenous people in such high esteem, but even those who hated them often recognized their intelligence and held them morally responsible as individuals for what the whites construed as acts of theft or unprovoked assault.

That the Creeks did not understand themselves and each other as modern moral persons is evident, however. One point of contention and misunderstanding between Creeks and whites in Georgia (both as a colony and then as a state) occurred in attribution of individual responsibility for crimes. In Creek country in the eighteenth century, if an individual of one town or clan killed someone of another town or clan, the aggrieved group would demand that the killer *or some other individual* from the offender's group be turned over to them for punishment. Responsibility for the killing seems not to have accrued to the individual alone, but to the group as a whole, and it was up to the group to make it right by sacrificing one of its members to regain the balance that had existed prior to the death. Following a raid on December 25, 1773, which resulted in the deaths of about a dozen members of two white families farming on the Georgia frontier, colonial officials demanded that the Creeks hand over to them the three perpetrators or face a trade embargo.[17] The Creek were a coalescent group with decentralized decision-making; headmen pointed out that the perpetrators were Coweta and argued that the embargo should only be imposed on them, not all Creek. The whites would not budge, so some Cusseta set out to capture the killers. They were unable to do so, however, because the men fled. They caught one and killed him on the run, but the whites were not satisfied that justice had been done. A few months later, Cusseta warriors killed two more men who had not participated in the Christmas

Day raid but were of the Coweta band. Three dead from the group whose members had killed whites, since the whites wanted three men brought to justice, would have sufficed in a Creek system of justice, even if two of them were not the actual perpetrators.[18] Justice among the Creek at that time seems not to have been a matter of punishing individual actors but of restoring some sort of balance among groups.[19] To white persons, predictably, this was not justice at all.

The most overwhelming evidence that Indigenous North Americans did not understand themselves as modern moral persons in the lineage of John Locke comes not from differences in concepts of justice and accountability, however, but in practices of ownership and concepts of property. As far as I am able to discern, despite all the variations of culture, language, and religion that existed in North America in the first decades of English colonization, there were very few aboriginal peoples there and then who would have believed that an "Indian" hunter who killed a deer made that carcass his personal property by way of having mixed his labor with it—or, indeed, by any way at all.[20] Meat was not property; deer were not property; land was not property. Individual human beings were not proprietors.

Tribes, bands, and nations had territories in which they lived, grew and gathered food and medicines, hunted, and buried the dead, and sometimes there were disputes over the extent of these areas. For example, in the 1810s there was a dispute between the Cherokee and Creek over a hunting ground in what is now the state of Georgia, which the Madison administration (represented by federal Indian agent R. J. Meigs) attempted to leverage in negotiations in 1816 as a means of taking the land for the United States (see Moulton 1978, 19). But even the hunting ground was not bounded property. Territorial boundaries were not surveyed and fixed; many were known by the course of a river or other natural feature, but often one group's territory shaded into another. Nor was there any superior authority to enforce whatever territorial distinctions existed. According to Leanne Betasamosake Simpson, Indigenous territorial frontiers are usually best understood as zones of overlap and occasions for diplomatic rituals and practices. She writes, "We don't have this idea of private property or 'the commons.' We practice life over a territory with boundaries that are overlapping areas of increased international Indigenous presence, maintained by more intense ceremonial and diplomatic relationship, not necessarily by police, armies, and violence, although under great threat we mobilized to protect what was meaningful to us" (Simpson 2017, 78). Territories are (or, at least, *were*) mapped not with measurements but with stories of events and cosmologies, some of which dictate locations of regularly repeated rituals and burial grounds.

Time and again, the choice that white officials put to Indigenous people who lived on land that whites had designated as property was either to leave or to accept the rules of proprietorship, with adult male heads of households becoming individual proprietors of parcels of land carved out of their group's territory.[21] In 1819 a Cherokee delegation met in Washington, DC, with President Monroe's Secretary of War John C. Calhoun in an attempt to get federal help to expel white squatters from their territory near the Georgia frontier. Calhoun refused to take decisive action to curtail white squatting. Instead, he asked the Cherokee to cede land in Tennessee and Georgia of equal size to what the United States had given to the small band that had agreed to emigrate to Arkansas after the Turkeytown Treaty of 1817. He also asked them to cede a piece of land in Alabama that the US government promised to hold in trust to generate money to fund a set of Indian schools. A treaty was signed on February 27, 1819; it contained Calhoun's points, and it also set aside 640-acre "reservations" for a few prosperous Cherokee men (many of whom were sons of white men) who had demonstrated an adoption of "American life-styles," such as plantation agriculture and slave ownership.[22] These men also had the option to work toward US citizenship and to purchase more land as individual owners, which some did (Moulton 1978, 21). Among the beneficiaries of these latter provisions were several members of the Washington delegation.

This would not be the last time that the US government dangled rewards for assimilation before Indigenous negotiators or individual members of Indigenous nations. And the basis—or price—of assimilation would be patriarchal household structures and individual male head-of-household land ownership, usually known as "allotment" (see Rifkin 2011, especially chap. 4).

On May 28, 1830, President Jackson signed the controversial Indian Removal Act, which passed Congress by only five votes. The Indigenous peoples occupying the states of Georgia, the Carolinas, Tennessee, Alabama, and Mississippi were to accept individual ownership of allotted land or be relocated beyond the US border to what was then known as Indian Country—now Arkansas and Oklahoma. The Cherokee responded with delegations, petitions, and litigation, managing to delay removal for eight years. Although most then joined the western band in Arkansas (those who survived the arduous trip, that is), some entrenched themselves in the Appalachians, some held on to individually owned land in North Carolina, and some fled to the South to join the Seminole who had declared war to stop their own removal to the West.

The Creek abandoned their efforts to hold on to the 5.2 million acres they still held as a nation in 1832 and accepted a system of individual allotments. Under the Treaty of Cusseta, each head of household was to receive

320 acres, with ninety headmen receiving 640 acres each, which they could keep or sell. The remaining 3 million acres would be opened to white settlers. The Creek were a matrilineal society, so there was some confusion over who would count as head of household and, hence, landowner. The US government refused, of course, to allot land to women. They did recognize white men married to Creek women as eligible for allotment, so some of the land went directly to white men, but they declared that Black men married to Creek women were not eligible for land, nor, apparently, were Métis men married to white women. Through the months it took the government to sort all this out, survey the land, and take a census of the Creek population, many white men rushed to marry Creek women in order to get acreage, taking some untold number against their will (Dupre 2018, 282). By the time the government finished its census and surveys in 1833, speculators had overrun the land, bilking Creek out of allotment by fraud, whiskey, and various illicit maneuvers. Those Creek living within the boundaries of the state of Alabama had been designated free people of color by law in 1827 and therefore, like Black Alabamians, were prohibited from testifying in court. It was easy for whites simply to take their land by force, and they did so, often forming local militias for the purpose. The federal government did little to challenge them except insofar as such militias might take states' rights to an anti-federalist extreme. Some Creek simply fled to the Cherokee (despite their history of animosity), but many stayed on allotments (in part out of distrust of the contractors the federal government had hired to oversee their trip). One group of Creek left for the western territory by 1835, but it was not until 1836 that most walked the three hundred miles to Memphis and boarded steamboats to Little Rock. From there, they walked to Oklahoma, the ten thousand survivors arriving at Fort Gibson in January 1837, where they were issued one blanket per family and little food (Dupre 2018, 288–90).

Over the next few decades, it became clear that the United States would occupy the entire continent coast to coast, including half of Mexico and possibly parts of western Canada. Removal of Indigenous peoples to a separate territory was no longer an option, therefore. How, then, to put Indigenous land into circulation in the colonial capitalist economy? One option was genocide, which was attempted in many states and territories, perhaps most notably in California. The other option was forced individual land allotment. If the land could be turned into private property, then negotiating with Indigenous nations would no longer be necessary. Instead, governments, speculators, and would-be homesteaders could simply negotiate with (or pressure or defraud) owners one man at a time. (And they were serious about the sex of Indigenous property owners; if Indigenous women were recognized as proprietors of land, white and free Black women protesting the laws of coverture could hardly be denied equal rights.)

In 1871 Congress officially put an end to the practice of treaty-making with Indigenous groups: "henceforth, no Indian nation or tribe . . . shall be acknowledged or recognized as an independent nation, tribe or power with whom the United States may contract by treaty . . ." (quoted in Hirsch 2014). This move paved the way for many changes in US Indian law and policy, including the General Allotment Act of 1887. This law, often called the Dawes Act after its sponsor Senator Henry Dawes, was intended to force Indigenous people to live like individual persons in a Lockean lineage. In Dawes's view, the problem with Indigenous peoples was that they were not individualistic. "There is no selfishness," he wrote, "which is at the bottom of civilization. Till this people will consent to give up their lands and divide among their citizens so that each can own the land he cultivates they will not make much progress" (quoted in Dunbar-Ortiz 2014, 158). The Dawes Act "allowed the president, at his discretion, to survey and break up the communal land holdings of tribes and to 'allot' land holdings to individual Indians" (Wilkins and Lomawaima 2001, 108). Commissioner of Indian Affairs John Oberly caught the spirit of the act well in his 1888 Annual Report when he wrote that the Indian "must be imbued with the exalting egotism of American civilization, so that he will say 'I' instead of 'We,' and 'This is mine,' instead of 'This is ours'" (quoted in Wilkins and Lomawaima 2001, 116). Clearly the intent was to force Indigenous peoples to become individual proprietor-persons.

The Dawes Act applied to reservation land but not to land still deemed Indian Territory, most notably the land occupied by the nations that had been removed from the Southeast in the 1830s. When oil was discovered there, Congress passed the Curtis Act of 1898 to end their sovereignty and make allotment mandatory. The Cherokee and Muskogee resisted privatization; even though Congress dissolved Indian Territory in 1907 to make Oklahoma a state, the Muskogee fought until 1912, when their leader Chitto Harjo (Crazy Snake) was killed by federal troops (Dunbar-Ortiz 2014, 158–59).

Most Indigenous people resisted privatization and individualization—meaning, too, that they resisted modern moral personhood—as long as they possibly could, and for many that resistance continues to the present day. They were and are intensely aware that personhood is an aspect of a regime of power that privatizes land and exploits natural systems and beings, human beings among them. The imposition of personhood was a tool in the project to divide them from each other and from themselves in their communality. It was a means of making them susceptible to condemnation and criminalization and to responsibilization and blame as individuals for their untenable living conditions in the aftermath of the devastation of their economies, lands, and cultures (which were for them inseparable).

IV. Conclusion

It should be obvious by now that moral personhood was never meant to free us to realize our visions of a just and beautiful world. It was meant to contain people, pin them to themselves, hold them to account, and encourage them not to think too deeply or creatively about their place in the world and the rightness thereof, and it continued to function that way even where those intentions were forgotten. The moral question to ask, then, is not: Can I be a good person? I cannot. None of us really can. The moral question to ask is: Can we work ourselves free of the personhood that has so thoroughly shaped and informed these self-aware living beings that we are? Can we be differently than we are? And can that differently being be in some sense good?

The next chapter considers the ways in which events of the nineteenth century in the United States altered personhood by attempting to include the notion of sovereignty (which was antithetical to the concept in the eighteenth century) and by greatly expanding corporate personhood (whose ancestry was described in chapter 1). The addition of sovereignty compromised the coherence of the concept, I will argue, while the material effects of an enhanced corporate personhood seriously undermined the rights and freedoms that individual human personhood purports to protect. The result is that moral personhood is now in crisis, which creates a socially pervasive uneasiness, if not outright anxiety, but which also presents an opportunity for dismantling a mode of subjectivity that has not served most of humanity, let alone the rest of the planet, particularly well.

[CHAPTER FOUR]

Sovereign Persons, Nonpersons, and Corporate Persons

The United States in the Nineteenth Century

Personhood in the present day owes much to Roman law, the Trinitarian controversies, and John Locke; it would not exist without them. However, it has not remained unchanged since 1694. Two changes in the nineteenth century, both of which occurred in the United States, reshaped personhood and the environment in which it must be enacted now in ways that Locke and his associates could never have imagined. Any genealogy of contemporary personhood would be seriously incomplete without examination of those significant alterations.

The first of these changes can be seen in the writings and efforts of white workingmen who began to claim that their personhood entailed not only individual rights but also individual sovereignty. As I will argue in section I of this chapter, not only did that claim, as it took hold, produce a certain degree of destabilization in the concept of personhood that over time has rendered it more difficult to inhabit, but it also indicates a major revision in the concept of sovereignty, a process that was occurring in Europe during the same time. Section II then recounts those developments by examining the work of a nineteenth-century mechanic named Josiah Warren and concludes with discussion of some implications for the present day.

The second change in the concept of personhood to be considered here began after adoption of the Fourteenth Amendment, which (along with the Fifteenth and Sixteenth Amendments) made formerly enslaved people full citizens of the United States with all the rights and liberties thereunto appertaining. (The amendment does not mention distinctions on the basis of sex, but in fact freedmen received guarantee of the rights and liberties of male citizens, and freedwomen received guarantee of the lesser rights and liberties of female citizens—more about the practical ramifications of this sex difference later on in the chapter.) When the Fourteenth Amendment was ratified in the summer of 1868, probably no one foresaw the use to which it would be put by what we now call Corporate America. Since the last decades of the nineteenth century, in part owing to how the amendment has been interpreted and deployed, the power of incorporated for-profit companies has grown so enormously that corporate interests can easily overwhelm the interests of flesh-and-blood people virtually anywhere in the world. And this state of affairs is, of course, a major factor in my and many other people's moral dilemmas and anguish about the personhood we have spent our lives trying to enact. The third and fourth sections of this chapter, which are also the final sections of the genealogical portion of this study, will focus on interpretations of the Fourteenth Amendment that allowed for the rise of the new corporate person, its phenomenally increasing power in the present century, and the ways in which it has made moral personhood an almost impossible position for mere mortals to inhabit. The last three chapters of this book will explore some non-genealogical strategies for distancing ourselves from personhood and some possibilities for living beyond it.

I. Sovereign Subjects?

Although few people today understand personhood to be a weapon of class domination, for Locke and his receptive readers that is exactly what it was.[1] Had it been otherwise, no doubt it would never have been so widely accepted. Why would powerful men extend genuine equality to their servants, especially after the violence against the hierarchies of church and state that they had seen in their youth? Commoners as individuals were no threat to the powerful. In fact, they were necessary. The threat was commoners as groups in rebellions and the religious sects that so often fed them. The threat was commoners insisting on commonality, living in common and sharing resources in common. Personhood helped to counter that threat with radical individuation of experience, belief, and action. It enacted and enforced individuation and subjection and tended thereby to obviate collective action.

Later commentators often miss or ignore this crucial aspect of Locke's concept, characterizing the modern moral person not as a subjected individual but as a sovereign individual, answerable only to the dictates of reason. "In its essence the individual of conventional liberalism is an altogether sovereign and rational agent bearing each of its accidental properties and ends by an act of will," proclaims Paul Fairfield in *Moral Selfhood in the Liberal Tradition* (2000, 4–5). Other contemporary theorists concur that sovereignty is a central feature of moral personhood. Siegfried van Duffel notes that "the conception of the rights-holder as a sovereign individual" has become a central feature of contemporary debates over rights (2004, 147). In fact, the idea that the moral person is a sovereign individual is so pervasive in twenty-first-century thinking that scholars and students fail to recognize that it is a relatively recent development. Moral persons were not sovereign in the seventeenth or eighteenth century. Sovereignty was incorporated into persons—unevenly and with the effect of destabilizing both concepts—in the nineteenth century. Theorists today are so sure of its longevity, however, that they tend to read it back into Locke's work and thereby misunderstand key aspects of his moral and political projects as well as the political history of their own fundamental concepts. In fact, personhood in no way guarantees freedom or self-determination. The assumption that it does, moreover, obscures the functions of subjection that it solidifies. Because of that tendency, more must be said here about the seventeenth- and eighteenth-century distinction between personhood and sovereignty and how blurring that distinction changed the meaning of both concepts in the nineteenth century.

In seventeenth-century England, both the concept and the institution of sovereignty were undergoing revision. Political thinkers were trying desperately to justify rebellion by countering the Stuart contention that kings ruled by Divine Right (and so should not be checked by earthly law), while at the same time vigorously resisting the populism and subversive disorder breaking out seemingly from every quarter as the country suffered the paroxysms of multiple institutional collapse and civil war. Their proposed compromise was that sovereignty (and, with it, legitimate subjection) was real, but that it was the product of collective human action, a historical achievement rather than a natural or supernatural phenomenon.

One of those mid-century thinkers was Thomas Hobbes, as we noted in a slightly different context in chapter 1. Hobbes argued that sovereignty is constituted through contract, or covenant, at the point where individual persons cede some of their natural rights to Leviathan.[2] Prior to that point, there is no sovereignty; individuals are not sovereign in themselves. We can see this in *Leviathan*, part II, chapter XVII. Leviathan is "*one person, of whose acts a great multitude, by mutual covenants one with another, have made themselves every one the author, to the end that he may use the strength and means of them all as he shall think expedient for their peace and common defense.* And he that carries this person is called SOVEREIGN and said to have *sovereign power*; and everyone besides, his SUBJECT." Sovereignty is an overwhelming power that is a product of the consolidation of natural powers. Leviathan "is more than consent or concord; it is a real unity of them in one and the same person, made by covenant of every man with every man . . ." (Hobbes 1958, 143, 142). The bearer of sovereignty is not a natural being but a humanly constituted person whose power is the result of a historical achievement.[3] That person, an artificial (though real) entity, is in turn borne by some select individual or assembly of individual human beings, but those who bear it are not themselves sovereign; they simply represent the sovereignty of the unified person that Leviathan is.

It is true, though, that what individuals cede through mutual covenant sounds something like what theorists nowadays call sovereignty. In covenant, Hobbes writes, it is "as if every man should say to every man, *I authorize and give up my right of governing myself to this man, or to this assembly of men, on this condition, that you give up your right to him and authorize all his actions in like manner*" (142). In the present day, self-governance may sound like autonomy, the practice of giving oneself laws or principles to live by. In Hobbes's time, however, the verb *to govern* had a very broad meaning: "to conduct oneself or others."[4] It could have a managerial connotation, as in to husband resources or supervise a staff, or it could involve caring for and educating children, from which we get the rather quaint word *governess*. It suggested running or overseeing an activity or enterprise, leading or guiding people. In the context of Hobbes's mutual covenant, to give up the right of governing oneself consisted in giving up one's right to set one's own course and conduct one's own affairs and, instead, to conform to the dictates of a mutually recognized sovereign authority.

Hobbes understands sovereignty much as Jean Bodin describes it in his 1576 work *The Six Bookes of a Commonweale*. There Bodin defines *sovereignty* as commanding power: "Maiestie or Soveraigntie is the most high, absolute, and perpetuall power over the citizens and subiects in a Commonweale: which the Latins cal *Maiestatem*, the Greeks *akra exousia*, *kurion arche*, and *kurion politeuma*; the Italians *Segnoria*, and the Hebrewes *tomech shévet*, that is to say, The greatest power to command" (Bodin 1962, 84). A command is a directive that must be obeyed; in other words, it is a speech act that imposes an obligation. For Hobbes as for Bodin, a command is issued by a superior to an inferior; although one can try, in fact no one can successfully command an equal, for a peer may freely comply with a directive or not comply.[5] It follows, then, that no one can command him-/herself. A person may *govern* him-/herself—that is, a person may choose to live in a certain manner or follow a certain regimen—but a person cannot be *sovereign over* him-/herself. Giving up the natural right to self-governance, on Hobbes's view, is not equivalent to giving up a natural right to self-sovereignty, because there can be no such thing.[6]

Likewise for Locke, no one could be sovereign over him- or herself; sovereignty entailed subjection *of another*. Furthermore, in the *First Treatise*, he argues vociferously against Sir Robert Filmer's claim that God gave Adam sovereignty as an individual. Filmer had claimed that Adam was the sovereign monarch of the whole world (see Locke 1960, 189; *First Treatise (FT)* III.19) and that his sovereignty was passed down to his descendants (and eventually to English royalty). In chapters III through VIII of the *First Treatise*, Locke critiques the four grounds upon which Filmer claims to prove Adam's sovereignty.[7] Of interest here is his critique of the claim that Adam was sovereign by "donation," based on Genesis 1:28: "And God blessed them, and God said unto them, Be fruitful, and multiply, and replenish the earth, and subdue it: and have dominion over the fish of the sea, and over the fowl of the air, and over every living thing that moveth upon the earth." Against Filmer, Locke maintains that the substance of this gift is not sovereignty; rather, it is property. It is clear, he declares, "that he [God] means nothing to be granted to *Adam* here but Property, and therefore he says not one word of *Adam's Monarchy*." If Filmer were a more careful writer, Locke continues, "he might, with much more clearness have said, that *Adam was hereby Proprietor of the whole World*" (192; *FT* IV.23). Sovereignty and property are not the same thing; a right of exclusive use is not the same as a power to command or rule.

Furthermore, Locke continues, this property was not given to Adam alone, but rather to "them," which might have been Adam and Eve together or might have been everybody. The previous verse, Genesis 1:27, says that "God created man in his *own* image, in the image of God created he him; male and female created he them." Taking into account that context, Locke asserts, we should conclude that when God blesses "them" and speaks to "them" in the next passage, the charge to multiply, replenish, subdue, and have dominion is directed to all human beings.[8] In any case, Adam did not receive this gift of property as his own, private estate. Indeed, this dominion was neither private ownership nor even full possession. It was simply what in Roman law was called *usufruct*, right of use. This is clear, Locke thinks, simply from the one passage; what "they" receive is dominion over fishes of the sea, fowl of the air, and terrestrial animals, not over everything. They are given the right to use those creatures, but even their use is limited, as the very next sentence reveals. In Genesis 1:29, God states: "I have given you every herb bearing seed, which *is* upon the face of all the earth, and every tree, in the which *is* the fruit of a tree yielding seed; to you it shall be for meat." Then in verse 30, he extends this gift to every beast, fowl, and thing that creepeth on the earth, which suggests that not only will humans not eat nonhuman animals, but no nonhuman animals will eat animals.[9] Noting this limitation on Adam's use, Locke writes:

> Should any one, who is Absolute Lord of a Country, have bidden our *A.* [Author, i.e., Filmer] *Subdue the Earth*, and given him Dominion over the Creatures in it, but not have permitted him to have taken a Kid or a Lamb out of the Flock, to satisfie his hunger, I guess he would scarce have thought himself Lord or Proprietor of that Land, or the Cattel on it: But would have found the difference between *having Dominion*, which a Shepherd may have, and having full Property as an Owner. (203; *FT* IV.39)

Locke here makes a distinction between simple dominion, by which he means what the Romans and later jurists called *usufruct*, and full property right, or ownership, which entails the right to dispose of or destroy/consume what one owns. Human beings did not even receive full ownership of the earth, according to Locke, let alone individual sovereignty.

For Hobbes, Locke, and their seventeenth-century contemporaries and eighteenth-century successors, sovereignty was the supreme power to command, the power to make and enforce law, and (subsumed under it) the right to repel any forces intent on destroying that power. Individual persons do not have that sort of power. In the seventeenth and eighteenth centuries, people, even as persons, were still *subjects*. They were subject to the commands of God and king. Although they could choose whether to obey those commands, if they chose to disobey, they were then subject to punishment. Subjects did not make the rules; sovereigns did. As long as persons were subjects, they could not be sovereigns. The notion of a sovereign subject was an oxymoron.

Some skeptics might suggest that my claim that Locke's person was not sovereign rests on a merely verbal rather than a conceptual difference. Their thinking might run like this: By *sovereignty* we just mean exclusive authority over what happens within a limited sphere, such as within a nation-state or, importantly in this connection, in one's body or in one's home; the government and other people ought not dictate how a person lives his/her private life. Similarly, Locke believes that people in the state of nature contract to bring about a government in order to cordon off and protect this same private sphere from intrusion and interference by other people; therefore, the government itself must not intrude in or attempt to regulate it, either. We and Locke are pointing to the same domain, my interlocutors claim; thus, we are merely using different words to articulate the same concept.

Not only do I think this interpretation is wrong, but I believe that it obscures a history that is crucial for understanding the untenable and sometimes excruciating ethical situation that is the focus of this book. To see this, we can turn to the nineteenth century and to John Stuart Mill.

Mill and Locke use the term *sovereignty* very differently. At the beginning of chapter 4 of his 1859 book *On Liberty*, Mill puts forward this question: "What, then, is the rightful limit to the sovereignty of the individual over himself? Where does the authority of society begin? How much of human life should be assigned to individuality, and how much to society?" (Mill 1978, 73). Mill assumes that there is an important boundary between public and private life, between civic accountability and personal choice. The public aspects of our lives are subject to social and legal regulation. The private aspects are ours, individually, to regulate on our own or with whatever advice and support we choose to accept, as long as we do not violate someone else's private domain. This idea that persons are, as Mill puts it, "sovereign" over their bodies, their real estate, their religious practices, and their private lives—however controversial the definition and parameters of "private" might be—pervades contemporary society in the United States. We hear similar claims from people as diverse as gun enthusiasts, pornographers, advocates of reproductive rights, and members of the LGBT community.[10] My body is my territory; my home is my castle; my conscience is my guide. Each individual person, many would agree, is sovereign in his or her respective domain. For Locke, what Mill is describing would have been considered property; each individual was a proprietor over his or her body, and so on. Sovereignty was distinct from proprietorship; sovereignty was the right to control subjects by command. For Mill and liberal thinkers after him, by contrast, sovereignty means control over a material object or space or a conceptual sphere. According to Joel Feinberg, "To say that I am sovereign over my bodily territory is to say that I, and I alone, decide (so long as I am capable of deciding) what goes on there. My authority is a discretionary competence, an authority to choose and make decisions" (1983, 453). This is a sovereignty without subjects, which Locke would have laughed at—and in fact did laugh at when Filmer proposed that Adam was sovereign of the world from the moment of his creation, before any other human beings existed (see Locke 1960, 187; *FT* III.16). For Locke, sovereignty implies subjection of others and does not exist without it; sovereigns cannot exist without subjects over whom they are sovereign. For these later thinkers, however, sovereignty does not imply subjection but only control over a circumscribed space and set of things and/or events—some sort of "private realm"—and it entails a right to defend that circumscribed territory (literal or conceptual) from intruders.

The skeptic's point, however, is not that Locke actually says individual persons are sovereign, but that his way of conceiving of personhood in effect makes persons sovereign by contemporary definition of that term, despite his using the term otherwise. Locke, the skeptic contends, leaves to individual persons a circumscribed "space" of control, namely, their bodies, their private beliefs, and their private property. Therefore, only the meaning of the term *sovereign* changed sometime between 1698 to 1859; the meaning of the term *person* remained the same. Nothing new has been predicated of persons. I disagree, and this is where I think something truly significant has been obscured.

Simply put, what is at stake here is the difference between responsibility and control. Lockean persons were responsible, accountable, judicable, and punishable, because they had dominion as proprietors of their own physical capacities through time. Every human being—excepting infants, idiots, and lunatics—was a person. But the vast majority of Lockean persons had little or no ability to repel intrusion into their corporeality, let alone exclude others from any physical space around them. They were neither legally nor morally entitled to exercise control over the boundaries of a private (bodily) domain such as Mill and twentieth- and twenty-first-century thinkers posit as individuals' sovereign sphere. Yet they were Lockean persons despite that inability.

Consider wives and servants. A wife might have no private space under her control at all, nor did she have control over her own body. Her husband had sexual access to her at all times, and if she displeased him, he could beat her. A servant was any person working under a labor contract for a period of time, such as a year, during which s/he had to be more or less constantly available for whatever work the master wanted done.[11] Servants were hired for work in households but also in businesses and farms. Since these institutions often occupied the same premises, one servant might work in the house, in the garden, in the stables, in the fields, and in the shop or office at different times of the day or year. Some servants lived in villages, but many lived in the master's house or somewhere else on his property.[12] Some were paid for their work, but some were merely given room and board. Servants—men, women, and children—were also regularly beaten for displeasing their masters.[13] While servants were responsible for their laboring to carry out the commands their masters issued—because they had dominion over their actions—by no stretch of the imagination could such people be considered sovereign over any kind of territory, including their own bodies. Locke, who knew full well what servants and women were and were not, declared them persons because they were proprietors of their bodies and bodily capacities, extending to their actions through time—proprietors, not sovereigns.

Now skeptics will no longer be dissatisfied with me only; they will question Locke: How can we say anyone has property in anything if they do not have the right to exclude others from it? One answer might be that wives and servants agreed to this constant access and the ever-present possibility of brutal punishment when they made their marriage or labor contracts. They relinquished their rights of exclusion in exchange for protection, keep, and/or payment. Another, at least partial, answer is that our concept of privacy did not exist in the seventeenth century or even in most of the eighteenth century. Historian Lynn Hunt (2007) has made the case that during the late eighteenth century a new sensibility of the self emerged. She locates this emergence in an increased modesty regarding excretory functions and sleeping arrangements, a new concern with individuated pain and suffering that resulted in criticism of torture, and a heightened awareness of personal emotional states, particularly those inspired by novels and music. Hunt's interest lies in tracing the conditions for the possibility of a discourse of human rights, but her research shows the historical, and rather late, emergence of something like personal privacy. If we take her argument seriously, we might conclude that corporeal propriety for Locke had to do with the responsibility to avoid harm and a right to dispose of one's labor by contracting it out, not with exclusive access to a private physical domain.

At any rate, Locke's person was not sovereign in either the seventeenth-century sense or the nineteenth- and twentieth-century sense. It was not sovereign at all. But if Locke did not attribute sovereignty over one's body and personal property to individual persons, where did the idea come from?

II. The Working Man's Sovereignty

Mill tells us where he got the phrase "sovereignty of the individual" in chapter 7 of his *Autobiography*, in the course of describing his collaboration with his beloved late wife, Harriet: "The 'Liberty' [meaning *On Liberty*] was more directly and literally our joint production than anything else which bears my name, for there was not a sentence of it which was not several times gone through by us together, turned over in many ways, and carefully weeded of any faults" (Mill 1924, chap. 7).[14] He notes the influences on their thinking, Johann Heinrich Pestalozzi and Wilhelm von Humboldt, and then he mentions the phrase "sovereignty of the individual." He and Harriet took that phrase, he says, from

> a remarkable American, Mr. Warren, [who] had formed a System of Society, on this foundation of the 'Sovereignty of the Individual,' had obtained a number of followers, and had actually commenced the formation of a Village Community (whether it now exists I know not), which, though bearing a superficial resemblance to some of the projects of Socialists,

is diametrically opposite to them in principle, since it recognises no authority whatever in Society over the individual, except to enforce equal freedom of development for all individualities. (Mill 1924, chap. 7)

Very few people in the world today have ever heard of the remarkable Mr. Warren, Josiah Warren, a mechanic born in Boston in 1798 who moved to Cincinnati in 1820 during the recession that followed the Panic of 1819. The Mills' knowledge of Warren most likely came from the 1852 edition of his book *Equitable Commerce*, although it might simply have come from mutual acquaintances in New York or Long Island, where Warren founded his "Village Community," which he called Modern Times. (Modern Times' name was changed to Brentwood after it got some bad press,[15] but it was still in operation in accordance with Warren's principles when he published *Practical Applications* in 1872, thirteen years after publication of Mill's *Autobiography*.[16])

Warren seems to have formulated his idea of individual sovereignty after the collapse of Robert Owen's socialist experiment at New Harmony, Indiana, 1825–27. He and his wife Caroline Cutter Warren were part of that experiment and were very disillusioned by it, as he states in his 1841 *Manifesto*.[17] Having observed that much of the disharmony at New Harmony centered on questions of equity in labor and use of material goods, Warren decided that pooling resources and holding property in common was the root of the problem. Instead, he thought, a community might work on the opposite principle, namely, each person would have full control over his or her labor and its products. Units of labor—whose value would reflect both duration and hardship—could then be exchanged, if individuals so desired, labor for labor. The price of all commodities would not be set by demand but by their cost in time to their producer. No one's labor would be undervalued, therefore; a washerwoman's labor of six hours would be equivalent to an attorney's labor of six hours. In fact, the washerwoman's labor might be valued somewhat more than the attorney's per hour because of the physical exertion and pain her labor cost her in addition to her time.[18] If a community were based on this idea, Warren believed, no one willing to work would live in poverty. Furthermore, he thought, most of the sources of interpersonal conflict would be eliminated, greatly reducing or even eliminating any need for a community to expend resources on institutions such as police, courts, and prisons.[19]

To test out his ideas, Warren opened what he called a Time Store in Cincinnati, where people could buy and sell on the basis of the time of a producer's labor. According to his account in *Equitable Commerce*, the system worked well (Warren 2011, 54–98);[20] it was both equitable and efficient, and through it he gained allies interested in establishing a whole community on similar principles. The group found land in Tuscarawas County, Ohio, where they established a village called Equity in 1835. Equity failed within two years because of illness; of its twenty-four residents, twenty-three were ill the first year and then twelve died of influenza. The group decided the location was unhealthy and disbanded. Warren returned to Cincinnati. In less than a decade, however, he and others of like mind founded another village, Utopia, in 1847 in Clermont County, Ohio.[21] Utopia was a success until land speculators drove up prices to the point that it was impossible for the settlers to afford their property. Interest among Easterners in Warren's principles led him to found a third village on Long Island, Modern Times, as mentioned above. As he describes them in *Equitable Commerce*, all three villages functioned well; the problems the communities faced all seemed to come from external forces—disease and the larger economic and social context.

Warren's ideas came from experience, reading (although we have no record of the extent of his reading), and experimentation. There is no evidence that he had any formal education, although obviously he was literate and had the mathematical skills necessary for making precise measurements, designing machinery, and keeping account books.[22] Undoubtedly in Boston he had been somebody's apprentice for several years and then, perhaps, somebody's employee. If he had lived in the seventeenth century, he would have been classified as a servant.

But Josiah Warren was not a servant. He was a white male US citizen with a newly opened frontier to escape to when the capitalist economy threatened him with poverty. Warren was a person. Had laboring people in seventeenth-century England read Locke's work, they might well have seen Locke's fine reasoning, his bloodless equality, and his radical individuation of responsibility as the power play that it was. As we saw in the last chapter, calling them persons was not a way of ennobling them. It was a way of shutting them up, both in the sense of making their voices inaudible in the parlors of power and in the sense of walling them in, isolating them in their individual bodies and destroying their communities as surely as the Parliamentarians' soldiers destroyed the Diggers' occupation. Things were different, however, for Warren. He was born into a world where personhood was assumed to be the universal state of self-aware individuals. More than a century after Locke's work, in a nation founded on successful repudiation of monarchy, a healthy young white man might be excused for imagining himself to be in charge of his own destiny. Why should he, or anyone, be subjected to a mortal master in a country where independence was the hallmark of freedom and freedom was the right of everyone?[23] Warren's experiences as an apprentice and a wage laborer in New England undoubtedly influenced his thinking as much as his contact with Robert Owen's ideas and his experiences at New Harmony did. We can see the former at work in his conception of sovereignty as he describes it in the *Manifesto*. There Warren proclaims that every individual must have "undisturbed possession of his or her natural and proper *sovereignty* over its [his/her] own person, time, property and responsibilities."[24] The sovereignty that Warren claims, then, consists in full and exclusive use and disposal of all of one's bodily capacities, one's hours and years, and all the products of one's efforts, and it entails sole responsibility for that use and disposal. These are the very things that every servant had to give up for the duration of a work contract; masters owned the servant's time, energy, and product for weeks, months, even years at a stretch and could demand service at all hours of the day and night throughout that span of time. In Warren's villages, everyone labored, but no one occupied the status of servant. Likewise, there were no masters or apprentices; people who wanted to learn a skill simply paid for lessons until the skill was acquired. Everyone had equal status as full proprietor of his/her own capacities and time. It would seem that the servant had accepted his personhood, and he drew the logical conclusion that, therefore, he was servant no more.

In Warren's villages and in his ideal world, no one is subject to any other person's command. His version of sovereignty is not the correlate of subjection. It consists simply in ownership. The concept of sovereignty has changed then but, much more importantly, so has the concept of personhood.

Warren's person, in the lineage of Locke, is an owner; the long history of personhood's connection with property carries forward from ancient Rome to the present day. However, Locke's grounding of moral personhood in natural law has disappeared. Warren's person is not a creature beholden to its Creator; its rights are not grounded in an inalienable duty to preserve God's moral creation in itself first and then whenever possible in others. Inalienable rights now need no such ground. Instead, Warren holds that individuals' inalienable rights rest simply on the observable propensity of all living beings to differ—both from each other and from themselves—over time. The natural world operates on a principle of unending differing, not remaining the same and certainly not converging toward unity. To expect a society to operate on a principle of sameness rather than difference is a recipe for misery, if not disaster. The only way people can live together productively and in peace is to allow that natural propensity to differ to take its course, whatever its course may be, which is inherently unpredictable. In fact, only one thing is predictable, namely that people will become more different from one another, more individual, over time. Warren writes, "Out of the indestructibility or inalienability of this individuality grows the absolute right of its exercise, or the absolute sovereignty of the individual" (58). Governments, religions, schools, and any other institutions that seek to unite people or enforce conformity violate the individual and perpetuate injustice.

Unlike Hobbes and Locke and even unlike the more practical-minded John Adams, Thomas Jefferson, and James Madison, Warren did not seek to establish a legitimate, workable system of government. Even in his very early essays in *The Peaceful Revolutionist* from April 5, 1833, he has harsh words for institutionalized government:

> Laws and governments are professedly instituted for the security of person and property, but they have never accomplished this object. Even to this day every newspaper shows that they commit more crimes upon persons and property and contribute more to their insecurity than all criminals put together. The greatest crime which can be committed against society and which causes poverty and lays the foundation of almost all other crimes is the monopoly of the soil. This has not only been permitted but protected or perpetrated by every government of modern times up to the last accounts from the congress of the United States. (Warren 2011, 108)

Warren seeks to establish not a government, but a just and prosperous society. People do not need government; they need an equitable system of material exchange that encourages productivity and division of labor. And there can be no equitable system of material exchange unless each person's labor—their time and exertion—is both under their control and is sufficiently rewarded under any contract. As he wrote in *The Quarterly Letter* in 1867, "Do justice to labor, and then we may see something of the bond of society and social order: not so much on paper as in every aspect of social life" (Warren 2011, 192). Locke would have been utterly appalled.

John Stuart Mill was not appalled, but however much Mill admired Warren and his principles and achievements, he did not take Warren's rejection of government, let alone his reasons for rejecting it, seriously. When Mill asks, "What, then, is the rightful limit to the sovereignty of the individual over himself? Where does the authority of society begin?" he means to be asking about the line between individual authority and governmental authority. Society, for Mill in this passage, includes socially instituted government. This is clear in the next two paragraphs when Mill asks specifically about imposition of law and society's "jurisdiction." Society has no jurisdiction, Mill asserts, "when a person's conduct affects the interests of no persons besides himself" (Mill 1978, 73). Otherwise, society does have jurisdiction and can command obedience under threat of lawful punishment.

Mill's view is that government is a necessary mechanism for the production of individual security: Without assurance that our lives and property will be protected against invaders and thieves, we could not carry on our personal affairs, and personal happiness would be impossible. A good government provides that protection, and those who benefit are indebted to and thus have obligations to support that government and obey its laws. Warren's view is that no government ever has provided that kind of security to working people whose labor is regularly stolen by an economic system based on money, speculation, and prices set by demand rather than by labor cost.[25] On the contrary, governments back up those economic institutions, and most government officials come from the class of people who benefit from them; "laws and governments still are what they have always been, viz. public means for private ends" (Warren 2011, 109).[26] Warren's answer to Mill's question would have been that there is no limit to the sovereignty of the individual over his/her time, bodily capacities, labor, and products and that society's legitimate authority over those things is nonexistent, precisely because government does not provide security for working people and their property.

It is Mill's question and not Warren's answer, however, that has set the agenda for liberal jurisprudence and political theory since the mid-nineteenth century. Yes, the individual person has acquired the quality of sovereignty, which for Locke it did not have, but that sovereignty is over a limited, so-called "private" realm, not over one's time and labor. And what counts as private is continually contested. Are religious practices private? Not if they involve certain forms of mutilation, drugs, reptile handling, or animal sacrifice. Are decisions about which medical procedures to undergo private? Not if they involve a fetus, genital reconstruction, or marijuana, or if FDA approval has not been secured. Individuals are not even free to purchase most medications unless they have a prescription from a state-licensed physician. What about sexual practices? I hardly need to elaborate. Even choice of domicile is subject to governmental approval if one has a felony record, is on probation, lives out-of-doors, or, within my lifetime, is not white. There was a time, not so long ago, when, within his own house, a man could beat his wife and children but could not read *Lady Chatterley's Lover*. The boundary frequently moves, and its placement in practice differs depending on one's age, race, sex, religion, sexual orientation, and gender identity. People argue continually over that boundary's location, but very few ever question the need for any boundary or the existence of the public and private realms it is supposed to separate.[27]

Warren did not speak in terms of public and private realms. He talked instead about control over how one spends one's time and over the product of one's effort. Warren, like Locke, is concerned with the power of an embodied individual to act through time. Such things are not best thought on the metaphor of bounded territory. But we have not inherited Warren's vision of individuation as unending process and of control over one's labor as the central fact of personhood and liberty. The workingman's perspective has been erased in its uptake and replaced by Mill's perspective, that of the corporate executive and member of Parliament.[28] The value of endless differing disappears into the value of clearly marked territory. In addition to self-enclosure, self-ownership, and sole responsibility for its actions, the modern person is now, in theory, sovereign over the ill-defined territory known as private life.

III. Legal Persons, Human and Not So Human

While individual persons were acquiring a new subject-less sovereignty and their numbers in the United States were growing as Indigenous people were forced to become Lockean individuals, the legal concept of personhood was developing in ways that would have much more impact on the lives of all human beings than any conferral of sovereignty or privacy rights could ever have. As we saw in chapter 1, legal personhood historically had nothing essential to do with being human; human beings could be legal persons (that is, they could have the status of legal personhood), but so could other sorts of beings. The other side of that coin was that legal personhood was not automatically granted to anyone just because Lockean personhood's moral worth and accountability was; one could be subject to moral judgment and punishment while having no legal standing at all, as was the case with enslaved people and, to a great extent, wives. Although Lockean and post-Lockean persons were always forensic beings, subject to judgment of both moral and legal authorities, most did not have property rights or civil rights, and some were actually property themselves. That began to change in the nineteenth century. Black men acquired the status of legal persons with civil and property rights under the Reconstruction amendments following the Civil War (although Jim Crow quickly evolved to make those rights extremely difficult to exercise). Black women gained some legal protections that they had not had while enslaved, but they, like women of all other races in the United States, had no right to vote in federal elections, run for office, serve on juries, enter into contracts without a male cosignatory, or in many cases even hold property in their own names, and any wage a woman earned was the property of her husband or father. Soon after the Fourteenth Amendment went into effect, feminists made plans to challenge women's inferior legal status on the premise that the amendment conferred legal personhood on all people born or naturalized in the United States.

In 1872 Virginia Minor claimed the right to vote in federal elections as a person under the Fourteenth Amendment. When the Missouri Supreme Court ruled against her, she appealed to the US Supreme Court. In 1875 in *Minor v. Happerscett*, the US Supreme Court explicitly ruled that women in the United States were not legal persons despite the wording of the Fourteenth Amendment (Gordon 2005); it was constitutional, therefore, for states to deny women civil and property rights. It would require another constitutional amendment to grant women voting rights, and that would not occur for another forty-five years. And it would be another forty-five years after that before women in the United States would gain full property rights.[29] Like women of all races and ethnicities, Indigenous people of all sexes were explicitly declared nonpersons under the Fourteenth Amendment. Even when the Nineteenth Amendment went into effect in 1920, Indigenous women were left out. Most Indigenous people did not acquire voting rights as US citizens until 1924 under the Indian Citizenship Act, which granted them eligibility to vote in federal elections. Many states, however, still prohibited Indigenous people from voting in state and local elections; New Mexico was the last to relent, in 1962. And, of course, Indigenous women, like all women, were denied many property rights and some civil rights under the legal doctrine of coverture into the 1960s.

During these many decades when no women or Indigenous men were legal persons and Black men were struggling against enormous odds to exercise their legal personhood, a species of nonhuman persons found the Fourteenth Amendment a sturdy platform upon which to claim not only new legal rights and protections but also tremendous political power (as the next section of this chapter describes in detail). Courts decided that the Fourteenth Amendment applied to a new group of persons, namely, corporate persons; corporations, unlike all women and Indigenous men, were entitled to equal protection and due process under the law. Over the next century and a quarter, corporations also gained freedom from double jeopardy and unwarranted search and seizure, and freedom of speech (specifically, the right to contribute money to political campaigns as a form of political speech). Indeed, in his dissenting opinion in *Citizens United v. Federal Election Commission*, Justice John Paul Stevens offered as a *reductio ad absurdum* argument against corporate free speech rights that a corporate right to vote in federal elections might be next: "Under the majority's view, I suppose it may be a First Amendment problem that corporations are not permitted to vote, given that voting is, among other things, a form of speech" (Stevens 2010, 33–34). A majority of his colleagues apparently lacked Stevens's sense of the absurd; they went on in 2014 to declare (in *Burwell, Secretary of Health and Human Services, et al. v. Hobby Lobby Stores, Inc., et al.*) that corporate persons have the right to free exercise of their religion. Currently, there is speculation that the Roberts court would affirm a Second Amendment right to bear arms for corporate persons, should a case come before them (Miller 2011). In fact, many corporations already employ security forces that amount to small armies.

The Supreme Court's deference to corporate persons is a significant departure from, if not an outright betrayal of, the founders' express intentions. Corporations were few and relatively unimportant in the US economy at the nation's founding, and men like James Madison and Thomas Jefferson sorely wanted to keep it that way.[30] Jefferson wrote, "I hope that we shall crush in its birth the aristocracy of our monied corporations, which dare already challenge our government to a trial of strength, and bid defiance to the laws of our country."[31] Jefferson strongly objected to government-chartered monopolies, but it was not only the monopolistic nature of British corporations (like the East India Company—the target of the Boston Tea Party and numerous other protests leading up to the Revolutionary War) that the founders wanted to avoid; many were also concerned about the concentration of wealth in entities, monopolies or not, that would in effect be immortal. As Madison wrote to James K. Paulding on March 10, 1827, "Incorporated Companies, with proper limitations and guards, may in particular cases, be useful, but they are at best a necessary evil only. Monopolies and perpetuities are objects of just abhorrence. The former are unjust to existing, the latter usurpations on the right of future generations."[32] Perhaps because of these fears, the founders did not grant the federal government the right to incorporate businesses, but they did leave the states free to do so, which, as far as they could foresee, meant that no corporation in the United States would operate beyond a small geographical region and none would ever grow to the size and have the political influence of the East India Company. Charters were granted by state legislatures for localized capital-intensive ventures deemed to be in the public interest, such as mines and mills, and those charters could be revoked if the public interest was violated.[33]

Despite these warnings and precautions—as will come as no surprise to modern Americans, jaded by the current state of national and state politics—political corruption ensued; state legislatures sometimes granted charters to friends and patrons while refusing them to would-be competitors, resulting in de facto monopolies. There were bribes and scandals.

States made efforts to clean up the corruption during the Jacksonian period by removing the power to incorporate from legislatures and relocating it in special state corporation commissions that simply processed applications and collected incorporation fees. Thus, access to the corporate form was made equitable, but the presumption remained that incorporation restricted the operation of a business to the mission specified in its charter. Activity beyond the chartered mission, known as *ultra vires*, was not only illegal but was held to be logically impossible for the corporate person itself. A corporate person having no life outside its legal description meant that its sphere of logically possible action was entirely defined by its charter. If an agent of the corporation overstepped the bounds of charter, he—not the corporation—was the guilty party. For example, if a railroad company bought and operated a steamboat or underwrote expenses for a music festival as a destination for passengers, there was a violation of the charter and thus of the law, but the guilty party was not the corporation per se; rather, it was the agent of the corporation who made the decision and (mis)appropriated corporate funds (Freund 1897, 64).

However, seeking to increase revenues from incorporation fees, state bureaucracies began to relax corporate chartering restrictions (Horwitz 1986, 195).[34] Not only did that increase the number of businesses within a state that decided to incorporate, but it also attracted businessmen from other states to headquarter their companies in congenial states. Changes in state law in 1875 made New Jersey a favorite for businesses seeking corporate charters; subsequently, in 1881 alone, New Jersey chartered 449 corporations, substantially more than any other state, including those with larger economies like Massachusetts and Pennsylvania. Further, in 1888 New Jersey granted corporations the right to own stock in each other, which legalized holding companies (and subsequently the practice of "pyramiding"—see Coleman 1974, 45) and facilitated "the transformation of controversial industrial trusts into ordinary business corporations" (Yablon 2007, 336). By 1896 so many corporations were chartering in New Jersey that the fees alone allowed the state to be virtually debt-free while imposing no statewide taxes, and other states were eager to acquire their own market shares (Yablon 2007, 324). Among the innovations on offer were the right to allow shareholders to vote by proxy (and the process for selecting proxies to be written off as business expenses), to hold shareholders' meetings in remote locations to encourage proxy voting, to issue stock without giving new shareholders voting rights, and even to allow a majority of voting shareholders to change the corporate charter. All these changes made it possible for corporate power to concentrate in very few human hands even as corporations themselves were expanding tremendously (Coleman 1974, 44–46).

Huge concentrations of capital—common by the end of the nineteenth century in railroads, insurance, sugar, tobacco, petroleum, and of course banking—could exert a great deal of economic and political pressure. Public animosity toward corporations in the first quarter of the nineteenth century was rekindled in the last quarter, leading to passage of the Sherman Anti-Trust Act in 1890, among other regulatory measures.[35] It seemed only federal authorities could rein in huge companies operating across state and even national boundaries. But the largest corporations had the wealth to influence federal policy as well; their campaign contributions reached a new high during the presidential race of 1896 as businesses sought to elect William McKinley over William Jennings Bryan. This high level of corporate political expenditure continued through the next two presidential elections (Lipton 2010, 1921). In response, Congress passed the Tillman Act of 1907, which prohibited corporate contributions to presidential and congressional general election campaigns. Nevertheless, by 1921, with pro-business Warren Harding in the Oval Office, corporations were relatively safe from regulation and trust-busting and remained so for half a century. Scrutiny of monopolies made a very brief comeback in the 1970s, with the US Department of Justice filing suit against AT&T and IBM, but the suits were not settled before Ronald Reagan became president. Reagan's Attorney General William Baxter dropped the case against IBM and broke up AT&T not because it was a monopoly but only because it, unlike IBM, was a *government-protected* monopoly—governmental market regulation, but not corporate monopolies, being against the principles developed by neoliberal economists like Milton Friedman at the University of Chicago.[36] What followed was a long era of deregulation, privatization, and corporate growth stretching into the present.[37] Large, powerful corporations have become a fixture of the American economy and political landscape. These remarkable changes in corporate status and power that commenced in the late nineteenth century have reshaped not only the US (and global) economy but also the moral landscape for human persons tremendously, leaving us to grapple with moral dilemmas like those described in the introduction to this study.

IV. How US Corporate Persons Took Over the World

In this final section of the genealogy, I will show that, although it might seem as if modern legal personhood has a life of its own, separate from the morally valorized personhood our tradition attributes to individual rational human beings, in fact it is the development of personhood in the Lockean lineage since the eighteenth century that has so dramatically empowered corporate personhood. As people came to believe that all beings of moral worth are also beings who must have legal status as persons, moral and legal personhood have become increasingly conflated (generating campaigns to confer legal personhood on more and more categories of beings deemed by some to have moral worth, such as chimpanzees and fetuses). This conflation has set the stage for advocates of business corporations, which are clearly legal persons, to claim rights of citizenship for them that were formerly reserved for those generally recognized to have moral worth, namely, people. As the right of chartering states to constrain them has dwindled, many corporations have become so wealthy and politically powerful that they can set the conditions—economic, governmental, and ecological—within which the vast majority of human and nonhuman beings now must do our best to live.

The rise of corporate personhood and power is an extremely complex history. Here we will consider two aspects of it. First, we will trace the history of the concession theory, which was devised to account for the nature of corporations in the Middle Ages. Then we will attend to a series of events that displaced that theory and gave US corporations civil rights against (and power over) the states that charter them.

A. MEDIEVAL CORPORATE PERSONS ARE CREATED BY LEGAL CONCESSION

In thirteenth-century Europe, a legal problem arose. German lords had built churches on their lands for their people, and they had installed their own priests. Over time, those priests began to claim that church buildings and surrounding land did not belong to the lords; the lords were simply the donors and patrons. The result in time was that lords lost legal rights over the churches they built. However, to whom did the buildings and lands belong? Various answers were advanced, such as that the saint for whom the church was named was its owner and the priest was his or her agent. But since these saints were deceased, people easily came to speak and act as each church itself was the owner of its building and surrounds. Jurists, trained in Roman law through the revival of Justinian's work in the twelfth century, began to treat churches like infant heirs with property rights that had to be protected (Coleman 1974, 16–17). In other words, they began to treat churches as something like underage Roman persons. Most scholars now attribute the formalization of this practice as doctrine, including what is now known as the natural/artificial person distinction, to the legal scholar Sinibaldo Fieschi, Pope Innocent IV.[38] Innocent was particularly concerned with the legal status of monasteries and the question of how they were to be "personated" at law, given that no members of monasteries were individually recognized as legal persons. (Recall that Roman legal persons were individual proprietors, a status monks renounced.) How could a monastery swear an oath (or enter a contract)? Could a monastery be excommunicated? He answered these questions by affirming that a monastery is a legal person with an identity apart from, although obviously in some sense contingent upon, the individuals who are its members at any given time. The people make up the monastery, but their association under the law generates an entity that is not those people in aggregate. Therefore monasteries, as legal persons, can enter into contracts despite the non-personhood of their members, he held, but they cannot be excommunicated: although human beings can create these corporate persons, unlike God, human beings cannot create souls. And, we might add, therefore they do not have the moral status of human individuals.

A second development also contributed to the shaping of medieval corporate personhood. Kings began to levy fines and rents against boroughs and to confer certain rights upon boroughs through their charters. For example, a borough might receive the right to take tolls and franchises and to sell them, meaning that the borough, as a borough rather than as an aggregate of its residents, could own property and dispose of it through contract (Coleman 1974, 18). Historian Phil Withington writes, "Incorporation perpetuated medieval concepts of political corporeality into the seventeenth century, the community of freemen, burgesses (in boroughs), and citizens (in cities) becoming a fictional person or body that could own property and be represented both at law and in Parliament" (2007, 1027). All of these corporate entities—churches, monasteries, boroughs, and cities—existed by grace of law and could be dissolved by law as well. Neither their human members nor their material existence as land and buildings constituted their personhood; only their status at law did that. Because a governmental authority creates a legal person by conceding it certain rights, this doctrine has often been called the concession theory of corporate personhood. Just as governments created corporate persons, governments could terminate them; unlike human beings, corporate persons had neither natural rights nor moral worth.

In addition to governmental, religious, and charitable institutions, English monarchs sometimes granted charters or patents to groups of merchants who formed for-profit joint-stock companies. In the mid-sixteenth century, for example, Commander Richard Chancellor requested a charter for a joint-stock company that was doing business overseas to the north. He had established diplomatic relations with the Russian empire and needed a formal status for the company so that, as an entity unto itself rather than as its several shareholders, it could own property and create an internal governance structure. Its charter, modeled to some extent on a municipal corporate charter, gave it a governor, four consuls, and twenty-four assistants elected from the shareholders. In 1566 it was officially christened the Fellowship of English Merchants for Discovery of New Trades, but it was more commonly known as the Muscovy Company or the Russia Company. As historian Philip Stern tells us, it became in effect the English government over Anglo-Russian commerce, and even though it was neither a branch of the English government nor under parliamentary control, it had de facto command of Anglo-Russian diplomacy and soon extended its operations into Persia (Stern 2023, 21–22).

Much of what we now think of as English colonization was actually the work of men like Richard Chancellor and their partners in joint-stock ventures. Most of Ireland was colonized by joint-stock companies who claimed land by patent and held governing authority over it, regardless of what the inhabitants of that land wanted. The intent was not to claim land for the Crown but to make money for the shareholders. Of course, many of those shareholders also happened to be members of Parliament and of the royal family; consequently, when corporations got into serious trouble, those interested parties would use the machinery of government and taxation to bail them out or send battleships and troops to defend them. Modern corporate form took shape in the context of Parliament and courts attempting to shore up and secure these often-sprawling operations.

Perhaps the most famous of these is the East India Company, chartered by Queen Elizabeth I in 1600 in her bid to rival the Dutch in the spice trade. As we saw in chapter 1, hundreds of merchants, landowners, and members of Parliament bought into the company, as did the queen herself. The returns on their investments were astronomical, and by the eighteenth century the company was a principal instrument of English colonization not only in India but also in North America. Many of the laws British Americans eventually found so objectionable were enacted by Parliament to protect their investments in the East India Company. The tea dumped into Boston Harbor during the famous Boston Tea Party was stolen from the company's ships.

Twelve years after the East India Company was chartered, in 1612 Sir Edward Coke rendered a decision that helped ensure its success. The case of Sutton's Hospital involved the status of property that Thomas Sutton had set aside to establish a hospital in Surrey, for which he had sought and obtained a charter from the king. Sutton had died before the hospital was built, so his human heir Simon Baxter laid claim to the land that Sutton had designated for it, claiming that since the hospital did not yet exist, the property was simply part of Sutton's personal estate. The question in the case was whether that property was indeed still part of the estate or belonged to the hospital itself as a corporate entity (Hallis [1930] 1978, xl–xlii). Was a hospital, chartered but unbuilt, actually a legal person? Coke ruled in favor of the hospital, declaring it independent of its founder and therefore not subject to dissolution upon his death. The corporation's property was its own property, apart from any human being who might have invested in it or otherwise contributed to its founding or operation. Coke's famous declaration is as follows:

> ... a Corporation aggregate of many is invisible, immortal, & resteth only in intendment and consideration of the Law; and therefore cannot have predecessor nor successor. They may not commit treason, nor be outlawed, nor excommunicate, for they have no souls, neither can they appear in person, but by Attorney. A Corporation aggregate cannot do fealty, for an invisible body cannot be in person, nor can swear, it is not subject to imbecilities, or death of the natural body, and divers other cases.[39]

Not only is the corporation independent of its founder so that it does not dissolve into his estate when he dies (so that it is effectively "immortal"); it is also "invisible." Coke insists on this because Baxter's attorney claimed that a corporation's founding only occurred when there was a literal laying of the cornerstone for the building. Coke said the "foundation" of the corporation occurred when the charter was enacted; it was created by a verbal act, not a physical one. Therefore, a corporation need have no physical presence whatsoever. For the East India Company and thousands of corporations to follow, this was an important point. East India was administered for several years out of Thomas Smythe's home, and its business was conducted at sea or along the coasts of foreign lands; there was no brick-and-mortar East India building for which a literal foundation stone could have been laid. Corporations, according to Coke, transcend any particular physical manifestation; any buildings they have are their property to dispose of at their discretion, not their essential being without which they would fail or cease to exist (see Coke 2003).

A century later, in 1819, Supreme Court Chief Justice John Marshall enshrined the English concession theory in US law, writing in *Trustees of Dartmouth College v. Woodward*, "A corporation is an artificial being, invisible, intangible, and existing only in contemplation of law. Being the mere creature of law, it possesses only those properties which the charter of its creation confers upon it either expressly or as incidental to its very existence."[40] Thus, according to Marshall, Dartmouth College was a rights-bearer, a person, because its legal charter (dating back to the colonial period) designated it as such. Furthermore, and in this case more importantly, that charter defined its very being; it did not exist apart from the description of it that its charter set forth. Thus, if it were to be substantially altered (in this case made a public entity as the state of New Hampshire desired), then that person would simply cease to exist altogether. This doctrine held sway in US jurisprudence through most of the nineteenth century.

B. THE CONCESSION THEORY DISPLACED

In many ways, the concession theory protected corporations from some forms of governmental interference, as well as from liability for actions of their officers. But it also placed limits on what corporations could do, because any change in mission required the conceding state to reconsider the charter. And as long as corporations were creatures of the chartering state, they were also subject to regulation by that state. States could issue time-limited charters and revoke charters for any number of reasons. State officials could come onto the premises and inspect machinery, labor conditions, or account books at any time. And, of course, states and their localities could tax corporate property, even if they did not impose similar taxes on non-corporate property, that is, on property owned by unincorporated legal persons, also known as human beings.

A dramatic change in corporate status, which eventually helped usher in alternatives to the concession theory, occurred in the 1880s. Many contemporary scholars cite events surrounding the case of *Santa Clara County v. Southern Pacific Railroad* as a turning point. That case stemmed from a decision of the government of Santa Clara County, California, to impose a tax on the property of the Southern Pacific Railroad at a higher rate than the tax it imposed on the property of individual human owners. From 1868 forward, Southern Pacific refused to pay. Santa Clara County took the corporation to court, Southern Pacific appealed, and finally over a decade later the case ended up on the docket of the US Supreme Court. The nature of corporate personhood was one of a number of issues in this case. The railroad's attorneys presented six separate lines of argument. One line posited that corporations are persons under the Fourteenth Amendment's Equal Protection Clause and therefore are entitled to equal protection under the law. Equal protection, the attorneys held, precluded deprivation of property in the form of taxation at a higher rate.

The intent of the Fourteenth Amendment was to enfranchise formerly enslaved people and to prevent states of the former Confederacy (or any others) from infringing on their civil rights or allowing others to violate those civil rights with impunity. Section 1 states: "All persons born or naturalized in the United States, and subject to the jurisdiction thereof, are citizens of the United States and of the State wherein they reside. No State shall make or enforce any law which shall abridge the privileges or immunities of citizens of the United States; nor shall any State deprive any person of life, liberty, or property, without due process of law; nor deny to any person within its jurisdiction the equal protection of the laws." The word *person* in this text obviously refers to human beings, beings who have the capacity for citizenship and who, as beings either born on US soil or naturalized through the federal government, are to be recognized as US citizens. In the 1880s, people did not commonly consider corporations to be either born or naturalized; they were chartered. Nor did they commonly consider corporate entities to be citizens with rights over against any government; under the concession theory and legal precedent to that point, they were creatures of state governments entirely. If the concession theory had held, legal personhood could never have been conflated with moral personhood, and corporate representatives would not have been able to assert corporate rights against the governments that created them. But it did not.

Even railroad lawyers prior to the 1880s had not argued that corporations were themselves persons under the Fourteenth Amendment.[41] In 1873 John Norton Pomeroy argued (in the *Slaughter-House* cases) that the Fourteenth Amendment applied to corporate property because ultimately it is shareholder property, the property of human beings who are entitled to equal protection. This view is sometimes called the partnership or contract theory of corporate existence. It has some theoretical and practical advantages, but because it runs the risk of compromising limited liability, it has not generally prevailed. And it did not succeed in the *Slaughter-House* cases. The Supreme Court majority disagreed with Pomeroy, construing the amendment to apply only to cases of racial discrimination. Justice Stephen Field, writing for the minority, argued for broader application, conceivably applying the amendment to shareholders, but did not assert that a corporation as such has a right of equal protection (Horwitz 1986, 177).

As of May 1886, when the Supreme Court handed down its decision in *Santa Clara County v. Southern Pacific Railroad Co.*, US corporations were legal persons under the states that chartered them, but they were not recognized as persons entitled to constitutional rights. The court held for the railroad, but not on the basis of equal protection. Justice John Harlan's majority opinion said nothing about the nature or status of corporate personhood; the court offered no official opinion on that topic. Nevertheless, within two years, *Santa Clara* was cited as precedent in rulings extending Fourteenth Amendment rights to corporations, and the court has used it as such a precedent ever since, despite the fact that it has never offered an argument for why corporations should be considered constitutional persons or why states' chartering actions confer federal rights on entities of the states' making (see Ciepley 2013, 223, 240).

How an opinion that said nothing about the meaning of personhood at all came to serve as precedent for extending constitutional rights to corporations is, to say the least, curious. In fact, it would not be a stretch to call it suspicious. The practice has been traced back to an incident that supposedly occurred prior to Justice Harlan's public reading of the opinion; according to the court reporter J. C. Bancroft Davis, Chief Justice Morrison Remick Waite turned to the railroad attorney Roscoe Conkling and his colleagues and said, "The Court does not wish to hear argument on the question whether the provision in the Fourteenth Amendment to the Constitution which forbids a state to deny to any person within its jurisdiction the equal protection of the laws applies to these corporations. We are all of opinion that it does."[42] Waite's alleged comment was not true, even though he and his colleague Justice Stephen J. Field wanted it to be.[43] (Waite, who had never held a judgeship before President Grant nominated him as chief justice, had spent his career representing large corporations, railroads in particular, and it may be worth noting that Grant had close ties to the railroad industry himself.[44]) But even if the comment had been true, it would only have been the private opinion of those several individuals at that point, not the opinion of the US Supreme Court. It became part of the official record of the court's proceedings only because court reporter Davis included it in the headnote—his own prefatory summary of the case—as part of the published record.

Nevertheless, writing for the majority in *Minnesota & St. Louis Railroad Co. v. Beckwith* in 1889, Justice Field cited *Santa Clara* as precedent for declaring that corporate persons had the constitutional rights of both equal protection and due process under the Fourteenth Amendment. Most members of the Supreme Court who have ruled subsequently on this and related questions have apparently (conveniently?) believed it was the official opinion of the Waite court in 1886 and have taken it as legal precedent.[45] Historians have tried to understand how such a gross error of legal interpretation could have occurred. Was it really a mistake, or was it some sort of conspiracy? Several theories have been put forth, the most recent one by Thom Hartmann, who believes that Davis, himself a Harvard-educated attorney with close ties to the Grant administration and railroad barons, deliberately inserted what he knew to be misleading words in the headnote to influence subsequent court decisions (see Hartmann 2010, 33–48). And so it did. Once subsequent judges, beginning with Stephen J. Field, began citing the headnote as if it were the stated opinion of the Waite court in *Santa Clara*, corporate persons no longer had only the privileges granted to them by state charters, privileges that states could revoke; they also had constitutionally guaranteed civil rights that they could exercise *against the states that chartered them*.

Whether Davis acted alone or in league with Justice Field and railroad attorney and former US senator Roscoe Conkling as some have speculated, this one event, momentous though it was, was not the only factor in the downfall of the concession theory.[46] As corporations grew in wealth and political clout, it was only a matter of time before they would find ways to sever or at least greatly weaken their ties to their chartering states, as well as their ties to their own shareholders. State corporation commissions required corporations to have a standard governance structure with the consequence that corporations behaved very differently from unincorporated partnerships. Whereas in a partnership, all partners must agree on a course of action—governance operates by consensus—these new incorporation templates established one-share, one-vote majority rule (note: one share, rather than shareholder) and centralized management as the norm. No longer were corporate actions clearly reducible to the conjoint actions of owners, both because shareholders could find themselves outvoted and because professional managers were beginning to run daily operations in large companies without consulting shareholders in most instances. Over time, especially as they grew in size, corporations began to seem more and more like real actors in and of themselves, not mere on-paper stand-ins for groups of shareholders. Eventually shareholders were thought of not as owners of incorporated businesses at all, but merely as investors in them (Horwitz 1986, 207) or as creditors (Nyombi and Bakibinga 2014, 97), and often simply as troublesome constraints on growth through reinvestment (Coleman 1974, 49) or as suppliers of inputs (Ripkin 2009, 160). Theorists were forced to admit that neither the concession theory nor *ultra vires* fits the facts. Corporate persons really did have some kind of life of their own distinct from the human individuals who owned shares or worked for them (Laski 1916, 407, 413–15) and the law that established them, and they were in fact capable of acting in ways that exceeded their charters.[47] The question for legal theorists (as well as for politicians and citizens) was what kind of life did they have?

The issue was debated in newspapers and political speeches throughout the 1880s (Hartmann 2010, 113). With as much as 75 percent of US wealth under corporate control by 1890, many legal theorists saw an acute need for a new theory of corporate personhood to replace the concession theory. Morton Horwitz delineates three theories in contention between 1880 and 1900: (1) the traditional concession view, which its opponent Otto von Gierke had by that time dubbed the theory of *persona ficta*,[48] (2) an analogy with partnership in which corporations were understood as aggregates of contracting individuals, and (3) what Horwitz calls the "entity theory," which held that the law merely *recognized* but did not *create* the corporation's existence at charter; this was the alternative that Gierke advanced (Horwitz 1986, 184–85). From the point of view of shareholders and corporate executives, each theory had pros and cons. They disliked the concession theory because it left corporations wide open to state regulation (which could involve inspections, audits, and demands for public accountability and service) and even to the possibility of revocation of charters. But it, unlike the contract theory, easily protected shareholders' limited liability for corporate debt. The contract theory might underwrite claims to equal protection and other civil rights, as Pomeroy had argued in the *Slaughter-House* cases, but if a corporation was nothing more than a partnership (albeit of hundreds of partners) then shareholders could be liable beyond their initial investment in case of bankruptcy. The entity theory, in turn, protected limited liability and might secure corporations equal protection and constitutional rights, but it also made possible lawsuits against and even criminal prosecution of corporations themselves. As long as corporations were assumed to be created by states, they were deemed incapable of any action not specified in their state charters; in particular, they were incapable of committing any crime (any act contrary to law had to have been committed by a human being, not the state-incorporated entity itself). But if they were not mere creatures of the state but rather independent entities merely recognized by the state, then they could act in ways contrary to both charters and law and thus could be guilty of criminal wrongdoing. Theorists fussed over the matter for over three decades more, but the question was never settled.[49]

Meanwhile, courts continued to render opinions, even in the absence of any agreed-upon doctrine to guide them. Those decisions were frequently contradictory as a result, even as late as the 1980s (Lipton 2010, 1917; Mitchell 1946, 96; Mark 1987, 1442).[50] But the general trend was toward erasure of Pope Innocent's natural-artificial distinction, giving the corporate person more and more of a legal presence as an entity unto itself—making it more and more like what Innocent had called a natural person and even what Locke had conjured into a moral person. As Harold Laski put in the *Harvard Law Review* in 1916, "It is purely arbitrary to urge that personality must be so finite as to be distinctive only of the living, single man" (1916,

416–17). The entity theory figured into lower court cases in the late nineteenth century; it made its first US Supreme Court appearance in 1905 with *Hale v. Henkel*, which conferred upon corporate persons Fourth Amendment protection against warrantless search and seizure (Horwitz 1986, 182–85).[51] Thus, corporate persons, like late nineteenth-century human (male) persons, obtained something like territorial sovereignty over their own private realms.

C. THE ENTITY THEORY, CORPORATE ENTITIES, AND THE WORLD THEY CREATE FOR THE REST OF US

There is something very right about the entity theory. Corporations do have a life of their own that surpasses the lives of the people who own shares in them, manage them, or work in them. The people are substitutable; the corporation transcends them all. As institutions, they have established goals, and they have guiding values, principles, procedures, and structures conducive to achieving those goals, some of which their stockholders and employees may not share. The character of an institution may shift somewhat over time in response to changes in the environment in which it operates, but major realignments are extremely slow; institutions are inherently conservative, resistant to dramatic redirection. Moreover, institutions shape the people within them far more than most of those people will ever shape those institutions. For these reasons, we can speak coherently of phenomena such as institutional racism, structural inequality, or systematic discrimination; even if no one living or working in an institution aims for inequitable or discriminatory outcomes, even if many actively seek the opposite, institutions that have produced them in the past can still operate in ways that produce them into the future. These things are true of all large, complex institutions, not just for-profit corporations. Trying to understand the social world without acknowledging that institutions have lives of their own in addition to the lives of their members is futile.[52]

Whatever their prior status (if we even want to grant that they have a prior status), once they are chartered, corporations are entities apart from the beings who make up their shareholders and workforces, and as chartered entities recognized by the various state governments, courts, and law enforcement officials as legitimate owners of property, they are legal persons just as individual human property owners are. That much is true. But those facts in themselves do not compel extension of any additional rights to corporate entities. Constitutional rights were established to protect people's lives and liberty, both of which were believed to exist prior to the Constitution's ratification and indeed prior to the enactment of any law or the establishment of any governmental institution whatsoever. Corporations, by contrast, have no mortal life to lose and no natural liberty.[53] They only exist within established frameworks of property law and rights.

Had it not been for the fact that by the late nineteenth century, most people were far more familiar with the concept of personhood from the Lockean lineage than with the older legal concept—put differently, had people remained people, individuals, souls, or *wights* apart from their roles as individual owners of property and had personhood remained simply a legal term for any entity with property rights—nobody would ever have been able to interpret the Fourteenth Amendment as limiting the authority of chartering states over the entities they themselves create, let alone as requiring them to respect corporations' First Amendment civil rights to free speech or free exercise of religion. Those rights would have been reserved to persons as deliberating, judging individuals, those held to have self-awareness and consciences to appease and exercise. It would be obvious that states and the federal government have the right, and indeed the duty, to regulate all forms commercial activity to protect the lives and liberty of their citizens. Wealthy and financially ambitious men seized upon the popular ambiguity of the word *person*—which in its application to human beings had come to encompass ideas of natural liberty and inherent moral value—to press for lifting limits on their corporately financed acquisition and retention of land, natural resources, and human labor.

One would think that if legislatures and courts really believed that corporations were constitutional persons, they would not be permitted to buy and sell each other. But of course, they do. The result over time in many sectors has been consolidation to the point where only a handful of distinct companies provide all the products of a certain type. The general public is probably most aware of this in the airline industry and in media. But it is true in many other industries as well, such as meatpacking and the manufacture of baby formula. When only a few companies control a market, prices rise. And when those few companies' supply chains and manufacture and distribution mechanisms are disrupted, as we saw throughout the COVID-19 pandemic, human beings suffer. But, as we also saw, stock markets and corporate profits can continue to soar.

Industry consolidation is not the only way that corporations control and manipulate the world that we and every other organic being must live or die in, however; it is not even the most significant. In the United States, corporations maintain memberships in large advocacy organizations such as the Chamber of Commerce, the National Association of Manufacturers (NAM), and National Federation of Independent Business (NFIB), as well as industry-specific groups like the National Grocers Association and the National Restaurant Association. Their financial support enables these organizations to support think tanks of experts to analyze existing laws and policies and develop proposals and strategies to build corporate power and wealth as well as to employ hundreds of lobbyists at the federal and state levels to push their agenda forward. These organizations participate, in turn (along with many wealthy individuals and politicians), in the American Legislative Exchange Council (ALEC), which writes model legislation that elected representatives then introduce into Congress and statehouses, changing laws to reduce the power of organized labor, to eliminate overtime pay and pensions, to roll back environmental protections, to privatize or eliminate social services (including Medicare, Social Security, and even public education), to reduce corporate and inheritance taxes to an ever-diminishing minimum, to resist governmental efforts to address climate change, and to criminalize various forms of public protest against these actions. ALEC's model Full Employment Act, for example, completely eliminates welfare, unemployment insurance, and food stamps, and requires that jobless Americans work at minimum wage to receive any benefits at all (Lafer 2017, 122). As of 2017, two thousand state legislators, which is about 25 percent of the total across the country, were members of ALEC, championing its agenda and striving to make it the law in their jurisdictions. Gordon Lafer quotes from ALEC's own promotional material, which asserts that "both corporations and legislators have a voice and a vote in shaping policy," and he elaborates: "Thus, state legislators with little time, staff, or expertise are able to introduce fully formed and professionally supported bills. The organization claims to introduce eight hundred to one thousand bills each year in the fifty state legislatures, with 20 percent becoming law" (2017, 13). The Chamber of Commerce, NAM, NFIB, and other affiliated organizations and major shareholders and CEOs can then direct corporate donations to cooperating legislators and to Political Action Committees mounting issue campaigns on behalf of ALEC's bills. The result is that states and the federal government are more and more under the control of corporate interests, not of voters, workers, consumers, parents, students, homeowners—in short, not of the vast majority of human beings who are the citizens and residents of this (or any) country.

Over the past century and a half, as corporate persons have gained and exercised more and more legal rights, human persons have become less and less able to exercise ours. Even if we are among the 50 percent of Americans with 401(k)s invested in corporations, we are not their masters; indeed, most of us are their servants. Unable to make a living without selling our time and energy, we contract ourselves out to corporations for thirty-five or forty or sixty or seventy hours per week. And those contracts place enormous constraints on our freedom, including on our civil liberties. Philosopher and social theorist Elizabeth Anderson puts this in perspective by asking her reader to imagine a government where inferiors take orders from superiors who are not accountable to them, where inferiors have no right to be consulted, and where rules can change at any time. No private or personal sphere is recognized, and there is constant surveillance and punishment for infractions. Inferiors can be made to submit to body searches and medical and drug testing with no grounds of suspicion. People can be sanctioned for consensual sex and choice of spouse, for political activity, for prohibited forms of speech or even for the language spoken. They can be required to engage in political advocacy for causes and candidates with which they disagree. The government owns all the nonlabor means of production and organizes production by central planning. We would certainly see such a government as undemocratic and even as tyrannical and its people as unfree. Yet this "government," Anderson says, is your corporate employer (2017, 37–38). And while each one of us is free to quit, we have few options but to seek out another, perhaps more benevolent dictator to sell our time and energy to.

Almost all of us who are not independently wealthy spend most of our lives as servants of a corporate person or as a dependent of somebody who is. Corporations, therefore, make a whole host of the rules human beings live under, no matter what the laws say our civil rights are. They also largely dictate the extent of our consumer choices: Will I buy the Honda or the Toyota, heat and light my house with Dominion Energy or sit in the cold and darkness? Corporate persons can exert far more control over state, local, and national governments than any of us humans could ever do, selecting and empowering political actors and often literally authoring their policies. Large for-profit corporate persons own almost all sources of political, social, economic, medical, scientific, technological, and historical information, as well as the means to communicate it. We human persons are morally responsible for what we do as individuals, subject to judgment and punishment as individuals, but as individuals we cannot do much to shape the conditions under which we deliberate and act; our individual personhood incapacitates us in the face of corporate personhood. The wealthy, the colonizers, the masters have joined together to create Leviathans, coordinated collectivities of forces answerable to virtually no one (perhaps not even to them), while allowing the rest of us only the tiny vehicles of our several, supposedly independent, individualities. This is where modern moral personhood has gotten us. And this is where my genealogy ends.

[CHAPTER FIVE]

Questioning Ownership

The first four chapters of this book presented what I have called a genealogy of modern personhood, a subject position that took shape in the midst of a particular set of political and theological conflicts occurring in a particular set of institutions, practices, and projects that existed in England in the late seventeenth and eighteenth centuries. It was articulated first as a way of reconciling scientific knowledge with Protestant Christian doctrine and secondarily as a way of justifying worldly practices of legal punishment and moral condemnation of individual people. Over time it proved to be useful, as well, in justifying dispossession of Indigenous peoples and in focusing criticism on individuals while deflecting it from social classes and institutions.

Genealogy is not standard history, because it does not assume the identity of its object and it does not strive to produce the real truth about that object. Personhood, I have assumed throughout, is not a single, given fact of the world, but a complex of elements that developed in different historical contexts and came together under specific political conditions in the late seventeenth century. In other words, as Foucault puts it, what lies at the origin—in this case of personhood—is disparity (1977, 142); it formed from fragments of older discourses in a time of crisis and change and was altered subsequently by many other changes, problems, crises, and practices. But genealogy differs from standard histories in other ways as well. It begins, as I said in the introduction to this book, in refusal, when a way of thinking and living becomes so untenable as to be intolerable. It is never, therefore, disinterested. It is always engaged in an effort to get free of what is oppressive. In all the work it does—all its curious attention to historical oddity and minute details—it hopes and aims for a crack in the edifice that leads not to the collapse of everything but to the possibility of something otherwise. Genealogy is, as Daniele Lorenzini (2020) puts it, a "possibilising" practice. It opens possibilities, not only incidentally but intentionally, although it never dictates how any possibilities that emerge must be seized or developed. By showing the contingency of a formation such as modern personhood, genealogy shows that life without personhood is possible. The question before us now is how to make that abstract possibility more concrete. Foucault called this sort of work innovation, but I will call it creative experimentation, which in this chapter and the next will take the form of playful probing of a couple of central elements of personhood that might be pulled apart and redistributed or dispersed to make openings for something new.

One of the fundamental features of modern person is proprietorship—of material goods but also of mental contents and actions. Persons have the capacity to reason, holding each step in a process in its mind as they move to the next step. A person can be said, therefore, to possess its past experiences and actions, as well as its current perceptions, as its mental contents. This capacity in turn gives the person both the right to appropriate and own material objects acquired through its labor and the moral responsibility for its deliberations and actions and their immediate consequences. Its moral responsibility is most highly manifest in the subjection of the person to moral and legal judgment, but what lies beneath it and supports it is the ability to possess, the capacity for ownership. In this chapter, then, I will consider, question, and attempt to unsettle ownership. I will proceed by focusing attention on ways in which ownership and related elements are relative rather than absolute, unstable or confused when placed under scrutiny, or simply inadequate to describe common human experiences. In the process, I hope to develop a heightened attention to aspects of self-in-world that exceed personhood's ownership and, as a result, find some ground for a different way of living for who and what we are.

I. What Exactly Does Ownership Mean?

On its face, ownership is a simple idea. Some things belong to me and some things belong to other people. I have different relationships with various things depending on whether they are mine or someone else's. It is good to share what I have, but sharing is not required. It is wrong to take what someone else has without that person's permission. If someone takes what I have, I am entitled to restitution. If someone shares with me, I should express gratitude. Even very small children grasp these concepts and navigate the social world with them in mind. Of course, we know that we also call things "mine" and "yours" or "hers" that are not owned by me, you, or her. For example, I speak of "my neighborhood" and "my birthday," although no one imagines that I own those things, let alone "my aunt Rosalie," "my supervisor," "my primary care physician," or "my parole officer." To take it to the extreme, an enslaved person could have spoken of "my owner," an obvious absurdity if we take the possessive pronoun to indicate ownership. Possessive pronouns express a relation between self and other, human or nonhuman, that is not always a relation of ownership. So what, specifically, is ownership?

I looked it up. The result of doing so was an intellectual paralysis that lasted about a month. I learned that one could study for a lifetime and still not master a respectable percentage of the scholarship on ownership, even of something as seemingly straightforward as land. There are theories. There is civil law. There is canon law. There is common law. There is case law. There are centuries of debates over the finest distinctions between ownership and possession.[1] There are disputes over whether land can be said to be jointly owned by lord and vassal or by husband and wife or by members of an aboriginal tribe, and if so how.[2] What is land, anyway? Is it two-dimensional or three-dimensional? Does owning land mean owning the airspace above it or the water or minerals beneath it?[3] What of the wildlife? Do I own my land's water filtration, carbon sink, and oxygen-generating capacities? And that is just *land*. Movable property is even more complicated. Then, consider intellectual property. Does a chef own his recipes? Who owns a dead poet's poems? How about a social media meme or a slang term? Can someone own a decoded genome? Can a scientist own a genetically engineered organism or an entire species? And don't even get me started on bodies and bodily tissues; kidneys, livers, hair, plasma, sperm, eggs, wombs, bone marrow, tumors, fetuses, corpses, frozen embryos—all can have monetary value, and you can find them all discussed and analyzed and argued about over and over again in legal, philosophical, and sociological scholarship as well as in the popular press. Does someone own my eyeballs? Well, it depends on what you mean by "own." And that is the question.

The correlate of ownership is generally presumed to be property, and most of the long millennia of scholarship on the subject is about what counts as property, what kinds of property there are, and then of course who owns the things that count as property and what duties non-owners have toward owners of those various types of property. A few things don't seem to be able to count as property under the law at the moment: living human beings,[4] the high seas, the moon, and the wind; but that could change.[5]

The dominant view of property in Anglo-American jurisprudence at the moment seems to be that something is property if someone has a "bundle of rights" in it. The rights in question are usually listed as possession, control, exclusion, enjoyment, and disposition. This does not mean that I actually do possess or enjoy my thing, only that I am legally entitled to, if I wish. But there are all kinds of exceptions. I may possess, control, enjoy, and have the right to dispose of something but not be able to exclude others from it—for example, private landowners in Scotland do not have the right to exclude people who want to hike on their land (Winchester 2021, 221). Here in Virginia, even if I put up "no hunting" and "no trespassing" signs, a hunter still has the right to come onto my land in pursuit of wounded prey. Hunters, in turn, are allowed to possess, control, and enjoy their dogs and their guns all they like, as long as doing so does not involve abusing said dogs or discharging said guns in urban areas. I possess a stash of cash in my wallet, and I can exclude anyone else from touching or taking it; indeed, I am entitled to dispose of it however I like—give it away, buy anything that is legally for sale, stuff it into a mattress—with one big exception: I am not allowed to destroy it. What about the e-book I bought online? I can enjoy it, but I cannot sell it or give it away.

One need not have all five rights in the bundle (or however many rights there are in the bundle; the literature is confusing) in order to be considered an owner. I own my land, no matter how many pursuers of wounded prey have the right to come onto it. I own my dog, even though I am not entitled to mistreat her and even though my attachment to her does not feel like ownership to me. No one single right in the bundle seems to be essential, nor is it clear how many of those rights one must have in order to be an owner.

II. Ownership in the Absence of Property

I gave up trying to understand the nature of ownership by researching property and property law. I leave all that to the lawyers (who have a keen interest in keeping it all very complex and contentious, lest their services not be needed nearly so often). After all, property is not the only kind of thing that persons are said to own. Whatever ownership is, it is apparently a lot more than the correlate of property or bundles of property rights. This fact is especially apparent in professional management scholarship, to which I turned next because it was the first thing to pop up in a JSTOR search for "ownership," oddly enough. Or maybe not so oddly. In fact, I found this literature both strange and familiar, probably because for many years I have worked for people who read it religiously and applied it to the employees they managed—in other words, me.

There is a whole body of management scholarship devoted to the phenomenon of "psychological ownership" that provides a very clear picture of ownership apart from property. People don't just possess, control, enjoy, exclude others from, and/or dispose of things, scholars in this field remind us (citing William James, Émile Durkheim, and disparate others); they also feel attached to the things toward which they behave in some or all of these ways, even if they have no legal title to them. The things—or "targets," as the management literature tends to call them—can even be other people or, more to the managerial point, work. If managers can get their employees to "take ownership" in their jobs and the companies they work for, they will likely get better results. (Another way this is sometimes put is that managers should aim to achieve employee "buy-in," to get employees to "invest themselves" psychologically in the job at hand, the new corporate initiative, or the firm itself. Presumably, "buying in" is a way of "taking ownership.") Pierce, Kostova, and Dirks (2001) conclude from their extensive literature review that psychological ownership grows out of three human needs: (1) to have some control over one's environment, (2) to define oneself or express one's identity, and (3) to belong somewhere or to have a home (and, in support of the last, they cite Simone Weil and Martin Heidegger[6]). They note that managers can use employees' efforts to satisfy these needs in ways that will benefit their organization. According to an empirical study conducted by Van Dyne and Pierce (2004), psychological ownership is allied with job satisfaction and organizational commitment (the latter being the likelihood that an employee will stay with the company), both of which seem from other studies to enhance job performance. But psychological ownership does something more. It motivates employees to step up their organizational citizenship; specifically, it induces them to do extra work that is not, strictly speaking, part of their job description (and so also likely not part of what they get paid for). Van Dyne and Pierce note that this is especially worth cultivating in the service sector; customers are happier when public-facing employees do more than just execute orders efficiently—when they are cheerful, friendly, extra helpful, and so on (Van Dyne and Pierce 2004, 455). College and university faculty employees will recognize this aspect of their jobs readily; it involves taking on extra advising and extra committee work, meeting more frequently with students outside class, mentoring junior faculty members, attending extracurricular events in support of students and colleagues, to name a few, and it is almost never quantified for the purposes of material reward.

Managers can do a great many things to get employees to take ownership of their work, such as provide them with more autonomy in structuring their time or workstations and with more information about how their work fits in with the bigger organizational picture or with more knowledge and skill about the work they do and the equipment they use. But managers must also be alert to danger. There is such a thing as "pathological" psychological ownership (Pierce et al. 2001, 303–4). Ownership, after all, typically involves rights (like possession, control, exclusion, enjoyment, and disposition). And while we want our employees to take ownership, we do not want them actually to behave as if they own the place. We do not want them to treat their tools and equipment as their property, taking them home after hours, using them for personal projects, or excluding others in the workplace from using them; we do not want workers to control workplace decision-making. In short, we do not want them to exercise such rights as possession, enjoyment, exclusion, control, or disposition with regard either to their equipment or to their work product, and certainly not to their department or the company as a whole. We want them to be owners, but not of any property.

It is tempting to say that employees' psychological ownership is sham ownership, a ruse to extract more surplus value from already exploited workers, especially those who are public facing and, in the pink-collar sector especially, woefully underpaid and generally without hope of advancement. It is tempting to say this managerial notion of taking ownership has arisen where jobs are too dirty, intrinsically pointless, or segmented for anyone simply to take pride in the quality of workmanship or where loyalty to the company is too obviously unreciprocated. Employees are tricked into forming affective attachments not for their own well-being but solely for the benefit of the company's bottom line. And all of that may be true, yet I still think we have to take this idea of psychological ownership—that is, of ownership in the absence of property—seriously. The very ubiquity of the concept—to which this literature's extensive citations from psychology, sociology, human development, and philosophy attest—suggests that for at least well over a century, people have indeed understood themselves to stand in relations of ownership toward things that are not property in the legal sense of the term (whatever that legal sense, or senses, might be—again, leaving it to the lawyers). Persons experience themselves as owners, even if they are penniless and unhoused.[7]

I chose to discuss the managerial notion of ownership because it illustrates how deep a chasm can exist between ownership and property. But management scholarship is not unique in employing the concept of ownership where there are no property rights. The concept pops up in all sorts of situations. On a few occasions, for example, I have been advised to encourage my students to take ownership of their educations. This seemed to mean that I should encourage them to disregard parental and peer pressure and choose their own course of study, but in truth I am not exactly sure what I was supposed to encourage them to do. More recently, I simply conducted an internet search for the phrase "take ownership." It resulted in 504 million hits. Among the top few of all these hundreds of millions was a website that lists fourteen ways that I can take ownership at work.[8] In fact, most of the top hits for "taking ownership" were about work, work projects, and careers. Some sites told managers how to get employees to take ownership (without, of course, treating their work as their property), but most were self-help websites and articles for people who wanted to win promotions or pay raises, get along with coworkers and supervisors, or just feel less bad about doing the work they are required to do. Scattered among the work-related articles and sites, however, were ones that advised taking ownership of other aspects of one's existence, such as one's health and well-being, one's retirement planning, and one of my favorites, a website that exhorted me to take ownership of my life.[9] Just living one's life is apparently subpar.

What does all of this come down to? Well, I hesitate to say that the notion of taking ownership has any sort of fundamental meaning, since it gets used in so very many and diverse contexts, but some ideas do recur in the literature with very high frequency. One is taking initiative. Another is taking control. Both of these involve acting decisively and relatively quickly to get a task done, to change a situation, or to solve a problem. Sometimes this is paired with the advice to "be proactive." Those promoting this often remind their readers that someone has to step up if anything good is going to happen, and that stepping up can pay off for the individual who does it. And that individual should be *you*! Don't wait for someone else to fix the problem or suggest a new approach! And certainly don't wait for somebody else to get control and take the credit. Be first to stake your claim on the situation! Grab the bull by the horns—or, in more contemporary parlance I suppose, *own* the damn bull.

The most commonly recurring idea, though, is not initiative, control, or proactivity; it is responsibility. A good example of this is an article by John Coleman in the *Harvard Business Review*. Coleman urges readers to take ownership of their actions. Doing so will not only make them better workers and business leaders and help them get ahead of the crowd, but it will also constitute "the first step to developing a healthy sense of self." He cites Nathaniel Branden, "the father of the self-esteem movement," who declared that if people want to have self-esteem, they should always assume that "help is not coming." Far from cause for panic or despair, Coleman views this assumption as "liberating." He elaborates: "The responsibility is yours, and it starts with developing a belief or habit of mind that you, as an individual, are accountable for the quality and timeliness of an outcome, even when you're working with others. It doesn't always mean you have the authority over a project. Nor does it mean that you shouldn't involve others. But it does mean you own the obligation to take action and deliver results" (Coleman 2012). To own something is to acknowledge responsibility for it—to claim credit or take the blame (although I do realize this means that Coleman's exhortation to own an obligation is a bit redundant).

We are not so very far from 1694 after all. According to Locke, the spinster may not own the wool she makes into yarn. She may not own her spinning wheel, let alone the premises upon which it and she sit to spin. But she owns the gestures that constitute the spinning. She can seek remuneration for them in wages or in food or shelter, but even if she is remunerated, she still owns those gestures, too, just not as her exclusive and private property. She owns those gestures just like she owns all her other conscious, deliberate gestures, all her actions. And when she dies and goes to stand before the Judge of the World, she will have to acknowledge her ownership and take the punishment for the times she fell short, just as she always did at her employer's or her master's or her husband's or the magistrate's hands. To own is to be subject to judgment. Maybe, as the managerial and self-help literature emphasize, that judgment will result in reward. Or maybe not. Maybe that bold initiative, that decisive taking of the bull by the horns, will produce an outcome quite different from the one that you planned or imagined, an outcome that other people do not appreciate. In that case, judgment may result in ridicule or scorn, demotion or termination, loss of self-esteem or jail time. Judgment can result in reward but also in punishment.

For some time now, the idea of self-ownership has been prominent in Anglo-American political theory. In a critique of that idea, philosopher Daniel Attas raises what I regard as a sincere and significant question. Why is it, he wonders, that theorists want to describe our right and need to protect ourselves from harm and adversity as a right of self-ownership? Why put this very genuine concern in economic, or quasi-economic, terms?[10] Indeed, why put any of this in economic terms? Why risk the confusion—and the "pathologies" of psychological ownership that managers fear—by speaking in these situations of ownership in any sense at all? We could so easily do otherwise.

What if we left ownership alongside property, a term to be used in situations where someone has a certain set of legal rights with regard to a thing, usually a tangible thing but, even when not tangible, at least a clearly circumscribable thing? And then suppose we leave that largely to the lawyers to sort out. Suppose that every time we felt predisposed to "take ownership" of our work, our problems, our emotions, our shortcomings, or our direction in life, we stopped and thought of some other words to describe what we are doing or want or need to do. Instead of taking ownership of my education, I need to resist pressure from friends and relatives to pursue a field of study that honestly bores me, or I need to tell my parents I want to leave school. Instead of taking ownership of my job, I should speak up for myself and make a case to the supervisor that I deserve a promotion or a pay raise. Instead of taking ownership of the work I do, I can simply acknowledge that I care what happens to the clients I serve, and I enjoy it when they recognize how hard I work for their well-being. Is the nature of my relationship best expressed by the concept of ownership, or do I just love my dog and want to provide her with what she needs to be happy and healthy and to live a very long time? Do I need to take ownership of my love life, or should I just find a way to let that special someone know how I feel? Own my feelings, or learn to dissipate my anger less destructively? Own my actions, or acknowledge the hurt I caused my colleague and apologize? I want to be a good and trusted friend, a faithful and loving spouse, a respectful neighbor, and a responsible citizen. I want to behave with integrity toward those with whom I work and live and to support them when they are in need. I want not to be subject to selfish tyrants or under the thumb of unyielding authorities. I want to contribute to the betterment of my community and to be appreciated for doing so. None of this needs to be expressed in terms of taking ownership, owning, or owning up.

But notice what happens if we drop those terms. Instead of focusing on unilateral acts and ourselves as individuals, we focus on networks of relationships and on bilateral, multilateral, or collective concerns. The language of ownership puts us in a world that is a mere aggregate of individuals, each competing to outshine or get ahead of the others or to exclude others from decision-making or control, each seeking to maximize individual preferences or, as the economists say, "utility functions." The alternatives generally don't prompt us to imagine ourselves as atomistic individuals. They put us in a world of connection and mutuality, interplays of desires, hopes, aspirations, needs, vulnerabilities, and care, with all its joys, fears, failures, and heartaches.

An easy step into the beyond of personhood is this rejection of ownership where the concept of ownership isn't true to the experience. In most aspects of our lives, and in the most important aspects, we are not owners in any sense at all. It is obviously in the interest of some people to encourage us to think that way about our jobs, but we can resist doing so and we can refuse to encourage other people to do so. We could make that resistance and refusal a regular practice in our lives, which would not take a tremendous amount of effort, but might make some real differences over time in how we feel about ourselves and how we are in the world. At any rate, it is certainly worth a try.

But what about the ways in which we are owners? What about the aspects of our lives in which we really do have bundles of legal rights in things and in which some of these things may seem to be central to our conduct and sense of self? Just changing how we talk about our ways of being in situations and contexts where what we are said to own really is property will not, of itself, be enough to change the real conditions of our existence after these three hundred years of proprietor-personhood.

III. Ownership in the Presence of Property

One option—and seemingly the cleanest—is simply to refuse to participate in structures and practices of ownership, to renounce property; I am not an owner if I simply do not own. A quick way to renounce property and cease to be an owner would be to get rid of everything we own and refuse to come into ownership of anything else. The first problem with that, however, is that the process of "getting rid of" cars, houses, jewelry, land, and whatever else one has that the law sees as property would be an exercise of ownership. If you sell them, all you do is transfer ownership to someone else; you don't change the property status of those things. Plus, you get something in exchange, money most likely. Even giving them away fails to address the practices of ownership that structure our society, from which virtually none of us can ever really withdraw. Destroying them, too, is an exercise of ownership, and with land it is impossible. You can destroy a piece of land's resale value by destroying its fertility and contaminating it with toxins, but the land remains, however despoiled. The fact is that we are caught up in a system of property rights and ownership that we are not at the moment in a position to overturn.

There is much to be learned, even so, from attempts to renounce property. Here I will consider two, one actually undertaken historically and well documented, the other historically conditioned but perhaps untried. First, in the early thirteenth century, Saint Francis of Assisi and his followers renounced property ownership in favor of living in poverty as they believed Jesus and his followers had lived. There were unanticipated problems and unintended consequences that anyone thinking of challenging ownership models of human existence must consider. A second situation worth pondering is that of the heirs of slave owners in the United States. Most of them simply became slave owners themselves, although a small number rejected that status. What did they do instead? What realistic options does one have if one owns property that one believes should not be owned? Thinking about this question in that context lends the issue a kind of urgency while allowing exploration of possibilities in a world of property law and values more similar to our own than was that of Italy in the Middle Ages. We can draw important lessons from both.

A. THE FRANCISCANS' RENUNCIATION

In the early thirteenth century, Giovanni di Pietro di Bernardone, heir to his wealthy merchant father Pietro's cloth trade and vast international business connections, decided to renounce all property and live as Jesus had. His father was not amused. First, he locked his son in a closet (or possibly a basement or a basement closet, from which at any rate his mother, Pica, eventually freed him) and then appealed to the bishop of Assisi to banish the young man from Umbria so that he could cause his family no more shame. Accused in the Piazza before the bishop and the townspeople, Giovanni stripped naked, tossed his fine clothing to his father, and declared himself answerable only to his Father God. The bishop did not banish him; instead, he (quickly, one imagines) wrapped his own mantle around the younger Bernardone's nakedness and then made his palace gardener give the man an old shirt and mantle. Thus did Giovanni Bernardone (or Francesco, as his father called him) place himself on the path to become Saint Francis of Assisi, founder of the Franciscan Order of Friars Minor, approved by Pope Innocent III in 1209. The Rule that Francis presented to the pope has been lost, but the formulation Francis produced in 1221 begins with these words: "The rule and life of these brothers is simple. Live in obedience and chastity, without property, and follow the doctrine and footsteps of our Lord Jesus Christ" (Francis of Assisi 2015, 207). This statement is followed by four passages from the Gospels of Saint Matthew and Saint Luke. In the first passage cited, Jesus declares, "If you wish to be perfect, go, sell your possessions, and give the money to the poor, and you will have treasure in heaven; then come, and follow me" (Matthew 19:21). Francis provided a similar Rule for the female counterpart of the Franciscans, often called the Poor Clares, founded by Saint Clare of Assisi and overseen by the Franciscans.[11] Members of the orders were to work for their bread, accepting gifts only if necessary and never in monetary form, as they traveled around the world evangelizing. They were to have only minimal clothing and no shoes unless absolutely necessary, as prescribed in the Rule, section 2. They built small huts for shelter on land held by others and granted to them for their use as a sort of base of operations.[12] When traveling, they stayed with friends or in caves, or they made shelters of cut boughs. They kept no animals, although they shared space and food with many, birds in particular, and only borrowed horses or donkeys to transport ill brothers and sisters when circumstances required, according to the Rule, section 15. Because they were to work, many possessed tools of their trades (sec. 7), but they were not to have any books. They were to keep moving to evangelize but also to prevent them from ever thinking of any place as belonging to them (sec. 7), and they were forbidden even to touch money except in the direst of circumstances to provide for care of an ill brother or sister. Francis, whose father's great wealth depended on international credit and finance (and possibly usury, see Frank 2008, 248), believed riches in general but money in particular to be an instrument of the devil. "If a brother even chances across money somewhere, he should give it no more regard than if it were dust trod underfoot" (sec. 8). Even to attribute any value to money was to court spiritual disaster.

Francis himself, Clare, and their early followers did manage to live this way, and did so with the blessing of the Church at first. But it did not last. There were a variety of reasons for this. For one, the rapid increase in the size of the Franciscan order and the diversity of people who came into it brought with it constant low-level pressure from within to make exceptions to the Rule.[13] For another, Francis's doubts about his own ability to lead the order (especially after a failed mission to Germany and Hungary) led him in 1220 to relinquish control to others.[14] Some commentators contend that these others were considerably less committed to absolute poverty than Francis was and more willing to make even more exceptions. Other commentators suggest instead that total renunciation of property was simply not feasible for an institutionalized order; relaxation of the Rule was inevitable. Church officials had practical concerns as well, namely, physical safety; Cardinal Ugolino, official protector of the order until he was elected Pope Gregory IX, was afraid that brothers traveling to hostile territory would be killed and that sisters traveling anywhere without male escorts or material means would be vulnerable to assault (see Northcutt 2018). He urged cancellation of brothers' trips on more than one occasion and tried to cloister the Poor Clares and force them to accept monetary donations for their upkeep. And there was increasing hostility from secular clergy (that is, parish priests who were not members of any order) toward the Franciscans, which undoubtedly affected the Church hierarchy's attitudes as well.[15] Over time, tensions were inevitable between the orders and the Church that sponsored them, if for no other reason than how it looked to have popes and bishops living in palaces while the rag-clad Franciscans wandered around preaching that poverty is holy and riches are the source of corruption.

There were conceptual issues as well. Was there really a distinction between having and using something and owning it? If someone gives you a loaf of bread and you accept it with the intention of eating it, don't you own the bread? As the popularity of the order brought in more and more donations, including bequests of land and buildings—which were needed precisely because of the ever-increasing number of brothers and sisters who had renounced all their own worldly goods—this question became pressing.

Officially, by an agreement reached prior to Francis's death in 1226 and fixed in Pope Gregory IX's bull *Quo elongati* in 1230, the Church owned these resources, and the orders merely had permanent use of them. But, practically speaking, isn't that a distinction without a difference? Furthermore, doesn't that mean that poverty for some is not possible without ownership for others—which would mean, in turn, that the Franciscan state of holiness depended on someone else's spiritual corruption?

Clearly, some casuistry was called for and, Catholics being Catholics, casuistry was forthcoming. The most important Franciscan to elaborate on the order's concept of poverty was Bonaventure. In 1269 he published his *Apologia pauperum*, which set forth a fundamental distinction between property, possession, and usufructus (all matters of legal right) and *usus simplex*, the simple use of things necessary to sustain life. The latter existed both logically and temporally prior to any positive law as a moral duty, pursuant to self-preservation, incumbent upon all people as God's creatures; *usus simplex* in no way implied property right. (Notice here that the ground has shifted from renunciation of property to renunciation of property rights.) In an effort to silence the Franciscans' critics, Pope Nicholas III affirmed Bonaventure's position in 1279 in his bull *Exiit qui seminat*. But critics were not silenced. I will spare readers the fascinating details of debate during the next five decades and skip straight to the culmination. In 1323, in his bull *Cum inter nonnullos*, Pope John XXII declared the doctrine of the absolute poverty of Christ erroneous and heretical. He refused to accept ownership of the order's goods and lands and exempted them from the Rule's ban on ownership in common. Franciscans could no longer claim to be following Christ in renouncing property (or property rights, as the case had come to be) and became, however unwillingly, legal owners of all the property that they had been using.

Meanwhile, Ludwig (or Louis or Lewis) the Bavarian got himself crowned Holy Roman emperor, installed Pietro Rainalducci as Pope Nicholas V, and declared John XXII a heretic. This complicated things somewhat for Pope John, but he persisted in his goal to get rid of the Franciscans who opposed him. By 1328 that group included the order's minister general, Michael of Cesena. Michael was reelected to his office in May 1328, despite the pope's efforts, but he, along with William of Ockham, Francesco d'Ascoli, Bonagratia of Bergamo, and a few others fled shortly thereafter to the protection of Ludwig. More pamphlets, letters, and bulls were issued, but things fell apart for the Franciscans in August when King Robert of Naples mounted an attack on Rome, causing Emperor Ludwig and Pope Nicholas to flee. Pope John XXII excommunicated Michael and his compatriots, and a majority of Franciscans declared their submission to avoid execution for heresy.[16] John then issued his final statement on Franciscan poverty in his 1329 bull *Quia vir reprobus*. He declared both individual and communal property a natural and unavoidable part of the condition of human beings, dating back to Adam and to Adam and Eve, respectively.

The most obvious lesson here is that renouncing all property in a world structured by property relations probably won't work. It may in fact be logically impossible. Even if it is not—and that of course depends upon the actual texts and court interpretations of property law in a given place and time—there will likely be strong opposition to and dire consequences for those who try. The four Franciscans who refused to submit to Pope John's statement on the issue were burned at the stake. In today's world, you are more likely to starve to death. Either way, your actions will not prevent ecological disaster or lead to a more just society.

But there are more lessons to be learned from the Franciscan example. The first is that their declarations and persistence actually strengthened the institution of property by provoking canon and civil lawyers to build a much more comprehensive and well-articulated system of property law than existed before the order.[17] And that set the stage for the sorts of legal arguments that have been made ever since to justify dispossession of Indigenous peoples as Europe expanded its reach to the Americas, Africa, Asia, and the South Pacific. In particular, the distinctions made between ownership and use and between ownership and possession became extremely useful as first popes and then various European explorers and sovereigns claimed land all over the world, in spite of Native peoples' clear use of it.

And not only did the Franciscans provoke the discussions with and among the rich and powerful that eventually generated these legal theories; they actually participated in colonization themselves. Franciscans were travelers, even after the order became the owner of land and buildings; they never stopped moving to evangelize. They sang, prayed, and preached all over Europe, North Africa, the Middle East, and the Far East even in the thirteenth century and roamed much farther afield later on. As Julia McClure recounts, "Before Maffeo and then Marco Polo went east, the Franciscan Giovanni da Plano Carpin traveled there in 1245. Flemish Franciscan William of Rubruck spent several months at the court of the Great Khan in Karakorum, 1253–54" (2017, vi). As a result of these experiences, many of them spoke multiple languages; were acquainted with traditions, mores, and leaders in many societies; and developed a great many practical skills associated with navigation, cartography, diplomacy, and related areas. In short, they knew how to get around. On his deathbed in 1226, Francis had warned against his brothers accepting money or positions as servants in households where they might handle money or supervise other staff. But their extensive knowledge and expertise as travelers made them attractive candidates for Vatican and royal diplomatic missions, during which they often had to do both. Franciscans served as advisers, as well, to explorers preparing to go to foreign lands; Christopher Columbus, for one, spent a good bit of time at the Spanish Atlantic Franciscan monastery La Rábida, where the brothers maintained an archive of knowledge from all over the world about what lay to the west (McClure 2017, vi, 62). In fact, Franciscans had sailed to and were familiar with at least twenty-five Atlantic islands already (as well as sub-Saharan Africa), but they never called discoverers because, under the Vatican's Doctrine of Discovery, that would automatically make them owners (McClure 2017, 69).

Franciscans accompanied Columbus on his second voyage to the Americas to evangelize its peoples. Thereafter, they went on many such voyages and set up missions in the newly claimed territories, thus becoming instruments of the Spanish conquests. Preaching holy poverty to people about to be dispossessed and enslaved, if not massacred, is a bit ironic, to say the least, but the Franciscans saw no problem with it. They embraced poverty and valorized it, so why object when entire peoples were divested of land? For colonizers, obviously, this theological stance was extremely useful. Likewise, the Franciscans' Inquisitorial Tribunals of the sixteenth century. It turned out that managing the rabble and keeping them under surveillance was something the Franciscans were very good at.

Fifteenth- and sixteenth-century Franciscans' skills and dubious accomplishments aside, my point here is that direct renunciation of all property or property rights is probably not a good strategy for undoing, dismantling, or disempowering personhood. It is both too difficult and too simple. Dismantling personhood will require a much more complex approach to institutions of property and ownership, as well as a refusal of the injustices of poverty. A simple unilateral renunciation is not sufficient to change oneself, let alone the world, even if thousands of people were to do it at the same time. Personhood exists as a network of practices, of which ownership practices and exercise of property rights is only a part. Insistence on a kind (or actually several shifting kinds) of radical individualization is also a major component of the network, which means we must beware of counter-practices that are rendered in equally individualizing terms. We will turn to that complex of practices and possible counters in chapter 6. First, we can continue thinking about practices of ownership and ways they might be modified by way of the thought experiment proposed in the next subsection.

B. THE DILEMMA OF INVOLUNTARY SLAVE OWNING

If you could stand outside of history or of any particular community, you might very easily condemn slave owning. But, then, you don't live in a society where slave owning is institutionalized in law and the economic system. What if you did? Imagine that you are a young person in the US South around the turn of the nineteenth century. (You need not be or even imagine that you are a white person to run this thought experiment. Although most slave owners were white, a small fraction was not. Slave owners included Native American members of the so-called "civilized tribes" in the Southeast, as well as free people of African descent.[18]) Imagine, further, that you have just inherited a piece of agricultural land and property rights in a set of human beings currently living and laboring on it. I will presume that you, being you, find this situation utterly morally repugnant and want to change it as soon as possible. But, realistically, what are your options? I raise this question, and will pursue it below, because it is the most drastic and uncomfortable example that I can imagine for exploring what it is to own, what owning involves, and how owning might be dismantled or reconceived.

One way to cease owning human beings is to sell them to somebody else or give them away. That would certainly be the quickest way to cease being a slave owner. But it does not change the status of the enslaved; they remain property, just as Franciscan monasteries and lands remained property even when the Franciscans did not hold title to them. The system remains intact, and those people remain fully subject to it. Furthermore, you now likely have no way to work the land and so must sell it and seek other employment. If you are a young man, you might go west (like maybe Ohio) to seek your fortune (if you don't find helping to dispossess Indigenous peoples morally repugnant as well). If you are a young woman, you will likely become dependent on (probably quite resentful) relatives.

Your own fate aside, another option is to give those people to themselves, that is, manumit them. That option has the virtue of changing the status of both the person who was the owner and the people who were the property. In some states at some times, however, the law prohibited manumission,[19] making it necessary to move the group to another place where manumission was possible or to dispense with the legal formalities and either help the people escape to a non-slave state (or country) or maintain the outward appearances of enslavement for the sake of authorities but treat the people as employees rather than as slaves—that is, pay them a wage, allow them to travel at will or leave altogether, and so on. Both these options require some financial liquidity, which many slave owners did not have, except perhaps shortly after a good harvest. It might be necessary, then, to hold the people in slavery and keep them working until sufficient money was accumulated. If your land is a large plantation in a fertile area, sale of land might bring enough money to resettle some or all of them as well as yourself, but you might well have inherited a smaller or less fertile farm. The particularities of the situation play an extremely significant role in what your options really are.

However you manage to acquire it, once there is enough money to send people somewhere that has no institution of slavery, there are logistical questions to be sorted out. One of the most obvious is how to equip them with means of survival during passage and once they arrive. Suppose none of them can read or write and they are ignorant of most of the rest of the world; they may easily be defrauded or exploited. Suppose the only sort of work any of them has ever done was agricultural; not one of them is a blacksmith or a seamstress who could set up in trade. Suppose some are small children or elderly or infirm and cannot get a job. Some provision for their futures must be made. This last set of issues arises even if manumission is legal where you are so that there is no relocation to finance. Wherever they will live as free people, they will need some skills that they may not have, and some may be unable to support themselves regardless. (In fact, some laws against manumission were enacted in part to prevent owners from freeing elderly people and people with disabilities and just abandoning them to destitution or the support of the local parish.) It would appear that you can't just renounce your inheritance like Saint Francis did; for some period of time, at least, you have to own these people. Their lives probably depend on it.

I leave it to the reader to imagine all the complications that might arise, but they would likely include such things as the hostility and possible violent responses of other area slave owners and relatives' legal attempts to block the loss of human capital to the extended family (no doubt a particularly difficult problem for a woman with few property or civil rights of her own). Whenever I run this thought experiment myself, I end up imagining that the process will take several years, will have to be executed in near secrecy, and will not be possible without a drastically changed relationship between owner and owned while the legal relation remains intact. It is this last condition that is of most interest in the context of this chapter. How does one remain an owner in a legal sense while working to dismantle the proprietorship that lies at the core of one's subjectivity as a person?

I believe that no matter what the particulars of the situation, this undertaking would be impossible without the active, informed, and willing participation of the enslaved people in question. They, or at least some of them, have to become partners in the enterprise. There are risks in making this so. Some of the ones most needed to help raise the money for the others—the strongest, healthiest, and smartest—may prefer simply to take their chances and leave immediately on their own. There is also the issue of secrecy; the more people who know the plan, the more likely it is that someone will accidentally or even willfully betray it. (Many slave revolts and escapes failed because an enslaved person gave the plan away.[20]) Enslaved partners will have to be chosen carefully, as will those selected to receive special training in literacy or other skills. These partnerships will require respect and trust, which undoubtedly do not exist at the beginning and will be hard to establish and maintain. Everybody involved will have to get to know each other deeply. The further along the plans get, the more everybody's life and future will depend on everybody else's behavior. Different people, with different strengths, skills, and legal positions, will have different contributions to make to the project. Each one's contribution is crucial. The slave owner's legal position has to become not a right over the other partners but a resource for the group's effort. The partners will have to decide together how to use that legal position, just as they decide how to use the farm and the available labor power to raise the necessary money, where and when to relocate, who and how many will go at a time, and how to keep everyone as safe as possible both through the process and after it.

Slowly, over the time that partnerships are established, resources assessed, and plans formulated, you the legal owner will give up more and more control of your own life as well as property and put yourself at greater and greater risk—of retaliation and violence from other enslavers, of failure of the plan that might bring financial hardship or legal punishment, of loss of other important relationships in your life, and more. Your fate will come to be very much in the hands of the people the law says you own, as theirs is in yours. If you stay committed to this process, you will change in some fundamental ways. And they likely will as well. As a group, you will come to belong together even as you approach the point where nobody belongs to anybody anymore.

Whether any such scenario ever occurred, I don't know. I do know the chances of succeeding in such a process would have been minimal, especially if we add in some of the complications mentioned above. The accounts I have seen of people ceasing to be slave owners (other than postbellum) are of sale or mass manumission where it was legal, done by white men with other means of support, and absent many details of what happened to the freed people afterward. The former owners' status changed, but it is not clear whether they themselves changed in any fundamental way.

Nevertheless, running the thought experiment has value, I think, because, among other effects, it forces you to think about how owning involves deep assumptions about control and about oneself as truly and rightfully in control. In manumitting, owners gave up control over people whom they had owned, but they never gave up control of their lives to people whom they had owned. But that is precisely what the experiment requires us to imagine. The most obvious lesson to be learned here, it seems to me, is that dismantling ownership in such a way inevitably brings with it an inescapable and unremitting vulnerability.

C. OF ANIMALS AND LAND

Back to the present. I am not, in fact, an involuntary owner of property. As a legal person, I have entered into contracts over the years to purchase houses and cars, appliances and furniture, the ordinary things of what since my late twenties has been a middle-class American life. I now own lots of things—no human beings among them, of course, but some of my "things" are living beings, both fauna and flora. And I will continue to own most of them until they die or break or wear out, or until I do. Can the above experiments give me any guidance for how to be a legal owner while dismantling my subject position as a proprietor who routinely exercises power of disposition and control over things?

i. What About My Dog?

If the property is human, partnership, trust, and sharing in decision-making are possible, even if the odds were stacked high against such a project in the historical circumstances. These possibilities don't seem to exist with houses, cars, jackets, or frying pans. But I wonder what possibilities do exist. Some owned things are easier to imagine becoming partners than others, for example, my dog. There is some trust between me and my dog, and sometimes we engage in activities together as partners, although, even when her preferences are taken into consideration, she is not a full partner in decision-making; my spouse and I are the ones with final say. Our behavior toward her could be construed as the actions of owners in that we enjoy, possess, and (to some extent) control her, and exclude some others from interacting with her; but here, too, there is some reciprocity: She also enjoys us and is possessive of us, at times trying to exercise a right of exclusion over us. (Just ask the cats.) We use our human abilities, including our legal rights, in ways that we believe will keep her happy and healthy for many years to come; in some abstract way that we presume she cannot understand, we try to be answerable to her. We also believe that she would exercise her canine abilities to protect and care for us if she perceived a danger or an emergency, as dogs have done for human friends for many centuries. We and our dog are not equal partners in our relationship, but maybe we are partners each in our own species-specific way. What would equality even mean, given the different capacities and incapacities of our two species? Between us there is mutuality, reciprocity, and care.

In *Land of the Spotted Eagle*, Luther Standing Bear has harsh words to say about Euro-Americans' attitudes toward animals in contrast to those of the Lakota. Whites make animals their slaves, he writes; they force them to labor or cage and torture them for fun or "study," although he cannot understand how knowledge of animals can be gained outside of their natural habitats and ways. The Lakota never engaged in "detached study but more the natural process of 'getting acquainted'—an exchange of friendship and the bounties thereof. The Lakota built no fences, cages, pens, corrals, nor prisons" (Standing Bear [1933] 2006, 171). They did share living space with dogs and, at some point after European invasion, horses, but he insists that this sharing was not ownership as Euro-Americans understood it. "The dog, it seems, became the helpmate of the Lakota far beyond all memory of the time. When, where, and how it came into the domestic life of the people does not appear to be known now" (171). Women trained dogs to pull their travois, but they seem to have regarded that as little different from training their children to make moccasins. Everybody in the band had skills and chores.

> According to the story of the Oglala band of Lakotas, the first horse they saw was already domesticated and appeared among them one early morning contentedly feeding within the circle of their tipis. It was a marvel to them—a beast of beauty and fascination. When the Lakota later captured the wild horse it was to make of him a companion and to decorate and ceremonialize him. Songs and dances were dedicated to the horse and it joined the warriors in the dances about the camp fire. (171)

Eventually, every band member old enough to ride had a pony or horse, and horses were given as gifts at ceremonies. But they seem not to have been bought and sold and to have roamed free over the plains when not being ridden. That Standing Bear perceived whites' animals as enslaved beings suggests that he and the Lakota more generally considered them as fundamentally entitled to freedom from usage against their inclinations. Although I am not sure that horses like carrying riders, especially into battle, it is easy to imagine that dogs loved pulling the travois, just as dogs in Alaska today clamor to be chosen for a sled team and as my dog clamors for a walk in the neighborhood or a run on the beach.

I chose to talk about the dog above, rather than the cats or the mule, because many people live with dogs and recognize that their relationships are not descriptively captured by the language of ownership. Many contemporary horse owners, too, love their horses as companions and relish the sense of harmony or even fusion that they feel when riding. If I had chosen to talk about one of the cats or the mule, the description of the relationship between us would have been different, because each of them is different. And that is another way in which these relationships exceed or defy the language of ownership—the supposed property, the animal, is not fungible. Each being is different not only because of species differences in bodies and modes of interactions but also because of differences in individual styles of behavior. Every pet "owner" knows this, but owners of food and work animals see things otherwise. Mules, for example, were once an important commodity in the United States, and breeders churned them out like Detroit did with automobiles. But to relate to a given mule as solely a commodity, it is necessary not to know that mule as anything except for its capacity for physical labor and the rudiments of its maintenance. If you know a mule in any other way, either in its muleness or in its this-muleness, its fungibility lessens. It may still be property, but it is also recognized as always more than property. Ours is called Buttercup.[21]

ii. What About My Garden?

This acreage is another matter. What is more clearly property than land, especially unmortgaged land to which one holds a legal title giving one rights of possession, enjoyment, exclusion, control, and disposition? In the eyes of the law, my spouse and I are proprietor-persons and this land is ours. Furthermore, land is not a conscious, deliberating, or even desiring being. The shared projects and mutual trust that can constitute relations between human partners are impossible, as are most of the sensual and empathic potentials that can bind a human and a nonhuman mammal such as a mule or a dog. What is left to mitigate the legally reinforced relationship that places a landowner in possession and control? Reasoning in the abstract will not yield any answers here, I suspect; we have to look at the particulars of a given situation.

My land comprises about five acres of pasture, about two acres of house, yard, and garden, and about one acre of woods. We leave the woods alone for the most part. It tends to be swampy, but when and where it isn't flooded, it is thick with cat briar and saplings. We bushhog the pasture a couple of times a year, so it maintains its grass and weeds, field mice and hawks. The groundhogs and deer graze there, and the foxes sun themselves. If we did not interfere at all, in a few years those acres would be woods too, as all this land was before it was colonized, although it would never return to its precolonial mix of species. The rest of the property shows the effects of human habitation—structures, fencing, mown grass, flower beds, and of course the vegetable garden. I will focus on the garden here because it is the part of the land where my impact is hardest to ignore, where it appears that I exercise my bundled rights of proprietorship most regularly.

I have been cultivating this particular garden for a quarter century, through summers so dry the well almost failed and springs so wet I would sink to my knees in mud. Air temperatures have been as high as 102 degrees Fahrenheit and as low as zero. Some days have been utterly still and clear, while others have brought hurricane-force winds and horizontal rain. I have watched this garden day after day, visited with individual plants, learned the look of need and the signs of attack as well as the happy expression of well-nourished, aerated, and irrigated roots. I have hauled water in buckets and dragged hoses when buckets couldn't bring enough. I have shoveled pound after pound of herbivore shit from pasture to wheelbarrow to bin to bed. I have eaten well, and so have the deer, the birds, the groundhogs, the rabbits, the squirrels, the moles, and the raccoons, as well as the hornworms, the squash borers, and the bean, cucumber, and potato beetles and the creatures who prey on them. I have made thousands of decisions about what would take place there, but not ever even once have I felt in control. While I have managed to exclude a few humans—hunters of deer, wild turkey, and relics of war as well as one owner of a crashed drone—I have never been able to exclude the hundreds of other beings who fly, creep, slither, hop, scuttle, and meander through that space, and certainly not the hundreds of thousands who are born there every year in the soil or on stalks and leaves of "my" plants or in trees nearby. Do I enjoy this garden? In the legal sense, this is not a question about my feelings at any given moment but rather one about whether I can extract benefit from this garden, but I do enjoy it in both senses, both pleasure and material benefit (although not income and not enough food to live on). My spouse and I could sell the land or give it away—to that extent we jointly have the right of disposition over it—however, land being what lawyers call an immovable, we cannot consume it or relocate it (the latter of which makes me sad when I think that in a couple of centuries it will once again be part of the floor of a sea). That leaves the question of possession, which strikes me as a strange word for how I am with any part of the land, even the garden.

I call it *the* garden, but it isn't really a thing. My relationship is not with what the garden *is* but with what happens there. What I mean by "the garden" is not the place itself but the taking place of ungraspably complex processes and events, aspects of which involve me, in which I both actively and passively participate. The same is true of the land in which *the* garden is embedded, including the groundwater beneath, the atmosphere above, the wildlife that inhabits it or passes through, and the microbial life that inhabits and enables all of it. How could I possess all that? I cannot comprehend it or even perceive it all, much less embrace it or preside over it. I am *in* it, not as owner-possessor but likewise as process and event, happening with it, sometimes as it. I find myself at a loss for words.

Looking for words, I read Brian Burkhart's *Indigenizing Philosophy Through the Land* (2019). Burkhart suggested to me that I read Luther Standing Bear's *Land of the Spotted Eagle* (1933), so I took a break from Burkhart to do that. These books, swirling together, gave me words that I use here, in combination with words from many other books and mouths that swirl around with me from my many years of reading and listening. I am aware that there are some people who will say that I should not use words from Standing Bear or Burkhart, who will say that using Indigenous peoples' words is a kind of theft made possible by centuries of colonialism and imperialism. So I want to say up front that I acknowledge that I would not have come across these particular words were it not for centuries of colonialism and imperialism. Standing Bear would not have written in English, or under the name Luther Standing Bear. He would not have had to recall old ways for young Lakota or indict malicious whites. I would not be seeking to know how to live in this land. I would not even be in this place. For that matter, I would not exist. Those are facts. All that I am and have emerged and is sustained under the conditions of centuries of colonialism and imperialism. Not just facts, then, but profound truths not to be outrun. But I also want to say to potential critics of my use: There is something fundamentally wrong about treating languages and cultures like intellectual property owned by the peoples who live within and through them. You are right to worry, but you need to cast your worries in different words. What I do with and in relation to the words I find in these Indigenous writings matters. But that I do something with them is not in itself a theft or even necessarily a wrong. It matters how my writing listens to theirs. And so I would ask potential critics to consider how they listen to my listening in my writing, and write their words from there.

Now, first, consider this source. Ota Kte was born in or about 1868, as Christians reckon time. For the first eleven years of his life, despite the atrocities and deprivations already suffered by his people (of which many more were to come), he received a more or less traditional Lakota boy's education. But things changed drastically when he was sent to Pennsylvania to be educated by whites at the Carlisle Indian Industrial School. There he received his father's name, Standing Bear, as a patronymic and Luther as a Christian name chosen at random. His hair was cut; his blanket, buckskin clothes, and moccasins replaced with woolen long johns, trousers, shirt, and boots; and his mother tongue forbidden. He believed then that it was his duty to die bravely as a Lakota in that place. But, as it happened, Ota Kte was among the 50 percent of the Plains Indian children in his Carlisle class who did not die over the next three years. The remarkable man who emerged from all that disruption, oppression, and death insisted that he was Lakota to the last, no matter what he took from the whites—name, clothing, language, wages, citizenship, legal rights. His books attest to the living man and to the living happening of languages and lifeways that clash and create themselves as they occur. Luther Standing Bear champions a Lakota past in order to carry it into a different but still Lakota future, arguing that absorbing foreign elements does not have to mean expelling or losing the crucially familiar and closely held. He writes for peers who despair and grieve and for their children and grandchildren who cannot remember. He writes for whites who imagine that they can shape and manage and assimilate and erase Indigenous peoples. And he writes for a future that he knows he cannot imagine. I don't think Ota Kte, Luther Standing Bear, would mind too much if I try using some of his words. I think maybe he was willing for something like that to happen when he let them go.

And so they have come to me, as a gift perhaps, and it is up to me, because he has let it be up to people like me, what I, and we, will make of them. Here is what I make of them.

As said above, starting with my garden, I began trying to think with land outside of, or at least in excess of, discourses of owning, managing, and producing. At first I focused on the land itself, meaning the plot and the soil and the life on and in the ground, but I couldn't see how to think about and around the fact of legal boundaries. Those boundaries operate to hem me in to ownership. How can I let them be—having no choice—without letting them be determinant? In *Land of the Spotted Eagle*, Standing Bear describes Lakota life on the land always in intimate relation with sky and sun. The land is not just below one's feet, but all around, with air and light inseparable from rock and dirt and darkness. I realized this was key. The surveyed plot is property, but the land exceeds the plot.

Reading Standing Bear's words made me think about the sunrise over the pasture here, and how I follow it through the seasons. Sunrise happens here, happens to/with/on/as this land. But it has nothing to do with legal boundaries. So I spent some time with sunrise.

Our house's largest windows look eastward, and the garden lies back there, just beyond the yard fence and before the pasture fence. There is a tree line beyond the pasture, and the oaks and pines there are very tall, maybe seventy feet. The pines' canopies are relatively small; their energy goes to upward growth rather than spread. The oaks' branches spread wider, but this late in the year their leaves are mostly gone. All this is to say that sunrises are visible early and at a longish distance. This isn't the Great Plains, of course. Horizons are close here. But the eastern horizon is the farthest and the one I attend to most of the time, even when I am not reading Standing Bear. Sunrise has moved closer and closer to its southern extreme over the past weeks, and I have watched its progress with a twinge of sadness. I knew the frost would come—which it did, although about three weeks late this year—and the garden plants would die. As the sun moves, so move the lives it illuminates, mine included. Thinking about the sun brings out many related lines of thought, seasons and mortality, surely, but also the seemingly more mundane. For example, thinking about the sun always entails thinking about that most quotidian of topics, the weather.

Standing Bear writes that Lakota never complain about the weather as whites do, because whatever each day brings is a gift from the Great Mystery ([1933] 2006, 48). I am not as accepting. I do see his point: To grumble about a spoiled outing, for example, just displays our Western sense of time—schedules, dates, and deadlines—our sense that we are entitled to manage the activities of the day, our refusal to let the world tell us what would be best to do in any given now. But all scheduling and grumbling aside, I can't help but worry: Is this weather the doing of the Great Mystery, or of Dominion Energy's coal-fired power plant that lies just over the western horizon?[22]

Although the east has most of my daily attention, this land's weather usually comes not from the east but from the west-southwest. The tree line in that direction is much closer and denser than it is in any other direction here, so clouds pile upon us suddenly. Still, we expect weather from there. When a strong wind does occasionally come not from the west but from the east, we know there is trouble, because the nearest ocean lies that way. A nor'easter from off the coast means lots of rain, sleet, or snow. From the south, which is also dense with trees, come hurricane winds and tropical storms. But even in the worst of storms, the wind rarely blows harder than sixty miles an hour, so the trees mostly stay where they are, only losing a few limbs if they are heavily canopied. From the north, what comes is whatever strays diagonally or down from weather that has already blown up to the north from the southwest along the mountains about seventy miles west, not very threatening although threatening enough that we made sure the horses' sheds were south facing, and we planted the fig trees where the house would provide some break from a winter north wind. All of this is very different from the land that Standing Bear describes. His nearest ocean is westward, and his north brings blizzards sometimes. He can see a long way in every direction, with a singular interruption arising as the sacred Black Hills. He seems not to think very much about tall trees and not at all about hurricanes. But for all the differences, and all the aspects of his thinking that I fail to grasp or feel, thinking with his words does help move me away from those stubborn legal boundaries and their power to determine how I am here. Legal boundaries are foreign, even nonsensical, in this living land. Thinking about weather means thinking about wind, and wind has no bounds.

Thinking in terms of the four directions, the winds, and the sun defies the notion that land is still, let alone delineable. There is locality, to use Burkhart's term, but there is no static space. If I were not educated in a Western worldview, I might know nothing of magnetic north, let alone truth north. Directions might not be compass points or coming and going of lines intersecting at me. Directions would be arcs of sunlight. East would be the arc of the dawn from summer to winter and back again, as west would be the complementary arc of the setting sun. South would be the arc of the light through the shortest of winter days. And north, here, would be the empty arc where the sun never mounts. The directions would be these moving circles of light, and they would form the clearing where the crisscrosses of comings and goings and intersections take place. I say they would be, but having thought myself to here, I suppose that this now is what they are. What do I know, anyway, of magnetic north, let alone true north? It's just hearsay. I can see and feel the moving sun and experience, every day of my life, how it moves me.

It was helpful and even invigorating to be carried along by this thinking with moving and changing, all yet happening here, making here to be this here, and so I tried to see how far I might go with Standing Bear. He mentions that the Lakota associate the four directions with four eagles. The east is associated with the golden eagle and the sun; the north is the bald eagle, the prevailing wind, and the snow; the west is the black eagle and darkness; and the south is the spotted eagle, which carries the dead to the land of happiness (122). I know of golden eagles and regularly catch glimpses of bald eagles, but black and spotted were new to me, not within my experience. Land is not everywhere the same, as Burkhart notes when he describes the different directional associations of the Arizona Diné (2019, 134–36). I need to think with the happening that is this land, here. So I tried thinking of land and direction in terms of the beings who inhabit this place here alongside me. Here the east is pasture grass, horse and mule, walking crows and running deer. There are bald eagles sometimes; they come from the south and return there, to where the James River runs with the fish that they eat, but the south, which is more wooded than any other direction, is also where the deer sleep and the turkeys hatch and the foxes hunt and the raccoons find cover. The west, beyond the high trees, is the city, and toward it runs the state highway. The north is the scattered houses and then the now-dormant soybean fields and then the airport and the white lines of contrails and vees of migrating Canada geese, coming and going. These relations are all the land in its being here, its happening here, its giving and taking place. Even the airport. Even the coal-fired power plant.

Brian Burkhart (a member of the Cherokee Nation, born in the Navajo Nation, and raised among the Lakota) not only draws on Standing Bear but also on Black Elk (who was also Lakota, like Standing Bear), whom he quotes at length regarding the four directions: "The east gave peace and light, the south gave warmth, the west gave rain, and the north with its cold and mighty wind gave strength and endurance" (2019, 125). Black Elk speaks of the four directions as a generous circle, or a circling of circlings. Using Black Elk's comments on the circularity of the four directions, sky, earth, and so on, Burkhart talks about Lakota knowing in contrast to Western philosophy's emphasis on propositional logic and universal truth. He writes, "The thinking of the circle of four directions . . . sees knowing or understanding as only one momentary part in the dawning of the East that moves (in one version at least) from the West (from the spark of passion and fear in the coming darkness in the setting sun as well as the joy of the coming life in the waters, thunders, and ocean) through the cold, quiet stillness and cleansing wind of spirit in the North and on to the bounty of the South and the summer (the body, the physical, the material world, or into action or practice)" (138). Illumination in knowing is only one arc of the circle, and not the first direction to turn even to reach that arc. The east of knowing is not a place; none of the directions is a place, as is already clear; all are movings along with moving beings—sun, wind, rain, and snow, living and dying. All of this moving takes place, makes places, but never yields anything like a geometric space whose dimensions might be knowable apart from any beings in relation. Moving is what land gives us to know. Knowing this land is living in the moving that takes place and is place. One knows the land as one knows friends (and enemies), not conclusively but continually.

In seeking to know this land, I hope that I give sufficient homage to the darkness and fear in which this circling begins and that I have gathered sufficient strength and courage from the long white stretch of memory that previous chapters have chronicled. I have not traveled in a straight line. And although I have moved, I am not sure that I have gotten anywhere at all. What do I know now? I know that the land moves, too. It happens in circles, with the sun and the wind. It takes and makes place, which is singular without discernible bounds. And neither I nor anyone else will ever own it, even if we hold titles that say we do.

IV. Four Lessons

Winter solstice is dawning now as I sit in the half-light, the dawning of the shortest day, the darkest day, the day that has, somehow, drawn me for weeks through the thinking of this strange chapter. I don't know why. Drawing toward a gathering darkness has not stood as a symbol to anything in this work; it has not meant anything, particularly, nor has it felt like a destination. It has been and is the force of the movement, I guess—just that; as Burkhart says, a sand painting never represents or symbolizes the healing powers but is their invocation and, therefore, their coming to presence (2019, 129). Neither sand nor sky is about meaning, but about moving. And so this is it, a short day dawning, a brief moving into a long darkness that will also move to another dawn. I can't actually see the sun rising this morning, because of the heavy bank of winter clouds that obscure the sky to the south and east. Yet the light comes, gradually, softly intensifying. Only a few hours before it will fade. Today feels urgent. What has happened in these last weeks? What can happen now?

I started by seeking cracks and fissures in the structures of ownership, the experiential excesses to those structures, ownership's nonsense. Could those structures be made to fracture or tear, even if slightly, to allow other ways of living besides within the proper proprietorship of Western personhood or without as its poor and despicable failures? Where might I press, where might I pull, and what would happen, if anything? The lines and indentations were scattered: management studies and psychological ownership, Franciscan renunciations and fourteenth-century papal bulls on the contents of Judas's purse and Adam's dominion in paradise, the logistics of nineteenth-century manumission, the colonial education of Plains Indian children. I had no idea where I was going. But I was moving. I knew that. I was moving as the sun was moving, as the wind was moving, as the season was moving, as the birds and deer were moving, as the land was moving, as everything exceeds what it was, even when it circles and returns.

I have not remade myself as a non-owner. We still hold title to this surveyed plot—and our cars and sundries and 401(k)s and I suppose even the dog. In that respect, legally, we are still persons. What, then, has been gained? (Gained? Watch the language here! The more important question could be: What has been lost?) In all the moving, what has changed?

Here is something I feel I learned: Structures of ownership are weakest where they operate in the absence of legal property and its close analogues. They take power from property relations, but that is borrowed power easily diminished with a little amused attention and a resolute refusal to play along with the game. And these efforts persistently practiced may go a good way toward upsetting the manners of modern persons who want to own their (and only their) choices and actions and to force others to own theirs as well. Stay creative in redescription. And above all, stay honest. In careful honesty, attention shifts, necessarily and profoundly, from unilateral action, competition, and individual success to relations, mutuality, and collectively if not particularly comforting community. The modern moral person falters in fellowship and even in multidimensional conflict where restoration of balance and reciprocity are sought. We can begin to live more fully in that excess to personhood's ownness, if we simply acknowledge it and speak of it as real. My first lesson was to speak plainly and attend the effects of words imposed.

My foray into the Franciscan world was an adventure of facts. All I really knew of Saint Francis—despite three summers in Tuscany and a good look at Giotto's frescoes in Assisi's Upper Basilica before the 1997 earthquakes—was a tonsured man with birds on his head, often depicted in poured concrete. Francis was a traveler, I learned; concrete hardly does justice to the man. He roamed, always barefoot, skin always bathed in the dust of the ground. He didn't command the birds, and he remembered the day they came to him on the road at Bevagna as one of the most beautiful of his life, a gift with no meaning beyond its simple occurrence. They just came.

Reading of Francis's work and translations of his words, I felt the joy and release of young Giovanni Francesco Bernardone's renunciation. Standing naked in the snow, he was free, free of his father, free of his society's expectations, free of the markets and account books and the demands of impending global capitalism and the foul sin of usury, free of everything except his passion for his God. He was a young man who wanted to live in the air and the light and the caves, to walk in the land, to sing, to pray through the darkness, and to give whatever he had or was, continually, to the giving power that he felt all around him. In Francis, there is pure joy. Little wonder that so many thousands were attracted to him and his vision of life. There is such power in joy.

Youthful, joyful Francesco was ignorant of the dangers that lay ahead, and, in any case, he had no means of managing them. All he wanted was freedom to live in his joy and to offer others some signposts by which they, too, could move beyond the structures that bound them. His Rule was never rule-like; it was always "do this insofar as possible, if you can, the more the better." Borrow a donkey only if you must, to transport someone who is too ill to walk. Only touch money to save a life. Rules of thumb, practical suggestions for the already committed—but use your own judgment as the situation demands. He never meant to control anybody, so how could the world, the Church, expect him to administer an ecclesiastical empire? There is even some evidence that his renunciation of real estate was not absolute, that he would have been willing to hold title to land if it were situated in such a way that entitlement could never involve exercise of exclusion.[23] But institutions need their rules and procedures to function like laws, and eventually his Rule was interpreted that way and altered to fit. And then the Rule was overturned, and other rules prevailed. It would feel like a tragedy to me, except that, even so, Francesco's joy permeates it all.

Still, there is a lesson here for those who seek release as Francesco did, even though it be release from a different set of institutions and demands. Direct renunciation is incredibly, overwhelmingly dangerous. It is to be weighed with utmost care and largely avoided. I both love and abhor the phrase "speaking truth to power." Young people believe in it so thoroughly, and I love them as I love Francesco for that. But gray-haired veterans know sometimes you just don't want power to know how much you know. Bide your time, find the cracks, hollow out the interstices, invaginate the firmaments. And always remember that secrecy has its place. I cherish those beautiful youths who believe so completely in the power of truth. I want them to believe in their vision of the world, even as I stand apart from them. And I stand only just a little apart, I know. Age and experience do not guarantee wisdom, or even just plain know-how. Even veterans can never anticipate all the dangers. All we can do is probe and watch and probe again.

Renouncing modern moral personhood outright is, I believe, impossible at the present time, both logically and logistically. Even attempting to do so would justify such irresponsibility that everything might be lost. But not doing so, working slowly and piecemeal, brings dangers of its own, many no doubt no more available to be anticipated than was the Franciscans' role in the conquest of the Americas and the dispossession, torture, and genocide of their peoples. The lesson I take from Saint Francis of Assisi is, then, be extremely wary and invariably humble, because even in our freedom we are never in control and because even joy may have a heavy cost and because even the greatest wisdom will never be protection enough.

With Francesco's story live in mind, I turned to the question of how one might work one's way out of a situation of involuntary slave ownership, a situation in which, it seemed obvious to me, direct renunciation was at best naive and even perhaps criminally irresponsible, because while the slave owner might be freed from an offensive property relation, the enslaved people would likely not be and might even be subject to worse conditions and injustices than they already endured. The scenarios I conjured called for the sort of careful, deliberate, slow planning that direct renunciation avoids. And therein I found a third lesson.

Renunciation separates self from property in things. Its appeal lies in part in this apparent purity, the clean break, the simple stepping away. My messy, ugly scenarios, by contrast, jeopardize and relativize every such separation in that they dissolve the boundaries that enable an owning self to remain distinct from owned things in the first place. As an involuntary slave owner seeking release, I imagined moving closer and closer to the enslaved and they to me, imagined us encroaching upon each other in networks of increasingly intricate and at times unspeakable dependencies as we worked in concert to change the conditions of all our lives. This dissolution of boundaries happened as and with both profound interdependence and tremendous risk. It was never a loss of difference or a loss of conflict; differences became crucial as every resource was inventoried and put to work, and conflicts grew inevitable where stakes mounted as hierarchies disappeared. The most prominent feature in these enactments of scenarios was not increasing indifference but intense alertness and extreme vulnerability. The owner's life—my imagined life as I ran the experiments—had to be placed in the erstwhile property's living hands, without any promise or guarantee. There was no other way but to run the risk of sacrificing everything. This third lesson is scary, but its frightfulness is mitigated by the exhilaration that such a yoking together of lives in such hard, terrifying, and creative work could bring, the freedom to be felt and lived in the intensity of such a powerful bond.

The first three lessons circle together in the fourth: Everything moves. In my real life, thank goodness, ownership extends only over nonhuman beings, beings who seem incapable of perceiving and receiving me as that imagined human property could and who therefore seem incapable of effecting their own transformation and release, let alone mine. It is all too easy to think that I will have to do it for them; I will have to find ways to treat my dog, my garden, my land as something other than mere property so that I can become something other than mere proprietor. But the other arcs of this circling tell me otherwise.

It is a grave mistake to think that the things we own are things, self-enclosed in their sameness and fixity, moving only when acted upon by beings such as we. Or is it a mistake—I mean, *just* a mistake? The histories I have traced in this book suggest something a little more deliberate, a fixing of things in categories and boundaries that were, in all honesty, foreign to them, an enforcement of their mere thingness. What is more real: the blowing wind and streaming sun or the lines on a survey map that mark out this land? If I choose the lines on the survey map, I can believe I am vulnerable to nothing here, resting assured in my self-enclosure, unquestionably dominant. But that's a lie. Everything moves, and everything moves with and against everything else, myself included. Differences, but no boundaries; no walls, but membranes opening and filtering in the valences playing and shifting across their surfaces. There are no real proprietors here, because there is nothing to own, just papers that say we do and thereby promise us rights in imaginary things drawn with imaginary lines.

Hours have passed. It is almost dark now on this shortest of days. I really have written this entire chapter section, these seven manuscript pages, in the clouded light of one brief day, as I had hoped to do. It hasn't been easy, what with groceries to unload and store in anticipation of an omicron wave (yet another surge in a now-two-year-long worldwide pandemic), a semi-annual trip to the dentist, cats and dog to tend, and in a couple of hours the weekly fundraiser to conduct so we can purchase food to give out Thursday to this city's many poor, unhoused, and hungry human beings. The writing has happened, as it usually does, in the interstices. This whole chapter, this whole season, has happened like that, writing while cooking, while ill in bed, while the TV is tuned to football, writing with a cat or a dog or a baby on my lap, between feedings, between changings, in the in-between. Writing, like living, has happened.

It is full dark now; the longest night has begun. And when it ends, I will look to the east again to follow the arc of the light back across the sky, above the farthest tree line, until the coming of the longest day, and back again. An endless circling, embracing all that happens as this land: the winds, the birds, the rain and snow, the writing, the thinking, and me.

[CHAPTER SIX]

Questioning Individuality

The night has passed. The sun itself is no more visible this dawn than it was yesterday—thick clouds to the southeast—but the light has returned. From this day on, for the next six months, the dawn and the sunset will arc northward. And if this is like other cycles—but with the disruption of our climate, who knows?—crocuses and wild onions will start up in eight or nine weeks, followed by the dandelions and daffodils, and I will turn dirt and sow seeds that will grow into plants and food for humans and birds and bugs and rabbits and deer, whether I want to share or not. And when the dawn peaks at its northernmost point, the pasture will be thick with grass for Buttercup and her horse friend Roo and alive with gawky juvenile turkeys and curious newborn fawns. For many peoples, including my own distant ancestors, the morning after winter solstice was and is a day of joy and anticipation of a beautiful, bountiful spring to come, despite the hardships of winter. But nowadays I think many people are unsure what to anticipate. Instead, we engage in a guarded hope—for a good snowy winter as well as a bountiful spring. In any case, here we are, on the move again, in a different direction this time.

In chapter 5, I explored several ways to disturb the proprietorship of modern moral personhood, to weaken that whole historical configuration of meaning and power by finding fault lines and applying pressures to assumptions, notions, and practices of ownership. I think—I feel—that that effort can disturb the historically generated network of meanings, expectations, comportments, and practice that I have been calling personhood, shift its alignments, and diminish its power in some ways in my life and maybe in the lives of people who read these words and think about their own places in the world. While there is no getting around the fact that I still legally own my 8.1 acres of surveyed, plotted, registered, colonized land, I can use whatever bundle of rights accrues to me with regard to it as resources for the flourishing of that much different, singular but unbounded land to which I, however contingently and unjustly, now feel that

I belong—and otherwise to disregard the law of property others apply to it as far as possible. I hope something similar might emerge in this chapter's examination of individuality, which is another of personhood's central features. I hope I come to some livable understanding of myself as an aware, acting being beyond the firmly bounded individuality that so much of our history subscribes to and demands of me.

Two issues should be acknowledged right away. First, this is not an entirely unfamiliar goal. Many, many people have critiqued individualism, sometimes as an inaccurate account of human life and sometimes as an ethically unsound approach to political and social existence, although usually not in an effort to challenge personhood per se. Second, the words *individualism*, *individuality*, and *individual* have been used in a variety of different ways and therefore name a variety of different things, which means that those many, many critiques are not necessarily mutually reinforcing, and some of them are not even pertinent to the project underway here. The first thing to do, then, is to clarify to the extent possible what sort of individualism characterizes and constitutes modern moral personhood in the lineage of Locke.

The word *individual* comes from the Latin *individualis* and *individuum*, denoting that which cannot be divided. Cicero used *individuum* to speak of Democritus's indestructible atoms, the smallest and most basic things in the universe and the building blocks of all other things. Persons are obviously not individuals in that sense. But modern moral persons do seem to be units—that is, each person is and remains one and the same being over time, as Locke took great care explain. Its durable sameness is essential if it is to function as a forensic entity, subject to moral judgment for past actions.

Furthermore, an individual of whatever sort is not only the same as itself over time; it is also not the same as anything else. A person, as an individual, is physically and mentally distinct from all others. Although persons' bodies interact and in doing so sometimes exchange material, nothing lost or acquired in that manner is normally thought to undermine each body's essential separateness from other bodies. Likewise, each person has its own emotions, thoughts, beliefs, aspirations, and memories. People sometimes speak of sharing beliefs or memories—for example, my sister and I share memories of our trip to Disneyland in 1976—but most people don't take such locutions to imply that there is just one memory to which more than one person has access; each person is presumed to have its own distinct set of mental "contents."

A person is an individual, then, in that it is separate from all other beings, the same as itself over time, and different from other persons and things. But in addition to these descriptive criteria, personhood includes a normative dimension that goes beyond simple separateness. Birth brings separation, but maturation is, in essence, a process of becoming more and more independent, needing less and less from elders, progressively taking control of one's own body and then one's own decisions and actions, and finally taking charge of the course of one's own life. To be recognized and treated as a full-fledged person, a human being must be physically, emotionally, and cognitively separate enough and financially, socially, and morally independent enough to make their own uncoerced decisions. Failure to achieve independence can mean fewer legal rights, and failure to maintain independence often means diminished respect. People whose disabilities or infirmities require attendants' assistance can be objects of pity (and sometimes of scorn). To be dependent on charity or on parents for one's livelihood in adulthood can be cause for shame. Elderly people are often construed as "burdens" on relatives, younger workers, and taxpayers. Dependence means failure or inferiority.

Of course, we all know that no one is ever totally independent of all others; everyone is constantly affected by other people's behavior as well as by the behavior of germs, weather, and gravity. Absolute independence functions as something like an ideal, something to aspire to. A person ought to strive to be as independent as possible. Successful persons are ones who grow up, leave home, make their own way in the world. Extremely successful persons are ones who become "independently" wealthy so that they no longer have to answer to employers or benefactors or adhere to the customs and mores of their communities if they choose not to. The ideal of total independence and the ubiquitous drive to approximate it grows almost naturally out of a deeply rooted belief in human beings' fundamental separateness, as does the common equation of independence (needing no one) with freedom (from everyone). If we did not believe in our separateness in the first place, independence would not be our goal. Our values and ethical lives would necessarily be different, and quite likely our social and economic orders and our political systems would be different as well.

The first three sections of this chapter endeavor to undermine that deep-rooted belief, the assumption that each person is a physically and mentally separate entity, by examining scientific analysis and common experience. Section I challenges the idea that each human being is physically separate from and genetically distinct to other beings. Section II challenges the idea that emotions are thoroughly individuated. Section III turns to the question of whether cognitive processes are always confined to individual minds. And, finally, section IV offers a sketch of an alternative way of thinking about our experiences as differentiated selves that takes those challenges and questions into account.

I. Hazelnuts and Holobionts: Questioning Physical Separateness

A couple of winters ago, we were very upset to discover that a workman had mistakenly cut down our two very large hazelnut bushes. In the spring, however, little hazelnut bushes sprang up throughout the area. I presumed that the previous year's scattered filberts had sprouted once they were free of the shadow of their large parents and was delighted to think that, as a result, we now had an abundance of hazelnut bushes that could be dug up and planted more widely apart to grow as large as their progenitors. But it was not so. When I began to dig, I discovered that all the little bushes were connected, having sprung not from seed but from the root systems of the original two plants. What appeared to be separate individuals were not really separate after all. I could sever a sucker from the rest of the system and care for it while it tried to establish itself, and it might possibly manage to live as an individual thereafter, but it was not an individual as I found it and would not likely ever become so if left to itself.

Relative to hazelnut suckers on a single root system, human beings are separate from each other. And that is an important fact about the world; some things are more individuated than others, and our expectations of and involvements with those various things must take those relative differences into account. But we should hesitate here. Once born, we humans are more individuated than hazelnut suckers; in comparison to them, we are relatively individual. But . . .

In 2012 the *Quarterly Review of Biology* published an article summarizing recent developments across the life sciences that call into question traditional ways of conceptually individuating living beings, humans in particular. The article was entitled "A Symbiotic View of Life: We Have Never Been Individuals," and in it the three authors—Scott F. Gilbert, Jan Sapp, and Alfred I. Tauber—assert, "Symbiosis is becoming a core principle of contemporary biology, and it is replacing an essentialist conception of 'individuality' with a conception congruent with the larger systems approach now pushing the life sciences in diverse directions that transcend the self/nonself, subject/object dichotomies that have characterized Western thought" (Gilbert et al. 2012, 326).[1] They looked at several different biological accounts of individuality and found that recent work challenges every one of them.

People typically assume that animals are numerically distinct wholes, the authors note, an assumption that has long informed the science of anatomy. I am one anatomical unit; my dog is another. Each of my organs, systems, and tissue types is integrated with the others and acts to structure and sustain my entire organism independently of other living organisms. Yet biologists now tell us that the bodies and even the cells of all animals contain numerous types and lineages of living beings that are crucial to the larger organisms' continued existence. Without those microbes, beings such as sponges, corals, cows, and humans would not be able to sustain themselves. According to Gilbert, Sapp, and Tauber and the scientists they cite, "In some sponges, nearly 40% of the volume of the organism is comprised of bacteria, which contribute significantly to host metabolism." Coral's algal symbionts provide up to 60 percent of the nutrients it needs to survive; otherwise, coral bleaches and dies. "Similarly, the entity we call a cow is an organism whose complex ecosystem of gut symbionts—a diverse community of cellulose-digesting bacteria, ciliated protists, and anaerobic fungi—informs its specialized anatomy, defines its plant-digesting physiology, regulates its behaviors, and ultimately determines its evolution" (Gilbert et al. 2012, 327). Human beings are no exception to this pattern; the space that is filled by us is not all or even mostly filled by human cells. Scientists have estimated that 90 percent of our bodies' cells are bacterial, and those bacteria in our digestive and neurological systems, on our skin, in all our orifices, and even in reproduction make essential contributions to our survival (327). Take away all the microbes, and not only would I die quickly, but my corpse would be quite a lot smaller and lighter than I am.

Gilbert et al. go on to consider developmental biology, beginning with Thomas Huxley's 1852 essay "Upon Animal Individuality," which characterized an individual not as a spatialized anatomical unit but as a continuous process of development unfolding in and of itself. We now know, however, that the life cycles of mammals do not unfold entirely from out of each animal "itself" but depend upon the action of microbial beings. In many species, microbes signal animal genes to activate or deactivate at appropriate points; in the absence of those microbial signals, the development process deviates or stalls. Biologists have raised laboratory mice without alimentary microbiomes and have found that their digestive systems and immune systems remain incompletely developed. (Such experiments are not done on human babies, for obvious ethical reasons, but mice are often used as analogues of human physiology; zebrafish, likewise used as a model for human physiology, also cannot develop complete digestive tracts without microbes.) "The coevolution of mammals and their gut bacteria has in effect resulted in the 'outsourcing' of development signals from animal cells to microbial symbionts. Thus, the symbionts are integrated into the normal networks of animal development, interacting with the eukaryotic cells of their 'host'" (Gilbert et al. 2012, 328).[2] Trends in this research also undercut the notion of genetic individuality, the "one-genome/one-organism doctrine of classical genetics" (330). Not only does it seem that what makes me human is not only human DNA but the DNA, RNA, and proteins of all the other little beasties that keep me alive—that make me *me*—but, additionally, I probably inherited some of that nonhuman DNA from my mother; the ancestors of some of "my" microbiome helped her develop and kept her alive, and some of their ancestors sustained her mother as well. Microbial genomes can be co-selected with the genomes of mammals, which means that "microbes provide a second hereditary system that enables holobiont survival and selection" (330), *holobiont* being the term coined by biologist Lynn Margulis for a being that exists in/as symbiosis.

The article goes on to consider several other functional accounts of individuality in the life sciences, but we need not rehearse them all to see the point: Whether considered as a body at a given moment in time or as a progression of development from a fertilized ovum or as a distinct genome, a human being is not one but many, not a unit but a complex interactive living system, or systems of systems.

Studies conducted over the past three decades have shown that not only are we humans made up of cells carrying genomes from microbial lineages as well as the unique combination of genes that came together at fertilization, but we are also made up of cells carrying the unique genomes of other human beings. A woman who has been pregnant—even if she miscarried or aborted—carries cells bearing the unique combination of DNA that arose at the moment of fertilization that initiated her pregnancy. These other human-lineage cell lines will likely persist in her body for decades. Her child will also carry cell lineages not only from the moment of its fertilization but also from the moment of hers—two distinct combinations of DNA arising from two distinct moments of fertilization many years apart. "The placenta was traditionally thought to be a barricade that keeps the genetically differing mother and child separate," write researchers Sean Maloney and his colleagues. "This assumption has recently given way, as a result of the application of molecular biological techniques to the study of human pregnancy. It is now recognized that fetal cells routinely pass into the maternal circulation during normal human pregnancy. Maternal cells can also be found in the fetal circulation" (Maloney et al. 1999, 41).

We might be tempted to dismiss this information as on par with the idea that we exchange some living cells with other people in other sorts of intimate contact, which, as already noted, is not taken to compromise our basic separateness. Deep kissing might result in exchange of some living cells between partners, for example, but those cells probably get expelled or die without ever affecting the physiological processes of each partner.

Wouldn't the exchange of cells through the placenta be similar? Apparently not. Just as embryonic cells probe into the endometrial tissue to begin to establish the placenta and its connection with the maternal circulatory system at the moment when the embryo is said to implant, the moment of conception, the same or similar cell types seem to push subsequently into the mother's blood and make their way purposefully into her bodily tissues. They have been found in breast, thyroid, and brain tissue, incorporating themselves into those organs' functions. They have also been found in their mothers' bone marrow, lungs, in general circulation in the blood, and congregated at the site of wounds and tissues associated with autoimmune disorders (see Boddy et al. 2015). Studies have shown that in breasts, thyroids, and brains, fetal cells can operate to enhance milk production, raise maternal body temperature to enhance heat transfer to the baby, and increase a mother's sense of calm and well-being. In breasts, fetal cells may simply signal glands to produce more milk, or, being similar to stem cells, they may produce daughter cells that become breast glands themselves and produce milk directly. At the site of wounds, fetal cells sometimes seem to facilitate the mother's healing. This all makes physiological and evolutionary sense during pregnancy and lactation, and it appears that the mother's immune system clears most of the fetal cells from her system in the weeks after pregnancy. However, cells descending from the fetus have been found in some of these tissues decades after childbirth, and cells of maternal lineage have likewise been found in children into their late forties. Transfer of cells from mother to fetus can involve not only maternal cells but also cells of previously gestated fetuses and even of maternal grandmothers (Boddy et al. 2015, 1107). As a product of my mother's third pregnancy, I may consist not only of cells with functioning microbial genomes whose mother cells were parts of my mother, but also cells with functioning human genomes from four other people. And my younger sister may carry cells with my genome passed from the fetus that became me to our mother and then to her.[3]

As much fun as it is to think about all that, though, does it really preclude my physical individuality, or does it just alter what I must consider to be its content? Maybe I am an individual created and sustained by a thousand different genomic cell types, a unity in genetic diversity, an individual holobiont. Even if I am much more than a human genome, I'm still not my dog. The system or ecosystem that constitutes and sustains me is distinct from the ones that constitute and sustain other individual living things. Complex and heterogeneous as it may be, I have a distinct inside as opposed to what is outside. I am sprawled at this end of the couch, and my dog is sprawled at the other—two distinct beings, not to mention the couch.

Of course, in some ways, while we are in proximity, we do overlap. Although bits of my dog are not likely to incorporate themselves into my tissues and begin replicating dog genes in me, they can have physiological effects. My allergist has persuaded me to have bits of dog injected under my skin twice a month to convince my immune system that dog bits are not foreign invaders but are somehow part of me, or at least guests whose presence should not evoke physiological protest. I suspect also that our bodies' microbial populations have become more similar to each other than they were before we met. The same is probably true of my spouse and me, our cats, and even our horse and mule. And after more than two decades of gardening one plot and eating produce from it, as well as some of what grows here without my help, my microbiome has been affected by the soil and compost in the backyard. I am of this place and its myriad inhabitants. If I were to be detached from these particular cats, dog, mule, horse, spouse, flora, and dirt, I would survive, but only if I were quickly attached to other dirt, flora, and human and nonhuman fauna. It seems that the physical individuality of any living being is purely relative.

These reflections help blunt some of the force of atomistic individualism, but they probably will not take us far enough. Modern moral and legal personhood actually do not require absolute physical separation. The example of Chang and Eng Bunker will make this point clear. The Bunker brothers were conjoined twins born in 1811. Their bodies were interdependent—or, perhaps, they were simply one body—yet each had his own thoughts and preferences, his own emotions and concerns. The brothers made a good bit of money by exhibiting their unusual body for the public's entertainment, and they used some of that money to set up two separate households for their two separate wives. Each owned his own property, including enslaved human beings, and each fathered several children. On January 17, 1874, Chang suffered a stroke and died. Eng did not have a stroke (at least not in the brain that was attributed to Eng), but he died on the same day a few hours later. The cause of Eng's death is said to be unknown. If we assume that both Chang and Eng had a body, were two bodies conjoined, then Eng's death seems to need an explanation; but if we assume they were one body, then it makes sense that when a significant portion of it died, the rest quickly followed. At any rate, whether we count Chang and Eng as one body with more or as two bodies with fewer than the usual number of parts, the life of the Bunker twins demonstrates that total bodily separation is not absolutely necessary for personhood. Chang and Eng were physically constrained by and dependent upon one another to a remarkable degree, but each had his own thoughts and desires, his own responsibilities, his own legal rights and property. Even though physically they were a bit like two hazelnut suckers sharing one root, somehow they were still separate; Chang and Eng were two individual persons.[4]

A counterexample, however, might be that of Christine Costner Sizemore, who was diagnosed in the 1950s with a condition then known as multiple identity disorder (now called dissociative identity disorder). Her psychiatrists, Corbett H. Thigpen and Harvey M. Cleckley, wrote a book about her case entitled *The Three Faces of Eve*, which became a movie starring Joanne Woodward. Sizemore's three distinct identities had their own names, characteristic gestures, personal tastes and styles, and perspectives on the world. They were as different as any three white, middle-class American women selected randomly might be, except that they shared one anatomically ordinary body. Nobody thought the three identities were three different persons. Instead, Sizemore was considered one person with a severe mental illness.[5]

Sizemore's case shows that bodily separation does matter for personhood to an important extent. Her various personalities shared one head as opposed to the two heads and two brains of Chang and Eng Bunker. The Bunkers were never seen as one man with two personhoods but rather as two, as conjoined twins. Their bodily twoness was assumed, even in their lifelong state of extreme interdependence, whereas the distinct personalities of Christine Sizemore's single head were not. Perhaps the difference is that separate heads are indicative of separate brains and, therefore, separate consciousnesses, whereas one head is indicative of one brain, which is normally assumed to be entitled to only one consciousness.[6] All the ideas and emotions in my one head belong to this one me, myself. My ideas and emotions are in my head, and yours are not. I don't share them with you, except via systems of signs or symbols. The thoughts and feelings in our respective heads don't seep out and mingle or blend, and they certainly don't originate beyond the boundaries of our skulls and subsequently pervade them. We reach the tentative conclusion, then, that it is the separate existence of heads or brains and therefore of what they do and contain that make for distinct personhood. What is most important, it seems, is the separateness of each individual's mentality. But . . .

II. Feelings and Perceptions

As a forensic being, a person must be able to experience, reason, and decide independently of others; otherwise, it could not appropriate its decisions and actions as its own (take responsibility for them), and it could not be judged blame- or praiseworthy for those decisions and actions and be justly punished or rewarded for them. A person's mental states and processes are and must be individuated, separated from the mental states and processes of others. Physical individuation may not be an essential feature of modern moral personhood, but mental individuation surely is.

Our mental states and processes are affected by the world, however. I may be sluggish and dull-witted when the air pollution level is high. A gloomy day can inspire a gloomy mood, while a sunny morning elicits a sunny perspective on the day ahead. And not just the environment, but other people's mental states can affect mine, blurring the boundaries between my feelings and theirs. Teresa Brennan gives the example of walking into a room of people and immediately "feeling the atmosphere" (2004, 1); people are excited, anxious or on edge, and suddenly so am I. Similarly, a coworker is depressed and, even though she doesn't tell me, after several hours with her, I leave work more than usually tired, flattened, vaguely sad.

We might account for some of this by positing visual cues—the group's rigid postures, the coworker's sagging shoulders; by such signs, people may guess how someone else is feeling. But what explains the resultant feelings—or, as Brennan would have it, the transmission of the affect that we learn to name as assorted emotional states—so that not only do we *know* someone else's feelings but we also, in some sense, *feel* them? If we believe that feelings happen within individual minds and can only be communicated if a mind then generates signs through its body that can be perceived by other bodies and conveyed to other minds who interpret them as indications of those feelings, then the phenomena are quite puzzling.

One way to account for this is to suppose that our minds are not always the source of the bodily changes that others take as signs of our emotional states. Suppose, instead, that at least some of the time our bodily states are the source of our feelings. Nineteenth-century psychologist William James suggested that physiological states generate mental states that we learn to identify as emotions. My fear does not cause my heart to race; rather, I feel fearful because my heart is racing. My body is already reacting to a threat before I can identify my current state as fearful.[7] Obviously emotions are not always generated in this way, but let us assume that sometimes they are. Now, add to James's claim that of Annie Murphy Paul: "When interacting with other people, we subtly mimic their facial expressions, gestures, posture, and vocal pitch. Then, via the interoception of our own bodies' signals, we perceive what the other person is feeling *because we feel it in ourselves*. We bring other people's feelings onboard, and the body is the bridge" (2021, 61).[8] By such a route, it seems, we could feel with other people, and the feelings we then shared would not be clearly individuated.

This kind of sharing may be a widespread phenomenon among social animals. Horses have extremely good hearing and can identify individual others' voices; when one horse in a herd sounds a danger, others will quickly react. But some evidence suggests that vocalization is not the only means of transmission. Horses also hear the heartbeats of other horses close by and tend to synchronize their own heart rates with those of herd mates, so a suddenly elevated heart rate in a herd member may spread quickly across the entire herd, putting the entire group on alert. The effect is not merely mechanical. As anyone who lives among them knows, horses feel, communicate, remember, and calculate; even without language, they are thinking beings (who can sometimes, and quite intentionally, outsmart humans). It is a stretch to say that these physiological changes also happen for them as what we call consciousness; if so, they have emotions like fear and anxiety, even though they do not use words to name what they experience.[9]

Some studies suggest that not only are horses sensitive to each other's heart rates, but they are also sensitive to the heart rates of other animals around them. They can hear a human heartbeat from four feet away, and they seem to be particularly attuned to a familiar rider's heartbeat. If a rider's heart rate increases upon perceiving a danger or difficulty up ahead from a vantage point above the horse's line of vision, the horse may react accordingly. At least one equestrian website encourages riders to learn how to control their own heart rates on the approach to a jump so as to keep the horse calm.[10] Likewise, according to some researchers, humans in close proximity to horses respond to equine heart rates. Human heart rates tend to slow down in proximity to horses, whose resting hearts beat about thirty to forty times per minute (whereas resting human heart rates are normally above sixty beats per minute). This effect may be one reason why horses often make good therapy animals.[11] Calm horses calm humans. This is not a result of humans hearing horses' heartbeats (since we usually don't), nor is it the result of humans mimicking the physical disposition of horses' bodies (since we can't), but is believed to be an effect of the electromagnetic fields that such large hearts produce around them, fields that affect the electromagnetic fields generated by smaller hearts nearby.[12] However it happens, though, people and horses influence each other's emotional states.

We might still want to say, even so, that the emotional states themselves are fundamentally individuated. The other people in the room each feel their excitement or tension, and when I enter their space what I feel is mine; the horse feels his calmness, and, although under his influence, what I feel is mine. The connection between two beings' emotional states may be causal, but their respective states are not mutually or even linearly constitutive.

Well, maybe. But consider now what happens when affective transfer is impossible. What happens to a human being who has no contact with human and nonhuman others? If our feelings are only influenced and not at all constituted by the feelings of others, people should be able to maintain a typical range of affective states even in isolation.

There is plenty of evidence to the contrary, however, drawn from studies of prisoners kept in solitary confinement for months and years on end (which is unfortunately still a common occurrence in the United States). All suffer. Most sustain lasting emotional impairments. Many simply unravel, a process that can begin within a few weeks and affect not only their emotions and bodies but even their perceptual faculties.

It is hard to know how many people in the United States are in solitary confinement at a given moment. Estimates vary from about 61,000 to over 100,000 men, women, and even some children, held in six-by-eight-foot (or, for the luckier, eight-by-twelve-foot) cells for twenty-three hours per day.[13] It is even harder to know how many remain in solitary confinement beyond the fifteen-day limit set by the United Nations Standard Minimum Rules for the Treatment of Prisoners (also known as the Mandela Rules), although there are likely many thousands. Psychiatrist Terry Allen Kupers (2017) has interviewed numerous prisoners, both male and female, who had been in solitary confinement for a decade or more. During their confinement, these people may never see another human being, because they are let into an exercise run or a shower room through doors opened and closed remotely, or they may only see other human beings when they are led in chains to and from those facilities (Haney 2003, 126). The only human touch they experience may occur during "cell extraction" or body cavity searches before and/or after their brief time outside their cells. Their surroundings never change: uniformly white walls, stark and immovable furniture, artificial lighting left on twenty-four hours, seven days a week. They experience no color, no vista, no smell of anything other than disinfectant, bad prison food, and human excrement. Any sounds they hear are likely to be generated by locks opening and closing, by prison employees slipping food trays through slots, or by other inmates screaming or raving in cells around, above, or below them at any time of the indistinguishable day or night.

If human beings were individuals—if they truly were psychically independent of any given milieu and physically self-contained—solitary confinement might be horrifically boring, but it would not precipitate the deterioration that occurs in people who spend more than a few weeks in supermax prisons and control units in lower-security prisons, jails, and immigrant detention centers. The effects documented for over a century support the view that human psychological health is unsustainable without significant contact with both human and nonhuman beings. As Milton Meltzer, medical director for several years at Alcatraz, wrote, "The sense of self, the ego and ego boundary phenomena are profoundly affected by isolation" (quoted in Grassian 2006, 344). Inmates lose track of time and have trouble maintaining alertness during the day and normal sleep patterns at night. Absence of sunlight and constant artificial light disrupt Circadian rhythms, affecting metabolism and often inducing or exacerbating clinical depression. Electroencephalogram data show that within a few days brain signal patterns shift toward patterns associated with clinical stupor and delirium (Grassian 2006, 331). Meltzer observed that after one week in solitary confinement, inmates became either extremely agitated and erratic or dissociated, withdrawn, in a state of hypnotic reverie (Grassian 2006, 344). Agitated prisoners paced endlessly around their cells, some banging their heads or other body parts repeatedly against cell walls. Stupor, approaching catatonia, seems to be the alternative. Stuart Grassian observed the latter condition in more than half of the two hundred prisoners he studied. Under-stimulation reduces an individual's ability to process stimuli and results in "hyper-responsiveness" to whatever stimuli are present. This intensified sensitivity quickly becomes unpleasant, leading people to avoid stimulation as much as possible; hence, the extreme psychic withdrawal that gives the appearance of catatonia. Short of that extreme, people became unable either to concentrate on a chosen object or task or to shift attention from one thing to another at will, the latter resulting in obsessive fixation, which sometimes becomes paranoia (Grassian 2006, 331). Hallucinations are commonplace.

Some of these symptoms are associated with serious psychopathology, according to Craig Haney, who conducted research at the Pelican Bay supermax facility in California, and they can occur in prisoners with no history of mental illness (2003, 134). Furthermore, as Grassian points out, some of these symptoms are rare even in people diagnosed with serious psychiatric illness. Loss of perceptual constancy is very rare, usually found only in people with brain tumors and seizure disorders. It is also rare for perceptual distortions to affect multiple perceptual modalities—auditory, visual, olfactory, tactile, and kinesthetic. So is hypersensitivity with a dysesthetic (subjectively painful) response—in fact, so rare that it suggests an organic brain dysfunction etiology (Grassian 2006, 337). But these prisoners had no documented brain injuries, tumors, or seizure disorders prior to or during confinement in isolation.

Why does this mental breakdown occur? Or, as philosopher Lisa Guenther puts it, "How could I lose myself by being confined to myself?" Human selfhood, she goes on to argue, "cannot be sustained in absolute solitude but only in relation to others" (2013, xiii). Haney's work supports her claim: "The virtually complete loss of genuine forms of social contact and the absence of any routine and recurring opportunities to ground one's thoughts and feelings in a recognizable human context leads to an undermining of the sense of self and a disconnection of experience from meaning" (2003, 139). And loss of social contact is not the only factor; human beings need nonhuman beings as well as human ones. We need sunlight; we need frequent and great variation in our perceptual field; we need to move through a richly varied world in order to maintain ourselves, in order not to disintegrate into a generalized background with no meaningful patterns or focal points. A human being removed from the world ceases to be a human being in all but the genetic and general anatomical sense. We are not and cannot ever be absolutely individuated—not cellularly, not genetically, not physiologically, not emotionally, not even perceptually. We are not hazelnut bush suckers, but we are not monads, either. We can be ourselves only under certain conditions; to be what we are, we require the ongoing dynamic accompaniment of a richly varied physical and social milieu.

Still, it might be hard to shake the sense that one is somehow still fundamentally individual. The fact that many people break down in solitary confinement does not *prove* that normal human mental life is socially or environmentally constituted; after all, some isolated people do manage to maintain themselves. And even if some of our emotions are prompted by the affects of other people or the bodily states of other living beings and influenced by environmental conditions, the feelings themselves still occur exclusively in the individuals who experience them, right? Besides, a person might want to insist, the real issue is not fleeting emotions but thoughts, judgments, choices, and decisions that we then put into action. Even if my depressed colleague gets me down, if I reflect on the source of my feelings, I can decide to manage them and put myself in a position to feel otherwise. How I choose to deal with the situations presented to me is under my control. And it is this ability to judge and act, perhaps despite the condition of my surroundings and others' effects on me, that makes me an individual person!

III. Cognition

The fallback position of personhood appears, then, to be that what matters is the individuality of deliberation and judgment, or what psychologists today call cognition. The previous two sections demonstrated that complete physical separation is not required for personhood, and emotional separation is, while generally assumed, not absolutely necessary either. Here, with individual deliberation and judgment, however, we may have found a form of individuality that modern moral personhood absolutely cannot do without.

How so? Individuation of deliberative processes as traditionally conceived involves two kinds of separation. First, each person's cognitive processes occur in separation from all others' cognitive processes; each person's judgments and actions belong solely to that person. Second, a person's cognitive processes occur in separation from the rest of the world. This second kind of separation is necessary to ensure the first; if people's cognitive processes were to extend into the world of things, those processes might overlap and even join across separate persons in one cognitive event. A modern moral person's cognition has to stay inside that person. Only the results can be publicly available, through action that generates signs and symbols for others to interpret. For example, suppose I work out a solution to a problem on paper. What is the cognitive status of the motions I make in the act of writing? Are the paper, the pencil, and the marks made components of the cognitive process, or are they simply records of what is happening in my mind that I may use as inputs for my own further cognizing or for communicating to someone else as inputs for their cognizing? If these objects are components of my cognitive processes, then the very same objects could also, and at the same time, be components of someone else's cognitive processes. In that case, cognition would no longer be fully individuated. Two or more people would actually be thinking together rather than simply communicating about what each of them was thinking individually. Those people and their papers, pencils, and marks would form one cognitive system engaged in one cognitive process. And that would make it difficult if not impossible for any one of them to claim exclusive ownership of whatever judgment or action emerged as the "output." But without exclusive ownership of judgment and action, a being is not a person.

Of course, people regularly collaborate. They bounce ideas off each other, build on each other's suggestions, generate new perspectives on problems, and imagine possible solutions in conversation with others. Groups of people can come up with designs, scripts, solutions, and strategies that no single one of them would have thought of on their own.[14] To maintain the traditional view that cognition is individuated, we must interpret collaborative engagement as communication between separate cognizers across non-cognitive space. Everything one group member says, writes, or draws becomes an "input" into the others' separate thought processes. It would then be the volume and variety of inputs that would explain the often-greater intelligence and creativity of groups over individuals, not some sort of merging of minds. We could interpret collaboration in this way and also insist that collaboration is not our usual means of deliberating, judging, and acting anyway and thereby save the individuation of cognition—and thus modern moral personhood as well.

But is this the only way to think about how thinking happens? For months, I searched for alternative accounts. I googled and browsed and shopped around in library and book catalogs. I wandered through discussions of neuroscientific findings using fMRIs, debates over artificial intelligence, memory enhancement strategies, military personnel studies, Polynesian celestial navigation, child development, and the inevitable reports on the activities of rats, chimps, and bonobos. And it turns out that, for at least four decades, there have been scientific challenges to the idea that cognition is confined to individual brains housed inside individual heads. Thinking is not just inside our heads, say some researchers; it is a bodily phenomenon inseparable from moving and doing.[15] Thinking spreads across environments and artifacts as humans interact with objects, tools, and changing situations, other researchers insist, positing those various non-mental things not simply as sources for "input" but as integral elements in cognitive processes. Thinking spreads across two or more conscious bodies, still others claim; groups of people sometimes form cognitive systems that engage in processes whose cognitive features are not fully attributable to any of the individual people in the group. Some theorists posit a mixture of these. I found many of these claims and theories very interesting. I will present two of them below, the so-called "extended mind" model of cognition and the model of "distributed cognition."

A. EXTENDED MIND

In 1998 Andy Clark and David Chalmers published a paper titled "The Extended Mind" in which they presented a hypothetical scenario about a man suffering from Alzheimer's disease who uses a small notebook to record information he might need later but fears he will forget. This man, Otto, carries the notebook with him everywhere and often refers to it when he has to decide on a course of action. The notebook, Clark and Chalmers argued, is deeply integrated into Otto's deliberative processes, so much so that researchers are justified in treating it as a component of those processes and not simply a tool external to them. What if we allow other items in the world to count as components of cognitive processes, they ask, even those used by people with no impairments? Might we find that we can explain some phenomena better, more readily, or more elegantly with the assumption that thinking can happen beyond the head rather than with the assumption that it never can?

Unless we have a fairly firm notion of what "deeply integrated" means, absurdity might ensue. After all, everybody uses grocery lists and address books and calculators all the time, and we don't consider them parts of our mental processing. There has to be a distinction between counting something as a component of a cognitive process versus as a prop or a tool. But where should we draw the line?

Clark offers a possibility in his 2011 book *Supersizing the Mind* when he points to a 2004 study in which monkeys learned to use a rake to pull food to them that was otherwise out of reach. Researchers Angelo Maravita and Atsushi Iriki wanted to find out if there were alterations in a monkey's body schema (its neurological awareness of its body's dispositions) as it became skilled with the rake. They focused on neural activity in the monkeys' intraparietal cortex, "where somatosensory and visual information is integrated," specifically on so-called "bimodal neurons" that respond to both types of information (Maravita and Iriki 2004, 79). These neurons activated in response to stimulation at and near the hand, but that changed as the monkeys grew proficient with the rake. Soon the neurons were responding to stimuli along the length of and at the end of the rake. This did not happen with monkeys who simply handled the rake, only the ones who learned to use it as a way of getting the food. It would seem, then, that over time the monkeys incorporated the rake into their body schemata. The rake became more than just a tool; it became part of the process of reaching itself. (Subsequent studies suggest that tool use alters humans' body schemata as well; see Cardinali et al. 2009 and Sposito et al. 2012.) What if, Clark asks, some tools that we use in cognitive processes become integral to those processes in analogous ways?

Clark acknowledges that "it is harder to know just what to look for in the case of mental and cognitive routines" (2011, 40). Just what would count as integration "in an analogous way"? But that difficulty is no reason to rule out the possibility, he says, much less to abandon the idea that cognition might extend beyond the skull. What we can say is that some tools seem indispensable to some thinkers in some situations. I know that there are some problems I simply cannot work out if I don't use pen and paper, and I am in good company. Clark introduces his book with a vignette about the famous physicist Richard Feynman. Historian Charles Weiner once referred to a batch of Feynman's notes and sketches as "a record of [Feynman's] day-to-day work," a record of what was going on inside Feynman's head. But Feynman insisted, "No it's not a *record*, not really. It's *working*. You have to work on paper and this is the paper. Okay?" (quoted in Clark 2011, xxv). Teachers of creative writing and composition take this position, too, when they urge students not to wait until they know what they want to say to start writing. Ideas emerge in the process of putting pen to paper, fingers to keyboard; arguments achieve clarity; conclusions draw themselves. Such events are part of ordinary experience.

A number of critics have accused Clark of claiming that objects like writing implements have cognition. But that is not what Clark maintains. In fact, no one believes that pens can think all by themselves. But, Clark asks, can brains? The answer seems to be: Sometimes, and sometimes not. Sometimes we need to make a sketch or sort things into piles or put marks on a map. The cognitive process seems to require physical movement, visual cues, spatial rearrangements. And if those actions and perceptions are integral components of the process, why not say the items moved, produced, and seen and even the marked or partitioned space itself are also components of the process? The models of cognition that Clark and others have put forth are of cognitive systems, not just cognitive processes. The idea is that cognitive activity occurs as an emergent property of certain sorts of systemic couplings and assemblages.[16]

Clark reminds his readers that even when cognition happens solely in the brain, it is a process that involves systems of variously conjoined components. Brains themselves are not homogeneous units. Brains have parts that do different kinds of things in different locations. Those parts also have parts, billions of neurons. Some regions of neurons are tightly connected and others are loosely connected or not connected to each other at all, and these connections can change with repeated or changing stimuli. Cognition happens across parts of the network in pathways of activation, involving some neurons and not others at various times. Most of this process is nonconscious. In the end, an idea or solution or decision emerges into consciousness, speech, or action, with or without some or any of the cognitive steps that led to it. Where is the thinking, then? It isn't in the pen or in the fingers, but it isn't in any particular neuron or bundle of neurons, either. It is in the variously coupled system of components, no single one of which could support thinking on its own. Clark insists that his extended mind model "gains in plausibility when the inner economy is itself seen aright: as multiple, fragmented, yet vastly empowered by an ill-understood capacity to form and re-form into a variety of surprisingly integrated (though temporary) wholes" (2011, 137–38). In cognitive processes where pens, paper, charts, astrolabes, slide rules, or anything else is coupled with some of the neural and physiological systems of an animal with a brain, there is no particular reason to accord any lesser status to the charts and slide rules than to the biological components. And it would seem that the more complex the cognitive process is, the more complex the processing system needs to be. According to Clark, a single person is a necessary condition for cognition to occur but, much of the time, one person is not a sufficient condition.

Clark brings forth many pages of evidence from his own research and that of numerous other cognitive and neuroscientists to help make this model plausible. Insofar as it is, the older model of thinking that locates deliberation entirely inside the mind (and separate from perception and action) has less power over how we see the world. But there are some theorists who believe that Clark has not gone far enough.

B. DISTRIBUTED COGNITION

Edwin Hutchins's model of distributed cognition departs from traditional views more radically than does Clark's extended mind. Hutchins agrees with Clark that cognition is a materially localized process that requires not just a material unit but a material system, of which artifacts like pens and slide rules can be crucial components along with neurons. But he doesn't think the extended mind model incorporates sufficient attention to social and historical factors and contexts. Clark holds, Hutchins points out, that it is the individually embodied, self-organizing neurological system that "recruits" the nonbiological supports it will couple to itself and to each other. For Clark, it is an "I" who picks up the pen, who searches for the scrap of paper, who places the ruler across the map. Rulers and maps do not seek me out to help them solve the problems they encounter. I organize my task world; it does not organize itself (Hutchins 2011, 438). But, Hutchins objects, this analysis is far too simplistic. It is just not the case, he insists, that a dynamic embodied thinker encounters a static world of things where the only source of organization is the individual mind. First, there are self-organizing dynamics in the material world at some levels. Second, and more important in this context, we humans constantly find ourselves in task worlds already organized by generations of predecessors. The tools we recruit to assemble our cognitive systems in the present moment are repositories of experience and information that far exceed anything any one of us could ever hold in mind. Indeed "recruitment" processes themselves precede our entry into the scene. It isn't just that I know how to solve a math problem because I went to school and learned to do so; it is that the very practice of counting and quantifying was discovered and learned by innumerable ancestors, gradually refined by them, passed along, and incorporated into countless other cognitive routines that are so basic to our existence that we can hardly imagine people living without them. But they did. And some still do. The Pirahã of the Amazon have no words for numbers, although they do understand one-to-one correspondence. The Munduruku of the Amazon count only up to five (see Tversky 2019, 177). Thousands of generations of *Homo sapiens* never counted anything. It never occurred to them, and it likely would never occur to me, either, if I had no number words. But if I had no number words, if my way of living in the world involved no notion or practices of quantification, what would my thinking be like? It is literally unimaginable that I could be who I am without any of that enormous set of words, concepts, skills, habits, and beliefs or any of the interactions and experiences that depend on them. This is Hutchins's central criticism of the extended mind model.

Like the extended mind model, the distributed cognition model assumes that cognition happens as a process supported by some sort of material "vehicle" (to use Clark's term) and that the material support is not a single unit but a system of components or elements that may be neurological and non-neurological and even nonbiological. But it does not assume that every cognitive system is assembled by an individual brain. Clark's examples of cognitive systems are relatively simple—brain, eyes, hand, pencil, notebook, for example—compared to Hutchins's examples, which are frequently analyses of important, complex, difficult workplace tasks such as piloting an aircraft or a ship.

Hutchins was employed by the US Navy in the 1980s as a personnel research psychologist studying workplace dynamics. His book-length analysis of distributed cognition, *Cognition in the Wild* (1995), originated in that work. He opens the first chapter with a description of an emergency that occurred while he was aboard an amphibious helicopter transport. As the ship was returning to San Diego Harbor, the steam engine that powers the propeller and generates the electricity to run many of its navigation instruments ceased to operate. A large ship has a lot of forward momentum, much more than can be countered simply by dropping anchor. With no power to reverse the propeller and slow it down, there was a very real possibility that the ship would crash into the harbor, damage itself and coastal structures, and injure many people. The navigation team had a key role to play to predict the ship's path, determine the length of time it would take to slow it, and try to steer it safely into a sufficiently deep side channel. Although collectively the crew knew how to use backup instruments to take readings and how to make the important calculations, no member of the crew had ever trained for precisely this emergency, and some members were still in training and had not yet achieved mastery under normal conditions in the positions they held. To make matters even worse, the broadcast and ship-to-shore communications also depended on that lost power source, so the crew could not even warn people in the harbor or the crews of any vessels that might lie in or sail into their path. The situation was dire. They had only minutes to make hundreds of observations, calculations, and decisions.

Coming into a harbor, a navigation crew must keep careful track of the ship's location, heading, and speed. This is called position fixing and is recorded on a chart, a sort of map of the ocean, continental shelf, harbor, and coastline. To fix the ship's position, as Hutchins described the procedure as it was followed in the 1990s, the navigator selects a charted landmark (e.g., a tower, lighthouse, or particularly tall building) and radios a sailor outside the bridge to find the landmark. The sailor visually locates the landmark and aims the hairline of a device called an alidade at it. The alidade hairline falls across an attached gyrocompass. The sailor then reports the angle formed by the line to the landmark and the line of the ship's direction. A sailor acting as recorder on the bridge writes down the angle numbers, and another acting as plotter uses a special protractor called a hoey to draw the angle on the chart. This entire procedure must be repeated every three minutes or less, with selected landmarks changing along the way.

When the steam engine failed in the approach to San Diego Harbor, so did the gyrocompass. Fixing the ship's position became a much more difficult series of computations. At the same time, the navigation crew had to locate a safe place to try to steer the ship as it coasted the several miles it would take to slow enough to drop anchor. Once a deep-enough target location was determined, they had to calculate the rudder angles necessary to get to that location without running aground and then issue rudder-angle commands to the helmsman far enough in advance of each turn to effect the proper change in direction. No one person could take all these readings, do all these calculations, and make all these decisions. Seconds mattered. There was no time to step back and design an efficient protocol; the crew scrambled to find a workable process through trial and error. Yet less than two hours after the engine failure, the ship was safely anchored in a side channel; no one was injured, and there was no damage (although the ship narrowly missed colliding with a buoy and a sailboat along the way). The navigation crew, the instruments they had that were still operational, and some tools not normally used in the fixing cycle (such as a handheld calculator) collectively averted what could have been a terrible accident with multiple casualties.

Hutchins counted sixty-six fix cycles during the crisis, with adaptations occurring more or less spontaneously until an expedient procedure was hit upon after the thirtieth cycle (1995, 322–23). Hutchins treats the entire navigation crew, their instruments, and the task space as the unit of cognitive analysis—in other words, as one cognitive system. That system, encountering an urgent novel problem, organized itself to respond. No single crew member designed an efficient response, but all participated in various ways in the production of it. Their collective project was only possible, however, because of the tools they had, tools that embodied the prior cognitive efforts of an untold number of human beings over generations. As Hutchins sees it, cognition had actually materialized in the tools, such as the harbor navigation chart and the practice of the fixing cycle. He spends several chapters prior to the analysis of the emergency discussing some of those tools and their development over the past five hundred years in great detail. In one chapter, he contrasts the navigational practices of European sailors (and their successors) with those of traditional Micronesian sailors, who rely on celestial position fixing, along with visual assessments of swells and currents and bird sightings. But whichever navigation practices, protocols, and instruments are used, the sailors engaging in and with them are themselves products of the cultural practices that generated them.

Cultures, according to Hutchins, can and should be seen as macro-level cognitive systems organized to provide general solutions to problems generations of ancestors have encountered. They can have cognitive properties that individual members of them do not have, Hutchins maintains (and demonstrates in his San Diego Harbor analysis). Furthermore, "the effects of group-level cognitive properties are not produced solely by structure internal to the individuals, nor are they produced solely by structure external to individuals. Rather, the cognitive properties of groups are produced by interaction between structures internal to individuals and structures external to individuals." He continues:

> All human societies face cognitive tasks that are beyond the capabilities of any individual member. Even the simplest culture contains more information than could be learned by any individual in a lifetime . . . , so the tasks of learning, remembering, and transmitting cultural knowledge are inevitably distributed. The performance of cognitive tasks that exceed individual abilities is always shaped by social organization of distributed cognition. Doing without a social organization of distributed cognition is not an option. The social organization that is actually used may be appropriate to the task or not. It may produce desirable properties or pathologies. It may be well defined and stable, or it may shift moment by moment; but there will be one whenever cognitive labor is distributed, and whatever one there is will play a role in determining the cognitive properties of the system that performs the task. (Hutchins 1995, 262)

Cultures are also systems for shaping the cognitive abilities of those born or brought into them. They impose a language, provide a set of artifacts and techniques, and train young people not only how to use those things but also how to approach the world more generally—for example, how to approach it quantificationally, or not. As noted above, brains do not simply learn cultural practices; they are literally, materially structured by many of them. If we leave out these macro-level cognitive systems, we will fail to understand fully the cognitive processes of any individual cognitive agent.

∵

Neither the extended mind model nor the model of distributed cognition precludes individuated deliberative processes located entirely within a single head (although from the perspective of the latter, such a thing is relatively rare). What they do challenge is the notion that deliberative processes are in essence totally separate from bodily movement, gesture, natural objects and artifacts, histories, and other human beings.[17] Abstract deliberation requires cognitive systems that extend across gestures and objects and often involve other people. Without extra-neural supports, people do not and to a great extent cannot manage complex cognitive processes. Insofar as average human beings can make complex calculations or generate logical trains of thought entirely "in the head," they employ practices, concepts, and words that they have learned from others and that they would never be able to devise on their own. It isn't just that *what* I think, believe, or feel is influenced by my surroundings and the people with whom I interact; it is that *how* I think, believe, and feel are thoroughly shaped by those surroundings and people over the course of my life, and especially during the earliest years when my neurological and physiological systems were forming in response to the living bodies of my relatives, the language they spoke, and the artifacts embedded in the practices that they brought me into over time. To isolate cognition in the head or even in the central nervous system is to misrepresent it, to attribute abilities to human beings that we do not have, and to fail to recognize abilities we do have or the crucial importance of them.

This is not to say we are somehow not really deliberating beings, only that we are deliberating beings in social, historical, and physical contexts and, as deliberating beings, largely inseparable from those contexts. Our bodies are not simply the media by which we take in perceptions and effect actions, a source of inputs and a tool for outputs; bodies are integral to cognition every step of the way. Our pasts and our cultural ancestors shape every aspect of our systems of cognition, as do the people around us. Individualistic models, whether from liberal political theory and economics or from updated versions in cybernetics, psychology, and cognitive science are not as good at accounting for cognitive or deliberative phenomena as other models might be. We are cultural products, so to speak, trained and equipped to couple ourselves to a wide range of cognitive assemblages.

IV. Rethinking Individuality

This chapter has explored several challenges to the idea that a human being is an individual—that is, some sort of clearly demarcated self-identical entity easily detachable from its surroundings. Contemporary findings in microbiology and genetics call into question any simple notion of human inside versus nonhuman (or other human) outside. Studies of affect and emotion suggest that my mind and my body are hardly distinguishable and that my body-mind is regularly affected by other humans' and possibly nonhumans' body-minds to such a degree that it isn't far-fetched to say that I sometimes feel others' feelings. Even my thoughts may not be best understood as located strictly in my head and may be more accurately described as shared in cognitive processes and systems that extend both through and well beyond this body in both space and time. It seems that what happens inside is also regularly happening outside and vice versa. And not only is the boundary between inside and outside porous and leaky; it seems the supposed inside disintegrates without a certain kind of reliable and supportive outside, bringing into question this whole inside/outside, identity/difference schema for understanding what human selfhood is.

There are plenty of reasons for distrusting what our Western philosophical tradition has taught us about ourselves. But the question remains: Practically, how can we depart from it? Where do we go from here? How can we think about selves without positing firm boundaries and fundamental separation?

Some of what I discovered in my meditation on ownership in chapter 5 could be of some help here. Land, for example, cannot be owned unless it has first been surveyed and parceled; boundaries must be established and officially recognized. But those actions and the boundaries and identities they establish do not reflect anything intrinsic to the land; the land is indifferent to them. Land is what it is because of the changes that constantly occur in, on, above, and below the ground, because of the cycles of seasons, the rotations and orbits of the earth and moon; the forces that make patterns of weather; rain, surface, and groundwater; the particular lives and deaths that shape and reshape its atmosphere, surfaces, and depths. Human beings may draw lines and call them boundaries, but the land knows no boundaries. The land knows only movements—movements that generate differences and relationships, the heres and the theres, the stuff of places.

Just as I am at one end of the couch and my dog is at the other, my garden is here and not at the South Pole. But "here" is not an individual, bounded piece of earth. Here is the patterned movement of sun, wind, water, of living and dying, generating and decaying, repeating and amplifying or dampening, dynamically, in these and not in other ways. These patterns and their histories give the garden its presence, which is never static, never the same, yet which is proximate and somewhat dependable within the temporality in which I encounter and participate in it. Even if there were no such thing as land ownership, no fixed boundaries indexed by lines on surveyors' maps, *here* would still not be *there*. And the difference is not simply relative to where I happen to stand. The Everglades is not the Badlands; the Sinai is not the Amazon. None of those places is precisely bounded, and none is static from moment to moment, much less year to year. But they are distinct places.

Similarly, even though I am not independent of other people and the world, I am still not my dog and not my couch. Is there some way to think about and experience people, including myself, as both unbounded and inseparable from the world and each other and at the same time as distinct? Instead of as a discrete and separate individual, can I experience my life and myself as a here in essential relation with but still distinct from a there, as a taking place? If I can think with the idea that the garden as the oscillating recurrence of patterns of relations, if that way of thinking does not feel nonsensical to me, then can I think with a similar idea of human beings?

For this, I knew I needed some new thinking tools.

After months of casting about, I came upon an alternative conception of individuality in a book called *Incomplete Nature* by neuro-anthropologist Terrence Deacon.[18] The title seemed to promise something other than bounded identities or static totality and, indeed, the book delivered. Deacon's thinking is much more oriented toward temporality, change, and process than toward constancy or sameness. In the course of a much larger argument about evolution, he uses the term *individual* to name a kind of event that occurs and recurs in a pattern that persists in relation to a set of environmental conditions (which of course are themselves patterned recurrences). Individuality, in his view, is not about being (what something is) so much as about occurring (how something happens). An individual is something that forms as a characteristic of certain sorts of complex recurring events—processes, he terms them, although, if I understand him correctly, they might be better termed organized or patterned change.

Deacon's analysis doesn't begin with systems or even with dynamic patterns, however; he advocates proceeding "from the bottom up." He starts, therefore, at the quantum level, where, he points out, there are no individuals; in fact, there are no things at all, just extremely rapidly oscillating energy fields. (And *extremely* doesn't begin to describe this speed; if we could perceive from the temporality in which these fields oscillate, the flex of a finger would seem to take eons.) A large portion of these oscillations cancel each other out statistically, resulting at a macro level in appearances of densities in relative stillness. Some of these events of density and stability occur and recur again and again, generating temporally prolonged patterns that sometimes generate, in turn, manifestations that can be identified as elements and compounds of elements. Human beings live and perceive at a (relatively) macro (and relatively temporally slow) level, where there are dense and stable things like trees and rocks. Such manifest, located, and roughly measurable things are, nevertheless, not static beings but organized or patterned occurrings, some of which recur more reliably and endure longer than others, but all of which are vulnerable to catastrophic disruption at any time. A rock resists completely eroding away for quite a while because the quantum attractions and repulsions that enable its recurring manifestation and the chemical bonds that keep its atoms and molecules in close proximity are stronger than the those of the gases and liquids bombarding it at a series of given moments. But the day will come. And the rock that we perceive as a whole, as a located and measurable thing, does nothing to protect itself, to keep itself together, to stave off that day. We might say that the rock is totally open to not-being-rock, both spatially and temporally.

So the rock happens as a thing, but it is not, as a thing, doing anything at all, happening in its repeated patterning in any way at all, to maintain itself as a thing; the various processes that give rise to its rockness do nothing to perpetuate that particular form or manifestation, that particular rock. Its component compounds and elements, atoms and molecules with their polarities and bonds, operate so as to recur as themselves, but their repeated happening contributes nothing toward a common future as this rock. On Deacon's view, therefore, the rock is a thing, but it is not an individual, whereas the tree is both.

For Deacon, to be an individual—or to occur as individuating—a thing must behave as a whole; or, more accurately, its component processes must happen together so as to resist the forces that could prevent their continuing recurrence as a whole. Each (sub-)process's occurrence feeds another or several other (sub-)processes. This systemic reciprocity constrains the whole set of (sub-)processes so that perturbation in one or some of them is countered by the others, producing a tendency to reestablish the same complex pattern of occurrence in disruption's aftermath. Thus, these recurring (sub-)processes happen together in ways that shield the whole system of recurrings against a total collapse of its organized repetition. A tree differs from a rock in many ways, but the way that matters here is that a tree's recurring processes will respond to disruptions in ways that promote the tree's continued existence as this particular thing. If a branch breaks off in a storm, an oak tree will grow bark over the exposed interior tissue, which reduces the possibility of further disruptions caused by invading bacteria and insects. If a giraffe eats some of its leaves, an acacia tree will immediately start producing ethylene, which makes the rest of its leaves taste bad and also signals, as a gas, to nearby acacia trees to produce ethylene prophylactically (Wohlleben 2016, 7). Trees' processes routinely respond to environmental events in ways that increase the recurrence not just of the component subprocesses immediately affected, but of the systemized patterns of processes as a whole tree—and in the case of the acacia tree of the grove as well.

In short, complex systems that generate resistances to certain disruptions or that, shall we say, "self-repair" when disruptions occur behave as if they were wholes (Deacon 2012, 465), even as they necessarily remain open to their environments and dependent upon them for inflows of energy and outflows of excess. But, Deacon emphasizes, this does not mean that trees have a desire to save themselves; he is not positing an intention or a will to systemic self-preservation, let alone any kind of life force. All he is saying is that some processes constrain spatially and temporally adjacent processes in ways that make continual recurrence of a system of processes highly probable and reestablishment of recurring patterns possible (and even more or less probable) after disruption. The systems these processes constitute—trees, for example—behave in some ways as wholes, whereas things like rocks do not. Deacon says these things that behave as wholes thereby "individuate"; their recurrent mutual patterning (not just their atoms' and molecules' polarities and chemical bonds) tends to keep them functioning together even in the face of environmental onslaught. Whereas the rock is totally open to the possibility of not-being-rock, the tree is not totally open to not-being-tree. Obviously there are serious limits to what any tree can withstand without total systemic collapse, but trees do close themselves off partially and systemically from many sorts of commonplace disruptions. No system is totally closed—nature is incomplete, as Deacon's title states—but those who fit Deacon's definition of "individual" include mechanisms that allow selective closures geared to risks typical of the environments to which they are also selectively open and upon which they depend.

My dog and I and the rosebushes outside the window are indefinitely recurring events of individuating; each one of us is a complex of processes that, among other things, tend to perpetuate our recurrence as interrelated wholes. We have no hard boundaries; we have, among the many repeating patterns of organization that constitute us, processes that regulate influx and outflux from and to the environmental processes in which we happen. If the environment lacks oxygen, the processes that generate this body will degrade. If the environment lacks patterned shifts in light and sound over time, the processes that generate these sensory experiences will degrade. And what if the environment lacks other living bodies that evince emotions and thought? Does it not make sense that the processes of feeling and thinking will degrade—not cease entirely perhaps, but become increasingly disordered?

Deacon's work helps me twist free the binary of inside/outside and of me/not-me. His terminology and explications of processes and organizations of reciprocally repeating processes give me a way to think of myself as a different being from the beings that are my dog and the couch without forcing me to think that I am utterly separate from and independent of those other beings, let alone all other beings. As systems of processes, we all interact, and we need to interact to continue being the systems of processes that we are.

Yet it still does seem like there is some kind of inside, doesn't it, or not really an inside so much as a feeling of a gap that cannot be spanned? There seems to be here, where this being now taking place happens, a feeling of loneliness, of a differing that cannot be surpassed. For all that is shared and circulated among us, in any given moment there still seems to be something that remains just here or just there, not merely a difference in angle of perspective but some unique quality of distinct experience here . . . or there. It is this feeling, this seeming, I believe, that makes us want to say that even when we are thinking or feeling exactly the same thing, there are still two thoughts or two feelings, not just one that is shared. How can I take account of that experience, so strong that it almost reaches the threshold of conviction, without positing hard-and-fast boundaries around isolated minds?

I found some help in the work of Peter Godfrey-Smith. If the picture he paints in his book *Metazoa* is accurate, he asserts, "then the storms within cells, the threading together of countless cells' activity, the perturbed rhythms of their electrical breathing, and their large-scale coordination *are* the stuff of mind. This is what we are to identify with—not to think that our minds are a *consequence* of this, but that our minds *are* such activities" (2020, 260). An imaginative leap is required, he says: "The imaginative leap is to the idea that we are not *extra*, not additions to the physical world, but aspects of its workings. We are *of* these activities rather than merely tied to them or made by them" (260–61). Yes, of course there is experience that is just yours and not mine, not the dog's nor the horse's. That experience "is the activity described above as felt *from the inside*. It is the way things feel for a system that has the right kind of activity in it. Experience is what it's like to *be* that system" (261). Thoughts, feelings, energy, and matter of all sorts can be shared across the different complex patterns of processes that are different being-wholes. Such things are not private possessions any more than is language, as Ludwig Wittgenstein made so clear. I can see your point, finish your sentence, feel your joy and your sadness, breathe your breath, share your microbiome. But I can never, ever *be* you. The individuating occurring that is me feels itself in its individuating.

Whether I will continue to think with Deacon or Godfrey-Smith or not, they have shown me an alternative to the individuality of personhood—a personhood that so much evidence examined through the course of this chapter has undermined. The existence of an alternative, along with the unsettling of self as ownership in chapter 5, tells me that there is life beyond personhood, whatever shape it may eventually take. The final chapter of this book turns from the task of reducing the power of personhood to define and order my life to the task of imagining how I might think, experience, and live otherwise. It is meant only to spark the imaginations of readers as they find themselves freed to whatever degree from personhood, not to offer a definitive ethical prescription; any operative ethos is a collective creation, a historical and social formation, not the product of a single author. I aim only to offer some elaboration on the ethical ideas that have begun to emerge for me through this long project.

[CHAPTER SEVEN]

Imagining Life After Personhood

Ten years ago, I began this book with a story about how I came to feel that bearing the responsibilities of personhood was untenable and, indeed, increasingly intolerable. What spoke in that beginning was a person, albeit an agonizing, failing person; it was a person who knew that no matter how much effort one might make, it was not possible to be a good person in this world. The question that arose out of that impossibility was whether another story was possible, whether it was possible to live otherwise than as a person. Was I doomed to be a failed person, or could a human being become something other than a person in this time and place and still lead an ethical life, whatever that might mean?

I believed then that the answer was yes. My philosophical training had convinced me that personhood, modern moral subjectivity in the Euro-American world and elsewhere, had to be a historical formation; it could not be a metaphysical given or a logical necessity. Furthermore, even as I was spewing out the very worst of the feelings of personhood, I knew that the fact that I could so objectify them in narrative prose meant that my life already exceeded the structures that generated them. The real question was how to get free of their definitive power.

The first step was acknowledging how thoroughly "personified" my life was, how deeply and fundamentally people in this culture and economy are subjectified as persons. While there was nothing described in the story that I told in this book's introduction that was not really me—I really did wail over succumbing to Dominion Energy by using the electric dryer; I really did worry over whether to own a Prius or a Subaru; and I really did feel horrible about the US invasion of Iraq, regardless of whether that made any sense—still, describing those feelings and their behavioral expressions sometimes to the point of the comedic and ridiculous not only was possible because I already had some emotional distance from them but it also worked to estrange me from them a little more. And that was an important thing to do.

I also hoped that some readers would recognize some of their own thoughts and feelings in those descriptions and thereby experience a similar sort of estrangement from their moral assumptions. It was a step toward making personhood an object that could be delineated and reckoned with.

The second step was more analytic. If personhood was not necessary and inevitable—if it was not the only way to live as a human being—then it had to be a historical formation. And if personhood was a historical formation, there had to be traces of those formative processes and what powered them. How did it come about that we think we are and should be persons rather than whatever it was our ancestors thought they were and/or should be? What forces coalesced or clashed as personhood formed itself? Who and what did those clashes and outcomes benefit?

In taking up that genealogical task, I was already beginning to speak in a voice that was not quite coincident with that of personhood, no longer grounded in it, though still in its orbit and bound by the pull of its gravity. Now, ten years and six chapters later, having traced the history and contingency of personhood and its deep entanglement with European colonization and industrialization, race and sex oppression, exploitation of the global working class (with criminalization as its flip side), and capitalistic commodification of damned near everything, it is time to give voice to what is not or is no longer personhood, to an incipient "otherwise," and to see what practices or lifeways might take shape. It is time to imagine and invent.

For a long time, I believed that the "otherwise" that this final chapter would explore and sketch out would offer a central place for responsibility. Bearing the responsibility of personhood was intolerable, but I was not looking to jettison responsibility altogether. I've never stopped wanting ecological devastation and injustice to end; I've never stopped doing whatever I could think of to bring that end closer to realization. And I believed that addressing devastation and injustice required taking responsibility for taking care, for creating change, for instituting better systems and policies and forming better communities. It did not occur to me for a long time that caring, working, creating, and building might grow out of anything other. And, so, I imagined that out of a genealogical critique of personhood, with its possessiveness and individualism and claims to sovereignty, a nonpersonal ethos of responsibility, a collective or collaborative responsibility perhaps, would emerge and would motivate, compel, and fuel the work necessary to solve the problems we face. Unlike sovereignty, individuality, and ownership, I thought responsibility could survive the death of personhood and, suitably reworked, serve as an important element in a different way of living, severally and communally. But now I'm not so sure.

It turns out that *responsibility* is something of a latecomer of a word. It has its origins in—what else?—legal proceedings. The accused must answer, must respond to the charge, must give some sort of account. Being responsible or answerable in a broader context does not come into general use in English and French until the last decades of the eighteenth century, with revolutionaries' proclamations that government must answer to them: The only legitimate government is a creature of the people, not of royals and aristocrats! Responsibility became the name of a kind of political ideal powerful enough to motivate armed struggle. The move from the courtroom to the barricades and battlefields altered the concept of responsibility somewhat, making it something that should occur in the normal course of things rather than only when some breach of normality has occurred; the government should be perpetually answerable to the people. (For more detail, see Vogelmann 2018, 6–9.)

As this brief history shows, the concept of responsibility does not come out of any ethical or theological tradition; it is a late Western legal and political concept. Its formative context was public contestation. Its center of gravity lay not with those being held responsible but with those doing the holding. It is bound up with the exercise of juridical forms of power. Only later did the idea come into being that one could voluntarily assume responsibility for something or someone in the present and into the future, only after modern moral personhood, forensic personhood, established itself (along with social contract theory and capitalism, I might add). Although I have not undertaken a full genealogical study of responsibility, these facts give me reason to believe that responsibility is deeply allied with personhood and may not be extricable from the individualism and ownership that personhood entails and the sovereignty to which it aspires. Therefore, I leave responsibility aside.

Instead, in the first two sections of this chapter, I will sketch out some affective and experiential openings toward an "otherwise" to lives shaped by personhood. Then, in section III, I will explore some possibilities for actually living (as/in) otherwise, which I will call an ethos of active belonging. In the fourth and fifth sections, I will address several hesitations or problems that an ethos of active belonging might inspire or seem to present. I will finish the chapter, and the book, with a meditation on a contrast between self-sacrifice and self-enactment.

My purpose in this chapter is not to argue for the rightness of a particular way of living, although my biases are evident, but simply to show that personhood is truly, concretely, and practically optional for our lives—not just in some fantastic future but right now in this world. It need not define us. In fact, for people who share my old ethical anguish and people who find this book's genealogical story plausible, it cannot define us, not completely, anymore. We are already moving toward something different. No one can say what that will eventually be, but all those who find ourselves in the midst of this movement can (and do and will) contribute to the new patterns that emerge. This chapter, then, is my contribution to our creative living beyond personhood.

I. Conspicuous Dependence

For most of my life I have understood myself and other human beings as persons and have tried to live in accordance with that understanding. But in these pages and in my thinking over these last ten years, I have become less and less able to do so. It is not so much that I have stopped believing in personhood—belief is not really the issue—but that, as its contingencies and investments and uses were systematically exposed, personhood has lost the power it once had to give structure and meaning to awarenesses of self, other, and world. Individuality and ownership no longer are central. Control and mastery have lost their allure, and the fact that they elude me is not cause for great fear or shame. Not only am I not able to be a good person; I am unable to be a person—self-contained, independent, autonomous, sovereign. But whereas before that could feel like failure, now I find that I am also just unable to worry over it. My energy is not flowing toward enactments of personhood.

Where does it flow, then? How do I find myself in self-awareness apart from personhood? So far, I have said that I'm not that, or I fall short of that, or I exceed that, but those are all just negative characterizations that are still bound tight to personhood. As self-awareness moves at least some distance away from personhood, how might it articulate its being and becoming?

The situation I find myself in now, given what I've undergone and learned in these ten years, is not exactly the opposite of, but is far from the autonomy that characterizes personhood at its strongest. Autonomy suggests a kind of individual sovereignty and presupposes that an individual has the ability to think—deliberate and judge—independently of others and of material contingencies. But chapter 6 rendered that kind of cognitive individuality profoundly dubious. Deliberating and judging depend on other mental processes; instead of input (perception), processing (deliberating, calculating, judging), and output (action), there is ongoing noticing, remembering, attending, directing, perspective shifting, manipulating, connecting, and disconnecting—forming and re-forming systems of cognition accomplished by elements of those systems in relation with each other. And all those processes depend on myriads of unthinking processes.

Indeed, the most conspicuous fact of my being is its dependence on dynamic processes that generate and sustain networks of others both human and nonhuman, not only for thinking but for existing at all. It isn't just that I have needs that must be met in order for me to thrive and that meeting those needs involves extracting certain items from the world, as Locke's Indian labors to appropriate a deer from out of the "stock of nature." Needs are episodic and therefore stimulate us to take specific actions to satisfy them. Dependence is not episodic, and no specific acts will ever put even a momentary stop to it. Dependence is a constant condition of my being, and it involves far more than just a few items in the world.

Just to take one of countless possible examples, consider water. I don't just need to appropriate some water from the stock of nature to quench my thirst and boil the beans I took from the garden this morning. I *am* largely water, and continuing to be me requires that water keep coursing through my tissues all the time. And this doesn't just happen in streams through my digestive tract and circulatory system or even in oozes and trickles around my cells. Water's moving is especially important inside each and every one of my cells (whether human, bacterial, fungal, or what have you). Water molecules darting around randomly inside cell membranes keep the various organelles and other molecules from clumping; they keep the interior of the cell in constant frenzied motion, colliding with cellular objects every ten-trillionth of a second (Godfrey-Smith 2020, 27). And that undirected frenzy is absolutely necessary for cellular life; without all that more or less random agitation, no cell could function. My life literally depends, from one ten-trillionth of a second to the next, on the movement of water. Every life that we know of, from the tiniest bacterium to the biggest of blue whales, depends on ongoing molecular frenzies of water. And if any of these lives are to persist, this planet must have water flowing across and beneath its soil and over its ocean beds, and falling from the sky, and coursing through the cells of plankton and plants and worms and birds and everything else. "Water is life," proclaimed the anti-pipeline protestors at Standing Rock; "WATER IS LIFE" say the placards so many of us have carried in marches ever since. And the same could be said of oxygen and carbon dioxide, of sunlight and soil, of chloroplasts and mycelia. These things are not tools or resources that people can master and own; we are their ongoing creation. In all sorts of ways, every nanosecond, our lives depend on them. And it's not just that each of these things must exist in some quantity for us living beings to exist. We don't just need them to be present. We need them to move, to circulate, to flow, and to flow through each other, transforming each other again and again in the process. Sunlight is transformed into vitamin D in skin or sugars in bean leaves. Oxygen is transformed into carbon dioxide as it is released from hemoglobin and passed through animal cells that are ripping apart carbohydrate molecules to release the energy of their chemical bonds to power muscle movements and brain waves. We human-holobiontic happenings are among the shapes and patterns those circulations generate. We don't use them. They project us and project through us and beyond us.

Reasoning and, in fact, self-aware processes in general are actually rare events in those dynamic patternings. Moreover, such processes are inessential, for the most part, to their repetitions and reconfigurations. The events, processes, and systems of the cosmos are almost completely indifferent to occurrences of thinking. Most of what really matters as far as the cosmos is concerned happens without any thought at all. Cells—even brain cells—don't have to think to give order to flows of water, oxygen, carbohydrates, enzymes, hormones, and so on. Worms don't have to cogitate to burrow through layers of soil, find food, and transform that food into movement and castings that serve as food for plants; mycelial fungi don't have to deliberate to reorganize their networks of hyphae when new food sources are found—which is not to say that their progress through life is fully preprogrammed or mechanical, either. Choices are made, somehow, of which way to go or grow, but those choices don't appear to arise through the deliberative mental processes humans have so valorized. Thinking is a real oddity, when you think about it.

I *do* think, although I don't have to think about thinking in order to think; it just happens, like it happens that fishes swim. I notice a recently opened morning glory; it suddenly occurs to me that I forgot to drop off a library book; I dream of showing a friend that I can fly by taking off and soaring around. Even when I wonder and question and try to find an explanation or an answer—in other words, even when I engage in very focused, goal-oriented thinking—the thinking happens without any supervisor in charge of it. Thinking is a process that brainy systems undergo, a process like diffusion, osmosis, digestion. There is no obvious reason to set off thinking from other processes like respiring or crystallizing or evaporating and proclaim it especially valuable and important, let alone declare it the mark of the most important and valuable way of being in the universe. The happening of thinking is one sort of pattern among many, and the holobiontic systems in which it occurs are just one (or a few) sort(s) of being among countless others.

Those who are persons will find that assertion outrageous. Persons are not one way of being among others. Persons are more important than anything else that is or ever was! There are persons—deliberators, actors, and owners; and there are things—the unthinking, the acted upon, the owned. In Rome, as we saw in chapter 1, personhood drew a dividing line between those who could own and those who could be owned. It still does. Personhood entails that all that is not defined as person be of lower status—own-able, manipulable, exploitable, consumable, available, and answerable to persons. Elevated status is an essential feature of personhood; whatever does not have such a status is not a person. But elevated status is not an essential feature of *Homo sapiens*, human being, or self-awareness. People can be one sort of being among trillions—among and not above. Thinking beings can find ourselves in a flowing awareness of the vastness of the cosmos and its temporality, of its overwhelming dynamism and complexity beyond comprehension, of the intricacies and complexities of even the smallest of unthinking beings and the entanglement of myriads of processes that have gone on without thought for eons, and yet feel no humiliation, let alone outrage, at all. Thinking—patterns of processes that support, undergo, channel, and regulate meaning flows—need be deemed no less wondrous for being utterly contingent and dependent and no less precious for being nothing more than a minor event on one tiny pebble of a planet in the vast ever-eventuating of the cosmos.

Rather than humiliation or outrage, I find myself experiencing relief, appreciation, and even exhilaration. As these feeling responses occur and recur, patterns of self-other-world have begun to reconfigure, generating different attunements and sensibilities, further diminishing the power of ownership, self-enclosure, and autonomy. Some description of those affective occurrences may help in this attempt at articulating an otherwise.

First, a great sense of relief attends a profound awareness of cosmic indifference. There is so little cause to fret. The cosmos absolutely does not need me to fuss over it. Nor does the galaxy, nor the solar system, nor the planet. Stars will burst or implode; photons will streak along at the speed of light; atoms will gain and lose electrons, tectonic plates will grind and heave, and lava will flow. I need not supervise.

And a good thing, too. For the most part, even if I fully understood them, I could neither initiate nor terminate the processes that generate the cosmos or even Earth's biosphere from moment to moment. As fleshy sometime self-awareness, I affect or direct processes only in small and local ways. For example, I can reduce the rate of increase in the population of anerobic bacteria in my compost bins and encourage the increase of aerobic bacteria and fungi by stirring and turning the yard waste and kitchen scraps to introduce more oxygen to the mixture. But I can't actually make compost; I can't turn kitchen scraps and yard waste into fertile soil all by myself. Like cellular structures that can only nudge torrents of molecular flows this way or that, with the knowledge and tools that I have and the gestures that I can set in motion, I can bring forces to bear, but I cannot generate those forces or their effects, nor can I put a final stop to them. My actions channel flows in relation to other flows, pushing processes into proximity so that they may augment or offset one another. I, one extremely complex and systematized entanglement of processes that includes meaning flows, affect other entangled processes. I flow among flows, a tiny ripple in a cosmic ocean.

As a child, I sometimes comforted myself with such thoughts of the vast cosmos and its indifference. After a day of missteps, failure, punishment, the anger or disappointment of adults, I would lie in bed in the dark and tell myself: "Over my head is the roof; over the roof are the clouds; over the clouds is the moon; over the moon are the stars of the galaxy; and over the stars is outer space. Way out there nobody cares what you did wrong today." And I would feel better, not worse, for being relatively insignificant. My guilt and responsibilities were limited to here and now, this day, this place, these people. Whatever burden I bore was neither universal nor eternal. Turning away from personhood and its valorization of rationality and autonomy, and embracing my dependence and limits, offers me the same sort of relief.

Relief isn't the strongest feeling that occurs, however. At times there is also a vague sensation of sinking as if sliding under water, of no longer viewing the world from above. Along with that feeling, a memory has repeatedly pressed for attention: It is forty years ago. I am with a group of people being led through Kentucky's Mammoth Cave. Deep underground, the tour guide tells us to stand still and prepare to experience utter and absolute darkness far more profound than night ever is anywhere on the surface of the earth. He then shuts off all the lights. Eyes wide open, I see nothing, nothing at all no matter how I strain. One might think that the result would be a disorienting distancing from the world, a sense of loss or suspension in an abyss. But it isn't like that at all. Instead of distance, I sense full presence, as if the world were right at my eyeballs, touching my retinas, pressing against me at every point. I can get no distance at all. Deep under the earth's surface, I felt more *in* the world than ever before, complete contact without respite. It wasn't that I felt imprisoned and immobile; I still felt perfectly free to move in every way (although the guide cautioned us not to). It wasn't that motile possibilities had disappeared, only distance. Streams of photons colliding with retinas allow us the illusion that we move through empty space, around and among objects. The absence of photons was the absence of the empty space between me and the things of the world. The world was everywhere, and I was right there in it, with it, inseparable from it.

Maybe these descriptions make it seem that the feelings attending them are uncomfortable or even frightening—as passive sliding underwater or concentrated staring into subterranean darkness might be—but, instead, they are warm, more like envelopment and safety. I am not actually underwater or under megatons of rock, places outside my daily life. This *is* my daily life. I am where I belong, but I feel this place now not as a surface on which I stand, rising up to look down and survey, but as a thickness and depth through which I move, touching, smelling, tasting, flesh and bones vibrating to sound and light as their waves flow around and through me. The world in which I take place enshrouds and permeates me, but more: It supports, sustains, and generates me moment by moment. I happen in this world, and I cannot happen without it. This sense of dependence does not feel like a state of impotence; on the contrary, it feels like home, where nourishment and support give strength.

We could focus on the vulnerability that such dependence entails, as have many writers over the past few decades who have explored vulnerability as a basis for developing an understanding of human interaction and relationships and for building a notion of ethics different from the theoretical traditions growing out of Aristotle, Kant, and nineteenth- and twentieth-century Utilitarianism. I will not follow that path here. Although there is much that is important and valuable in that body of work, there are drawbacks. Emphasizing vulnerability involves foregrounding the possibility of pain, harm, violation, betrayal, and death in order subsequently to think about trust and care. But before we are vulnerable to forces that can hurt or even destroy us, we first of all have to *be*. Before there can be vulnerability, there must be viability. Feeling in the world as movement with and through the currents of the world is what vitality feels like. Vulnerability is nothing in itself; it is just the ever-present possibility that vitality might diminish.

Viability comes from the world—cosmic, biospheric, and social processes—that give rise to the local processes that are my living body, including the flows of self-awareness that occur in its midst some of the time. That world and those processual flows generate this tiny region where I can and do live and where my self-aware feelings and thinking and actions take place. This region is not isolated from anything, although it has varying proximity to and entanglement with other regions of self-aware and non-self-aware patterning events. Whatever a good life might be for any human being, it will happen in the midst of these shifting proximities and entanglements, in the temporality of action-generated recognition and self-aware confluence, influence, effluence, and affluence.

In addition to relief and vital belonging, there is a third feeling, a rush of exhilaration and release. The image that comes to mind is of ripping my shirt open and baring my chest to the wind—full on contact. In that fleshy fantasy, an old, almost-forgotten anger falls away with the fabric. I remember the day that I acquired that anger, the day that I was closed up inside a body with only a few paltry portals for external data entry. It was the second grade. My teacher Miss Burleson told us pupils that we each had five senses. She listed them. I was sure she was wrong, not because I thought I had six or seven senses, but because the whole schema of discrete sensory portals linking my (interior) self to the (exterior) world seemed totally wrong. That was not how the world occurred for me, not how I found myself in the world. Mentally, I sputtered in vociferous protest, though I said precisely nothing. I didn't know what to say. After school, I racked my brain for a different account of how I knew the world. But I couldn't come up with one. I didn't know how. I was only seven, after all. I was no match for this metaphysical onslaught.

Much of my life since second grade has been lived from behind my eyes and inside a skin that I wear like clothes. Miss Burleson's lesson has been reinforced in every conceivable way by spokespeople in every institution I ever inhabited or encountered—school, church, media and advertising, the medical profession, financial experts, computer geeks—a huge chorus of cacophony that somehow sounds the same note: Each human self is enclosed in a body; the body extracts data that the hidden self then pieces together to think, feel, and compose commands to send back to the body to implement. That is, until our rational spirits ascend from the fleshly cave into the light of disembodied truth (or some really sophisticated computer hardware).

But in that memory of Mammoth Cave and in my garden reaching through leaves and vines for peppers and beans, things happen otherwise. When height and distance disappear, the parts of my body that feel most alive (besides my eyes, as always) are the sides of my face and neck, across the fronts of my shoulders, my chest, and down both my arms. The feeling is like a hum, an almost electric vibrancy, a dynamism of full contact full force forward. I wonder if this is what it felt like, millions of years before books and philosophies, when naked primates first began to stand on their back feet and reach, back when standing and reaching were new. I wonder if this is what ordinary life would always have felt like if I had never been to the second grade.

It is remarkable, when you stop to consider it, how much energy it takes to sequester a seven-year-old behind a wall of flesh and keep her there for the rest of her life—how much experience must be discounted, how much ignorance must be maintained, how much numbing is required. The "knowledge" that I sample the world through five sorts of perceptual data ports—maybe seven if you count proprioceptual and interoceptual circuitry—has to be kept ever before me, at least pre-reflectively, lest I begin to attend to humming surfaces of differential awareness that might suggest an ever-occurring otherwise.

Those humming surfaces attract my attention more and more, especially in late summer when I do a lot of harvesting in my always untidy and by that point severely overgrown garden; for about an hour every morning, I search bushes and vines for beans, tomatoes of all sizes, and jalapeño peppers, extending my hands among the leaves of those plants and the okra stalks and asparagus ferns they have overgrown and the squash and Malabar spinach vines that have in turn entwined with and overgrown them, feeling for the textures of pods and skins. In this effort, my eyes don't register distance so much as depth and variations in movement, shadow, and color. They are in service to my hands. Fingers in front, eyes farther back for wider-angled guidance, muscled back and bony feet behind for balanced propulsion. Where am "I" in all this? I jut into the surrounding world foremost with my fingers, hands, arms, front upper torso, cheeks, and eyes.

I don't have to think much, but thinking happens anyway, and on these days it usually happens to fasten onto the wonder of what I am doing—in particular the wonder of coordination between eyes and arms and fingers—and the wonder of bean and okra pod growth from one day to the next (evidence of the mind-boggling speed of water molecules, energy conversion, and cell division second to second). I appreciate the coordinated precision of a bumblebee's flight path into one squash blossom after another and the quiet patience of the praying mantis who lives among the pole beans, its head turning toward me only when I mistake its long green abdomen for a bean pod. The processes that are me and that are characteristic of beings like me are incomprehensibly complex and amazing, but so are the other processes occurring beyond the tips of my fingers and the soles of my boots. And all those processes are vital not only to me but to each other. If one is precious, they all are. These intermingling flows of light and meaning and flesh and breath and water may well involve multiple distinct awarenesses and selves, some of which say "I," but all of which are conspicuously dependent.

II. A Nonpersonal Story About How (and Where) Selves Happen

Ever since Locke, the standard account of human selves in world has been that selves are persons who receive sensations (or impressions, information, data, or qualia) from their surroundings, cogitate over them, and then tell their body parts what to do about them. This story has varied through the centuries, especially with the rise in the twentieth century of cybernetics, robotics, and cognitive sciences, but the basic input-output model has persisted. Consequently, there is always a gap between a person and the world, a gap bridged by the receptive and active body with its sensors and what I've recently learned to call its effectors. By contrast, living mostly in and as my face, chest, arms, and hands is living molecule to molecule, surface to surface with the world; there is no distance or gap, just the press of difference.

There are other accounts of selves in the world, though, and I found what felt like a more appropriate one in Peter Godfrey-Smith's writings. Godfrey-Smith is an Australian philosopher of science and an avid scuba diver whose sensibilities are profoundly shaped by worlds where beings have quite variable and often indefinite surfaces and where notions of empty space between them are hard to maintain.[1] His underwater awarenesses led him, and then me, to Fred Keijzer and his colleagues' very provocative work on the evolutionary origins of nervous systems. Taking up a phrase coined by Nicholas Holland (2003), they propose and develop what they call the skin brain thesis, or SBT (Keijzer et al. 2013). They suggest that the first nervous systems developed as conductive cells in contractive tissue, enabling coordinated locomotion in tiny multicellular organisms. Precambrian sea creatures had no brains, of course, nor had they any need for abstract thought. What they did need, increasingly as the number of cells in their makeup increased, was some way to move around, or, as Marc van Duijn, Fred Keijzer, and Daan Franken put it, to react "to the environmental dispersal of metabolic requirements" (Duijn et al. 2006). Specifically, because sufficient food wasn't coming to them, they needed to go to the food. Just tumbling around randomly on the ocean floor wasn't getting the job done. They did better to crawl or slither or something. Sheets of contractile tissue—muscle or proto-muscle or just sheets of a kind of contractible cell called myoepithelium (the last of which humans and others have in or around sweat, salivary, and breast glands)—were useful for locomotion, but they could be made even better if their contracting was extensively coordinated, giving them rhythmic traction along surfaces like sand and rocks or maybe the ability to propel themselves through water in just one direction for a second or two. The ones who developed these abilities of course got more food and were statistically likely to make more babies. Eventually there were animals with these conductive cells throughout their contractile tissues inching along the ocean floor and squirting through the depths. These animals had (and have) neural nets, excitable, conductive cells dispersed throughout muscle tissue. And not only did these nets enable them to move in coordinated and metabolically effective ways; they also enabled them to feel the surfaces they slid through or over. This sensory development would have been concomitant with the development of contractile cellular coordination; to work effectively, coordinated change in tissue either at or just beneath the organism's surface—the contraction and relaxation of the tissue that produces whole-body movement—would have to be distinguishable from changes in the tissue brought on by something other than the coordination effort itself, something such as a rough spot on the seabed or collision with an obstacle (see Keijzer 2015, 324). For moving to continue, then, a new pattern of coordination had to be initiated; the contractile tissues had to be able to alter the rhythm of their contractions in response to their milieu. Coordinated movement thus entailed sensation of both the muscle sheet and the surface of contact in their differing. Keijzer calls this emergent system the animal sensorimotor organization (ASMO), and he argues that it is not best understood on the now-traditional model of sensation as input through special receptors and action as output through special effectors. Instead, the body itself functioned as a sensing device independent of input or external sensors. The organism differentiated between external surfaces structures directly, not with sensory input as a precondition (Keijzer 2015, 325). In sum, as he and his collaborators put it, "early nerve nets did not evolve as a clumsy way to connect sensors to effectors, but, rather, as a dedicated structure for organizing a new kind of effector" (Keijzer et al. 2013). The world was felt immediately by naked muscle and skin as it moved. Feeling, experience, began at this dual surface, this interface, this frontier at the convergence of the one being and the other.

Godfrey-Smith calls such accounts of the development of nervous systems and awareness "action-shaping models" (in contrast to input-output models). In action-shaping models, he explains, the "central idea is that rather than mediating sensory input and behavioral output, the first nervous systems came to exist as solutions to a problem of pure coordination within the organism—the problem of how to coordinate the micro-acts of parts of the body into the macro-acts of the whole" (2016, 71). His interest in and knowledge of octopuses leads him to reject any account of nervous system evolution that sets the brain apart from the rest of the body. It seems much more plausible to imagine that as a large nervous system evolved to coordinate a large body (and to distinguish between experiences resulting from that coordination and experiences resulting from environmental encounters), "the result is so much neural complexity that eventually other capacities arise as by-products, or relatively easy additions to what the demands of action-shaping have built" (72). In the garden, I feel that *I happen* in among the leaves, and maybe that is because I do.

Hundreds of millions of years have passed since those first tiny wormy things stretched and pulled their way across seabed sand. At some point, conductive tissue developed specialized neural cells, which then developed axons and dendrites, elongations that enabled conductivity across non-contractile tissues so that sheets of muscle not directly adjacent to each other could engage in coordinated movement. Thus it became possible for organisms to operate new appendages like legs, fins, and jaws, and coordinated movement became extremely complex, requiring astounding amounts of signaling to occur at lightning speed.[2] Those elongated neurons could also be buried deeper in larger organisms' flesh, away from the body's surface, so that they were much more protected from disruption and harm.[3] Eventually, some of the nervous systems coordinating all that movement benefited from a bit of spatial concentration, and brains were born. Not all of them were in heads, though, by any means; the anatomical locations, as well as the degree of braininess, differed as did the bodily structures to be coordinated. For example, an octopus has about the same number of neurons as a dog does, but they are very differently distributed, and while a dog has but one brain, scientists disagree over whether an octopus has one brain or nine, one in each of the eight tentacles and one in the ring around its mouth.

Sometime over all those millions of years, some parts of some of those many and varied nervous systems, with or without brains, did develop into more specialized sensors that could signal directly to more specialized receptor regions. Human bodies have retinas, for instance, that send signals to the back parts of the brain. And we also have brain and spinal cord regions that send signals to specific body parts, too (our "effectors"). But these developments and formations remain in the service of the body's activity in direct contact and interaction with its immediate surroundings. Despite the importance of these specialized circuits in large bodies, Fred Keijzer, Marc van Duijn, and Pamela Lyon do not think their functioning should be the sole or even primary model for how we think about neurological or mental activity; they believe that there are so many reasons to question the explanatory power of the input-output model that it must be carefully scrutinized and critiqued, and other models must be evaluated for their perhaps superior explanatory power (Keijzer et al. 2013).

Keijzer et al.'s evolutionary story lends scientific support to the idea that the body is not a possession of the self but is, in its dynamic patterning, the occasion (along with what psychologists call the "peripersonal space," the region of a body's surroundings in which immediate physical action is possible) of the self's very occurring. Godfrey-Smith insists that the self is neither the body's possessor nor its product. The self *is* this spatiotemporally occurring and recurring.[4] Furthermore, this body-self's recurring depends upon influent and effluent water, energy, air, light, meaning—flows whose fluctuating specificities give its recurring processes their changing character and potentialities, even as its constituent processes draw on those flows to reinstate their dynamic reciprocal patterning in the midst of perturbation and disruption. This dynamic reciprocal patterning functions as a whole (as an individual in Deacon's sense)—as a self—but it is not encased inside something that is distinct to it. Self-awareness occurs in immediate contact with differences, *right where it feels like it occurs.*

III. An Ethos of Active Belonging

Jutting into the thickness of leafy bean stalks, probing and fingering long slender pods and occasionally a mantid's abdomen, I am reminded of how Leanne Betasamosake Simpson characterizes her people's (the Anishinaabe's) historical experience of land. In the absence of landownership, the places where one tribe's territory met another was not a boundary where one parcel ended and the other began; instead, Simpson tells us, it was a region of intensified diplomacy, communication, ritual, and ceremony.[5] It was where difference was felt and made, and, thus, in a sense it was where each culture was most overtly expressive of itself as a whole. The analogy between bodily surfaces and contiguous lands is a stretch, I know, but I still like the thought that the skin of my palm grasping the walnut as I pull it from the tree is engaging in intensified communication, negotiation, and diplomacy with the walnut skin. Surface to surface, density to density, undergoing the play of difference, is how I happen in the world, and how other beings happen too. And I am aware, as Simpson is, that how things happen can sometimes depend on the stories we tell.

To the extent that this other story of thinking, attunement, and awareness takes hold, the question that opened this book—How can I be a good person?—seems irrelevant, even nonsensical. What says "I" here and now is not an owner of thought and action, not an individual cognizer independent of others, and certainly not a sovereign master of anything at all. No being can be good at being what it is not. From this emerging perspective, what says "I" here and now is not a person; it may be better understood as a dynamic, ongoing holobiontic event occurring in a world that itself takes place with and as its constituent processes. If we feel sufficiently moved by that characterization or something close to it, the question becomes: How might these selves—these holobiontic wholes in the midst of and dependent upon so many other processual beings and nonbeings—live good lives?

Dare we take a cue from the ethos of personhood? Living a good life as a person meant affirming and enacting personhood, engaging self-reflectively in individuated practices of calculation, deliberation, judging, and owning all the while respecting other deliberating, judging beings—mostly if not exclusively human beings—and their rights of individual ownership. All these practices together marked the domain of ethical life. Although it is dangerous to take personhood as a model for ethical life, maybe a way to start thinking about living otherwise is to imagine how to live so as to affirm holobiontic patterning taking place in and dependent upon networks of systems of patterned processes in the enacting of it. If living a good life as a person means actively exemplifying autonomy, reasoned judgment, proprietorship, and respect for others who have those capacities, maybe living a good life otherwise means actively exemplifying holobiontic place-taking in awareness of selves and worlds in profound dependence and inter- (or intra-)dependence. In other words, maybe it means living like I belong to the world rather than like the world belongs to me.

Something like this contrast occurs in Robin Kimmerer's 2013 book *Braiding Sweetgrass*, in a chapter entitled "The Honorable Harvest." There Kimmerer recounts a conversation she had with a European engineering student who had recently visited an Ojibwe friend's family. The young man described a wonderful day spent out on a lake gathering wild rice. Despite having enjoyed the experience tremendously, however, he was critical of the Ojibwe's harvesting technique. "It didn't take long to collect quite a bit," Kimmerer quotes him as saying, "but it's not very efficient. At least half the rice just falls in the water and they didn't seem to care. It's wasted" (2013, 181). Grateful to his hosts, he told Kimmerer, he applied his expertise to the perceived problem and presented them with a design for a grain capture system that he estimated could get 85 percent of the rice. To his surprise and dismay, however, his hosts declined his help, choosing their less efficient method instead.

Kimmerer relates this conversation as fact and, we must assume, as she seems to, that the young engineer who told her of his experience was also relating facts. These are real people, then, who have their own beliefs, attitudes, and values, and I don't know any of them, so it would be a mistake to believe that I could possibly know their real ethical positions or self-understandings. I propose, instead, to treat this anecdote as a parable that reveals possibilities, not as an account of what those real people actually think or how they truly live.

As I interpret the story, then, the young engineer is a good person. He responds to his hosts' generosity with gratitude. He wishes to reciprocate by offering a gift of his skills and time in the form of a plan for a technical object that would enable them to appropriate a valuable resource more efficiently. The Ojibwe family members, by contrast, are not good persons; they do not appreciate efficient methods of appropriating resources. On the contrary, they waste resources (as Locke and others believed "Indians" wasted land that could have been logged, fenced, and farmed in service of accumulation of wealth), and they clearly choose to do so, expressing a firm preference for their profligate ways. The engineer is frustrated and confused by their lack of interest in his design. It seems that they are not even trying to be good persons! But that is not because they are bad or evil persons, as I read the story; it is because they are not persons at all. Their way of living is some sort of otherwise, which I am not in a position to know in fact, but which appears in Kimmerer's brief sketch as at least a bit like what I am trying to describe as an ethos of active belonging.

The engineer imagines that beings who are not persons—lakes, rice plants, and so on—are resources for persons; that is, they are things that can be made into property. All the world is there to be owned, to belong to someone. The perspective that supports these presumptions seems to be one of standing on the earth and surveying it, subject over against object. The Ojibwe perhaps view the world from a perspective more like the one that befell me forty years ago in the cavernous darkness and that I enjoy in the dense summer garden: They are right there in the thick of the world, not surveying it as a set of objects but enmeshed in it in their immediate occurring. Their taking place happens in and with a world to which they belong. And the others happening in that world are beings, processes, and flows with whom they belong, together and alongside, in intricately patterned occurrings and recurrings.

From such an *otherwise* perspective, a good life isn't a life of efficient labor, accumulation, and proprietorship and of respect for others' living likewise. It is not about autonomous decision-making in pursuit of logical consistency or the greatest benefit for the least cost. It is not about preparing to give an account of oneself in the end to make a case for everlasting life in heaven as opposed to oblivion or hell. Those are all attitudes and practices that presuppose a fundamental separation of self from world and selves of all sorts from each other that isn't visible from the perspective of dependent belonging. Instead, from the perspective of dependent belonging, a good life is one lived in gratitude for the flows and processes and systems that make that life possible. It is about safeguarding the conditions—the flows, processes, and systems—that sustain dynamic patterns that generate and constitute a world season to season, moment to moment, nanosecond to nanosecond. It is about acting to enhance those patterns and working to restore the conditions for their repetition where they have been disfigured.

If we appropriate 85 percent of the rice, we will destroy the conditions for those patterns to repeat. There will be much less rice next year, not enough for humans but also not enough for any other creatures that might depend on it. Without so many decaying rice plants, what will happen in the lakebed? Will the chemistry of the water change? The ducks won't come back, the Ojibwe tell the young engineer, which might allow the other lake plants that they eat to run rampant and choke out the light and leave the turtles that eat little ducklings to go hungry. How many other beings who live in the lake or around its edges will die or leave and not come back? All these beings make up dynamic patterns that will be disfigured or possibly irreparably disrupted if every summer we take 85 percent of the rice. What persons perceive as perfectly reasonable, those who belong perceive as an exponentially increasing existential threat. "What we leave is not wasted," the Ojibwe explain, and Kimmerer adds, "Our teachings tell us to never take more than half" (2013, 181–82).

The engineer might have responded, probably in exasperation, that if they insisted on leaving half the rice in the lake, then at least his device would allow them to gather it faster, saving labor and time for doing other things. How might the Ojibwe respond? I don't know, but Kimmerer offers a possibility when she describes her own harvesting practices a few pages before the rice story. She uses a less-than-sharp trowel to harvest wild leeks, she writes, because "while a sharp trowel would make digging more efficient, the truth is that it makes the work too fast. If I could get all the leeks I needed in five minutes, I'd lose that time on my knees watching the ginger poke up and listening to the oriole that has just returned home" (178). The engineer views the work of gathering rice as nothing more than labor that can be saved or reallocated like a resource. But for the Ojibwe, it is likely something quite other. Perhaps it is a time of engagement with each other, with the water, with the rice, with the ducks, with the sunshine, with whoever else might gather at the watering hole or cross the sky. Perhaps it is a time colored and textured like no other, unlike the generic time of labor that can be allocated and reallocated without changing its color and texture at all.

IV. But What About . . . ? Some Hesitations

While the young engineer might merely have been baffled, some persons would be positively appalled at the attitude of the Ojibwe. People who won't work to accumulate are lazy, they might say, which is not just a disvalued personality trait but a serious moral failing, and people who prefer inefficient means of appropriating because those activities give them pleasure—listening to singing birds, floating around in a quiet canoe—are just plain selfish, an egregious moral failing. This was in fact the view that Locke articulated and presumably the view of his patron Shaftesbury and the other investors in the Carolina Colony. Furthermore, Locke held, when selfish, lazy people have a resource that they neglect to develop, they ought to be dispossessed of it in short order, not just for the enrichment of European gentlemen but for the expansion of the colonial market and the emerging nation-state. Dispossession is a matter of public good.[6]

For men like Locke and Shaftesbury, their peers, and their successors, ways of living that did not evince respect for a hard distinction between person and thing, subject-owner and objects there for the owning, were either immoral or irrational or both—indeed the two are often hard to distinguish. The world belongs to persons, not people to worlds. But you don't have to be an English gentleman with wealth in your sights to suspect that the Ojibwe in the story were in some ways as self-interested and anthropocentric as Locke was in his. Maybe they were just smarter about it, realizing that continued appropriation over the years would require some self-restraint and that labor-saving devices might make that self-restraint a little more difficult to maintain. Maybe they *say* they leave plenty of rice out of a sense of kinship with the other denizens of the lake country, but they seem perfectly aware that their long-term self-interest as individuals and as a family is best secured by taking less rice than they could. And the same might be said for their concern with the ducks; one suspects that they might also eat ducks and duck eggs and use duck feathers and down to insulate their clothes and bedding. Doesn't this talk of the rice and ducks and turtles as our kindred just mask that same old drive for individual self-preservation, that same acquisitive self-centeredness that so many liberal theorists posit as the truth of human nature? Are we really moving toward an ethos of active belonging, or are we just refusing to acknowledge our fundamental selfishness?

Again, I cannot speak for the actual, living Ojibwe. But if we take the people in the parable version of the story to exemplify something like an ethos of belonging, we can't construe what grounds their lifeways as self-interest. Insofar as actions contribute to the viability and vitality of a world, they will benefit the beings dependent upon that world; therefore, yes, they are likely to benefit the actors. Actors are not separate from worlds; world systems, processes, and flows are not discrete objects upon which a discrete subject acts. But if the acting self is aware that it occurs and can occur only within certain patterns of world processes, then it cannot understand itself to have interests that are not bound up with a world and the beings it generates and sustains. An ethos of active belonging is one of attention to and care for the processes that constitute the world, which includes the selves given viability within it, but the individual self isn't the focus of such an ethic, because there is no truly individual self. Viability and vitality are world concerns, in that the occurring of a world is the occurring of a region of beings in and as dynamic interrelated patterns. There is no individual viability, let alone vitality. An ethos of active belonging gives rise to lifeways that invigorate the patterns in which they occur or at the very least do not fatally disrupt, deplete, or sunder them.

An ethos of active belonging is not about self-interest, then, but it is also not about self-denial. It does not entail giving up anything that sustains our viability. Enacting our belonging means caring for ourselves in the process of caring for others. And just as there is no true individual interest, there is no true species interest apart from the world systems that generate us all. An ethos of active belonging cannot be exclusively concerned with human well-being, because there is no human well-being apart from world. Neither individualism nor anthropocentrism have any place here.

I dismiss the worry about selfishness, then, but a much bigger worry presents itself to me as I imagine an ethos of belonging: Will this way of thinking and living end up being fundamentally conservative? Of course we talk about conservation, but we don't really want to conserve everything, do we? To put the issue bluntly, don't some of us want to change or even to destroy some of the worlds we inhabit, even though we might well be nourished by them some of the time? What if the world upon which my life at present depends promotes inattention, exploitation, hoarding, ruthlessness—as neoliberal capitalism, for example, surely does? Aren't there systems and processes and even whole worlds that ought not be conserved, that ought to be disrupted instead? What about authoritarian regimes that imprison, torture, or disappear people who dissent? What about carceral systems that keep people isolated in cages for years on end? What about legal systems that give huge corporations the right to blow up mountains and pollute groundwater for profit? What about global banking systems that require governments to sell off their people's collective assets, and therefore their future, in exchange for desperately needed loans? What about systems of taxation that extract from the poor through sales and income taxes while the well-off pay little to nothing on their wealth and corporate earnings? What about whole societies structured by sexism and racism? How, from the perspective of an ethos of active belonging, can we think about and conduct ourselves with regard to systems that maintain injustice and oppression? We belong to many of those systems as surely as the Ojibwe belong to the lake country.

Consider heterosexism, for example. The profundity of belonging to a heterosexist world was deeply impressed upon me a little over thirty years ago when a fellow named David Scondras came to speak at the university where I worked. A decade earlier, Scondras had become the first openly gay Boston City Council member. One of his first acts in office was to sponsor the ordinance that created Boston's human rights commission. Several years later, he sponsored the Family Protection Act to allow same-sex couples to register as domestic partners for health insurance, hospital visitation, and bereavement rights. He was an interesting and compelling fellow, so I tagged along with the group that took him out to dinner after his talk, and at some point that evening he turned to me as the only other openly gay person in the party (we were still gay then, not yet queer), and he asked me what I imagined the world would be like if there were no more homophobia. I stared at the table in silence for a long moment. Then I confessed that I couldn't. I couldn't imagine it. There was so much, and it was so very, very deep; every institution in our society, formal and informal, assumed heterosexuality and scorned everything else. Scondras wasn't surprised that I couldn't imagine a world without heteronormativity (as we soon learned to call it). He just said we all ought to work hard to try, because that is a world worth striving to create.

Surely a just world is worth trying to create, and the structures, institutions, practices, and assumptions that militate against justice are worth tearing down. White supremacy, heteronormativity, sexism, poverty—yes, if those systems and patterns were powered by wild rice, I would take up that young white engineer's proffered efficiency in a heartbeat and encourage everybody I knew to scoop every last grain out of that lake. I am not in principle opposed to destroying worlds, even worlds to which I so profoundly belong that I cannot imagine an otherwise. But doesn't that inability to imagine suggest that I, as I am and have been constituted, have no place in a non-racist, non-heterosexist world? And, again, wouldn't an ethos of belonging lead me to conserve the unjust world rather than to destroy it? I don't believe it would, but not for the reasons a logical person might expect.

A logical person wants criteria for how to decide which worlds to conserve and which to destroy. But as self-aware holobiontic happenings dependent on flows, processes, and systems that far exceed their capacity to comprehend and control know quite well, I realize that there is something very wrong with the way the issue is framed. I am neither a destroyer nor a conserver of worlds. I don't have that power, and I don't exist on that plane of abstraction. I select, when I can, what effects to produce in the systems, processes, and flows within the sphere of my influence, which are just a tiny few of those within which I live. The Ojibwe rice harvesters cannot conserve their world, despite their conservative practices; it is crumbling because of forces and processes and systems they do not control. And just as they can't protect their rice world from destruction, I can't destroy my racist, heterosexist world, no matter how my practices counter the processes and systems that enable those patterns to repeat. Worlds do get perpetuated and destroyed, but no being does that on its own, so no being is ever faced with that kind of choice.

I can only choose and act locally, day to day. My choices and actions occur at the level of practices, not worlds. I can choose to act as if I belong to a world to which people of many races, genders, sexualities, and abilities contribute to the viability and vitality of the community in which I find myself—because they do; that *is* the world I belong to. I can choose to respect people, work alongside them, learn from them, honor their contributions, and receive their being and doing not as my due but as a gift for which I am grateful, much as the Ojibwe receive the gifts the lake and rice plants offer. And if I do that, some of the flows that feed white and hetero supremacist systems might be slowed, diluted, or diverted. A racist, heterosexist world is founded in and depends on continual denial of dependence and belonging. Active belonging inhibits patterns that sustain such worlds, even when it does not eliminate them. We can hope that eventually different patterns will emerge. But, fortunately, we don't have to be able to imagine new worlds in advance to create possibilities for them to form, all due respect to Mr. Scondras.[7]

Meanwhile, as the paragraph above shows, it is possible to discern a difference between systems, institutions, practices, ways of living that disavow our radical dependence and ones that acknowledge and affirm it. Insofar as I can see those differences, I may condemn some of those systems. An ethos of active belonging does not compel me to support any institution or conserve any configuration of forces just because it exists, even if I am somehow implicated in it. In fact, it may compel me to resist conforming to the dictates of an institution and seek to change or dismantle it. If I want to be effective in my opposition, though, I will have to rely on others for help. In chapter 5 I imagined what would happen if an involuntary slave owner joined with "their" involuntarily enslaved people to transform their collective situation. I imagined that the slave owner went into the project with some ideas about what needed to be done, given the particular legal and economic circumstances of the group, but how the project would play out, would evolve and shape itself, would be the result of the collaboration, not of any individual's dictates. The people—owner and enslaved alike—would come to affirm and enact their belonging together, changing all of them as they worked to change their places in the world. Something like this happens in any process of collective action aimed at situational or structural change.

Here is a very limited and mundane example from my own experience. In the United States, most people buy medical care (if they get any); it is not considered a public good to be financed with tax money. Most of the entities that sell medicine and medical advice and procedures are for-profit corporations, many of them traded on stock markets and obligated to make as much profit as possible for their shareholders. The high price of medical care under this system generates a profitable market for insurance corporations that pool risk across groups of customers and are thereby able to offer prices for care that are lower than providers' prices. But then the availability of insurance enables providers to raise prices and still keep customers. As a result of this feedback loop, over time, the retail cost of medicine and medical care has climbed so high that almost nobody can afford even the most basic diagnostics and treatments. That, in turn, generates more need for insurance and pushes up its price, so that many people cannot afford it, either. Fewer and fewer employers offer it as a benefit to their workers as prices rise, and people who lose their jobs also lose their coverage. This system bespeaks radical individualism; it denies that people—all people—depend on other people for their well-being and that illness and injury affect whole networks of people, not just individual bodies in pain. Support of such a system is antithetical to an ethos of belonging. I condemn it, but I can't abolish it. What I could and did do was join with a lot of other people who condemned it, too.

We would like to eliminate the profit taking and make medicine and medical care available to everybody at an uninflated cost subsidized by tax money, but so far we haven't been able to make that happen. Instead, in 2010 Congress passed and President Obama signed the Affordable Care Act, a tax-supported insurance subsidy for people whose incomes are too high for Medicaid (which in some states is limited to mothers and their dependent children) but not high enough to afford private insurance. There were several other provisions of the act as well, one of which was to transfer federal money to states with low funding for Medicaid so that more people (those too poor to afford even government-subsidized insurance but too well-off to qualify for meager state-subsidized health care) could get free health care. This was called "Medicaid Expansion." In a number of state legislatures, including Virginia, politicians who opposed all sorts of public benefits refused the federal money, leaving hundreds of thousands of people with no medical coverage. Collectively, we decided to force the Virginia

General Assembly to expand Medicaid coverage. It took several years, but it happened. The result was not a health care system that avows and affirms radical dependence. But the work we undertook together did do so. We accomplished what we did not as individuals but as people together who recognized our belonging together in solidarity. And that awareness of belonging together intensified through the years of collaboration.

There may be a place for the question of which worlds to conserve or destroy. But if so, that place is with people together, not with me by myself. I can perceive wrong, injustice, or oppression, and I can join with others who perceive it too. But plans for altering the conditions that produce it will be made collectively, and the vision of what to foster in their stead will emerge as conditions change. Nobody will dictate, because nobody can. People together can and do conserve and destroy worlds and therefore can and should entertain questions about what sorts of worlds they want to live in. Provisional collective answers to such questions can result in undertakings to change systems, structures, and institutions in ways that avow our dependence and belonging, as in our efforts to change health care, or in ways that deny it, as projects of colonization and racial segregation have done. My point here is simply that, whether we avow our belonging or deny it, we need each other to do whatever world changing we do. That is why the question of which worlds to conserve or destroy raised at the level of any particular one of us is misplaced.

V. The Inevitability of Violence

In the previous section, I considered and addressed several critical questions about an ethos of active belonging: (1) Is it just a cover for selfishness or anthropocentrism? (2) Is it fundamentally conservative? (3) If it is not fundamentally conservative, then how does anyone decide which worlds or systems to conserve or destroy? Now I want to consider one last point of contention.

Every follower of a diet that excludes red-blooded mammal flesh has at one time or another been told that their principles and the decisions and actions to which they lead are self-contradictory (as well as antisocial, unhealthy, and possibly un-American). All eating involves killing something: If it's wrong to take one life, then isn't it also wrong to take any other? If it is wrong to kill cows, is it not also wrong to kill beets and lettuces? Some people discriminate on the basis of intelligence; a pig is smarter than a potato. But so what? People who reject intelligence as a criterion of moral worth might suggest the capacity to feel pain as a criterion; a pig would suffer whereas a potato would not. But then it isn't the killing itself that gives pause, only the prelude to it, which conceivably could be eliminated. The question of killing itself has not been answered. And if just comes down to the assertion that one has to eat *something*, well, the next question is why choose your own life over any other life at all? Why not starve yourself to death if doing so could save thousands of potatoes?

There are all sorts of problems with the line of thought that generates these questions and supposed dilemmas, notably the assumption that moral worth resides exclusively in individual beings, but there is a serious concern here for an ethos of active belonging. It is this: If I am to live, I must do violence. I will address that concern in detail below. I want to start, though, by contextualizing and thereby politicizing this sort of call for logical consistency.

Most of the people who pursue these lines of questioning based on a demand for consistency do not do so innocently. The motive is not to learn from someone or to help them clarify their thoughts and values; it is to change their practices or at least to embarrass or belittle them. The demand for logical consistency—to treat all lives as of equal worth, for example—is really meant as a demand to abandon vegetarianism in favor of anthropocentrism or individualism or capitalism or whatever the questioner thought was threatened by refusing to eat meat.

Ethnographer Naisargi Davé considers demands for logical consistency in a story she tells of tagging along with an employee, Dipesh, of an agency called Welfare for Stray Dogs, which provides basic veterinary care for loose dogs on the streets of Bombay. One day she was with Dipesh when he came upon a dog with an infection in its rectum. The dog was very old and not likely to live much longer regardless of treatment. Nevertheless, Dipesh carried it to some shade, laid down an old newspaper, extracted dozens of maggots from its anus, applied medicine, and let the dog go to whatever fate it might meet. He then squashed the maggots. Davé notes that her leftist colleagues and friends are quick to charge animal activists like Dipesh with inconsistency: Isn't it a contradiction for Dipesh to kill maggots to save the old dog?

Leftists in India tend to be very suspicious of animal welfare activists, she explains, whom they see as elitist, reactionary, and allied with neocolonial capitalists, and she makes clear that there is good reason for those characterizations in many instances. But when it comes to this charge of inconsistency, Davé will have none of it. She makes two points. First, the old dog and the maggots are only equivalent under the abstract concept "animal" or "living thing," and there is no such abstraction in the world. Ethical practice is not abstract; it is a continual attending to and negotiating with what actually, concretely, is. Second, Davé notes that the situations wherein these accusations of inconsistency arise are often highly politically charged, situations in which speech is strategic action. In such a context, the accusation of ethical self-contradiction "has one primary, and deceptively ordinary, function: *to exhaust*—and I mean literally, *to make people so tired that they give up*" (Davé 2023, 59). If you help one dog, then you must help all dogs; if you help dogs, then you must help all animals, maggots included; and so on. If those accused then try to be consistent, they are overwhelmed, so they do give up and just stop helping, leaving the status quo intact. In such contexts, enforcing an abstract law of non-contradiction is a highly interested act, not a purely logical one. A disingenuous demand for abstract logical consistency, if heeded, makes careful, world-attuned ethical practices impossible.

For people with genuine, concrete ethical concerns, however, there are good reasons to take up this issue of inescapable violence. If we are to live, we have to kill. The question is who to kill, and when and where and by what means. These questions are very present for me because of the amount of time I spend in the garden. An awful lot of gardening involves killing, and not just the harvesting of lettuces or beets. I don't use poison to kill weeds or insects, but I do kill them. I pull hundreds of plants up by the roots in just a few minutes' time, or I hack them to bits with my hoe. I knock hornworms off tomato plants and squash them with my boots. I pinch asparagus beetles to death and crush dozens of potato beetle eggs with my fingers. If I don't do these things, there soon won't be a garden anymore. Gardening requires carnage.

If I am a gardener, I kill things. Likewise, if I am a raptor, I kill things. If I am a hornworm, I kill things. If I am a whale who eats only plankton, still, I kill things. No animal can live without killing (or having another kill for them, as do scavengers and most humans). When it comes to killing, human beings differ from raptors, whales, and hornworms only in that we usually have a wider range of options than they do about which beings we kill (or have killed for us). The hawk perched in a pine tree above the pasture can kill this or that rabbit, squirrel, cotton rat, or snake, depending on who comes along at feeding time. I, however, can kill or refrain from killing just about any being (leaving aside the bacteria and fungi my immune system kills every nanosecond, which is outside the realm of self-aware selectivity, or the fact that just walking across a lawn kills countless organisms). My acts of killing are more discretionary than the hawk's, but no less necessary. The systems, processes, and patterns that constitute the world in and to which I belong involve dying as well as living, dying inseparable from living. Belonging as a human animal in and to this world means acting in ways that have effects, some of them deadly. Ethical practice takes place in this world, not in an abstract logical realm. As Robin Kimmerer puts it, "I am a mere heterotroph, a feeder on the carbon transmuted by others. In order to live, I must consume. That's the way the world works, the exchange of a life for a life, the endless cycling between my body and the body of the world" (2013, 176–77). Kimmerer puts the question not in terms of logical law but in terms of justice. How do we do justice to the lives we take? "This was a question of profound concern for our ancestors," she writes (177). Presumably here she is speaking of her ancestors, the Potawatomi, but undoubtedly it has been of concern to many peoples around the world through our few hundred thousand years as a thoughtful species. And it remains paramount. Whether to kill is not the question. But who, when, and how to kill is. Who and how shall I kill within an ethos of active belonging?

In grappling with these questions, I caution myself against the old habit of dividing the world into discrete entities shorn of their dependencies and relations. Just as I have been taught (as a person) to do that with people (to divide the world into individual persons and aggregates thereof), I have been taught to do that with actions. Each act is to be considered for itself, apart from its dependencies and relations. When Santa (or God) tallies up the times you've been naughty or nice, he is counting individual acts like beads on an abacus. But in an ethos of belonging, it would make more sense to look at choices and actions in contexts of the practices to which they belong and upon which their meanings depend. I believe the question of how to do justice to the lives we take is best considered in relation not to particular actions but in relation to our consumption practices and the range of choice we have about which practices, not which discrete acts, to engage in—practices, not individual acts.

I'll restate the question, then: By means of what practices will I acquire what I eat? Will I forage? Will I bow hunt? Will I keep chickens? Will I fish? Will I buy food from local markets or supermarkets? Will I order my groceries from Amazon? No matter which of these I choose (and of course it is also possible to choose some combination of these), beings will be killed. I can avoid supporting the killing of birds, mammals, and fish by refusing to eat meat. But grain and vegetable production methods also kill beings, and not just the plants harvested. In addition to all the plants ripped out to make room for vegetables and grains, protecting crops to maturity means directly or indirectly killing whatever would feed on them. And depending on what means are used to do that killing, death may radiate up the food chain.

My choice to raise some of my food in a backyard garden entails tearing out grasses, slicing up some worms as I turn the soil, and pinching bugs to death. If I don't weed and cultivate and kill the insects that would kill the crops, I won't have a garden for long. But I have no doubt that the practice of gardening is more consonant with my belonging to this world than ordering food from Amazon would be. Supermarkets sell food harvested by fossil-fuel-burning machines and transported by fossil-fuel-burning ships and trucks. Most of that food was raised in the presence of chemical herbicides or insecticides, which kill not only plants and insects but also the birds and butterflies that eat them and, sometimes, the human farmworkers too. And transporting that food burns fossil fuels that alter the climate and pollute the air. By contrast, the bodies of the plants I kill go into the compost to return to the soil they sprang from as unpoisoned nourishment for worms and microbes. The compost bin also receives food scraps and yard waste, keeping all that out of landfills (where it would generate methane) and putting carbon back into the soil. I plant crops suitable for local temperature and moisture variations, so that mechanized climate control is absent and irrigation is minimal. And I transport the food to the kitchen not with diesel engines but with my arms and legs. These practices bespeak awareness of belonging to and dependence upon the world—air, sunlight, rain, and so on—in ways that practices of supermarket shopping are hard-pressed to do.

Of course, since gardening and farmers' markets are seasonal, I do shop at supermarkets too. There are three in my vicinity. How do I choose? One chain is unionized, so the full-time employees are likely better paid than those at the other stores, but it also limits many employees to part-time work. One chain's owners poured money into efforts to elect a candidate who opposed restrictions on AR15 assault rifles even after a massacre in a school near their corporate headquarters took the lives of seventeen people. The third sometimes carries a few items from local farms but stocks very little food raised organically. There is no way to formulate a rule to cover all this complexity, and certainly no principle that would be generally applicable across people differently placed. There is simply ongoing thinking, learning, weighing, and negotiating. An ethos of active belonging is about choosing practices that best express belonging, not about refraining from doing any violence or causing any pain. But it remains attuned to violence and pain as well as vitality and joy, to living and dying in their concrete occurrence in dynamic patterns of the worlds to which we belong.

This attunement will involve serious efforts to learn about the economic, political, and biological patterns and flows in which we find ourselves and the ways various practices affect them. But this is not obligatory learning; it is learning propelled by curiosity and wonder, open-ended discovery that generates practical experimentation and invention. Nor will learning be a solitary undertaking, first, because it will involve listening to anybody with anything to teach. By any "body" here, I mean any being at all—human, nonhuman, living, dead, or inorganic; in this attentiveness, lines drawn between humans and nonhumans blur, as do lines between living and dying and being without living at all. And, second, because learning often gives rise to collective practices. I learn from the garden and from my reading related to it, but I also learn from my visits to the farmers' market and its many information booths and the people who staff them; in the process, I come across ideas for strengthening vital patterns and decreasing disruptions through collaborative action with other humans. That leads to new garden experiments and techniques but also to attending community meetings to organize opposition to fossil fuel infrastructure expansion, corporate data centers, and impermeable surfaces and industrial-scale groundwater extraction. While learning about dangers and threats to local and extended systems can be daunting and depressing, strategizing and acting collectively are not. On the contrary, those practices often delight and excite. People who come together to create community gardens or food cooperatives or farmers' markets or to design rainwater storage and distribution systems or programs for soil rehabilitation or to prevent commercial rezoning of farmland, wetland, and woodland belong not only to the world of soil, sun, and rain but also to each other. Such work, such discovery, such collective effort and resonance is joyful.

Learning will be an ongoing project, and prosaic as well as critical questioning will be crucial. Attentiveness, patient listening, and willingness to try and touch and see are likely to be virtues in this venture. Decisions will be local and often tentative, based on either gathered knowledge or, just as importantly, acknowledged ignorance. The practices we engage in will vary and differ, even in our collectivity. Not everybody can garden. Not everybody can go to zoning board meetings and speak in favor of protections for wetlands. Not everybody can babysit other people's kids while they go speak at zoning board meetings. Everybody has limitations of skill, time, stamina, mobility, and material resources, especially those who must work two or three jobs to keep food on the table at all. There is not one single thing that everybody can do. The question of how to enact belonging to the world will have different answers for differently situated people, even when they are acting collectively, and the answers will change for everybody over time as our capacities and locations and worlds change. We can appreciate each other's contributions and admire each other's ingenuity without expecting any uniformity in practice, and we can find ways to support and relieve those currently prevented from contributing as they would like because of the burdens they bear. What could be common to us is engagement in active belonging—to each other as to common worlds—each as differently endowed, abled, and situated. There are no commandments or universal rules.

And mistakes will be made. That is inevitable, given the level of ignorance and the capacities for action and influence that human beings have. Persons seek not to be guilty, to avoid moral failure. People who live in an awareness of belonging acknowledge their limitations and seek to learn from their mistakes. Limit and error are not evidence of ethical failure. The only ethical failures come of enacting denial of our profound dependence.

∴

In the course of considering various questions and hesitations in the preceding two sections, I also sketched several features of an ethos of active belonging, which I'll summarize here. I said that it plays out primarily (although not exclusively) at the level of practices rather than either the level of choices of worlds or that of particular actions. It involves ongoing learning in multiple contexts and from and with a wide variety of beings. It requires experimentation and expects decisions to be provisional and ever revisable. It blurs distinctions between humans and nonhumans, even as it gathers us into communities and collaborative projects. It accepts mistakes as inevitable. It opposes systems, practices, and actions that deny dependence and belonging. I note that this provisional sketch is offered only as a possibility for living otherwise, not as a prescription. My aim in offering it is not to dictate how things should be or what people ought to do, but to demonstrate that living beyond personhood is a genuine possibility in the present, in the world as it is right now.

VI. Self-Sacrifice Versus Self-Enactment

To me, the prospect of living beyond personhood comes not only as a relief, but as much of the foregoing has suggested, a cause for excitement and even joy. It is a relief not only from the unbearable burdens of personhood but even from much of what has called itself environmentalism over the last few decades. Living a good life morally is not all about the comforts, luxuries, and pleasures that people ought to give up. It is not about taking and using and having less, shouldering more responsibilities, bearing more burdens, and asking for as little as possible from others. It is not about suffering, even while it attends to suffering. An ethos of active dependent belonging does not center on sacrifice. In fact, much of what an ethos of individual personhood construes as sacrifice looks like something else entirely. I will illustrate this with a commonplace observation.

As my circle of human acquaintances ages, various ones of us suffer with illness, temporary and chronic disability, and grief. I've observed that many people are very reluctant to ask for help or even to accept it if offered. I suppose for some it is hard to acknowledge their loss of strength and ability, especially when it heralds steep decline, perhaps eventual institutionalization, and death. For others, it is a lifelong habit instilled in childhood; one should not impose, should not speak up, should not occupy more literal or figurative space than absolutely necessary, lest one be resented or punished. Women and queer people may have a deep-seated fear of being the focus of attention. Some straight men feel emasculated, perhaps imagining that anyone who helps will also condescend. Overall, need and the undeniable dependence it can entail can be hard things for people in this society to accept in their own lives. But I have also observed that, contrary to so many people's expectations, friends and neighbors and even simply nearby acquaintances are eager to help. They want to be asked to pick up groceries or provide a ride to the doctor. They are more than willing to wash some dishes, clean the litter box, scrounge up a few box fans, or walk the dog. They are honored to be trusted with an expression of grief. These acts are embodiments of belonging together in a community. They are affirmations that our lives are interwoven and that we matter to each other when we are in need and when we are not. And they are flows of meaning, energy, and material vital to the patterns that sustain a world. The lesson of this is that people who belong tend to offer what they have, be it money or skill or a listening ear. In fact, they look for ways to enact their belonging with others. They don't sacrifice themselves in doing so, although what they do may cost them money and time and may in and of itself be arduous or unpleasant. They *are* themselves in doing so; they are the selves who are generated and sustained in the belonging and who draw power and meaning in the awareness that this is so. How much more we find we have to contribute when awareness of belonging expands beyond the human, when we find ourselves contributing to the vitality of soil, air, the wild things that share this place.

Closely allied with the notion of sacrifice is that of limit. People don't want to sacrifice any more than they have to, so much of the research, writing, and public discussion of pollution, greenhouse gas emissions, groundwater extraction, ocean acidification, and so on focus on finding the limits beyond which it is unsafe to go. Once the limits are revealed, we can go ahead and pollute and extract and emit right up to those limits. But when the limits are reached, the experts warn, whatever desires or needs we have must go unsatisfied or else—and we are invited again and again to contemplate what that "or else" will be like, a terrible time of pain, want, and death. This is the message: sacrifice now or be sacrificed later. That is what the ethos of personhood has brought us to. And of course there is truth in these assertions of limits. Flows of poisons can overwhelm vital systems that might be able to deflect or incorporate them at lower speeds or volumes. Vast patterns can destabilize, deteriorate, and fail to repeat. Limits are real. But sacrifice need not be the salient concern.

I want to turn to Kimmerer once again to highlight this further aspect of the shift away from the ethos of personhood. Toward the end of the chapter "The Honorable Harvest," she repeats a story told to her by an Algonquin ecologist named Carol Crowe, who requested funding from her tribal council to attend a conference on sustainability.

> They asked her, "What is this all about, this notion of sustainability? What are they talking about?" She gave them a summary of the standard definitions of sustainable development, including "the management of natural resources and social institutions in such a manner as to ensure the attainment and continued satisfaction of human needs for present and future generations." They were quiet for a while, considering. Finally, one elder said, "This sustainable development sounds to me like they just want to be able to keep on taking like they always have. It's always about taking. You go there and tell them that in our way, our first thoughts are not 'What can we take?' but 'What can we give to Mother Earth?' That's how it's supposed to be." (Kimmerer 2013, 189–90)

Limits and the dangers of exceeding them are very real. But that is not a new phenomenon. There have always been limits. Limits mean sacrifice and despair only if our desire is not to have to live in the world those limits make possible. But we belong to that world. An ethos of belonging is not about finding ways to push as far as possible and then restrain our desires so as not to destroy the world, but about finding ways to enact belonging within them. As I understand what the Algonquin elder was saying from my emerging and coalescing perspective as dependent holobiontic happening, I'm aware that belonging is contributing however we can to the collective being and becoming of the world. And doing so is the enactment not only of dependent belonging but also of self. Indeed, it is the being of self.

It is possible that, in the end, the limits will be breached, that we will not succeed in maintaining or restoring or creating a world that will sustain human and other living beings, just as we have already failed to maintain a world that could sustain Pinta Island tortoises, Bachman's warblers, and Tasmanian tigers. I don't know. But what I do know is that persons and their privatized rational individualism will never manage to do it. Persons, in fact, are one of the barriers to a sustainable world. I hope this book has gone some way toward dismantling that barrier both by exposing its fault lines and by imagining a possible otherwise.

However we do it, though, getting ourselves free of personhood would be a significant step toward learning how to be with/of/as a world together, humans and nonhumans, living and nonliving. Our lives collectively probably depend on it. All lives collectively and the worlds to which they belong may depend on it. In the vast cosmos, what happens on this tiny pebble of planet probably does not matter at all. But as long as we live here, it matters infinitely to us, all of us, together. Let us enact ourselves in contributing what we can.

Acknowledgments

Sometimes I think that an author is nothing more than a node in a network of thinking relays, a place where normally fast-moving ideas get stalled and, however briefly, coagulate. I, at least, feel more like a contingent locus than a creative source of what unfolds in this book. Thoughts came here from many directions. With deep gratitude, I will here put some names to those directions.

Todd May read every word of every chapter every time I rewrote them, which was many. He contributed some of those words, too, as well as his wit and wisdom and his unending encouragement from the first stirrings of this project to its end. I have no idea what this book would look like, or even if it would exist, without him. My spouse, Carol Anderson, also read every word—or suffered through my reading of them to her on every road trip we took for the last decade-plus—and her probing questions and practical advice gave this book much more clarity than it ever would have had otherwise. Her patience and emotional support made this and all work possible, and sometimes made me possible, day to day. I am grateful to and for her beyond all words.

Charles Scott and Nancy Tuana read versions of chapters 1 through 5 and offered detailed analysis and suggestions to which I returned again and again as I revised. To say they were generous with their time and attentiveness would be a major understatement. The book also benefited from frequent conversations with Nancy about related texts and of course from all the guidance and inspiration that Charles and his work have given me since he directed my dissertation forty years ago. My debt to him is far greater than I could ever describe, much less repay.

Scores of other people have contributed to this project. Somewhere along the way, Verena Erlenbusch-Anderson and Colin Koopman organized the Critical Genealogies Workshop, a small group of scholars who meet every eighteen months to discuss our works in progress. Since this work was in progress for so long, members of that group plowed through many pages of it, some of which have survived to publication. I am deeply grateful to Verena and Colin in particular for their kind attention, always sound suggestions, support, and general goodwill, and to Verena for attending to and reviving thoughts and theses that I had let fall to the side. Special thanks, also, to Andrew Dilts, who has been among my most trusted auditors and readers for many years and often seems to know what I am saying even when I do not.

I owe much of my sanity, such as it is, to my colleagues in the WGSS program at the University of Richmond, especially those who served with me on the program board, Dorothy Holland, Lucretia McCulley, Crystal Hoyt, Mariela Mendez, Erika Damer, Julietta Singh, Nathan Snaza, Melissa Ooten, Holly Blake, Nancy Propst, Andrea Simpson, Sydney Watts, and MariLee Mifsud. They not only listened to my ideas but buoyed my spirits time and again through all the upheavals in our collective academic, social, and political lives through the first decades of this century. I am grateful, also, to the anonymous donors who made possible the Stephanie Bennett Smith Chair in Women's, Gender, and Sexualities Studies in 2015, which I held from that year until I retired from the university in 2023 and which funded three semester research leaves during that time.

Finally, I want to thank Kyle Wagner and Kristin Rawlings at the University of Chicago Press for their enthusiasm, time, and encouragement and Erin DeWitt for her thorough and perceptive copyediting. Obviously, this book would not have been possible without their support and efforts.

Notes

INTRODUCTION

1. For those readers living in the future, DSL stands for Digital Subscriber Line. At the time that I signed the book contract, it was the highest speed internet connection available for residences in my neighborhood.

2. Yes, at that time I still wrote checks for all our utility bills and mailed them in, because I'd be damned if I would give such elusive and untrustworthy entities direct access to our bank account. However, with the onset of the coronavirus pandemic and the installation of Louis DeJoy as postmaster general, the US mail service became so unreliable that I gave in. Chalk up one more defeat for the little guy.

3. There is a philosophical debate over the question of whether citizens really bear any moral responsibility for their governments' actions, and there is plenty of room to question this. I report only that I felt implicated in the actions and responsibility toward the people who are victimized as a result of them, such as the people of Iraq.

4. Or perhaps I should say I am a Unitedstatesian, a rough translation of the Spanish *estadounidense*.

5. Or even, "a majority of us voted against that guy."

6. I fear that some of those crazies are actually in charge of aspects of our government since the 2016 presidential election, however.

7. The article was by James Howard Kunstler (2005a). Soon after, Kunstler published a book by the same name (2005b).

8. Actually, Indigenous people had used the stuff for centuries, apparently primarily for medicinal purposes, and white settlers had taken up the practice. Oil was seeping into Oil Creek at a rate subsequently estimated to be about twenty barrels per year, so it was readily accessible in small quantities.

9. A history of the oil industry can be found in Yergin (1991).

10. For example, the International Energy Agency estimates that Canadian oil sands produce 5 to 15 percent more carbon emissions than conventional crude oil, calculated on a "well-to-wheels" basis, although the production itself is much dirtier than production of conventional crude. See page 49 of their *World Energy Outlook 2010* executive summary online at https://www.iea.org/reports/world-energy-outlook-2010.

11. The Deepwater Horizon blowout in 2010 was in deeper water than the framers of US permitting regulations ever imagined possible. It was 18,360 feet (5,600 meters) below sea level in 5,100 feet (1,600 meters) of water forty-one miles off the coast of Louisiana. Eleven workers died in the explosion. The well spewed oil into the Gulf of

Mexico from April 20 to September 19, 2010. The well's construction simply could not withstand deep pressures, and the fail-safe mechanism failed to shut the well off.

12. In addition to Kunstler (2005b), I also read Simmons (2005).

13. Kjell Aleklett maintains that there was a text of a 1999 speech that Cheney (then chairman of Halliburton) gave at the London Institute of Petroleum in which he evinced a fairly clear understanding that peak oil would be upon us within the next decade (see Aleklett 2004; personal copy provided by the Aleklett, who can be reached at Aleklett@tsl.uu.se or www.peakoil.net).

14. Centers for Disease Control, 2013, https://www.cdc.gov/suicide/facts/data.html.

15. Excerpts are available on Michael Bess's website: https://michaelbess.net/foucault-interview/.

CHAPTER ONE

1. Ongoing political movements to treat human fetuses as persons under the law are surely familiar to every reader. Human embryos are also persons, some have argued; since 1992, activists have drawn on a Tennessee Supreme Court case, *Davis v. Davis*, 842 S.W.2d 588, to make their case for the personhood of embryos frozen after in vitro fertilization procedures. The Nonhuman Rights Projects tried for several years to win the status of personhood for chimpanzees to protect them from experimentation and other forms of cruelty; see, e.g., Gorman 2013. Some legal theorists are concerned that scientists may soon be able to combine human and nonhuman DNA to produce humanoid species whose members might be enslaved if they are not recognized as persons; for arguments for transgenic humanoid personhood, see Rivard (1992). A perhaps more current issue is the status of artificial intelligence; for discussions of whether some artificial systems should be considered persons, see Solum (1992) and Bayern (2016). In 2019 Lake Erie became the first natural feature to have the status of personhood in the United States when the city of Toledo passed the Lake Erie Bill of Rights (Daley 2019). (For an overview of efforts to grant legal standing to non-genetically discrete natural entities, see Kolbert 2022.) Tribal governments within US territory have granted personhood to some natural entities such as the Klamath River (Yoruk Tribe) and wild rice (White Earth Band of Ojibwe) (Smith 2019). As Anna Smith (2019) notes, such rights have already been established in other countries such as Colombia, Ecuador, New Zealand, and India.

2. Realizing that one's own way of living and thinking is historically conditioned opens one's mind to the possibility—indeed to the fact—that people in non-European traditions and lineages have other ways of understanding human and nonhuman lives, some of which are less painful and more tenable than what the dominant modern Euro-American tradition has to offer. Some of these alternatives will be explored later in this book.

3. Christopher Hill's *The World Turned Upside Down: Radical Ideas During the English Revolution* (1972) is a much-cited classic.

4. Hill informs us that the Diggers of 1649 were not the first to be so named. There had been a Digger (as well as a Leveller) movement in 1607. They also opposed land enclosure (Hill 1972, 117–18).

5. Interestingly, this passage is not rendered in this way in the earlier Tyndale translation, which was begun in 1522, finished in 1524, and revised in 1534 and 1536. In

that translation, God is simply not "parciall." The Revised Standard Version does not include the phrase, nor does any other translation I have come across except the Amplified translation of 1965. The Saint Joseph edition of the New American Bible (revised, 2010), for example, translates the passage thusly: "Then Peter proceeded to speak and said, 'In truth, I see that God shows no partiality. Rather, in every nation whoever fears him and acts uprightly is acceptable to him.'" I am very grateful to my colleague Dr. Julie Laskaris for tremendous help in identifying these and other Greek sources and English translations.

6. Here the word is πρόσωποληπτέω (*prosopolēpteo*).

7. See also Mark 12:14, Romans 2:11, Galatians 2:6, Colossians 3:25, James 2:1–4, 1 Peter 1:17, and Jude 16. It occurs in the Old Testament also. See Leviticus 19:15 and 26:9; Deuteronomy 1:17, 10:17, and 16:19; 2 Samuel 14:14; Job, 13:8, 13:10, 32:21, and 34:18–19; Proverbs 18:5, 24:23, and 28:31; Lamentations 4:16; and Malachi 1:9. Obviously this locution was common in the seventeenth century and generally meant valuing some—usually the wealthy—over others.

8. Tyndale does use the phrase in question to translate the passage from James, however: "Brethren have not the fayth of oure lorde Iesus Christ the lorde of glory in respecte of persons."

9. Students of British empiricism will also recall that the eighteenth-century philosopher George Berkeley's last name is pronounced *Barkley* (Maitland 1975, 226). Same principle.

10. Historian David Underdown notes, however, that there were commoners on all sides of the complex religious issues of the day; there was no uniform class position. Regional differences in political behavior were more marked, he claims, than class differences (Underdown 1996, 91–92).

11. Laud and members of his faction liked to call themselves priests rather than parsons—a trend that reached back to the 1620s (Cressy 2006, 136)—but most people still referred to clergymen as parsons.

12. Throughout the seventeenth and eighteenth centuries, of course, many of these radical sects were exported to the colonies, where they caused trouble for the Anglicans and for each other, and where they often grew and flourished.

13. Thomas J. Farrell says the noun form of *wight* occurs in Chaucer's corpus 355 times (2015, 190).

14. *Phersu* is the transliteration most common in dictionaries, but Marcel Mauss spells it *farsu*. He lists his source as Antoine Meillet and Alfred Ernout's *Dictionnaire Etymologique*. He says that he learned of the possible derivation from the older Greek word in a personal communication with M. Benveniste, presumably Émile Benveniste, the linguist (Mauss 1938, 274).

15. My source for this Greek etymological history is my colleague Dr. Erika Zimmerman-Damer, personal communication, August 7, 2012. Subsequently I have found corroboration in Schlossmann (1968, 38ff.).

16. Siegmund Schlossmann (1968) makes an extended argument for this view through the first quarter of his book..

17. An English translation of *The Grammar of Dionysios Thrax* from 1874 is available at https://archive.org/details/grammarofdionysi00dionuoft/page/n3/mode/2up. See page 12 of the translation for the relevant passage: "There are three *Persons*: First, Second, and Third. The First is the person *from* whom the assertion is; the Second, the one *to* whom it is; and the Third, the one *concerning* whom it is."

18. The rule did not limit the number of non-speakers who could be onstage simultaneously, and it did not apply to the chorus.

19. Colin Morris notes that Cicero's *De Officiis* was among the most popular of Latin texts among the educated members of Western European society, including the English, in the twelfth century, around the same time that Justinian's Code was rediscovered (Morris 1987, 14–15).

20. This insight can be found in Trendelenburg (1910, 346).

21. The Roman Empire had attained its greatest geographical extent more than four centuries earlier, by 117 CE under Trajan; at that time, the empire had encompassed about 2.2 million square miles, 5.7 million square kilometers (by comparison, the continental United States encompasses about 3 million square miles [a bit under 7.7 million square kilometers], and it was home to about 120 million people, close to 40 percent of the population of the world at that time. Trajan's successors Hadrian and then Antoninus Pius consolidated the empire, which reached its height of peace and prosperity under their rule (Cheilik 1969, 206–9). The empire's decline began almost immediately, however. By Justinian's time, Italy was a kingdom of the Ostrogoths, Gaul was split between the Burgundian and Frankish kingdoms, the Iberian Peninsula was divided between the Suevian and Visigoth kingdoms, and North Africa was ruled by Vandals (Cheilik 1969, 232). We might note, however, that many of the barbarian rulers were happy to understand themselves as subservient to the emperor in the East and as still part of the Roman Empire in a sense. They often needed the much wealthier Eastern emperor as an ally (Moorhead 1995, 119).

22. The price—in addition to wealth and human lives—was the loss of some Eastern lands to the strengthening Persians.

23. Before Justinian's project, there had been several efforts to codify Roman law. The first had occurred almost a thousand years before, in 451 BCE, as a result of a conflict between Rome's two ancient classes, the populous and the plebeians. The populous had controlled government and religious affairs exclusively until about 493 BCE, when the growing plebeian class forced a move to extinguish all debts and create tribunals that could offer plebeians some legal protections. (Thomas Collett Sandars speculates that the plebeian class was formed over time by freed slaves, people living in territories that Rome conquered, and foreigners who simply settled in Roman territory [1941, xi].) But this change did not end the conflict, and revolution eventually ensued. One of the plebeians' demands was that customary law, known as the *ius civile*, be written down. Upon conclusion of hostilities, therefore, the Romans formed the Decemvirate, a body consisting of equal numbers of plebeians and patricians that was charged with compiling and disseminating the law. The result is known as the Twelve Tables. No complete copy exists now (apparently the Twelve Tables were destroyed in the Celtic invasion of the fourth century BCE), but the content remained well known to Roman officials, and there remain enough fragments to give a good sense of the whole. Implementation still tended to favor the patricians, however, and equality remained elusive until at least 287 BCE (Sandars 1941, xviii). The Twelve Tables did not synthesize all of the *ius civile*, however, only the parts of most concern in the class conflict. Much of customary law remained unwritten but still in force well into the imperial era. Neither the Twelve Tables nor the remaining unwritten *ius civile* was considered applicable to non-Romans, however, which meant that, as Roman territory had expanded, more or less ad hoc local arrangements had to be made to afford official recognition of the property of conquered peoples and to provide some protections for those people. Over time provincial

magistrates issued edicts covering their territories, and this body of law became known as the *ius honorarium*. In the second century CE, at the height of the empire, a number of renowned jurists—including Gaius, whose *Institutes* served as a model for the later work of Justinian—produced commentaries and interpretations that were used extensively in applying the law. Then, in addition to all this, beginning in 285 CE under Diocletian, there was direct imperium legislation (Patterson 1983, 90). Justinian's commission had a huge task to perform.

24. Moyle's translation of the relevant passages in Justinian can be found in Justinian (1913, 7–9).

25. For more extensive discussion of this point, see Esposito (2012b, 76–80).

26. Roberto Esposito maintains that the only way that some individuals could be legal persons at any time was for others not to be, either some of the time or all of the time. "A category defined in juridical terms, no matter how broad, becomes meaningful only thanks to the comparison and indeed the opposition with another category from which all other categories are excluded" (Esposito 2012a, 23). Further, "it isn't possible to personalize someone without depersonalizing or reifying others, without pushing someone over into the indefinite space that opens like a kind of trap door below the person" (2012a, 24). I am not convinced of this claim as a logical necessity, although I believe that the concept did indeed function much as Esposito describes.

27. Similarly, the idea that some human beings are not persons persisted in European jurisprudence into the Renaissance and beyond. Esposito offers several sixteenth- and seventeenth-century examples of this latter phenomenon:

> ... Hugues Doneau (Donellus, 1517–91) noted that "a slave is a man, not a person; man is term of nature, person is a term of civil law" (*servus homo est, non persona, homo naturae, persona iuris civilis vocabulum*), Hermann Woehl (Vulteius, 1565–1634) later limited personhood to "a man possessing civil status, as it exists in the tribe, in personal freedom, in citizenship, and in the household" (*homo habens caput civile, quod positum est in tribus, in libertate, in civitate, in familia*). Finally, Arnold Vinnen (Vinnius, 1588–1657) brought the distinction to completion when he argued that "a man is anyone for whom a human mind connects with a human body" (*homo dicitur cuicumque contingit in corpore human omens humana*), whereas "a person is a man with a certain status, just as if he had been clothed in it" (*persona est homo statu quodam veluit indutus*). (Esposito 2012b, 81)

This juridical use of the term *persona* leads Esposito to assert, "Not only is *homo*—the word generally reserved in Latin for a slave—not a *persona*; the word *persona* is the *terminus technicus* that separates the juridical capacity from the naturalness of the human being" (2012b, 81). Hence his claim that "person" must be understood as a *dispositif*, an apparatus of power, and must be critiqued as such.

28. The legal status of slaves was not absolutely depersonalized; slaves were not simply things. First off, *things* were not just things in Roman law. As Sandars puts it in his commentary on the *Institutes*, "As person comprehends every legal being that has rights and is subject to them, so thing comprehends all that can be considered as the object of a right" (1941, xliv). There were incorporeal things, then, such as walking across a field, which could be the object of a right of way. There might also be corporeal entities that could not be the object of a right, and they would not have been classed as things. Of course, slaves *were* objects of their owners' rights, so they were things, but they also had some very limited rights as persons. Sandars notes, "Slaves were *personae* in the sense that they were

not merely things, and they could go through some legal forms and were entitled in later times to a certain amount of legal protection; but although they are thus treated under the law of persons, it is chiefly their want of legal capacities that attracts attention" (xxxvi, 13).

29. We might have expected Roman law to have made a mark on England during the time that part of the island was a Roman province (from 43 to 410 CE), but the law seems to have left along with the legions themselves. Nor did the eleventh-century Norman conquerors bring Roman law to the island. Initially, they just tried to write down and systematize existing Anglo-Saxon law (Turner 1975, 4).

30. Corporations had their ups and downs in Rome. In 64 BCE all Roman *collegia* were officially abolished because of public disturbances created by newly formed political groups. The ban continued for six years, after which incorporation was again allowed and continued until the first years of the Imperial period. Julius Caesar revoked incorporation for all but professional and religious associations. Then, under Augustus, any group desiring to form a *collegium* had to seek licensure through the Senate, and membership in an unlicensed *collegium* was punishable as treason. Incorporation was legally systematized and monitored. Under Marcus Aurelius, corporations were recognized explicitly as juridical persons and could own slaves. The nature and purposes of these organizations were varied as they had been during the Republic; in addition to religious associations, there were associations of businessmen, tradesmen, and craftsmen (Patterson 1983, 94).

31. Scholars differ over the degree to which explicitly recognized Roman law persisted in the West over time. A copy of Justinian's *Digesta* was preserved at Pisa and a copy made in the eleventh century for the scholars in Bologna. There was also a copy of the *Code* in Verona (Ullman 1975, 68–69). These documents had a great impact on canon law, and clerics disseminated Roman law throughout the West (Ullman 1975, 72). The Visigoths in Spain were great legal scholars and preserved much of Roman law until being conquered by the Arabs in 711; despite the conquest, however, their legal influenced persisted. Not all scholars agree with Walter Ullman, but many do believe Roman law survived implicitly in altered form in Germanic codes and in purer form in some localized governmental institutions; for example, much of Roman property law seems to have remained intact in Lombardy into the eighth century, as charters of transactions show (Fouracre 1995, 8).

32. There was a great deal of controversy over this in Hobbes's time having to do with the question of the status of a corporation sole (Maitland 1975, 210ff.).

CHAPTER TWO

1. An account of Boyle's paper and its connection to Locke's work can be found in Uzgalis (2018). William Uzgalis cites the paper "Some Physico-Theological Considerations About the Possibility of the Resurrection" from its print source in *Selected Philosophical Papers of Robert Boyle*, ed. M. A. Stewart (Manchester University Press, 1979), 198. It is worth noting that Boyle and the other members of the Royal Society assumed that cannibals were also subject to divine judgment. The peoples of Africa and the Caribbean, where cannibals were thought to exist, had not yet been denied souls or deemed members of a lesser species.

2. And there are still commentators who reject Locke's distinction between person and thinking substance. See, for example, Lowe (2005, 94).

3. If Kirstie McClure (1996) is correct to view punishment as the primary motivation for and function of government on Locke's view, the stakes here could not be higher.

4. Not to mention the glaring philosophical problem: If persons are immaterial, how could they possibly have material effects in the first place?

5. There are a number of good summaries of Locke's argument in *Essay*, II.xxvii. A particularly clear and detailed one is Yaffe (2007). Another very interesting one is LoLordo (2012).

6. For the oak example, see *Essay* II.xxvii.4. Paragraph 5 applies this argument to animals before paragraph 6 goes on to make the argument for humans and then persons.

7. Étienne Balibar tells us that the English word *organization*, meaning "organized body," first appeared in 1450 and in French in 1488. Life began to be conceptualized as a fact of organization only in the latter half of the seventeenth century, which Locke would have known through his medical training (Balibar 2013, 94).

8. For an interesting discussion of this point, see Zack (1996, chap. 5). Zack, like many other commentators, equates this extension of consciousness into the past as memory. See also, for example, Radin (1982, 963). Harold Noonan has pointed out that Locke never actually uses the word *memory* in his discussion. Instead, he repeatedly refers to consciousness (Noonan 1989, 52–53). I have worded my description of Locke's position to avoid slipping into the assumption that awareness of past actions as one's own is the same as remembering those actions. What seems most important for Locke is the "mineness" of those actions, not their memorial status. Locke also says that brutes have memory, but they are not persons (*Essay* II.x.10, 151), as Yaffe points out (2007, 220).

9. Locke likely was unfamiliar with cases of repressed memories or with interrogation techniques that leave people genuinely confused about what they really did and did not do. He simply lumped people who could not keep up with their own behavior into the categories of lunatics and idiots (non-persons) and left it at that. But if we are not too deeply committed to the idea that a given consciousness's extent is totally dependent on that individual's memory, we could address the issue by looking not at the mistakes per se but at the ways people avoid making such mistakes. There are ways to reinforce consciousness, ways to check facts and prod memories, and people engage in these practices daily. In such practices, we depend on the people around us as well as available configurations of material objects to keep consciousness as extensive and consistent as possible. Consciousness is never entirely private, then, despite its individual identity. And just as we regularly rely on extra-mental supplements to keep our self-identities intact, parents, peers, magistrates, and courts can investigate events and assess guilt by drawing on those same social and material networks to reconstruct what a given consciousness probably includes. In this way, even if an accused person does not confess, a court can pass judgment. This system is not perfect, but earthly justice can never be perfect as God's justice is. That fact does not render earthly justice impossible. We must do the best we can. Locke might have balked at this way of supplementing his view, however, because it does tend to undermine radical individualism, to which he was apparently unquestioningly committed.

10. Although for many reasons I am skeptical of John Yolton's account of Locke's personhood, I agree with him that personhood is an achievement. He writes, "I think we can say that Locke's man is not born a person, but that the man can become a person, can develop into one" (2004, 9). Yolton refers especially to Locke's work on education to substantiate this view.

11. For an extensive textual analysis of Locke's person as a subject of accountability, see Boeker (2021, esp. 71ff.).

12. Karen Armstrong holds that Paul himself did not believe in the divinity of Jesus of Nazareth (1993, 96).

13. At first *Christian* was apparently a term of derision, but the followers of Jesus took it up and gave it a positive value. Personal communication from Ellen Armour, December 2013.

14. Marian Hillar suggests 150 CE as the culmination of the process, with the teachings of Justin Martyr (2012, 106).

15. As Hillar points out, Jews are (or at least were) not strict monotheists in that they did not rule out the idea that other peoples also had gods (2012, 221). Other deities might exist then, but for Jews there was only one deity.

16. Armstrong says Tertullian's dates are 160–220 CE (1993, 97). Ullman puts his dates as 150–230 (1975, 33). Hillar puts them as 170–230 (2012, 190). To me, it doesn't matter, although I imagine it mattered to Tertullian.

17. In fact, Tertullian could read Greek and early on wrote in Greek, but his preferred and usual language was Latin (Fortman 1972, 108).

18. According to Armstrong, "In the early years of the [third] century in Rome, one Sabellius, a rather shadowy figure, had suggested that the biblical terms 'Father,' 'Son,' and 'Spirit' could be compared to the masks (personae) worn by actors to assume a dramatic role and to make their voices audible to the audience. The One Godhead thus donned different personae when dealing with the world" (1993, 99). What for Sabellius might have been a helpful metaphor became something more nearly literal in Tertullian's writing.

19. Edmund Fortman contends that Tertullian was probably not the first to use the word *persona* in this way. He suggests that Hippolytus used it first (1972, 113).

20. Fortman asserts this (1972, 71), and Sarah Mortimer concurs (2010, 75).

21. However, it only occurs five times: Corinthians 9:4 and 11:17, where it means state or condition; Hebrews 1:3 and 3:14, where it means reality or being; and Hebrews 11:1, where it means something between realization and reality (Turcescu 2005, 20).

22. The Cappadocians may have drawn on Aristotle's early work the *Categories*, although it is uncertain whether they had direct knowledge of that work or only indirect knowledge through other writers such as Porphyry. Nevertheless, a quick review of Aristotle here will facilitate comprehension of the Cappadocians' intellectual strategy. In that early text, Aristotle sets out ten categories, one of which is substance, and further divides substance in two—namely, primary substance, which is both individual and indivisible, and secondary substance, which is species or genera and which can encompass or be divided into many individuals. (In his later work in the *Metaphysics*, Aristotle defines substance as that which cannot be a predicate, thereby denying that universals are substantial and eliminating the concept of secondary substance, but here we may set that aside.) Like the early Aristotle, the Cappadocians divide substance in two. For them, first substance is οὐσία (*ousia*), that which is common. Second substance is ὑπόστασις (hypostasis), that which is proper and concrete. The Godhead is first substance, οὐσία, and is common to all ὑποστάσες, which are second substances, each with a proper name and real, concrete existence. For discussion of this issue, see Phan (2011, 8), and Turcescu (2005, 26–40). This became generally accepted in Constantinople, although apparently the Cappadocians themselves had some reservations about the terminology.

23. The most relevant section of Augustine's *De Trinitate* is probably book 7, chapter 6.

24. Subtle, no? So subtle that, try as I might, I do not understand what I have just written, nor do I understand what I am about to write about Boethius's views. Fortunately, this is a genealogical account, not an explication.

25. When Theodoric, who was an Arian Christian, began to suspect that the Catholics in his service were conspiring with the Catholic emperor Justin to depose him, he imprisoned them, Boethius included, and ordered their execution. While in prison awaiting his fate, Boethius wrote his perhaps most famous text, *De Consolatione Philosophiae*, a philosophical classic that was translated into English as early as 1609.

26. Much of the information in this paragraph comes from McInery and O'Callaghan 2013.

27. Hans Hillerbrand notes that Calvin's actions can be "explained neither by the general intolerance of the age nor by the medieval Catholic legacy of the inquisition and persecution of heretics. In the extensive discussion that followed Servetus's death, Calvin remained adamant. His treatise *Defensio Orthodoxae Fidei de Sacra Trinitate* (*Defense of the Orthodox Faith Concerning the Holy Trinity*) conveys that the death penalty for heretics was an integral part of his theological thought" (2007, 135).

28. My primary source for the preceding two paragraphs is Mortimer 2010, especially chapter 1.

29. The title is apparently a reference to the vision of the prophet Ezekiel. In the midst of the vision, in which there is a lot of fire and things flying, God commands Ezekiel to ingest a scroll (a rolled-up book). See Ezekiel chapters 3 and 4. Beyond this, your guess is as good as mine.

30. Actually, the question was already open for discussion in 1648 when New Model Army leaders began to deliberate over a new state constitution. In that process, the groundwork could have been laid for a new state church. It soon became clear, however, that agreement on the religious issue was not possible. Many, including the Levellers, wanted a commodious settlement that would confer freedom of conscience on the people, but many others insisted on giving magistrates authority to compel an established doctrine and form of worship. Henry Ireton (1611–1651), a Calvinist who was at that time commissary general of the New Model Army and Oliver Cromwell's son-in-law, vehemently opposed liberty of conscience; he and his allies insisted that enforced belief in the Trinity and the Incarnation were essential to a national church (Mortimer 2010, 190–96). But this debate was soon displaced. The trial and execution of King Charles took center stage, followed by rebellion in Ireland, followed by the attempt of the executed king's son, Charles Stuart, and his Scottish military allies to retake the realm. Not until the fall of 1651 was Charles Stuart's incursion stopped.

31. The number nine hundred comes from Wroughton (2006, 35), but other sources suggest higher numbers.

32. James, then Duke of York, had secretly converted to Catholicism in 1668 or 1669, but this did not become known until 1673. At that time, because of the passage of the Test Act of 1673, all military leaders had to swear to Protestant oaths or resign their position. James resigned his admiralty rather than swear.

33. I am ever grateful to Paul C. Lim at Vanderbilt Divinity School for alerting me to this text and to the similarity of Sherlock's views to Locke's, in a conversation I had with students and faculty at Vanderbilt on April 8, 2014.

34. The Anglo-Germanic term was an option he implicitly acknowledged: "*Person*, as I take it, is the name for this *self*. Wherever a man finds what he calls *himself*, there I think another may say it is the *same person*" (Locke, *Essay* II.xxvii.26, 312).

35. We know that Locke commented on one of Boyle's manuscripts in that year, and his written notes are extant. Peter Anstey (2020) has done a comparative study of Locke's comments and Boyle's published text to make a plausible argument that, indeed, an early version of *The Christian Virtuoso* was the text that Locke reviewed.

36. In this, Boyle was merely following the received account of natural law that goes back at least to Francis Suárez's 1612 work *De legibus, ac Deo legislatore* (Haakonssen 1996, 19).

37. We are accustomed to reading Locke as speaking primarily not of a duty but of a right to life and consequently to the appropriation of resources required for sustenance. But it is in seventeenth-century natural law theory, natural rights were always derivatives of natural duties (Haakonssen 1991, 20) and were nothing more than means for fulfilling duties. Where no duty existed, there was no right; if we subtract the *duty* to preserve our lives, along with it we lose the *right* to preserve them as well. Today, in stark contrast to Locke, duty or no duty, most people assert the primacy of a person's right to life; a fundamental feature of personhood seems to be the right to life. Indeed, were it not the case that a claim to personhood entails a claim of a right to life regardless of the existence of duties to fulfill, there would be a lot less controversy over whether fetuses, chimpanzees, and brain-dead hospital patients are persons at all. Obviously, some very fundamental shift in meaning has occurred since Locke's time. Now, rights seem to stand logically first, with duties deriving from them—if I have a right, then you have a duty to respect that right. As Joseph Raz puts it, "Rights are grounds of duties in others" (Raz 2006, 41); they are decidedly *not* a set of tools granted to their bearers only because of some duty those bearers already had. One can look back at more than two centuries of US history and see documents that boldly assert inalienable or natural rights but say absolutely nothing about any natural duties from which those rights might have arisen. Consider the second paragraph of the Declaration of Independence of 1776: "We hold these truths to be self-evident, that all men are created equal, that they are endowed by their Creator with certain unalienable Rights, that among these are Life, Liberty and the pursuit of Happiness." Not a word here about what duties we are supposed to fulfill by means of these rights. Also, Thomas Paine's 1791 pamphlet *Rights of Man*: "Natural rights are those which appertain to man in right of his existence. Of this kind are all the intellectual rights, or rights of the mind, and also all those rights of acting as an individual for his own comfort and happiness, which are not injurious to the natural rights of others" (Paine 1791, 36). Who says anything about duties? If we read these eighteenth-century works outside of their eighteenth-century context, we can easily get the impression that rights have always been understood—in Anglo-America at least—as a sort of property we possess *sui generis* rather than as a power bestowed upon us so that we can meet an obligation. In these famous American documents, we find none of Locke's chain of reasoning from a duty to preserve God's moral creation to the right of appropriating resources for survival. Yet, a broader survey of that eighteenth-century context would show us that rights were still understood as powers granted in the service of fulfilling duties. Eighteenth-century writers and readers of these documents would have assumed that these rights existed only as means to that end. Nothing about human individuals in and of themselves implied any rights at all; individuals had rights only as deliberating *creatures*—that is, only as they stood in relation to the superior authority that Jefferson called "Nature and Nature's God." The severing of right from its roots in duty had not yet occurred. Good government required recognition of those rights and protection of them, to be sure, and that was

the basis for the American critique of the British Parliament and Crown. In violating American rights, the British government prevented American colonists from fulfilling their duty to preserve the moral creation and pursue its happiness.

38. The term "private property" here might be a bit misleading for some readers. As my friend Andrew Dilts reminds me, since Marx political theorists typically distinguish between private property and personal property, with the former referring to ownership of the means of production rather than to possession of objects we use in our daily lives. If we want to adhere to that distinction, we should probably say that Locke is talking about personal property. In a Lockean state of nature, prior to the invention of money, there would have been no private property in that strict Marxian sense, although there would have been plenty of personal property, some of which would have been productive of the means of subsistence for individuals, families, or even communities, but would not have been productive of surplus value.

39. Even readers who seriously misinterpreted Locke understood the distinction he was making between *person* and *body* in his *Essay*. Although the two treatises were published anonymously in 1689/90, everyone knew their author's identity well before Locke's death, so cross-referencing the two works should have been the norm. Opposition to Locke's claims in the early eighteenth century focused in part on his rejection of the body as fundamental to personhood (Felton 1725, 5).

40. Although the *Two Treatises* and the *Essay* were published in tandem, it is known that Locke actually composed the former sometime around 1680, whereas he composed II.xxvii of the *Essay* in 1693 (Woolhouse 2006, 329–31). One might question whether the understanding of personhood that he presents there is operative in the much earlier text. Still, Locke does closely ally the activities of reasoning and laboring throughout the *Second Treatise*, thus suggesting that accumulation of wealth is evidence of superior intellect put to good use.

41. For a discussion of this point, see Huyler (1995, 110–14).

42. Knud Haakonssen suggests that Jefferson used the broad phrase "pursuit of happiness" instead of asserting an inalienable right to property, because what is required for people to pursue happiness might be different in different societies (1991, 49–50). Margaret Radin argues that modern American law assumes that persons have fundamental rights to property. She writes, "The premise underlying the personhood perspective is that to achieve proper self-development—to be a *person*—an individual needs some control over resources in the external environment. The necessary assurances of control take the form of property rights" (1982, 957).

CHAPTER THREE

1. It may seem odd here to include plants, but see Matthew Hall's book *Plants as Persons: A Philosophical Botany*. Hall urges us to consider plants as persons: "The earned, practical recognition of plants as persons releases us from the dichotomy of regarding nature either as a combination of *processes* or *things*. Instead, it puts forward the view that nature is a community of subjective, collaborative beings that organize and experience their own lives" (2011, 169).

2. My argument here bears some resemblance to Saidiya Hartman's suggestion that recognition of enslaved individuals' humanity did nothing to reduce the violence done to them and even, in fact, made that violence more likely. Hartman asserts that humanizing enslaved people served the purpose of criminalizing them rather than liberating

them. She writes: "However, suppose that the recognition of humanity held out the promise not of liberating the flesh or redeeming one's suffering but rather of intensifying it? Or what if this acknowledgement was little more than a pretext for punishment, dissimulation of the violence of chattel slavery and the sanction given it by the law and the state, and an instantiation of racial hierarchy?" and "It was often the case that benevolent corrections and declarations of slave humanity intensified the brutal exercise of power upon the captive body rather than ameliorating the chattel condition" (1997, 5). I argue here that attributing moral personhood to enslaved people simply made them responsible in ways that supposedly justified punishment.

3. According to Brad Hinshelwood, the Carolina Colony was the only one of the British North American colonies to begin with a preference for African slave labor. Enslaved Africans were among its first settlers (2013, 577).

4. Wayne Glausser (1990) investigates three interpretations in the secondary literature prior to 1990: (1) The discrepancy between Locke's theory and practice represents a "minor lapse" that does not affect the worth of his theory. (2) Locke uses "tortured logic" to make his practice seem aligned with his theory. (3) In fact, Locke's theory does accommodate chattel slavery.

5. In 1697 as commissioner on the Board of Trade, Locke proposed that the poor law be more strongly enforced and amended to create "working schools" for children between three and fourteen, which in fact were not schools but wool-spinning factories, wherein they would work for nothing but shelter, bread, and water (and warm gruel in winter if it could be made with the same firewood used for heating). Landowners, farmers, and craftsmen could take any boy of their choosing out of the industry and put him into an unpaid apprenticeship until he was twenty-three. All boys not chosen by age fourteen would be forced into farmwork without pay until age twenty-three or sent to shipmasters for a nine-year tour at sea. Adult males caught begging would be sent to sea for three years or to houses of correction for three years—longer if not found to be diligent at the end of their sentences. Adult females would be sent to houses of correction for six weeks. (One could imagine that many people would have been subject to these temporary enslavements repeatedly throughout their lives.) People absolutely not able to work at all would be housed four to a room and fed by way of a poor tax. See Locke 1697, at https://pols2900.files.wordpress.com/2011/01/poorlaw.pdf. Locke also proposed a procedure for dealing with people who went to the parish guardian of the poor asking for relief payments on what he called the "pretense" of not being able to find work. Needless to say, it involved forcing them to work. Locke's proposal was not the only one at the time. In 1698 Andrew Fletcher, a political theorist and member of the Scottish Parliament, proposed to Parliament that Scottish vagabonds (he estimated that there were about 200,000, which would have been about a sixth of the total population) should be enslaved by the state and parceled out to landowners. Bishop George Berkeley proposed enslaving the Irish poor in 1735, and Francis Hutcheson proposed a similar scheme in 1755 for the English poor (Rozbicki 2001, 30–36). Hutcheson also argued that merchants who purchased slaves in Africa for trading in the American colonies were actually saving the lives of those people, indebting them to their European owners (Rozbicki 2001, 38).

6. For some of these details, see Armitage (2004), Glausser (1990), and Dupre (2018), 62.

7. For those who worked in industries and institutions other than agriculture, much depended on individual owners' or supervisors' proclivities, so conditions could vary

considerably. For that reason, I will stick with the relatively more uniform and more common conditions of agricultural workers.

8. It is hard to know what to say about the way in which white interviewers rendered Black interviewees' vernacular in the WPA texts. I refer the reader to Hartman's comments on the problematic nature of these documents and her use of them (1997, 11).

9. The most brutal memoir that I have read is that of Frank Bell, who was never employed as a field hand. He was the only slave of a saloon owner in New Orleans in the two decades before Emancipation. When his master, Johnson Bell, discovered that young Frank had secretly married, he caught the young woman, beheaded her in front of Frank, and forced Frank to dispose of her body by throwing it in the Mississippi River (Yetman 2002, 9). But there are many just as terrifying and grisly.

10. Patsey's infraction consisted of going on a Sunday to visit a female friend on a neighboring plantation. Epps, who had been raping Patsey for years, believed she had left in order to "cheat on" him with the other planter and would not be persuaded otherwise. Epps's wife blamed Patsey for her husband's "infidelity" and hated her. Northup reports that she watched the beating with "heartless satisfaction" (1859, 183). He does not record the children's reactions, but presumably they were not terribly distressed by what they heard and saw.

11. I am not qualified to speak of the situation in South America, although I suspect it was similar in this respect.

12. There were vast differences across tribes and times, however. For a wide range of those differences, see Graeber and Wengrow (2021).

13. If you can stand some horrific reading (and you really should think first, because horrific it is), you can learn about some of these bloodbaths in Dunbar-Ortiz (2014), especially chapter 4. Dunbar-Ortiz suggests that the term "redskin" comes from the mutilated corpses white "rangers" routinely left in fields and woods (65).

14. This attitude appears to have prevailed primarily where Indigenous peoples had no economic worth to whites and presented barriers to capitalist accumulation. Perhaps the economic value of enslaved people—which made living in proximity to them necessary for many whites—helped to generate practices of management and judgment that a concept of moral personhood aided.

15. During the Pequot Wars (1636 and 1638), Connecticut and Massachusetts paid colonists for every Pequot head they turned in to authorities. Scalp bounties first appeared in colonial law in the 1670s. During King Philip's War (1675–78), the Plymouth Colony offered five shillings' worth of trucking cloth for every "head skin" a colonist brought in. In July 1689 during King William's War, Massachusetts offered eight pounds for each scalp (Grenier 2005, 39). Unwilling to send militia to aid the North Carolina Colony in its war against the Tuscaroras in 1711, the Virginia House of Burgesses offered a bounty of twenty pounds for every Indian scalp brought to them (Grenier 2005, 44).

16. Frightened Delaware, who had declared themselves neutral, asked for protection from the British authorities but received nothing other than a warning to stay away from colonists (Grenier 2005, 158).

17. The Creek were not an ethnically or linguistically homogeneous tribe. After the collapse of the Mississippian civilization (which may have been the result of disease), smaller groups formed alliances and confederation. According to Kevin Kokomoor, Creek ethnogenesis occurred between 1718 and 1776 (2018, 18). Dupre says that by 1715, the English referred to the Coweta, Cusseta, and Hitchiti as the Lower Creeks and the Abihka, Tallapoosa, and other groups to the west of the Chattahoochee River as the

Upper Creeks. But they had no overarching governmental infrastructure and were still organized as autonomous talwas (towns) (Dupre 2018, 65). Daniel Dupre says most of the groups spoke a version of Muskogee, but not all did.

18. For details of these events, see Kokomoor (2018, 1–13, esp. 12–13).

19. This is not to say that Creek and other tribes did not attribute actions to particular people and honor or disdain (or even punish) them as individuals as a result. Of course they did. But it is to say that responsibility for wrongdoing and for restoring right balance, at least across groups, in the wake of it was not individualized as it was in the European discourses and practices that make personhood a central category.

20. The one exception that I am aware of is described in Graeber and Wengrow (2021, chap. 5). The Yurok of the Pacific Northwest seem to have formed in opposition to their neighbors' practices of capturing people and enslaving them. They may have coalesced as a group after escaping from enslavement. At any rate, they were adamant that each individual should have his or her own property and that no one be enslaved.

21. Never mind that, among most groups of Indigenous peoples, males had never been heads of households, and figuring out which males were to assume that status was chaotic and confusing to all concerned.

22. All US treaties signed with North American Indigenous groups can be found here from GovInfo: https://tinyurl.com/bdhbzu2e.

CHAPTER FOUR

1. Which is not to say that class domination was what Locke had in mind when he formulated it. He was solving a set of philosophical, theological, and ethico-theoretical problems. But he solved them in a way that would not disturb his class biases or endanger his and his friends' and patron's status and wealth. In fact, he solved them in a way that would secure their status and likely enhance their wealth.

2. While the words *contract* and *covenant* may be interchangeable for us and might have been for Hobbes, the history of *covenant* differs from that of *contract*. A covenant historically was an agreement between a stronger and a weaker party wherein the weaker pledged fealty to the stronger in exchange for protection. This is the reason the agreement between God and the Israelites was a covenant, not a contract (an agreement between supposed equals), and the reason that agreements between lords and vassals were covenants, not contracts. It seems that Hobbes's notion partakes in some of the connotations of covenants and some of the connotations of contracts.

3. According to Arihira Fukuda (1997, 93), Bodin, Hobbes, and James Harrington all saw the sovereign as a unity of wills. It could not be a single will.

4. Michel Foucault refers to and employs this older sense of the term *government* through much of his late work. See, for example, Foucault (2014, 12).

5. The idea that sovereignty consists in the power to command is still very present today. See, for example, Jacques Derrida's 2001–2 seminar, published as *The Beast and the Sovereign* (2009, 4). In that seminar, Derrida considers many different meanings of *sovereignty*, including medieval meanings such as "excellence," "first rank," and other such adjectives in application to anyone who evinced superiority in any skill or area. The primary meaning throughout the seminar, however, is that of command; sovereignty is the correlate of subjection.

6. Of course, many people who are not sovereign command others. Generals command soldiers; masters command servants and apprentices; parents command

children; husbands command wives. For Hobbes, these examples of superiors obligating inferiors fall short of sovereignty both because they are not the final rung of superiority in the hierarchy of the state and because they are not constituted by the unification of individual governing powers.

7. These are sovereignty by creation (as opposed to birth), sovereignty by donation (God gave man dominion in Genesis 1:28), sovereignty by Eve's subjection (Eve's curse is to be ruled by her husband), and sovereignty by begetting. Locke devotes a chapter to each of these.

8. Locke and Robert Filmer both assume that Genesis is a unified account of creation, whereas modern scholars believe it is two different stories compressed into one text. The first story concludes in Genesis 1:31: "And God saw every thing that he had made, and, behold, it *was* very good. And the evening and the morning were the sixth day" (King James translation, 1611). The second story begins in Genesis 2 with God's seventh day's rest followed by his planting of the garden and creation of Adam and Eve. This would reinforce Locke's claim that God gave dominion to humans in common, not just to Adam, although Locke would undoubtedly have trouble with the idea that Genesis is not a unitary narrative.

9. Locke points out that Noah and his sons did receive the right to eat the fishes, fowl, and animals after the Flood in Genesis 9:2–4. There God tells them, "[T]he fear of you and the dread of you shall be upon every beast of the earth, and upon every fowl of the air, upon all that moveth *upon* the earth, and upon all the fishes of the sea; into your hand are they delivered. / Every moving thing that liveth shall be meat for you; even as the green herbs I have given you all things. / But flesh with the life thereof, *which is* the blood thereof, shall ye not eat." Their dominion, while still limited, is closer to full ownership in that they can destroy the fish, birds, and animals in consuming them, something Adam was apparently not allowed to do.

10. Granted, one could fit into all these categories simultaneously, but the public discourses of each group appear to arise and draw sustenance from some very different political departure points.

11. William Blackstone declared that, unless a contract specified otherwise, it was assumed to be for a year "'that the servant shall serve and the master maintain him, throughout all the revolutions of the respective seasons; as well as when there is work to be done as when there is not.' Authority over the servant's time was perpetual: the employer had obtained the day-in, day-out attentions of a servant in a relationship of some reciprocity" (Steedman 2004, 5–6). The employer owned the servant's time twenty-four hours a day for however long the employment lasted.

12. C. B. Macpherson (1973) has argued vigorously, against Peter Laslett in particular, that the category of servant included all wage earners in the seventeenth century. He also asserts that all wage earners in seventeenth-century England (and presumably in the English colonies in North America) were nonpersons (216–17).

13. Examples abound, but here are a few from the *Diary of Samuel Pepys*. From December 1, 1660: "This morning, observing some things to be laid up not as they should be by the girl, I took a broom and basted her till she cried extremely, which made me vexed, but before I went out I left her appeased." From June 21, 1662: ". . . hearing from my wife and the maids' complaints made of the boy, I called him up, and with my whip did whip him till I was not able to stir, and yet I could not make him confess any of the lies that they tax him with. At last, not willing to let him go away a conqueror, I took him in task again, and pulled off his frock to his shirt, and whipped him till he did

confess that he did drink the whey, which he had denied, and pulled a pink, and above all did lay the candlestick upon the ground in his chamber, which he had denied this quarter of a year. I confess it is one of the greatest wonders that ever I met with that such a little boy as he could possibly be able to suffer half so much as he did to maintain a lie. I think I must be forced to put him away. So to bed, with my arm very weary." From June 23, 1663: "... calling, as I have of late done, for my boy's copybook, I found that he had not done his task; so I beat him, and then went up to fetch my rope's end, but before I got down the boy was gone. I searched the cellar with a candle, and from top to bottom could not find him high nor low. So to the office.... So home to dinner alone, and there I found that my boy had got out of doors, and came in for his hat and band, and so is gone away to his brother; but I do resolve even to let him go away for good and all." Pepys's *Diary* can be found online in its entirety, searchable by date, at https://www.pepysdiary.com/.

14. My copy of the autobiography is so old that it does not include a publication date. It is not a first edition, but I have no way of knowing what edition it is. However, for what it is worth, the references in this paragraph are from pages 251–56.

15. Warren's partner in this venture was Stephen Pearl Andrews, a polymath abolitionist attorney who championed "free love." All of Warren's communities allowed and even encouraged personal experimentation, so although Warren thought polygamy was unworkable, he did not object to residents trying it. Nor did he object to nudism or a variety of other "experiments" conducted in Modern Times. Many people outside the community did object, however, and some of their objections found their way into the press, not only in New York but also back in Ohio and elsewhere. There were even some attempts to sabotage the community by planting people in it who would intentionally run afoul of neighbors and local law enforcement with the aim of giving it a bad reputation and limiting its growth.

16. The town of Brentwood still exists today and maintains an archive documenting its principled history. For accounts of all three of Warren's villages, see Warren (2011, 202–29).

17. The *Manifesto*, which is a very short document, is available online at http://dwardmac.pitzer.edu/Anarchist_Archives/bright/warren/WarrenManifesto/Pages/3.html.

18. Warren says this at least as early as 1852 in *Equitable Commerce* (2011, 89).

19. Ultimately there might be no need for attorneys.

20. The 2011 collection, edited by Crispin Sartwell, corrects much of Warren's odd and usually emphatic punctuation. One can see Warren's preferred punctuation in the online edition, edited by Stephen Pearl Andrews, at https://archive.org/details/equitablecommerc00warr.

21. Some sources say he was a founder of Utopia (see Sartwell 2011, 4), but others, such as Ann Caldwell Butler's 1978 dissertation at Ball State University, say he joined a newly established community there. A village had been established by Charles Fourier and his followers in 1844. But by 1847, the Fourier community was gone, and the property had been purchased by spiritualist John Wattles for a new community. This new version of Utopia operated according to Warren's principles. Butler writes, "Utopia had no government, no laws, no police and was based on Warren's philosophy of voluntary subordination or mutual aid. This, coupled with the labor-for-labor system, was to create a sovereign individual" (Butler 1978; abstract online at http://cardinalscholar.bsu.edu/handle/handle/175361?show=full).

22. In 1821 he acquired a patent for a lamp that burned lard instead of more expensive tallow (Sartwell 2011, 4). In 1820 he started setting up a small factory in Cincinnati to manufacture it for sale.

23. In his young adulthood, Warren seems not to have thought much about chattel slavery. When he did begin to think seriously about it in the years prior to the Civil War, he was clearly very troubled by it. His principles set him utterly against it, but he struggled to think through any way to mount and justify collective action to dismantle it. His principles also set him firmly against coverture; in his communities, women and children were to have as much control over their labor and products and men did.

24. Let it be noted here that Warren uses what we, since the early 1970s, have called "gender-inclusive language." Women and men are equally sovereign. He supported the women's movement of his time and repeal of coverture.

25. He does agree, however, that the purpose of any social organization is the happiness of that organization's members (Warren 2011, 104, 135).

26. See also Warren (2011, 138), his essay "Money" from August 1873: "All government issues of money are so many drafts upon labor akin to forgeries or burglaries. They get the product of labor by trick, by stealth, or else by force of arms like highway robbery: extorting by bodily fear; such are all 'legal tender' laws and all statutes forbidding individuals from issuing their own notes." The last clause is a reference to his villagers' practice of issuing labor notes to use for exchange. These could not circulate; they could only be redeemed by the person to whom they were issued in exchange for that person's equivalent amount of labor. Warren's solution to violations of people's rights was ad hoc community action on a case-by-case basis, not sitting legislatures but councils formed to deal with specific issues as they arose, as he describes in 1863 in *True Civilization* (see Warren 2011, esp. 147–50). As editor Sartwell notes, this text evinces Warren's personal struggle with the secession, Civil War, and slavery. He needed to find a principled way to justify coordinated action to free the slaves. As strange as his proposal of councils and regional decision-making sounds, it is not altogether different from the ways in which colonists came together to raise armies and make war against England.

27. And the few exceptions are scary: on the one hand, a police state with constant surveillance and, on the other, something like the domestic terrorists on the FBI watch list known as the Sovereign Citizens who recognize no laws, including those against murder. See the FBI website: https://archives.fbi.gov/archives/news/stories/2010/april/sovereigncitizens_041310/domestic-terrorism-the-sovereign-citizen-movement.

28. It must never be forgotten that John Stuart Mill was an apologist for the East India Company. In 1858, having been promoted to chief examiner, Mill wrote a long petition to Parliament to stave off nationalization of the company. In that document, Mill claimed that the East India company had at its "own expense, and by the agency of their own civil and military servants, originally acquired for this country its magnificent empire in the East," thereby glorifying the then-failing company as a mechanism of British colonialism, and then he went on to claim that the company's rule in India was "the most beneficent [government] ever known among mankind" (quoted in Robins 2012, 195–96). Mill was a company man above all.

29. Things were similarly explicit to the north; the Supreme Court of Canada ruled in 1928 that women were not persons under Canadian law. The next year, however, the Judicial Committee of the British Privy Council ruled on appeal that the word *persons* in section 24 of the British North America Act included "members both of the male and female sex" (Benoit, n.d.).

30. This remained the case for several decades. Before 1890 most businesses were owned by individuals or partners; incorporation was a fairly rare occurrence (Yablon 2007, 354).

31. This is from an 1816 letter to George Logan and is available online at https://founders.archives.gov/documents/Jefferson/03-10-02-0390.

32. This letter is available online at https://founders.archives.gov/documents/Madison/04-04-02-0304.

33. The Supreme Court did not consider whether a corporation might operate across state lines until 1839 (*Bank of Augusta v. Earle*) (Mark 1987, 1456).

34. New Jersey's law allowed companies to own stock in other companies and to incorporate for any lawful business purpose, not just those deemed to be in the public interest (Horwitz 1986, 195).

35. The Sherman Act did not prohibit companies from merging, however, and after its enactment, they went on a buying spree, resulting in far greater concentration of market power (Cerri 2018, 260).

36. Baxter was "devoted to Chicago-School economics with the same intensity that others worship a deity" (Galambos 2004, 157).

37. I should note that some commentators, Bernard Harcourt in particular, contend that "deregulation" is a misnomer; in fact, neoliberal policies have actually dismantled regulations that constrained corporate activity while re-regulating, or differently regulating, markets, non-corporate institutions, and people's lives. See Harcourt (2011, esp. 191–96, 242).

38. At least one scholar has suggested that Innocent was not the actual author (Conard 1976, 417n5). What difference this makes, I don't know, but I like to be thorough, just in case it turns out that it does matter upon further investigation. At any rate, Innocent or the true author drew a bright line between that which God made, persons with souls, and that which man made, persons without souls, corporations. Only two passages in Innocent's *Apparatus* bear specifically on the ontological status of a *collegium* or *universitas* (both terms designating legally recognized corporate personae). In the first, Innocent notes that when a *collegium* is required to swear an oath, it can do so either by having each member swear or by having one member swear on its collective behalf. The latter option exists, he says, because "the College is in corporate matters figured as a person" (*cum collegium in causa universitatis fingatur una persona*) (Koessler 1949, 437). In the second passage, Innocent considers whether a *universitas*, such as a monastery, can be excommunicated. He answers that it cannot be, "because Corporation as well as Chapter, Tribe, and so on, are legal terms rather than names of persons" (*quia universitats secut est capitulum, populous, gens et haec nomina sunt juris et non personarum*) (Koessler 1949, 438). Innocent acknowledges in the first passage that the law treats a *collegium* as it treats an individual person; in law it *is* an individual person. Then in the second passage, where he is concerned about excommunication, he uses the genitive plural of *persona* as if it normally applies only to individual people, not to groups no matter how organized.

39. Coke's argument and his definition of corporate person can be found online at https://oll.libertyfund.org/titles/shepherd-selected-writings-of-sir-edward-coke-vol-i.

40. The full text of the decision can be found at www.law.cornell.edu, as well as several other internet sites.

41. They preferred what some refer to as the contract theory, the idea that a corporation is really a bundle of contracts among the shareholders, so even though the

corporation holds and disposes of property independently of those shareholders (who also have limited liability), that property ultimately belongs to them, those real people with the same rights as unincorporated real people (see Cerri 2018, 246–49).

42. This comment was part of the headnote inserted by the court reporter, not part of the actual opinion read by Justice Harlan. See the case at http://supreme.justia.com/cases/federal/us/118/394/. Although the court has since used *Santa Clara* as a precedent for application of the Fourteenth Amendment to corporate persons, Thom Hartmann has argued that this was not the *Santa Clara* court's intent (see Hartmann 2010, chap. 1). Whether all the justices were of Chief Justice Waite's opinion on this matter is highly unlikely (see n. 43 below), but it is known that Waite and Justice Stephen Field held this view (see also Horwitz 1986, 177).

43. Justice William Burnham Woods, for one, did not believe the amendment covered corporate persons (Winkler 2018, 152).

44. After his presidency, Grant helped to create the Mexican Pacific Railroad (see Hardy 1955).

45. With a few notable exceptions such as Hugo Black and William O. Douglas (Hartmann 2010, 24). For a long quotation from Black on the matter, see Clements (2012, 72–73).

46. Luigi Cerri, for one, rejects the headnote story as a minor factor in the growth of corporate power (2018, 262).

47. Legal literature from the first four decades of the twentieth century is replete with articles on corporate personhood; this debate was very lively and sometimes acerbic. By 1930 Frederick Hallis declared that "the Fiction Theory is worse than useless" ([1930] 1978, 243); "the conception of corporate personality supplied by the orthodox Fiction Theory has broken down completely in its attempt to give legal form to the facts of corporate life, and it is the theory which must be abandoned" (xxxiii).

48. Otto von Gierke, a German legal scholar, held that the concession theory construed corporate legal personhood as a fiction, whereas he believed corporations had a real existence apart from the state. In fact, however, neither Innocent nor Coke had said the corporation was not real, only that its reality was conferred by law (see Deiser 1908, 136; Koessler 1949, 437).

49. For a discussion of the Supreme Court's shift away from any attempt to settle these issues, see Mayer (1990, esp. 25–27).

50. Radin mentions a particularly interesting set of cases in which courts found that corporations, unlike their shareholders, were not raced. In *People's Pleasure Park v. Rohleder* (1908), a court held that a corporation was not a Negro although all its members were. This allowed the corporation to lease a park whose deed prohibited leasing to Negroes. In *People v. Awa* (1865), a court declared that the state of California is not white (see Radin 1932, 660–61).

51. By the 1920s, the so-called "M-form," or multidimensional form of corporate structure, enabled firms to manage national and international operations and provide diverse products efficiently (Galambos 2004, 153)—something nineteenth-century theorists had thought was impossible. So they grew even bigger, richer, and more politically powerful. But their political influence was only one of the concerns jurists and policymakers voiced in the first decades of the twentieth century. There were also questions of corporate interest that ran counter to the interests of consumers and workers. In 1909, in the case of *People v. Rochester Railway & Light Co.*, the New York Court of Appeals considered the possibility that a corporation could be guilty of

second-degree manslaughter for negligence in installation of a machine (88 N.E. 22, N.Y. 1909). The court found for the corporation, but Judge Hiscock noted that under other circumstances, he might find a corporation guilty of a crime, as long as it did not involve "personal, malicious intent." After all, as Ernst Freund had pointed out in 1897, the beneficiary of such crimes was not the individual employee, as would be the case if a person had embezzled money, but the corporation itself as a common stock of property and bundle of shareholder interests (Freund 1897, 64–68). Corporations themselves might well be liable then, but if they were in fact devoid of emotion or intent, they could not be vicious (see Lipton 2010, 1931–32). In 1909 the Supreme Court seemed to agree; in *New York Central & Hudson River Railroad Co. v. United States* (212 U.S. 481, 494, 1909), it upheld criminal liability against a corporation for paying rebates to corporate patrons in violation of the Elkins Act. Thus, the court endorsed the idea of criminal liability, but the question of *mens rea* remained open as jurists vigorously debated the existence of a corporate mind, will, and intentions. In 1916 Harold Laski urged acceptance of the idea that the corporation has a mind distinct to the minds of its members and that it "must bear the responsibility for its actions" (Laski 1916, 415, 413). If corporations were real persons and not fictional ones, not only should they have the rights of persons, but they should also bear the responsibilities. It was becoming clear that, insofar as it could be made to support the idea of corporate mentality and, hence, *mens rea*, the entity theory posed as much of a threat as a promise to corporate growth and power. Perhaps in part for that reason, the theoretical questions were never settled. Instead, the issue simply dropped from sight in the late 1930s and was omitted from legal textbooks by 1976 (Mark 1987, 1441; Bratton 1989, 1508–09). Peter French (1984) has tried to give a philosophical foundation for holding corporations, as such, morally responsible for their actions.

52. As James Coleman puts it, "It is the corporate actors, the organizations that draw their power from persons and employ that power to corporate ends, that are the primary actors in the social structure of modern society" (1974, 49).

53. They can, of course, cease to exist, but as we saw with the transformation of bankrupt WorldCom into Verizon, big ones tend to transform or sometimes divide but rarely dissolve entirely. Their lifespans are indefinite; they do not age. For obvious reasons, they cannot be imprisoned or subjected to corporal punishment or execution. It is extremely rare for a state to revoke a charter, and there is nothing to stop a corporation from simply chartering elsewhere if one does.

CHAPTER FIVE

1. Perhaps the most famous modern example is Friedrich Karl von Savigny's treatise on the *Jus Possessionis* (1848). It is divided into six books, and all of book I is on the definition of *possession*, a total of 141 pages. Read it if you dare.

2. For discussions of husband and wife and lord and vassal, see, for example, Rüfner (2010). Apparently, the Romans did not allow common ownership (although Savigny says there were disputes over this—see Savigny [1848, 112–15]). Medieval jurists wanted to reconcile their laws with Roman law, but they also needed to explain how a lord and his vassals both owned the same land, so, according to Thomas Rüfner, Bartolus de Saxoferrato, and others developed superior and inferior ownership, a legal hierarchy of owning.

3. All three of these have generated voluminous scholarship and case law. The answer is no or not necessarily to all three, with myriad conditions and exceptions. For some real fun, look into the scholarship on oil ownership in Texas. Water rights, both surface and ground, have been in dispute all over the world for a very long time. After all, water is life. It is especially contentious right now in the southwestern United States, Central America, and the Middle East; and India, despite its very long history of communal water management, is not far behind. Airspace rights only came into legal scholarship with the invention of airplanes and was settled in favor of airline companies. However, the recent availability of small drones has brought the issue to the fore once more. For a discussion of that and much, much more, see Winchester for airplanes and drones (2021, 215).

4. Although there is much controversy over whether slavery is in effect legal in Sudan. Since 1995 a number of reports have suggested that the government of Sudan has backed and armed slave-taking militias and has failed to enforce kidnapping laws and laws against forced labor. Some sources say enslaving ended in 2002, but an unknown number of people remained in conditions of slavery.

5. Yes, even the wind. It turns out that very large wind turbines disturb airflow so much that they can interfere with the working of turbines downwind, in some cases making them non-operational. This has led to disputes over, yes, the wind. Imagine what will happen when companies start vying to sell climate-changing technologies.

6. If there is a heaven, and if Martin Heidegger is in it, and if I go there too (all very big "ifs"), I want to be the one to tell him.

7. It is important to remember that in the United States today, there are many people with steady jobs who are both penniless and unhoused. Some estimate that about 25 percent of the US homeless population is employed. According to endhomelessness.org, in 2019 on any given night, 567,715 people were without housing. Of course, the numbers have risen since the coronavirus pandemic began the following year.

8. Jamie Birt, "14 Ways That Employees Can Take Ownership at Work," Indeed.com, https://www.indeed.com/career-advice/career-development/taking-ownership-at-work.

9. Michelle Rees, "How to Take Ownership of Your Life and Get Everything You Want," https://www.wholelifechallenge.com/how-to-take-ownership-of-your-life-and-get-everything-you-want/.

10. Daniel Attas not only raises the question. He also attempts to provide an answer saying that these theorists (and libertarians in particular) believe that if I don't own something, somebody else does. Therefore, if I can't be said to own myself, someone else owns me; I am a slave. Attas calls this the "fallacy of exhaustive ownership," the idea that everything that can be identified can and will in fact be or become someone's property. Attas illustrates the operation of this fallacy with an examination of the work of Robert Nozick (Attas 2000, 7–8). I am unsatisfied with Attas's answer to his question, however. It seems to me to be nothing more than a redescription of what these theorists do, not an account of why they do it or why most of us do it so much of the time.

11. Saint Clare wanted the sisters to constitute an order unto themselves, but in 1215 the Fourth Lateran Council put a moratorium on new orders, making their independence impossible (see Northcutt 2018, 6).

12. According to Malcolm Lambert, the Benedictines would have been happy to give the chapel and space to the Franciscans, but Francis was determined not

to own anything. The orders agreed that the Franciscans would pay the Benedictines rent consisting of one basket of fish per year for the pleasure of using the area (1998, 45).

13. One might wonder at this; why would thousands of mostly young men and women renounce property to live in the open with insufficient clothing and the poorest of food? Genuine belief in the Christian Gospels was no doubt a huge factor, but I cannot help but imagine that it was supported by others. Wealthy families exercised tremendous power over their children, both sons and daughters. Luxurious accommodation does not always compensate for such lack of freedom. And Francis's message was always that renunciation of property was the path to freedom. As Michael Heller and James Salzman explain, "For much of human history, individuals didn't matter so much for ownership. Wealthy 'owners' were merely their generation's guardian of family estates, obligated to transmit their ancestors' landholdings down to descendants. Though this may be hard to imagine today, in an important sense, the family was the owner, not any individual member" (Heller and Salzman 2021, 216). Young noblemen might well have wanted something else from life—a lofty purpose, perhaps, a mission, open air, travel, solitude, and the companionship and love of like-minded peers. Francis was not of the nobility, but he was especially sensitive to the link between money (and the emerging international money economy) and earthly power, which was manifest in his early life as his wealthy merchant father's violence and tyranny. By contrast, the freedom Francis's order embraced and offered was, according to his nineteenth-century biographer Paul Sabatier, "the freedom that leads each soul to obey the divine and mysterious power that the flowers of the field adore, that the birds of the air bless, that the symphony of the stars praises, and that Jesus of Nazareth called *Abba*, or, Father" (2015, 117–18). And so they flocked to the order, giving up their titles and riches and refusing to take the place in society that their families demanded of them. Women, whether of the nobility or the merchant class, had even more reason to seek that freedom, because they would have had none of it within their families or the families of those to whom they would be given in marriage. Little wonder that Chiara Offreduccio ran away at age sixteen after hearing Francis preach in the cathedral in Assisi, or that her younger sister Agnes fled to join her three weeks later. Their family, like Francis's a few years before, made every effort to retrieve them, but they refused to go back to their old lives as young noblewomen (Sabatier 2015, 84). The multitudes who joined the Franciscans and Clares were not all wealthy, however; many were poor. They chose a life not so terribly different, materially at least, from what they left. But they exchanged a life of denigration and abuse on account of their poverty for a life in which poverty was shared and valorized.

14. Lambert says Francis really lacked the skills to oversee a large, dispersed order. He writes, "Francis was a supreme spiritual master of small groups; but he was unable to provide the impersonal organization required to maintain a world-wide order. His genius was alien to all abstraction" (1998, 37).

15. Francis and Clare always saw themselves as supplements to the missions of parish priests and worked to cultivate good relations with them. But the growth of the orders undoubtedly strained such relationships. The orders pulled people as well as donations away from parish churches, and the Franciscans' and Poor Clares' valorization of poverty undoubtedly made some parish priests and layman look bad in the eyes of some of their parishioners.

16. For sordid details, including the execution of four Franciscans for heresy, see Lambert (1998, chap. 10).

17. On this point, see McClure (2017, 23).

18. Carter Woodson's research is the foundation for much of the work in this area (see Woodson 1924 and 1925). For some later sources and examples, see Koger (1985) and Lightner and Ragan (2005). Larry Koger notes that at the end of the Civil War, when all slave owners were required to release the people who had been enslaved, there were still 171 Black slave owners who held 766 people as slaves in Charleston, South Carolina. Koger gives ample evidence that these owners were not all simply relatives who had bought enslaved people to save them from exploitation by whites (although of course some were) but actual entrepreneurs profiting from these people as investments and as laborers.

19. In fact, the majority of Southern states made manumitting enslaved people very difficult or impossible. "In 1830 a master who wished to emancipate a slave could do so without significant legal constraint only in the states of Maryland and Missouri and in the Arkansas Territory. Everywhere else there were barriers. In Delaware and Kentucky, the master had to post a bond in order to ensure that the freed slave would not become a public charge. Virginia demanded that all slaves who were freed must either move out of the state within a year or be re-enslaved. North Carolina allowed manumission only as a reward for meritorious service and by permission of a county court. Tennessee had a procedure similar to North Carolina's but allowed its courts more discretion. In South Carolina, Georgia, Alabama, Mississippi, and Louisiana, slaves usually could be emancipated only by a special act of the legislature, which was not easily obtained. Alabama, for example, freed an average of only twenty slaves a year between 1819 and 1829. Florida Territory prohibited manumission altogether until 1829 and thereafter required removal from the territory within thirty days" (Lightner and Ragan 2005, 536).

20. A couple of the best-known examples are Gabriel's Conspiracy in Richmond, Virginia, in 1800 (for details, see Nicholls 2012) and Denmark Vesey's Revolt in Charleston, South Carolina, in 1822 (see Lofton 2013).

21. We do not have legal title to Buttercup; I don't know whether anyone does. She just showed up one night and took to our horse Peanut (hence her name), and once a mule decides to settle down somewhere, there is no good way to remove her. Plus, Peanut liked her, and he had been very lonely since his pasture mate Teaspoon died. A year or so later, an irate animal control officer led me to believe that we have legal liability for Buttercup, simply because we did not expel her from our land when she arrived. But maybe he lied, because, come to find out, he was the officer who had failed to arrest her the night she wandered all over East Henrico County looking for a new herd; he just abandoned the chase and left her to Peanut, while we were out of town. So I don't know, but this is where she lives now, and we have to keep her out of the road. It's not so much ownership as responsibility, but that's a subject for another chapter, book, or perhaps author.

22. This morning, we are still receiving updates out of Kentucky, Arkansas, Illinois, Missouri, and Tennessee about the line of tornados that moved through that area less than forty-eight hours ago. Authorities say this is the worst outbreak of December tornados ever recorded. It looks like well over a hundred people died, but no one yet knows how many more there are. The line of storms stretched about 250 miles. Deadly tornados a few days before winter solstice, like a hurricane season that now starts before June 1 and stretches past November 30 and a wildfire season that now lasts all year, is enough to make any reflective weather watcher uneasy.

23. Lambert says there is some indication that Francis was willing to accept a gift of land, but only if he could be sure that it was remote and undesirable enough that the order would never have any reason to exclude anyone from it who wanted to be there. This suggests that what he objected to was not the formality of legal ownership but practices of treating land, and so on, as out of the common. Certainly his Rule emphasized practices that would prevent Franciscans and Poor Clares from falling into old ways of behaving as if they had exclusive control over any material thing (see Lambert 1998, 52).

CHAPTER SIX

1. I am very grateful to Nicolae Morar for calling my attention to this article.

2. I believe the word "outsourcing" is a misnomer here. Human cells likely never evolved to do this work on their own. Microbes predate human cells by eons so have likely been there doing that work for human cells always. It is not outsourcing so much as it is receiving.

3. I have not seen studies that included subjects older than forty-nine, so I do not know whether maternal, sibling, or fetal cell lines persist in people throughout their life spans. Also, the studies I have seen tracked sons' genomes in mothers and mothers' genomes in sons, for the obvious reason that identifying sex chromosomal differences is far easier than identifying genetic differences directly. But researchers assume that the sex of the fetus is not a factor in the passage of cells through the placenta; XX cells will pass as readily as XY.

4. Things can get very complicated with conjoined twins, as one anonymous reader pointed out by way of the example of Abby and Brittany Hensel, born in 1990 with two heads, conjoined torso with separate organs above the navel, and a single pair of (separately controlled) arms and legs. The twins are considered by law and by those around them as two separate persons. They hold two separate driver's licenses, two separate college degrees, and Abby is married while Brittany is single. The question the reader raised—which has legal, moral, and metaphysical dimensions—is, to put it bluntly, whether Abby's husband is having sex with Abby only or with Brittany also (and whose children any future offspring might be). I can imagine this might become legally and morally difficult if Brittany objected to the situation, which to my knowledge she has not done. As of late 2024, the three people involved seem to have worked things out among themselves, and thus it remains their private business. Should it become otherwise, this is one of those sets of issues that I will happily leave to the lawyers.

5. Although Locke might have agreed that Sizemore was a "lunatic," his treatment of personhood might have allowed for her disjunctive personalities to count as persons in their own right. See his discussion of whether two or more persons might occupy the same body in the *Essay* II.xxvii.12, 15, 19–23, and see Boeker (2021, 148).

6. Or maybe personhood is not a well-delineated concept at the margins and generates contradictions in practice. Or maybe there are such significant contextual differences in the two cases that they really cannot be considered counter to each other. My analysis from this point takes the path of what I think most people would see as common sense.

7. The same affective state can generate different emotions, depending on cultural or subcultural labeling. For example, the physiological state of arousal that some experience and label as fear could be experienced and labeled as excitement by others. As

children, we learn how to label our emotions from the people around us who interpret our affective states for us. Labeling, therefore, can vary, and since labeling occurs in language where words like *fear* and *excitement* participate in webs of meanings that may take our experiences in different directions, our conscious emotional experiences may vary culturally or subculturally as well.

8. I do not mean to claim that the only source of our emotions is physiology. Thoughts clearly inspire feelings and, in fact, bodily states. What we think can raise or lower blood pressure, tighten or relax muscles, affect digestion, and so on. I do not mean to imply that emotion, let alone mentality more generally, is epiphenomenal.

9. Animal researchers do attribute emotions to horses. Scopa et al. (2019) discuss horses' emotional intelligence and physiological means by which they are able to discern humans' emotions: facial recognition and recognition of human facial expressions as positive or negative, voice recognition, and olfactory perceptions of human body odors (indicating either fear or happiness).

10. This is coming out of a California institute called HeartMath, specifically studies by Ann Baldwin and Ellen Gehrke. They can be found at the website www.heartmath.org. The studies on the site have not been peer-reviewed and have been challenged—see Henderson (2024).

11. Horses also respond physiologically to human body odors (Lanatà et al. 2018). Affective states are bodily states, and bodily states sometimes involve production of chemical substances that can leave the body in exhalation or through the skin. Although human beings are not particularly good at attuning to and actively considering aerosolized substances (compared to dogs, we have a poor sense of smell), those molecules do enter human mouths and noses just as they enter the noses and mouths of horses and dogs, and similar chemical reactions occur in those human tissues. Therefore, Brennan (2004) suggests, some transmission of affect among humans may occur not through the eyes and ears (or heart) but through the nose.

12. For information on how a beating heart generates an electromagnetic field, see Burleson and Schwartz (2005, esp. 1111–12).

13. A Liman Center and Yale University Law School report from 2018 suggests that the number of inmates in solitary during the course of 2016 might have been around 61,000, but even this study, while perhaps the most authoritative currently available, has limitations. (For a discussion of the available data and its limitations, see Manson (2019). Terry Allen Kupers, a psychiatrist who often serves as an expert witness in class action suits on behalf of prisoners, asserts in his 2017 book that even an estimate of 100,000 people was too low: "I believe that figure is a gross underestimate (for example, it does not include the number of prisoners on lockdown)." He also noted that the Bureau of Justice Statistics reported that 20 percent of prisoners had spent some time in solitary confinement in the past twelve months (2017, 8).

14. A very interesting example of collaboration that produces results when individuals alone likely could not is code breaking during World War II. Liza Mundy describes it in *Code Girls*, "Code breaking during World War II was a gigantic team effort. The war's cryptanalytic achievements were what Frank Raven, a renowned naval code breaker from Yale who supervised a team of women, called 'crew jobs.' These units were like giant brains; the people working in them were a living, breathing, shared memory" (2017, 22).

15. One interesting version of this view is called Enactivism and was championed by Francisco Varela. For a good overview of his work, see Lanfranco et al. (2023).

16. There has been a great deal of scientific and philosophical controversy over how to define "emergent property." For a taste of this controversy, see Clayton and Davies (2006). The best account I have seen is in Deacon 2012, chapters 5 and 6.

17. Francisco Varela and others have argued for Enactivism, whose central idea is that cognition is inseparable from perception and motion. Varela insists that corporeal specificity, sensory and motor processes, perception and action "are fundamentally inseparable in lived cognition, and are *not* merely contingently linked in individuals." He argues strenuously against any view that makes cognition separate from action: "Cognitive structures emerge from recurrent patterns of perceptually guided action"; cognition consists, then, "not of representations but of *embodied action*" (1992, 329–30, 336).

18. Who knew there were such beings as neuro-anthropologists? Can you imagine a college student telling their parents they wanted to major in neuro-anthropology? The world is just way bigger than I thought.

CHAPTER SEVEN

1. In particular, I recommend Peter Godfrey-Smith's books *Other Minds: The Octopus, the Sea, and the Deep Origins of Consciousness* (2016) and *Metazoa: Animal Life and the Birth of the Mind* (2020).

2. Fred Keijzer holds that synapses predate axodendritic processes, possibly by quite a long time (see Keijzer et al. 2013 and Keijzer 2015, 319–20).

3. These new appendages, jaws in particular, also made active predation possible, which in turn spurred the evolution of countless defensive capacities.

4. This identity of self and particular occurring is why, Godfrey-Smith suggests, my moods, emotions, thoughts, and beliefs happen here and not there where someone else occurs, why "minds" do not merge with one another in any direct way (see Godfrey-Smith 2020, esp. chap. 10).

5. Leanne Betasamosake Simpson writes, "We practice life over a territory with boundaries that were overlapping areas of increased international Indigenous presence, maintained by more intense ceremonial and diplomatic relationship" (2017, 78).

6. Through the eighteenth century, this view was widespread, as Elizabeth Anderson details in her book *Hijacked: How Neoliberalism Turned the Work Ethic Against Workers and How Workers Can Take It Back* (2023, esp. chap. 3).

7. I was saddened to learn as I researched this section of the chapter that David Scondras passed away on October 21, 2020. My criticism of him here is gentle. My respect for him is great.

Works Cited

Adams, John. 1977. *Papers of John Adams*. Vol. 1. Edited by Robert J. Taylor. Belknap Press.
Aleklett, Kjell. 2004. "Dick Cheney, Peak Oil and the Final Count Down." Unpublished manuscript.
Anderson, Elizabeth. 2017. *Private Government: How Employers Rule Our Lives (and Why We Don't Talk About It)*. Princeton University Press.
Anderson, Elizabeth. 2023. *Hijacked: How Neoliberalism Turned the Work Ethic Against Workers and How Workers Can Take It Back*. Cambridge University Press.
Anstey, Peter R. 2020. "Boyle's Influence on Locke." In *The Bloomsbury Companion to Robert Boyle*, edited by Jan-Erik Jones. Bloomsbury Academic.
Aquinas, Thomas. 1945. *Introduction to St. Thomas Aquinas: "The Summa Theologica," "The Summa Contra Gentiles."* Edited by Anton C. Pegis. Random House.
Armitage, David. 2004. "John Locke, Carolina, and the *Two Treatises of Government*." *Political Theory* 32, no. 5 (October): 602–27.
Armstrong, Karen. 1993. *A History of God: The 4,000-Year Quest of Judaism, Christianity, and Islam*. Ballantine.
Assisi, Francis. 2015. *The Complete Francis of Assisi: His Life, The Complete Writings, and "The Little Flowers."* Edited and translated by Jon M. Sweeney. Paraclete Press.
Athanasius. 2021. *De Synodis 26*. Translated by Cardinal Newman. In *The Acts of the Early Church Councils: Production and Character*. http://www.elpenor.org/Athanasius/councils.asp.
Attas, Daniel. 2000. "Freedom and Self-Ownership." *Social Theory and Practice* 26, no. 1 (Spring): 1–23.
Augustine. 2002. *De Trinitate, Books 8–15*. Edited by Gareth B. Matthews. Translated by Stephen McKenna. Cambridge University Press.
Balibar, Étienne. 2013. *Identity and Difference: John Locke and the Invention of Consciousness*. Translated by Warren Montag. Verso.
Baptist, Edward E. 2014. *The Half Has Never Been Told: Slavery and the Making of American Capitalism*. Basic Books.
Bayern, Shawn. 2016. "The Implications of Modern Business–Entity Law for the Regulation of Autonomous Systems." *European Journal of Risk Regulation* 7, no. 2 (June): 297–309. https://doi.org/10.1017/S1867299X00005729.
Benoit, Monique. n.d. "Are Women Persons? The 'Persons' Case." Library and Archives Canada. No. 119. http://www.collectionscanada.gc.ca/publications/002/015002-2100-e.html.

Bess, Michael. 1980. "Foucault Interview: Power, Moral Values, and the Intellectual." https://michaelbess.net/foucault-interview/.
Boddy, Amy M., Angelo Fortunato, Melissa Wilson Sayres, and Athena Aktipis. 2015. "Fetal Microchimerism and Maternal Health: A Review and Evolutionary Analysis of Cooperation and Conflict Beyond the Womb." *Bioessays* 37: 1106–18.
Bodin, Jean. 1962. *The Six Bookes of a Commonweale*. Edited by Kenneth Douglas McRae. Translated by Richard Knolles. Harvard University Press.
Boeker, Ruth. 2021. *Locke on Persons and Personal Identity*. Oxford University Press.
Boethius. 1962. *The Theological Tractates and The Consolation of Philosophy*. Translated by H. F. Stewart and E. K. Rand. Harvard University Press.
Boyle, Robert. 1690. *The Christian Virtuoso*. www.openlibrary.org/books/OL139999 36M/The_Christian_virtuoso.
Bratton, William W., Jr. 1989. "The New Economic Theory of the Firm: Critical Perspectives from History." *Stanford Law Review* 41, no. 6 (July): 1471–527.
Brennan, Teresa. 2004. *The Transmission of Affect*. Cornell University Press.
Burkhart, Brian. 2019. *Indigenizing Philosophy Through the Land: A Trickster Methodology for Decolonizing Environmental Ethics and Indigenous Futures*. Michigan State University Press.
Burleson, Katharine O., and Gary E. Schwartz. 2005. "Cardiac Torsion and Electromagnetic Fields: The Cardiac Bioinformation Hypothesis." *Medical Hypotheses* 64: 1109–16.
Butler, Ann Caldwell. 1978. "Josiah Warren, Peaceful Revolutionist." PhD diss., Ball State University. http://cardinalscholar.bsu.edu/handle/handle/175361?show=full.
Cardinali, Lucilla, Francesca Frassinetti, Claudio Brozzoli, Christian Urquizar, Alice C. Roy, and Alessandro Farne. 2009. "Tool-Use Induces Morphological Updating of the Body Schema." *Current Biology* 19 (12): R478–R479. https://doi.org/10.1016/j.cub.2009.05.00.
Carey, Daniel. 2006. *Locke, Shaftesbury, and Hutcheson: Contesting Diversity in the Enlightenment and Beyond*. Cambridge University Press.
Carrithers, Michael, Steven Collins, and Steven Lukes, eds. 1985. *The Category of the Person: Anthropology, Philosophy, History*. Cambridge University Press.
Cerri, Luigi. 2018. "Birth of the Modern Corporation: From Servant of the State to Semi-Sovereign Power." *American Journal of Economics and Sociology* 77, no. 2 (March): 239–77.
Chaucer, Geoffrey. 1977. *The Complete Poetry and Prose of Geoffrey Chaucer*. Edited by John H. Fisher. Holt, Rinehart, and Winston.
Cheilik, Michael. 1969. *Ancient History from Its Beginnings to the Fall of Rome*. Harper & Row.
Cicero. 1991. *On Duties*. Edited by M. T. Griffin and E. M. Atkins. Cambridge University Press.
Ciepley, David. 2013. "Neither Persons nor Association: Against Constitutional Rights for Corporations." *Journal of Law and Courts* (Fall): 221–45.
Clark, Andy. 2011. *Supersizing the Mind: Embodiment, Action, and Cognitive Extension*. Oxford University Press.
Clark, Andy, and David Chalmers. 1998. "The Extended Mind." *Analysis* 58, no. 1 (January): 7–19.
Clayton, Philip, and Paul Davies, eds. 2006. *The Re-Emergence of Emergence: The Emergentist Hypothesis from Science to Religion*. Oxford University Press.

Clements, Jeffrey D. 2012. *Corporations Are Not People: Why They Have More Rights than You Do and What You Can Do About It*. Berrett Koehler.

Coke, Edward. 2003. *The Selected Writings and Speeches of Sir Edward Coke*. Vol. 1. Edited by Steve Sheppard. Liberty Fund. https://oll.libertyfund.org/titles/shepherd-selected-writings-of-sir-edward-coke-vol-i.

Coleman, James S. 1974. *Power and the Structure of Society*. W. W. Norton.

Coleman, John. 2012. "Take Ownership of Your Actions by Taking Responsibility." *Harvard Business Review* (August 30). www.hbr.org/2012/08/take-ownership-of-your-actions.

Conard, Alfred. 1976. *Corporations in Perspective*. Foundation Press.

Coppe, Abiezer. 1649. *A Fiery Flying Roll: A Word from the Lord to all the Great Ones of the Earth, whom this may concerne: Being the last Warning Piece at the dreadfull day of Judgement. For now the Lord is come 1. Informe 2. Advise and warne 3. charge 4. Judge and sentence the Great Ones*. https://archive.org/details/fieryflyingroll00coppuoft/page/n3/mode/2up.

Cressy, David. 2006. *England on Edge: Crisis and Revolution, 1640–1642*. Oxford University Press.

Daley, Jason. 2019. "Toledo, Ohio, Just Granted Lake Erie the Same Legal Rights as People." *Smithsonian Magazine*, March 1. https://www.smithsonianmag.com/smart-news/toledo-ohio-just-granted-lake-erie-same-legal-rights-people-180971603/.

Davé, Naisargi N. 2023. *Indifference: On the Praxis of Interspecies Being*. Duke University Press.

Deacon, Terrence W. 2012. *Incomplete Nature: How Mind Emerges from Matter*. W. W. Norton.

Deiser, George F. 1908. "The Juristic Person—I." *University of Pennsylvania Law Review and American Law Register*, o.s. vol. 57, no. 3; n.s. vol. 48 (December): 131–42.

Derrida, Jacques. 2009. *The Beast and the Sovereign*. Vol. 1. Translated by Geoffrey Bennington. University of Chicago Press.

Duijn, Marc van, Fred Keijzer, and Daan Franken. 2006. "Principles of Minimal Cognition: Casting Cognition as Sensorimotor Coordination." *Adaptive Behavior* 14 (2): 157–70.

Dunbar-Ortiz, Roxanne. 2014. *An Indigenous Peoples' History of the United States*. Beacon Press.

Dupre, Daniel S. 2018. *Alabama's Frontiers and the Rise of the Old South*. Indiana University Press.

Esposito, Roberto. 2012a. "The *Dispositif* of the Person." *Law, Culture and the Humanities* 8 (1): 17–30.

Esposito, Roberto. 2012b. *Third Person: Politics of Life and Philosophy of the Impersonal*. Translated by Zakiya Hanafi. Polity Press.

Fairfield, Paul. 2000. *Moral Selfhood in the Liberal Tradition: The Politics of Individuality*. University of Toronto Press.

Farrell, Thomas J. 2015. "The Meaning of Middle English Wight." *Chaucer Review* 50 (1–2): 178–97.

Feinberg, Joel. 1983. "Autonomy, Sovereignty, and Privacy: Moral Ideals in the Constitution?" *Notre Dame Law Review* 58, no. 3: 445–92.

Felton, Henry. 1725. "The Resurrection of the same Numerical Body, and its Reunion to the same Soul; Asserted in a Sermon Preached before the University of Oxford, at St. Mary's on Easter-Monday, 1725. In which Mr. Locke's Notions of Personality and Identity are confuted. And the Author of the *Naked Gospel* is answered." Oxford. https://archive.org/details/bim_eighteenth-century_the-resurrection-of-the-_felton-henry_1733.

Fenwick, Paul J. 2005. Foreword to *Gregory of Nyssa and the Concept of Divine Persons* by Lucian Turcescu. Oxford University Press.

Fortman, Edmund. 1972. *The Triune God: A Historical Study of the Doctrine of the Trinity*. Westminster Press.

Foucault, Michel. 1977. "Nietzsche, Genealogy, History." In *Language, Counter-Memory, Practice: Selected Essays and Interviews*. Edited by Donald F. Bouchard. Cornell University Press.

Foucault, Michel. 1997. *"Society Must Be Defended": Lectures at the Collège de France, 1975–1976*. Translated by David Macey. Picador.

Foucault, Michel. 2014. *On the Government of the Living. Lectures at the Collège de France 1979–1980*. Translated by Graham Burchell. Palgrave Macmillan.

Fouracre, Paul, ed. 1995. *The New Cambridge Medieval History*. Vol. 1: *c. 500–c. 700*. Cambridge University Press.

Francis of Assisi. 2015. *The First Rule (1209)*. In *The Complete Francis of Assisi: His Life, The Complete Writings, and "The Little Flowers."* Edited and translated by Jon M. Sweeney. Paraclete Press.

Frank, Thomas. 2008. "Exploring the Boundaries of Law in the Middle Ages: Franciscan Debates on Poverty." *Law and Literature* 20, no. 2 (Summer): 243–60.

French, Peter A. 1984. *Collective and Corporate Responsibility*. Columbia University Press.

Freund, Ernst. 1857. *The Legal Nature of Corporations*. University of Chicago Press. Reprint, Leopold Classic Library.

Fukuda, Arihira. 1997. *Sovereignty and the Sword: Harrington, Hobbes, and Mixed Government in the English Civil Wars*. Clarendon Press.

Galambos, Louis. 2004. "The Monopoly Enigma: The Reagan Administration's Anti-Trust Experiment in the Global Economy." In *Constructing Corporate America: History, Politics, Culture*. Edited by Kenneth Lipartito and David B. Sicilia. Oxford University Press.

Gilbert, Scott F., Jan Sapp, and Alfred I. Tauber. 2012. "A Symbiotic View of Life: We Have Never Been Individuals." *Quarterly Review of Biology* 87, no. 4 (December): 325–41.

Glausser, Wayne. 1990. "Three Approaches to Locke and the Slave Trade." *Journal of the History of Ideas* 51, no. 2 (April–June): 199–216.

Godfrey-Smith, Peter. 2016. *Other Minds: The Octopus, the Sea, and the Deep Origins of Consciousness*. Farrar, Straus and Giroux.

Godfrey-Smith, Peter. 2020. *Metazoa: Animal Life and the Birth of the Mind*. Farrar, Straus and Giroux.

Gordon, Ann D. 2005. "The Trial of Susan B. Anthony." In *Federal Trials and Great Debates in United States History*. Federal Judicial Center, Federal Judicial History Office.

Gorman, James. 2013. "Considering the Humanity of Nonhumans." *New York Times*, December 9. http://www.nytimes.com/2013/12/10/science/considering-the-humanity-of-nonhumans.html.

Graeber, David, and David Wengrow. 2021. *The Dawn of Everything: A New History of Humanity*. Farrar, Straus and Giroux.

Grassian, Stuart. 2006. "Psychiatric Effects of Solitary Confinement." *Washington University Journal of Law and Policy* 22: 325–84.

Grenier, John. 2005. *The First Way of War in the Seven Years' War, 1754–1753*. Cambridge University Press.

Guenther, Lisa. 2013. *Solitary Confinement: Social Death and Its Afterlives*. University of Minnesota Press.

Haakonssen, Knud. 1991. "From Natural Law to the Rights of Man: A European Perspective on American Debates." In *A Culture of Rights: The Bill of Rights in Philosophy, Politics, and Law—1791–1991*. Edited by Michael J. Lacey and Knud Haakonssen. Cambridge University Press.

Haakonssen, Knud. 1996. *Natural Law and Moral Philosophy: From Grotius to the Scottish Enlightenment*. Cambridge University Press.

Hall, Matthew. 2011. *Plants as Persons: A Philosophical Botany*. State University of New York Press.

Hallis, Frederick. (1930) 1978. *Corporate Personality: A Study in Jurisprudence*. Oxford University Press. Reprint, Scientia Verlag.

Hamilton, Alexander, James Madison, and John Jay. 2008. *The Federalist Papers*. Edited by Lawrence Goldman. Oxford University Press.

Haney, Craig. 2003. "Mental Health Issues in Long-Term Solitary and 'Supermax' Confinement." *Crime and Delinquency* 49, no. 1 (January): 124–56. https://doi.org/10.1177/0011128702239239.

Harcourt, Bernard E. 2011. *The Illusion of Free Markets: Punishment and the Myth of Natural Order*. Harvard University Press.

Hardy, Osgood. 1955. "Ulysses S. Grant, President of the Mexican Southern Railroad." *Pacific Historical Review* 24, no. 2 (May): 111–20.

Hartman, Saidiya V. 1997. *Scenes of Subjection: Terror, Slavery, and Self-Making in Nineteenth-Century America*. Oxford University Press.

Hartmann, Thom. 2010. *Unequal Protection: How Corporations Became "People"—and How You Can Fight Back*. Berrett-Koehler.

Heller, Michael, and James Salzman. 2021. *Mine! How the Hidden Rules of Ownership Control Our Lives*. Doubleday.

Henderson, Antonia J. Z. 2024. "Human/Horse Heart Math: Does It Add Up?" *Horse Sport* (February 8). https://horsesport.com/magazine/behaviour/human-horse-heart-math-does-it-add-up/.

Hill, Christopher. 1972. *The World Turned Upside Down: Radical Ideas During the English Revolution*. Penguin.

Hillar, Marian. 2012. *From Logos to Trinity: The Evolution of Religious Beliefs from Pythagoras to Tertullian*. Cambridge University Press.

Hillerbrand, Hans J. 2007. *The Division of Christendom: Christianity in the Sixteenth Century*. Westminster John Knox Press.

Hinshelwood, Brad. 2013. "The Carolina Context of John Locke's Theory of Slavery." *Political Theory* 41, no. 4 (August): 562–90.

Hirsch, Mark G. 2014. "1871: The End of Indian Treaty-Making." *American Indian Magazine* 15, no. 2 (Summer/Fall): https://www.americanindianmagazine.org/story/1871-end-indian-treaty-making.

Hobbes, Thomas. 1958. *Leviathan, Parts I and II*. Edited by Herbert W. Schneider. Bobbs-Merrill.

Holland, Nicholas D. 2003. "Early Nervous System Evolution: An Era of Skin Brains?" *Nature Review/Neuroscience* 4 (August). https://www.nature.com/articles/nrn1175.pdf.

Horwitz, Morton J. 1986. "*Santa Clara* Revisited: The Development of Corporate Theory." *West Virginia Law Review* 88, no. 2: 173–224.

Hunt, Lynn. 2007. *Inventing Human Rights: A History*. W. W. Norton.

Hutchins, Edwin. 1995. *Cognition in the Wild*. MIT Press.

Hutchins, Edwin. 2011. "Enculturating the Supersized Mind." *Philosophical Studies* 152: 437–46.

Huyler, Jerome. 1995. *Locke in America: The Moral Philosophy of the Founding Era*. University of Kansas Press.

International Energy Agency. 2010. *World Energy Outlook 2010*. https://www.iea.org/reports/world-energy-outlook-2010.

Jefferson, Thomas. 1816. "Thomas Jefferson to George Logan, 12 November 1816." Founders Online. National Archives. https://founders.archives.gov/documents/Jefferson/03-10-02-0390.

Justinian. 1913. *Imperatoris Iustiniani Institutiones*. Edited by J. B. Moyle. 5th ed. Oxford University Press.

Kant, Immanuel. 1996. *The Metaphysics of Morals*. Translated and edited by Mary Gregor. Cambridge University Press.

Keijzer, Fred. 2015. "Moving and Sensing Without Input and Output: Early Nervous Systems and the Origin of Animal Sensorimotor Organization." *Biological Philosophy* 30 (March): 311–31. https://doi.org/10.1007/s10539-015-9483-1.

Keijzer, Fred, Marc van Duijn, and Pamela Lyon. 2013. "What Nervous Systems Do: Early Evolution, Input-Output, and the Skin Brain Thesis." *Adaptive Behavior* 21 (2): 67–85. https://doi.org/10.1177/1059712312465330.

Kimmerer, Robin Wall. 2013. *Braiding Sweetgrass: Indigenous Wisdom, Scientific Knowledge, and the Teachings of Plants*. Milkweed Editions.

Koessler, Maximilian. 1949. "The Person in Imagination or Persona Ficta of the Corporation." *Louisiana Law Review* 9, no. 4 (May): 435–49.

Koger, Larry. 1985. *Black Slaveowners: Free Black Slave Masters in South Carolina, 1790–1860*. McFarland & Co.

Kokomoor, Kevin. 2018. *Of One Mind and of One Government: The Rise and Fall of the Creek Nation in the Early Republic*. University of Nebraska Press.

Kolbert, Elizabeth. 2022. "A Lake in Florida Suing to Protect Itself." *New Yorker*, April 11. https://www.newyorker.com/magazine/2022/04/18/a-lake-in-florida-suing-to-protect-itself.

Kunstler, James Howard. 2005a. "The Long Emergency." *Rolling Stone Magazine*, March 23, https://webpages.uidaho.edu/core125/Kunstler_The_Long_Emergency.pdf.

Kunstler, James Howard. 2005b. *The Long Emergency: Surviving the Converging Catastrophes of the Twenty-First Century*. Atlantic Monthly Press.

Kupers, Terry Allen. 2017. *Solitary: The Inside Story of Supermax Isolation and How We Can Abolish It*. University of California Press.

Lafer, Gordon. 2017. *The One Percent Solution: How Corporations Are Remaking America One State at a Time*. Cornell University Press.

Lambert, Malcolm. 1998. *Franciscan Poverty: The Doctrine of the Absolute Poverty of Christ and the Apostles in the Franciscan Order, 1210–1323*. Rev. ed. Franciscan Institute.

Lanatà, Antonio, et al. 2018. "A Case for the Interspecies Transfer of Emotions: A Preliminary Investigation on How Humans Odors Modify Reactions of the Autonomic

Nervous System in Horses." *2018 40th Annual International Conference of the IEEE Engineering in Medicine and Biology Society (EMBC)*: 522–25. https://doi.org/10.1109/EMBC.2018.8512327.

Lanfranco, Renzo, Andrés Canales-Johnson, Boris Lucero, Esteban Vargas, and Valdas Noreika. 2023. "Towards a View from within: The Contribution of Francisco Varela to the Study of Consciousness." *Adaptive Behavior* 3 (5): 405–22.

Laski, Harold J. 1916. "The Personality of Associations." *Harvard Law Review* 29, no. 4 (February): 404–26.

Lavin, Chad. 2008. *The Politics of Responsibility*. University of Illinois Press.

Lightner, David L., and Alexander M. Ragan. 2005. "Were African American Slaveholders Benevolent or Exploitative? A Quantitative Approach." *Journal of Southern History* 71, no. 3 (August): 535–58.

Lim, Paul C. H. 2012. *Mystery Unveiled: The Crisis of the Trinity in Early Modern England*. Oxford University Press.

Lindsay, Brendan C. 2012. *Murder State: California's Native American Genocide, 1846–1873*. University of Nebraska Press.

Lipton, Daniel. 2010. "Corporate Capacity for Crime and Politics." *Virginia Law Review* 96: 1911–64.

Locke, John. 1697. "An Essay on the Poor Law." PDF at https://pols2900.files.wordpress.com/2011/01/poorlaw.pdf.

Locke, John. 1960. *Two Treatises of Government*. Edited by Peter Laslett. Cambridge University Press.

Locke, John. 1980. *Second Treatise of Government*. Edited by C. B. Macpherson. Hackett.

Locke, John. 1997. *An Essay Concerning Human Understanding*. Edited by Roger Woolhouse. Penguin.

Locke, John. 1999. *The Reasonableness of Christianity as Delivered in the Scriptures*. Edited by John C. Higgins-Biddle. Clarendon Press.

Lofton, Peter C., and Peter C. Hoffer. 2013. *Denmark Vesey's Revolt: The Slave Plot That Lit a Fire to Fort Sumter*. Kent State University Press.

LoLordo, Antonia. 2012. *Locke's Moral Man*. Oxford University Press.

Lorenzini, Daniele. 2020. "On Possibilising Genealogy." *Inquiry* 67, no. 7: 2175–96. https://doi.org/10.1080/0020174X.2020.1712227.

Louth, Andrew. 1995a. "The Byzantine Empire in the Seventh Century." In *The New Cambridge Medieval History*. Vol. 1, edited by Paul Fouracre. Cambridge University Press.

Louth, Andrew. 1995b. "The Eastern Empire in the Sixth Century." In *The New Cambridge Medieval History*. Vol. 1, edited by Paul Fouracre. Cambridge University Press.

Lowe, E. J. 2005. *Locke*. Routledge.

MacPherson, C. B. 1973. "Servants and Labourers in Seventeenth-Century England." In *Democratic Theory: Essays in Retrieval*. Oxford University Press.

Madison, James. 1827. "From James Madison to James K. Paulding, 10 March 1827." Founders Online. National Archives. https://founders.archives.gov/documents/Madison/04-04-02-0304.

Maitland, Frederic William. 1975. *The Collected Papers of Frederic William Maitland, Downing Professor of the Laws of England*. Vol. 3. Edited by H. L. A. Fisher. Cambridge University Press.

Maloney, Sean, Anajane Smith, Daniel E. Furst, David Myerson, Kate Rupert, Paul C. Evans, and J. Lee Nelson. 1999. "Microchimerism of Maternal Origin Persists into Adult Life." *Journal of Clinical Investigation* 104, no. 1 (July): 41–47.

Manson, Joshua. 2019. "How Many People Are in Solitary Confinement Today?" *Solitary Watch*. https://solitarywatch.org/2019/01/04/how-many-people-are-in-solitary-today/.

Maravita, Angelo, and Atsushi Iriki. 2004. "Tools for the Body (Schema)." *Trends in Cognitive Sciences* 8, no 2 (February): 79–86.

Mark, Gregory A. 1987. "The Personification of the Business Corporation in American Law." *University of Chicago Law Review* 54, no. 4 (Autumn): 1441–83.

Marshall, Mary Hatch. 1950. "Boethius' Definition of Persona and Mediaeval Understanding of the Roman Theater." *Speculum* 25, no. 4 (October): 471–82.

Mauss, Marcel. 1938. "Une Catégorie de l'Esprit Humain: La Notion de Personne Celle de 'Moi.'" *Journal of the Royal Anthropological Institute of Great Britain and Ireland* 68 (July–December): 263–81. This essay is available in English translation in Carrithers et al. 1985, on pages 1–25.

Mayer, Carl J. 1990. "Personalizing the Impersonal: Corporations and the Bill of Rights." *Hastings Law Journal* 41, no. 3 (March). http://reclaimdemocracy.org/mayer_personalizing/.

McClure, Julia. 2017. *The Franciscan Invention of the New World*. Palgrave Macmillan.

McClure, Kirstie M. 1996. *Judging Rights: Lockean Politics and the Limits of Consent*. Cornell University Press.

McDowell, Gary. 2010. *The Language of Law and the Foundations of American Constitutionalism*. Cambridge University Press.

McInery, Ralph, and John O'Callaghan. 2013. "Saint Thomas Aquinas." In *Stanford Encyclopedia of Philosophy* Winter ed. Edited by Edward N. Zalta. http://plato.stanford.edu/archives/win2013/entries/aquinas/.

Mill, John Stuart. 1924. *Autobiography of John Stuart Mill*. New York: Columbia University Press. Available at https://babel.hathitrust.org/cgi/pt?id=uiug.30112045978720&seq=15.

Mill, John Stuart. 1978. *On Liberty*. Edited by Elizabeth Rapaport. Hackett.

Miller, Darrell A. H. 2011. "Guns, Inc.: *Citizens United, McDonald*, and the Future of Corporate Constitutional Rights." *New York Law Review* (October): 887–957.

Mitchell, E. T. 1946. "A Theory of Corporate Will." *Ethics* 56, no. 2 (January): 96–105.

Moorhead, John. 1995. "The Byzantines in the West in the Sixth Century." In *The New Cambridge Medieval History*. Vol. 1, edited by Paul Fouracre. Cambridge University Press. Pp. 118–139.

Morris, Colin. 1987. *The Discovery of the Individual, 1050–1200*. University of Toronto Press.

Mortimer, Sarah. 2010. *Reason and Religion in the English Revolution: The Challenge of Socinianism*. Cambridge University Press.

Moulton, Gary E. 1978. *John Ross: Cherokee Chief*. University of Georgia Press.

Moyle, J. B. 1912. "Editor's Introduction." In *Imperatoris Iustiniani Institutionum*. Clarendon Press.

Mundy, Liza. 2017. *Code Girls: The Untold Story of the American Women Code Breakers of World War II*. Hachette.

Nicholls, Michael L. 2012. *Whispers of Rebellion: Narrating Gabriel's Conspiracy*. University of Virginia Press.

Noonan, Harold W. 1989. *Personal Identity*. Routledge.
Northcutt, Emily. 2018. "The Battle for Poverty: Pope Gregory IX Against Saint Clare of Assisi." *Magistra* 24 (Winter): 4–21.
Northup, Solomon. 1859. *Twelve Years a Slave*. C. M. Saxton.
Nyombi, Chrispas, and David Justin Bakibinga. 2014. "Corporate Personality: The Unjust Foundation of English Company Law." *Labor Law Journal* (Summer): 94–103.
Paine, Thomas. 1791. *The Rights of Man*. Part 1. https://archive.org/details/PaineRights OfMan.
Patterson, Jeffrey L. 1983. "The Development of the Concept of Corporation from Earliest Roman Times to A.D. 476." *Accounting Historians Journal* 10, no. 1 (Spring): 87–98.
Paul, Annie Murphy. 2021. *The Extended Mind: The Power of Thinking Outside the Brain*. Mariner Books.
Phan, Peter C., ed. 2011. *The Cambridge Companion to the Trinity*. Cambridge University Press.
Pierce, Jon L., Tatiana Kostova, and Kurt T. Dirks. 2001. "Toward a Theory of Psychological Ownership in Organizations." *Academy of Managerial Review* 26, no. 2 (April): 298–310.
Radin, Margaret Jane. 1982. "Property and Personhood." *Stanford Law Review* 34, no. 5 (May): 957–1015.
Radin, Max. 1932. "The Endless Problem of Corporate Personality." *Columbia Law Review* 32, no. 4 (April): 643–67.
Raz, Joseph. 2006. "On the Nature of Rights." In *Theories of Rights*, edited by C. L. Ten. Ashgate.
Rifkin, Mark. 2011. *When Did Indians Become Straight? Kinship, the History of Sexuality, and Native Sovereignty*. Oxford University Press.
Ripkin, Suzanne K. 2009. "Corporations Are People Too: A Multi-Dimensional Approach to the Corporate Personhood Puzzle." *Fordham Journal of Corporate and Financial Law* 15: 97–177.
Rivard, Michael D. 1992. "Toward a General Theory of Constitutional Personhood: A Theory of Constitutional Personhood for Transgenic Humanoid Species." *UCLA Law Review* 39, no. 5: 1425–510.
Robins, Nick. 2012. *The Corporation That Changed the World: How the East India Company Shaped the Modern Multinational*. Pluto Press.
Rozbicki, Michal J. 2001. "To Save Them from Themselves: Proposals to Enslave the British Poor, 1698–1755." *Slavery and Abolition* 22, no. 2 (August): 29–50.
Rüfner, Thomas. 2010. "The Roman Concept of Ownership and the Medieval Doctrine of *Dominium Utile*." In *The Creation of the Ius Commune: From Casus to Regula*. Edited by John W. Cairns and Paul J. du Plessis. Edinburgh University Press.
Sabatier, Paul. 2015. *The Road to Assisi: The Essential Biography of St. Francis*. In *The Complete Francis of Assisi: His Life, The Complete Writings, and "The Little Flowers."* Edited and translated by Jon M. Sweeney. Paraclete Press.
Sandars, Thomas Collett. 1941. *The Institutes of Justinian with English Introduction, Translation, and Notes*. Longmans, Green and Co.
Sartwell, Crispin. 2011. Introduction to *The Practical Anarchist: Writings of Josiah Warren*. Edited By Crispin Sartwell. Fordham University Press.
Savigny, Friedrich Karl von. 1848. *Von Savigny's Treatise on Possession; or, the Jus Possessionis of the Civil Law*. 6th ed. Translated by Sir Erskine Perry. Reprint, Law Book Exchange.

Schlossmann, Siegmund. 1968. *Persona und Πρόσωπον im Recht und im Christlichen Dogma*. Wissenschaftliche Buchgesellschaft.

Scopa, Chiara, Laura Contalbrigo, Alberto Greco, Antonio Lanatà, Enzo Pasquale Scilingo, and Paolo Baragli. 2019. "Emotional Transfer in Human-Horse Interaction: New Perspectives on Equine Assisted Interventions." *Animals* 9, no. 12 (November 26). https://doi.org/10.3390/ani9121030.

Sherlock, William. 1690. *A Vindication of the Doctrine of the Holy and Ever Blessed Trinity, and the Incarnation of the Son of God Occasioned by the Brief Notes on the Creed of St. Athanasius, and the Brief History of the Unitarians, or Socinians, and containing an Answer to both*. https://archive.org/stream/avindicationdoc00shergoog#page/n3/mode/2up.

Simmons, Matthew R. 2005. *Twilight in the Desert: The Coming Saudi Oil Shock and the World Economy*. John Wiley & Sons.

Simpson, Leanne Betasamosake. 2017. *As We Have Always Done: Indigenous Freedom Through Radical Resistance*. University of Minnesota Press.

Sirota, Brent S. 2013. "The Trinitarian Crisis in Church and State: Religious Controversy and the Making of the Postrevolutionary Church of England, 1687–1702." *Journal of British Studies* 52, no. 1 (January): 26–54. https://doi.org/10.1017/jbr.2012.7.

Smith, Anna V. 2019. "The Klamath River Now Has the Legal Rights of a Person." *High Country News*, September 24. https://www.hcn.org/issues/51.18/tribal-affairs-the-klamath-river-now-has-the-legal-rights-of-a-person/print_view.

Solum, Lawrence B. 1992. "Legal Personhood for Artificial Intelligences." *North Carolina Law Review* 70, no. 4: 1231–87.

Sposito, Ambra, Nadia Bolognini, Guiseppe Vallar, and Angelo Maravita. 2012. "Extension of Perceived Arm Length Following Tool-Use: Clues to Plasticity of Body Metrics." *Neuropsychologia* 50: 2187–94. https://doi.org/10.1016/j.neuropsychologia.2012.05.022.

Standing Bear, Luther. (1933) 2006. *Land of the Spotted Eagle*. New ed. University of Nebraska Press.

Steedman, Carolyn. 2004. "The Servant's Labour: The Business of Life, England, 1760–1820." *Social History* 29, no. 1 (February): 1–29. https://www.jstor.org/stable/4287043.

Stern, Philip J. 2023. *Empire, Incorporated: The Corporations That Built British Colonialism*. Belknap Press of Harvard University Press.

Stevens, John Paul. 2010. Dissenting Opinion in *Citizens United v. Federal Election Comm'n* 558 U.S. 310 (2010). PDF available at https://www.supremecourt.gov/opinions/boundvolumes/558bv.pdf.

Taylor, Elizabeth Dowling. 2012. *A Slave in the White House: Paul Jennings and the Madisons*. St. Martin's Press.

Trendelenburg, Adolf. 1910. "A Contribution to the History of the Word Person." *The Monist* 20, no. 3 (July): 336–63.

Turcescu, Lucian. 2005. *Gregory of Nyssa and the Concept of Divine Persons*. Oxford University Press.

Turner, Ralph V. 1975. "Roman Law in England Before the Time of Bracton." *Journal of British Studies* 15, no. 1 (Autumn): 1–25.

Tversky, Barbara. 2019. *Mind in Motion: How Action Shapes Thought*. Basic Books.

Ullman, Walter. 1975. *Law and Politics in the Middle Ages: An Introduction to the Sources of Medieval Political Ideas*. Cornell University Press.

Underdown, David. 1996. *A Freeborn People: Politics and the Nation in Seventeenth-Century England*. Clarendon Press.
Uzgalis, William. 2018. "John Locke." In *Stanford Encyclopedia of Philosophy*. https://plato.stanford.edu/entries/locke/.
Van Duffel, Siegfried. 2004. "Natural Rights and Individual Sovereignty." *Journal of Political Philosophy* 12, no. 2: 147–62.
Van Dyne, Linn, and Jon L. Pierce. 2004. "Psychological Ownership and Feelings of Possession: Three Field Studies Predicting Employee Attitudes and Organizational Citizenship Behavior." *Journal of Organizational Behavior* 25, no. 4 (June): 439–59.
Varela, Francisco. 1992. "The Reenchantment of the Concrete." In *Incorporations*. Edited by Jonathan Crary and Sanford Kwinter. Zone Books.
Varro. 1938. *On the Latin Language*. Vol. 2. Translated by Roland G. Kent. Harvard University Press.
Vogelmann, Frieder. 2018. *The Spell of Responsibility: Labor, Criminality, Philosophy*. Translated by Daniel Steuer. Rowman & Littlefield International.
Warren, Josiah. 1841. *Manifesto*. Available at http://dwardmac.pitzer.edu/Anarchist_Archives/bright/warren/WarrenManifesto/Pages/3.html.
Warren, Josiah. 2011. *The Practical Anarchist: The Writings of Josiah Warren*. Edited by Crispin Sartwell. Fordham University Press.
Welchman, Jennifer. 1995. "Locke on Slavery and Inalienable Rights." *Canadian Journal of Philosophy* 25, no. 1 (May): 67–81.
Wilkins, David E., and K. Tsianina Lomawaima. 2001. *Uneven Ground: American Indian Sovereignty and Federal Law*. University of Oklahoma Press.
Wills, Garry. 1978. *Inventing America: Jefferson's Declaration of Independence*. Doubleday.
Winchester, Simon. 2021. *Land: How the Hunger for Ownership Shaped the Modern World*. Harper.
Winkler, Adam. 2018. *We the Corporations: How American Businesses Won Their Civil Rights*. Liveright.
Winstanley, Gerrard, et al. 1649. *The True Levellers Standard Advanced: Or, The State of Community opened, and Presented to the Sons of Men*. Available at https://www.diggers.org/diggers-ENGLISH-1649/True-Levellers-Standard-Advanced-1649.pdf.
Winstanley, Gerrard. (1652) 1973. *The Law of Freedom and Other Writings*. Edited by Christopher Hill. Penguin.
Withington, Phil. 2007. "Public Discourse, Corporate Citizenship, and State Formation in Early Modern England." *American Historical Review* 112, no. 4 (October): 1016–38.
Wohlleben, Peter. 2016. *The Hidden Life of Trees: What They Feel, How They Communicate; Discoveries from a Secret World*. Translated by Jane Billinghurst. Greystone Books.
Woodson, Carter G., ed. 1924. *Free Negro Owners of Slaves in the United States in 1830, Together with Absentee Ownership of Slaves in the United States in 1830*. Association for the Study of Negro Life and History. Negro University Press.
Woodson, Carter G. 1925. "Free Negro Ownership of Slaves in the United States in 1830." *Journal of Negro History* 9 (January): 41–85.
Woolhouse, Roger. 2006. *Locke: A Biography*. Cambridge University Press.
Wroughton, John. 2006. *The Routledge Companion to the Stuart Age, 1603–1714*. Routledge.

Yablon, Charles M. 2007. "The Historical Race, Competition for Corporate Charters and the Rise and Decline of New Jersey: 1880–1910." *Journal of Corporation Law* (Winter): 324–80.

Yaffe, Gideon. 2007. "Locke on Ideas of Identity and Diversity." In *The Cambridge Companion to Locke's "Essay Concerning Human Understanding."* Edited by Lex Newman. Cambridge University Press.

Yergin, Daniel. 1991. *The Prize: The Epic Quest for Oil, Money, and Power*. Simon and Schuster.

Yetman, Norman R., ed. 2002. *When I Was a Slave: Memoirs from the Slave Narrative Collection*. Dover.

Yolton, John W. 2004. *The Two Intellectual Worlds of John Locke: Man, Person, and Spirits in the "Essay."* Cornell University Press.

Zack, Naomi. 1996. *Bachelors of Science: Seventeenth-Century Identity, Then and Now*. Temple University Press.

Index

action, 5, 9, 20, 22, 25, 41, 42, 45, 49, 50, 51, 64, 72–73, 75, 76, 81, 85, 86, 91, 93–94, 104, 106, 117, 168, 181, 185, 199, 200, 203, 204, 208–9, 210, 214, 217, 219, 221, 222, 224, 225, 231n3, 244n19, 250n51, 256n17; collective, 104, 105, 218, 247n23, 247n26; corporate, 120, 126, 129, 130; ownership of, 41, 45, 52, 71, 75, 80, 95, 110, 136, 141, 142–43, 163, 169, 175, 181
affect, 140, 176, 178, 180, 190, 254n7, 255n11
ALEC (American Legislative Exchange Council), 133
allotment, 99–101
Anglican. *See* Church of England
Aquinas, St. Thomas, 30, 31, 58, 61–62
Arian Heresy, 56–57, 239n25
Aristotle, 59, 204, 238n22
Athanasius, 56–57, 79
Augustine, 58–59, 238n23
autonomy, 9–11, 12, 106, 139, 199, 202, 203, 211

bacteria, 171, 193, 200, 202, 221. *See also* microbes
Baptist, Edward, 87–89, 93
Black Elk, 161
Bodin, Jean, 106, 244n3
Boethius, 30, 58–62, 70, 239nn24–25
Bonaventure, 147
bounties, 96, 243nn15–16
Boyle, Sir Robert, 48–49, 73, 236n1, 240nn35–36
Brennan, Teresa, 176, 255n11

Bunker, Chang and Eng, 174–75
Burkhart, Brian, 157, 160–62

Calvin, John, 62, 239n30
Calvinism, 62, 63, 66
canon law, 36, 37, 38, 65, 137, 236n31
Carolina Colony, 80, 81–83, 214, 242n3, 243n15
Charles I, 25–26, 65, 239n30
Charles II, 67–69, 239n30
Chaucer, Geoffrey, 27–28, 233n13
Cheney, Richard, 1, 4, 8, 232n13
Cherokee, 98–101, 161
Church of England, 24–26, 46, 64, 66, 67, 69–70, 233n12
Cicero, 30, 32–33, 55, 60, 168, 234n19
Citizens United v. Federal Election Commission, 24, 38, 118
Clare of Assisi, 145–46, 251n11, 252n13, 252n15, 254n23
Clark, Andy, 182–86
climate change, 7, 8, 133, 167, 223, 251n5
cognition, 180–85, 188–89, 199, 256n17; distributed, 185–86, 188–89; extended mind model of, 182–85, 186
Coke, Sir Edward, 124–125, 248n39, 249n48
colonialism, 85, 157, 247n28
colonization, 79, 80, 82, 95, 97, 98, 100, 124, 134, 148, 149, 156, 162, 167, 197, 214, 219, 243n15
concession theory, 122–26, 127, 129–30, 249n48
conjoined twins, 174–75, 254n4
Coosa, 83

corporate personhood, 24, 38, 40, 42, 102–4, 118–23, 126–31, 133–34, 248nn38–39, 249nn42–43, 249n47

corporations, 3–4, 10–11, 37–39, 67, 118–34, 215, 218, 236n30, 236n32, 248n30, 248n33, 248n41, 249n48, 249nn50–51, 250n53. *See also* corporate personhood

Council of Nicaea, 56–57

coverture, 101, 118, 247nn23–24. *See also* women

Creek, 97–98, 99–100, 243n17, 244n19

Davé, Naisargi, 220–21

Deacon, Terrence, 191–95, 210, 256n16

dependence, 169, 199–200, 203–4, 211, 217, 219, 223, 225, 226

Diggers, 17–26, 36, 40, 46, 65, 74, 77, 113, 232n4

Divine Right, 40, 41, 105

Doctrine of Discovery, 149

dog(s), 92, 138, 143, 153–55, 162, 165, 166, 170, 173–74, 191, 193–95, 209, 220–21, 226, 255n11

Dominion Energy, 3, 134, 159, 196

East India Company, 39–40, 119, 124–25, 247n28

Elizabeth I, 39–40, 124

emergent property, 184, 256n16

enactivism, 255n15, 256n17

English Civil Wars, 15, 18, 25, 36, 40, 46, 64, 65, 105

entity theory, 130–31, 250n51

Esposito, Roberto, 35–36, 235nn25–27

ethos of (active) belonging, 198, 210–25, 226–27. *See also* dependence

Filmer, Sir Robert, 107–8, 109, 245n8

Foucault, Michel, 12–14, 16, 17, 40, 135–36, 232n15, 244n4

Fourteenth Amendment, 103–4, 118, 126–28, 132, 249n42

Francis of Assisi, 38, 144–48, 151, 164, 251n12, 254n23

Franciscans, 145–49, 150, 164, 251n12, 252n13, 254n23

Gaius, 33, 34, 64, 235n23

genealogy, 13, 16, 17, 18, 34, 103, 121, 134, 135–36, 197

genocide, 96, 100, 164

Gierke, Otto von, 130, 249n48

Godfrey-Smith, Peter, 194–95, 200, 207–8, 209, 210, 256n1, 256n4

grammar, 31–32, 233n17

Guenther, Lisa, 179–80

Haney, Craig, 178–80

Hobbes, Thomas, 40–43, 45, 105–6, 108, 115, 236n32, 244nn2–3, 245n6

holobiont, 170, 172, 173, 201, 210–11, 216, 227

homoousia, 55–57

horse(s), 145, 154–55, 160, 161, 167, 174, 177, 195, 253n21, 255n9, 255n11

Horwitz, Morton, 120, 127, 129–31, 248n34, 249n42

Hutchins, Edwin, 185–88

hypostasis, 54, 57, 60, 238n22

identity, 40, 44, 49, 50, 77, 123, 135, 139, 175, 190, 237n9; personal, 46, 47, 48, 50, 51, 53, 77; self, 14, 256n4

Indian Removal Act, 99

individualism, 14, 95, 168, 174, 197, 198, 215, 218, 220, 222, 228, 237n9

individuality, 77, 109, 112, 114, 134, 167–68, 170–74, 180, 181, 190, 191, 195, 197, 199

individualization, 101, 149

individuation, 72, 86, 104, 113, 117, 176, 181, 182, 192

Innocent IV, 123, 130, 248n38, 249n48

James, William, 139, 176

James I, 17, 20–22, 63

James II, 68–69, 239n32

Jefferson, Thomas, 47, 115, 119, 240n37, 241n42, 248n31

joint stock company, 37, 39–40, 123, 124

judgment, 9, 16, 23, 42, 45, 48, 73, 76, 77, 79, 85, 86, 117, 134, 136, 142, 164, 168, 180–82, 199, 211, 237n9, 243n14; divine, 48, 50, 52, 236n1

Justinian I, 33–34, 36, 38, 64, 122, 234n19, 234n21, 234n23, 235n24, 236n31

Kant, Immanuel, 4, 9–10, 45, 46, 50, 204
Keijzer, Fred, 207–9, 256n2
killing, 9, 19, 89, 95, 97; necessity of, 219–22
Kimmerer, Robin, 211–13, 222, 227
King James Bible, 19, 21–23, 245n8

labor, 7, 11, 25, 76, 81–83, 86–91, 93, 110–17, 126, 132, 133, 136, 150, 152, 154, 155, 188, 212–14, 242n3, 246n21, 247n23, 247n26, 251n4, 253n18; Locke on, 75, 77–78, 80–83, 98, 113, 200, 241n40; plantation management systems of, 87–90
Lakota, 154, 157–61
land, 4, 19–20, 23, 75, 80, 81, 83, 84, 98, 108, 113, 122, 123, 125, 132, 144, 150–51, 153, 156–63, 165–66, 190–91, 212, 234n22, 253n21; colonization of, 94, 98–101, 124, 148, 149, 156, 167; Diggers' view of, 17, 18–20; enclosure of, 17, 18, 29, 232n4; Franciscan, 145, 146–48, 163–64, 254n23; Indigenous, 80, 84, 86, 96, 98–99, 101–2, 210; as property, 19–20, 23, 26, 29, 37, 38, 77, 79, 80, 81, 92, 95, 99–101, 124, 137–38, 144, 150, 155, 165, 190, 250n2, 254n23; Standing Bear on, 158, 160
Laud, Archbishop William, 25–26, 233n11
Lindsay, Brendan, 96
Locke, John, 17–18, 23–24, 45–53, 61, 62, 65–66, 68–79, 81–86, 91, 96, 98, 103, 104–5, 108, 206, 214, 236nn1–3, 237n5, 237nn7–11, 239nn33–34, 240n37, 241nn38–40, 244n1, 245nn8–9, 254n5; and Boyle, 236n1, 240n35; *Essay Concerning Human Understanding*, 46, 47, 49–51, 72, 73, 75, 239n34, 241nn39–40, 254n5; on labor, 75, 77–78, 80–83, 98, 113, 200, 212, 241n40; on poor laws, 242n4; on property, 74–76, 107–8, 110; on slavery, 81–85, 242n4; on sovereignty, 106–9, 111, 116; *Two Treatises of Government*, 47, 48, 74–75, 241nn39–40
Lorenzini, Daniele, 135

Madison, James, 88, 98, 115, 119
management scholarship, 138–40

manumission, 150–52, 162, 253n19
Margulis, Lynn, 172
Marshall, John (chief justice), 125–26
mask, 30–31, 41, 55, 60–61, 62, 238n18
Mauss, Marcel, 30, 233n14
microbes, 8, 171–72, 223, 254n2. *See also* bacteria
microbiome, 171–72, 174, 195
Mill, John Stuart, 108–12, 115–17, 247n28
Modalism, 55, 57, 59, 62
mule(s), 155, 161, 174, 253n21
multiple identity disorder, 175

natural law, 63, 73–76, 83, 85, 114, 240nn36–37
natural right, 74, 76, 82, 105, 106, 123, 240n37
Nietzsche, Friedrich, 16–17
nonpersons, 10, 15, 17, 35, 37, 42, 103, 118, 123, 197, 237n9, 245n12, 247n29
Northup, Solomon, 90–94, 243n10

oil, 4, 5–8, 101, 231nn8–11, 232n13, 251n3
Ojibwe, 211–14, 215, 217, 232n1
ownership, 29, 41, 45, 72, 75, 76, 79, 86, 98, 107, 108, 114, 135–44, 147–49, 153, 154, 155, 158, 162–65, 167, 190, 202, 211, 241n38, 245n9, 250n2, 251n3, 251nn8–10, 252n13, 253n21, 254n23; of actions, 41, 52, 75, 76, 141–42, 181; as component of personhood, 14, 197–99; enslaved people, 81, 90, 99, 164, 253n18; Franciscan, 145, 147–49; land, 26, 29, 46, 77, 99, 191, 210; psychological, 139–40, 142, 162; self, 117, 142, 195

person, as word, 17, 24–25, 27–31, 37, 45, 46, 57, 75, 127, 132, 239n34, 247n29. *See also* persona; personhood
persona, 23, 28, 29–36, 37–38, 40–41, 54, 55, 57–61, 235nn27–28, 238nn18–19, 248n38
persona ficta, 130
personal identity, 47–51, 53, 77
personate, 40–43, 123
personhood, 9–17, 18, 20, 23–24, 26, 29, 34, 37, 35, 36, 41–46, 48, 50–53, 59,

personhood (*cont.*)
61, 64, 79–80, 84–87, 90–91, 93–95, 96, 101–5, 109, 113–14, 117–18, 121–23, 127–28, 132, 134, 135–36, 143, 144, 149, 162–64, 167–68, 174, 175–76, 180–82, 195, 196–99, 202, 203, 211, 225–28, 232n1, 235n27, 240n37, 241n42, 242n2, 243n14, 244n19, 254n6; as consciousness, 45, 46, 50–51, 70–72, 75, 77, 78; of God, 53, 58–62, 64, 67, 70–72, 233n17; in King James Bible, 21–23; legal, 16, 37, 39–40, 45–46, 117–18, 121–23, 125, 126–27, 131, 153, 174, 235n26, 249n49; Lockean, 17, 47–52, 69–82, 84–86, 96, 98, 101, 108, 110, 111, 117, 237nn8–11, 239n34, 241nn39–40, 254nn5–6; natural, 41–43, 130; nonhuman, 37, 39–40, 42, 45, 232n1, 241n1; Roman, 35–38, 40, 45, 77, 235nn27–28. *See also* corporate personhood; nonpersons; respect(er) of persons
Poor Clares. *See* Clare of Assisi
privacy, 87, 111, 117
property rights, 36, 38, 40, 95, 108, 117, 118, 122, 132, 138, 140, 144, 147, 149, 150, 241n42
prosopon, 30, 31, 32, 54, 55

Quakers, 26, 65, 67, 68

respect(er) of persons, 15, 19–23, 43, 233n8
responsibility, 4, 5, 9, 13, 23, 44, 45, 46, 50, 52, 63, 73, 75, 78, 79, 85, 91, 93, 97, 101, 110–11, 113, 114, 117, 134, 136, 141–42, 143, 175, 176, 197–98, 202, 225, 231n3, 242n2, 244n19, 250n51, 253n21
Roman law, 24, 34–38, 45, 64, 103, 107, 122, 234n23, 235n28, 236n29, 236n31, 250n2

Santa Clara County, 126–29, 249n
Scondras, David, 216–17, 256n7
self-esteem movement, 141–42
servants, 20, 77, 82, 87, 104, 110–11, 113–14, 133, 134, 148, 244n6, 245nn11–13
Servetus, Michael, 62, 239n27

Shaftesbury, First Earl of (Anthony Ashley Cooper), 68, 81, 83, 214
Sherlock, William, 46, 53, 69–72, 239n33
Sherman Antitrust Act, 121, 248n35
Simpson, Leanne Betasamosake, 98, 210, 256n5
Sizemore, Christine Costner, 175, 254n5
skin brain thesis (SBT), 207–8
slavery, 77, 79–81, 86–88, 90–94, 103, 117, 127, 150–52, 165, 174, 217–18, 232n1, 241n2, 242nn3–5, 243n14, 244n20, 247n23, 247n26, 251n4, 253nn18–19; of Indigenous people, 83, 149; Locke and, 80–85, 117, 242n5; of nonhumans, 154
Socinians, 62–64, 66, 69
solitary confinement, 89, 178–80, 255n13
sovereignty, 9, 18, 26, 40, 41, 68, 73, 82, 91, 101–6, 108–10, 114, 116–17, 131, 148, 197, 198, 244n3, 244nn5–6, 245n7, 247n24; Derrida on, 244n5; Hobbes on, 40–43, 105–6, 108, 244n3; Indigenous, 101; individual, 9, 103–5, 109–12, 114–16, 131, 198–99, 210, 246n21, 247n27; Locke on, 106–9, 111; Mill on, 109–11, 115–16
Standing Bear, Luther, 154, 157–61
state of nature, 84–85, 108, 241n38
subjection, 45, 84, 86–87, 91, 104–5, 109, 114, 136, 245n7
subject(ivity), 13, 15, 22, 43, 45, 47, 52, 72, 76, 102, 108, 135, 151, 153, 196, 214, 237n11; of attributes, 61; correlate of sovereign(ty), 28, 40, 42, 82, 91, 104–6, 108, 109, 117, 244n51; as opposed to object, 170, 212, 214; subject to, 38, 77, 78, 82, 86, 108, 109, 113, 114, 125, 126, 127, 134, 142, 143, 150, 165, 168, 235–36, 242n5, 250n53
Sutton's Hospital, 124–25

Tertullian, 55–56, 57, 238nn16–19
Trinity, 46, 52–53, 58–62, 64–67, 69–72, 239n27, 239n30

ultra vires, 120, 129
Unitarianism, 53, 66, 69–71

vegetarianism, 219–20

Warren, Josiah, 103, 111–17, 246n15–18, 246nn20–21, 247nn23–26
Water is life, 200
wight, 24, 27–29, 30, 37, 132, 233n13

Winstanley, Gerrard, 17–20
women, 18, 84, 85, 87, 88, 91, 96, 100–101, 154, 175, 178, 226, 247nn23–24, 252n13, 255n14; as nonpersons, 35, 118, 247n29; as persons, 77, 81, 110; status of, 95, 103, 117, 118; as wives, 110, 117, 174, 245n6. *See also* coverture

www.ingramcontent.com/pod-product-compliance
Lightning Source LLC
Chambersburg PA
CBHW022042290426
44109CB00014B/956